CITIZENS AND COMMUNITY

The related subjects of political legitimacy and system support are key theoretical concerns of students of democratic societies. They have received very little scholarly attention, however, because of the conceptual and methodological complexities they engender. In this book the authors address these concerns through systematic multivariate analyses of the sources, distribution, and consequences of variations in citizen support for key political objects in one such society, Canada. Although the authors do so within a comparative context, their primary focus is on Canada because it is one of the world's oldest democracies and is a country that has experienced support problems that periodically have reached crisis proportion. Many of the problems facing Canada are more extreme examples of difficulties that have vexed other democracies. This study helps illuminate both the conditions under which democracies in general are able to sustain themselves and those under which they could flounder.

The authors demonstrate that political support has its origins in people's political socialization experiences and their instrumental judgments about the operation of key political and economic institutions and processes. They find that political support is not "of a piece." Average citizens are able to distinguish among and ascribe different degrees of support to key objects such as parliament, the bureaucracy, judiciary, political parties, federalism, political authorities, and the national political community itself. Support also is dynamic and can vary markedly over relatively brief intervals of time. For example, periodic national elections, changing economic conditions, and the activities of political parties have a significant impact on support levels. And, differences in support for authorities, regime, and community do matter. They affect the levels of public participation in a variety of conventional and unconventional political activities as well as the relative willingness of people to comply with the authoritative edicts of government.

This series publishes comparative research that seeks to explain important cross-national domestic political phenomena. Based on a broad conception of comparative politics, it hopes to promote critical dialogue among different approaches. While encouraging contributions from diverse theoretical perspectives, the series will particularly emphasize work on domestic institutions and work that examines the relative roles of historical structures and constraints, of individual or organizational choice, and of strategic interaction in explaining political actions and outcomes. This focus includes an interest in the mechanisms through which historical factors impinge on contemporary political choices and outcomes.

Works on all parts of the world are welcomed, and priority will be given to studies that cross traditional area boundaries and that treat the United States in comparative perspective. Many of the books in the series are expected to be comparative, drawing on material from more than one national case, but studies devoted to single countries will also be considered, especially those that pose their problem and analysis in such a way that they make a direct contribution to comparative analysis and theory.

CITIZENS AND COMMUNITY

POLITICAL SUPPORT IN A REPRESENTATIVE DEMOCRACY

ALLAN KORNBERG
Duke University

HAROLD D. CLARKE
University of North Texas

CAMBRIDGE
UNIVERSITY PRESS

Published by the Press Syndicate of the University of Cambridge
The Pitt Building, Trumpington Street, Cambridge CB2 1RP
40 West 20th Street, New York, NY 10011-4211, USA
10 Stamford Road, Oakleigh, Victoria 3166, Australia

First published 1992

Printed in the United States of America

Library of Congress Cataloging-in-Publication Data
Kornberg, Allan.
Citizens and community: political support in a representative
democracy/Allan Kornberg and Harold D. Clarke.
  p. cm. – (Cambridge studies in comparative politics)
  Includes bibliographical references (p.).
  ISBN 0–521–41678–7 (hardback)
  1. Allegiance – Canada. 2. Legitimacy of governments – Canada.
  3. Political socialization – Canada. 4. Political stability – Canada.
  5. Canada – Politics and government – 1945– . I. Clarke, Harold D.
  II. Title. III. Series.
  JL27.5.K67   1992
  320.971 – dc20
                                    91-34374
                                        CIP

A catalog record for this book is available from the British Library.

ISBN 0-521-41678-7 hardback

Contents

Tables and figures

FIGURES

Acknowledgments

Many individuals and organizations helped to make this book possible. We are pleased to have this opportunity to acknowledge their assistance. First and foremost we thank the National Science Foundation (NSF) for its generous financial support, and Dr. Frank Scioli, Political Science Program Director, for his encouragement of our work. An initial research grant from the Foundation in 1983 and a second project continuation grant in 1988 enabled us to conduct five national cross-sectional and panel surveys in Canada over the past seven years. This study would not have been possible without the data gathered in these surveys.

We also thank the NSF, as well as the Canada Council and the Social Sciences and Humanities Research Council of Canada for their support of related studies conducted during the 1970s and early 1980s. The NSF generously funded survey research by Allan Kornberg and Joel Smith on the development of political attitudes during the 1980 sovereignty-association referendum. The two Canadian councils funded Harold Clarke, Jane Jenson, Larry LeDuc, and Jon Pammett for their 1974, 1979, and 1980 Canadian national election surveys and their study of voting in the sovereignty-association referendum. The data gathered in these surveys proved invaluable for mapping the dynamics of political support in Canada over the past two decades.

Our research has also been facilitated by generous financial support provided by the Institutional Research Grant Programme of the Public Affairs Division, the Canadian Embassy in Washington, D.C. We particularly wish to thank Dr. Norman London, Academic Relations Officer of the Embassy, for his interest in our project. We acknowledge with thanks the support of Duke University's Canadian Studies Center, Clark Cahow Director, and the Ford Foundation Grant Program in International Political Economy, Robert H. Bates Director. Research grants from these organizations and programs enabled us to conduct a national survey in 1987. Similarly, grants from the Duke University Research Council and Provost's Funds allowed us to carry out related surveys in 1985, 1986, and 1989. The data from these surveys did much to enhance our understanding of political support in Canada in the periods between national elections.

We thank colleagues who provided valuable comments and suggestions. William Mishler and Jon Pammett took time from their busy schedules to read a draft of the manuscript. Their insightful criticisms and those provided by three anonymous reviewers helped us to clarify our prose and, more importantly, to clarify our thinking. At various times during the development of our work we benefited from discussions with Bob Bates, Hy Bursten, Euel Elliott, Mike Gillespie, Bill Keech, Peter Lange, Joel Smith, Paul Whiteley, and Gary Zuk. Marianne Stewart's many comments and suggestions were especially helpful. Although we gratefully acknowledge their assistance, none of these people bears responsibility for any of the analyses and interpretations presented here.

Many others assisted us with various aspects of the project. Especially important was Mary Auvinen, Senior Project Director, Canadian Facts Ltd., who assisted us with the construction of our survey instruments and supervised the fieldwork for our several surveys. Her wide-ranging expertise and tireless efforts proved invaluable. Nitish Dutt and Rose-Marie Zuk helped to construct the codebooks for the 1983 and 1984 data sets. Nelly Hodge at VPI & SU, Bob Jackson and Jim Granato at Duke; and Phil Baczewski, Phanit Laosirirat, George Morrow, Dave Molta, Panu Sittiwong, Neal Tate, and John Todd at the University of North Texas patiently and skillfully answered many questions concerning the intricacies of the computing systems at these institutions.

Those who helped us get our words on paper also deserve special recognition. Jo-Ann Lutz at the University of North Texas and Patricia Tackney and Dot Weathers at Duke shared the burden of manuscript processing; Jo-Ann prepared the tables. Their prompt, efficient, and cheerful responses to repeated requests for secretarial assistance proved invaluable.

Finally, we thank the thousands of Canadians who took the time to answer our many questions. Some of them spoke to our interviewers on several occasions. We deeply appreciate their willingness to share their thoughts with us. Their roles in the unfolding drama of political support in one of the world's oldest continuously functioning democracies is the principal theme of this book.

Introduction: Political support and representative democracy

Prognoses about the health of representative democracies have changed markedly during the twentieth century. During the 1930s and again in the 1970s and early 1980s the democracies seeming inability to cope with economic distress engendered by unemployment, sluggish growth, soaring national debt and, in the latter period, stagflation and an inability to pay for costly social programs made their future appear problematic. In several cases, additional threats were posed by apparently irreconcilable differences based on various combinations of class, ethnolinguistic, racial, religious, and regional cleavages in their populations. For some observers these compounded difficulties signaled the onset of a generalized "legitimacy crisis" to which democracies, in varying degrees, were in danger of succumbing.

At other times optimistic appraisals were the norm. The virtues of democracies were widely proclaimed after their victories in two world wars and throughout the period of protracted economic prosperity that followed the second of these conflicts. The revitalization of the economies of many Western countries in the mid-1980s, the collapse of Communist dictatorships in Eastern Europe at the end of the decade and in the Soviet Union itself in the summer of 1991 made earlier predictions of the imminent demise of democracies appear both short-sighted and invalid. They seemed based on unwarranted interpretations of public discontent produced by short-term social and economic dislocations. The discontent was real, but it was focused on governing political parties and their leaders. A more general legitimacy crisis existed only in the minds of disaffected right- and left-wing intellectuals. Among ordinary citizens support for representative democracy remained strong and stable.

In our view, both types of forecasts have been too easily rendered, because despite the vast literature on public attitudes and behavior, much remains to be learned about support for democratic political systems, their components, and the factors that influence them. Also, surprisingly little research exists on how variations in support affect crucial attitudes, such as the willingness of people to voluntarily comply with the edicts of duly constituted authorities, or their periodic proclivity to engage in confrontational protests. Our study addresses such questions through a case study of political support in Canada, one of the world's oldest, continuously functioning democracies, but one which also has experienced support problems that have occasionally reached crisis proportions. The most serious crises were the referendum of May 1980 advanced by a separatist provincial government in Quebec and the June 1990 failure of all the provinces to ratify the Meech Lake Accord. Had it succeeded, the referendum would have given the Quebec government a mandate to begin the process of establishing a sovereign Quebec and, by so doing, dismembering the Canadian political community. If the provinces and the federal government are unable to resolve the constitutional crisis generated by Meech Lake, the 1990s may well be the decade in which Canada in its current form ceases to exist. For these and other reasons Canada provides an excellent locale for investigating the complex of factors that have been said to threaten the viability of democratic polities. Such an investigation into the Canadian experience can also illuminate the conditions under which democracies can be sustained.

The story we tell in this book is that political support in a democracy such as Canada is not "of a piece." We find that average citizens, no less than political philosophers, distinguish among and ascribe different degrees of support to key political objects. Thus, even in a country having Canada's history of integration problems, support for the national political community is markedly higher and more stable than that for major regime institutions and top-level political authorities. Support for the latter two not only is significantly lower, it also is compressed. In our view, this compression occurs because the presence of a Westminster-model parliamentary system, cohesive legislative parties, the brokerage electioneering strategies practiced by competing party elites, and long periods of one-party dominance at both the national and provincial levels of the federal system tend to obfuscate the distinction between government-of-the-day and government-as-regime. Despite these inhibiting factors, citizens *do* distinguish between the political regime and the authorities who are the temporary occupants of its various positions. Moreover, they also distinguish among regime structures, separating their feelings about policy-making and policy-implementing institutions (parliament and bureaucracy) from feelings about institutions that adjudicate those policies and pass judgment on their constitutionality (the judiciary).

We argue that political support has its origins in people's political socialization experiences and their instrumental judgments about the operation of key political institutions and processes. Each of these "twin pillars" of support, in turn, has two principal components. Those are individual and group identities and democratic norms and values in the case of socialization experiences, and effectiveness and equity–fairness judgments in the case of the operation of the political system. We demonstrate that the relative importance of these determinants varies. Socialization experiences have their greatest direct impact on community support, whereas instrumental judgments have their strongest effects on the regime and authorities. Moreover, although support is not a seamless web, its components are interrelated and, in the Canadian case, support flows "upward" – from authorities, to regime, to community.

Although the normative and instrumental bases of political support are conceptually distinct, the former factors provide the context in which the latter judgments are made. Support also is dynamic; it can vary markedly over relatively brief intervals of time. We find that periodic national elections are events that stimulate increases, albeit temporary ones, in support for political authorities, institutions and processes, the political community, as well as promoting attitudes such as political efficacy, interest, and trust, which are hallmarks of democratic citizenship. Changing economic conditions or, rather, public evaluations of those conditions and attributions of responsibility to government, especially the government-of-the-day, also have significant effects. However, the impact of these judgments is asymmetric; citizens are more likely to blame than to praise government for its handling of the economy, and are more likely to credit themselves than government for their own material well-being. Asymmetry also characterizes people's judgments about national conditions and their own circumstances. Faraway pastures do not "look greener." Just the opposite, is the case. We attribute this condition to the tendency of people to make judgments about their own condition and that of their local community largely on the basis of personal experience. Global judgments about the country as a whole, in contrast, rest more heavily on information from, and interpretations by, the mass media.

In contemporary democracies such as Canada, a healthy economy and its effective management by government are not enough. People expect government to undertake a wide variety of other initiatives, and evaluations of its success in doing so have important effects on support. Equally significant, however, are public perceptions of how fair and equitable government is in discharging its many responsibilities. Conventional wisdom might suggest that combinations of extremely positive or negative effectiveness and equity–fairness judgments would interact and, in so doing, have particularly strong effects on support levels. In fact, however, they constitute separate streams of influence.

Periodic, constitutionally sanctioned, free and competitive elections are the principal mechanisms whereby people express their effectiveness and equity–fairness judgments and choose among governing and opposition parties. Democratic theory ascribes a variety of functions to elections. We argue that perhaps the most important is that free, competitive elections demonstrate to citizens that their political system is indeed a democracy and, in so doing, elections stimulate significant, albeit temporary, increases in support for key political objects as well as attitudes such as political efficacy and trust that are hallmarks of a democratic citizenry. Although elections help to generate support, the quality of the choices that citizens make in any election in part is affected by the kinds of strategies competing parties pursue. In Canada the brokerage strategies traditionally employed by the national parties have tended to obfuscate policy differences among them and thereby to decouple societal cleavages from their articulation by the party system. One important result is that the direction and intensity of psychological attachments to parties and their leaders are highly volatile. The volatility of support for political authorities, in turn, has important consequences for the political support process more generally.

The last part of the story we tell is that differences in support for authorities, regime, and community matter. Democratic theory holds that extensive citizen participation is fundamental to the continuing good health of a democratic polity. Over time, both the democratization of political institutions and processes and the repertoire of legitimate citizen political action have expanded greatly. We demonstrate that political participation in Canada is multimodal and is the preserve of overlapping groups of active minorities. Differences in support influence involvement in both conventional, electorally related forms of behavior and unconventional behavior, ranging from signing petitions to participating in potentially violent protests.

Democracies are like other systems of governance in that they require their citizens to comply with laws and regulations promulgated by duly constituted authorities. In Canada there are two types of compliance orientations, which we have labeled "laws and regulations" and "service and obedience." Both types vary over relatively short periods of time in response to changes in levels of political support, and evaluations of the performance of the political system and its leaders. We may infer from this that political authorities in contemporary democracies cannot take public compliance for granted. Compliance is a renewable resource, but it is one that must be continually replenished by actions that animate and sustain the institutions and processes of democratic government.

Our study of political support is based on evidence from a now lengthy series of national surveys, which are described in the Appendix. We began our inquiry in the late 1970s, using data gathered in several federal election studies. Throughout the 1980s research funding provided by the National Science Foundation and other agencies enabled us to expand our data base by conducting a set of national cross-sectional and panel surveys focusing on political support, its correlates and consequences. The materials gathered in these surveys, together with those from the earlier election studies and other sources, provide an extensive portrait of public political attitudes and behavior in Canada during a period when the country was experiencing economic problems that waxed and waned, but which always had an impact on support for the political system and its leaders. This is because representative democracies such as Canada are a special breed. The market-oriented economies that generate wealth and great strength also produce a plethora of continuing problems. In Canada the economic problems of the 1970s and the early 1980s were conjoined with an ongoing series of integration crises that threatened to tear the country apart. These crises continued into the early 1990s. Consequently, the Canadian experience reflected in the story we tell will help us to comprehend both how representative democracies are able to sustain themselves and the conditions under which they may fail.

1

The problem of political support

The government of Quebec has made public its proposal to negotiate a new agreement with the rest of Canada, based on the equality of nations; This agreement would enable Quebec to acquire the exclusive power to make its laws, administer its taxes and establish relations abroad – in other words, sovereignty – and at the same time, to maintain with Canada an economic association including a common currency; Any change in political status resulting from these negotiations will be submitted to the people through a referendum; On these terms, do you agree to give the government of Quebec a mandate to negotiate the proposed agreement between Quebec and Canada?

December 20, 1979 announcement by the Quebec government of a referendum on political sovereignty for Quebec.

The sun shone brightly throughout most of Quebec on May 20, 1980, warming long lines of voters waiting throughout the day to cast their ballots in a historic referendum on sovereignty-association. The heavy turnout among the province's 4.3 million voters had been foreshadowed by a record level of voting in advance polls the previous Friday and Saturday. At the end of the day, 59.5 percent of those voting had said "no" to the Parti Québécois government's proposal that it be given a mandate by the people of Quebec to enter into negotiations with the government of Canada for a new status for Quebec – political sovereignty coupled with an economic association with the rest of Canada.

Although the outcome of the referendum gave the Canadian federal union a new lease on life, the leaders of both sides of the bitterly contested five-week campaign predicted that this was not the end, that fundamental constitutional changes must occur – and quickly. In fact, during the debate on the referendum Prime Minister Pierre Elliott Trudeau already had offered the Quebec electorate a "renewed" federal system if the proposal were defeated. In return for voting no, Trudeau promised that the British North America Act, the written segment of the Canadian constitution, would be patriated from Great Britain, a formal amending procedure would be established, and a Charter of Rights and Freedoms would be added to it.

After the referendum's defeat the prime minister began to put his promises into effect. However, eight of the ten provincial governments balked at his threat to proceed unilaterally if agreement could not be reached on an amending procedure. The governments of Quebec, Manitoba, and Newfoundland appealed to the Supreme Court to prevent the federal government from acting unilaterally. In a September 1981 decision the Court stated that the federal government could unilaterally patriate the British North America Act, establish a formal amending procedure and add to it a Charter of Rights and Freedoms. However, it went on to assert that although the federal government was legally entitled to do so, such an action would seriously contravene constitutional convention. As a consequence, in November 1981 a First Ministers Conference was held, at which a compromise agreement was reached between the federal government and all the provinces, except Quebec, concerning an amending formula and a "notwithstanding" provision (Section 33) for the proposed Charter.

Quebec remained opposed and refused to sign the constitutional accord, but the process continued, culminating on April 17, 1982 with the Queen's signature on a British House of Commons bill ceding formal control over the Constitution to Canada.[1] Because of possible problems, the Equality of Rights provision in the Charter did not take effect until 1985. During that year the Parti Québécois was defeated in a Quebec provincial election and replaced by the Liberal government headed by Robert Bourassa, a change that helped pave the way for the Meech Lake constitutional accord reached by Prime Minister Brian Mulroney and the ten provincial premiers at two meetings at a federal government retreat at Meech Lake on April 30, 1987 and June 3, 1987.

The Meech Lake Accord dealt with the constitutional status of Quebec, the Senate, immigration, the Supreme Court, compensation to provinces by the federal government for shared-cost social programs in areas of provincial jurisdiction but in which a province did not wish to participate, and provisions for the amendment of the constitution through annual federal–provincial conferences.[2] The most contentious issues were the first two,

1 Quebec refused to sign the 1982 agreement largely because it was refused a veto over the amending formula. For accounts of the process by which the constitutional accord was reached and discussions of its impact on Canadian politics see Banting and Simeon (1983); Romanow, White, and Leeson (1984).

2 Under Meech Lake, the regional distribution of Senate seats would have remained unchanged, i.e., there would have been twenty-four Senators each for Ontario and Quebec, ten each for New Brunswick and Nova Scotia, four for Prince Edward Island, six for Newfoundland, and six for each of the four Western provinces of Manitoba, Saskatchewan, Alberta, and British Columbia. The Yukon and Northwest Territories each would continue to have one Senator. With regard to the immigration provision, since 1971 there has been an agreement between Quebec and the federal government to ensure a role for Quebec in choosing potential immigrants. Since that time only Ontario, Manitoba, and British Col-

recognition of Quebec as a "distinct society," and reform of the Senate. Supporters of the distinct society clause argued that it merely reflected current social and political realities in Quebec. Critics contended that the legal implications of the concept of a distinct society were unclear, and it could facilitate the ability of the Quebec government to override minority language rights. The Senate provision called for nominations for the Senate to be made by provincial governments, but with the actual appointment power to be retained by the federal cabinet. The Accord also called for Senate reform to be a topic on the agenda of future constitutional conferences. It fell far short, however, of the demand made by Western provincial premiers for a popularly elected Senate with equal representation from each of the ten provinces.

Although the Accord was eventually signed by the Prime Minister and the ten provincial premiers, it failed to be ratified by the Manitoba and Newfoundland provincial legislatures within the prescribed three-year period that ended on June 22, 1990. The failure to ratify sparked a constitutional crisis that many observers believe jeopardizes the viability of the national political community. Stark (1990), for example, contends that the crisis "poses a potentially far greater threat to national survival than the sovereignty-association referendum." Whatever the immediate threat Meech Lake poses, the acrimonious disputes it has generated vividly illustrate the continuing problematic nature of political support in Canada.

Canada is not the only Western democracy to have encountered problems of political support in the past two decades. Britain, Switzerland, Spain, Holland, Italy, and France come immediately to mind as countries that have experienced national integration problems of varying severity because of cultural, ethnolinguistic, or economic particularisms. Like Canada, they also have been concerned with complex social and economic issues and intergenerational value differences. As a consequence, Jean François Revel was moved to complain that, "The third quarter of the twentieth century, the period when they grew richest and most free, was

---

umbia have failed to sign such an agreement with the federal government. Meech Lake ascribed limited constitutional status to these agreements and protected them from unilateral change by the federal government. The Supreme Court provision granted the Court full constitutional status, entrenched the reservation of three of the nine court appointments for Quebec, and required that the federal cabinet select new judges from lists of nominees provided by the provincial governments. The social programs provision confirmed the federal government's right to initiate such programs although any province that chose to opt out of any particular program would still receive its share of federal funding, if it implemented an appropriate program of its own. Finally, the Accord set an agenda for the evolution of the constitution, but made it more difficult to change it by broadening the number of topics (e.g., the establishment of new provinces) that would require unanimous approval to be implemented. For a comprehensive treatment of the complex issues surrounding the Accord, see Behiels (1989).

also the period in which the industrial democracies became increasingly unstable, explosive and ungovernable" (Revel, 1984:18).[3] However, despite the gloomy assessments by Revel and others and their pessimism about the future, all of the Western European and Anglo-American democracies are still with us. As the 1980s ended, it was the Soviet empire in Eastern Europe that collapsed rather than any of the Western democracies, with former Soviet satellites such as Poland, Hungary, Czechoslovakia, and the German Democratic Republic beginning rapid transitions toward democracy. Indeed, the Soviet Union itself has begun a very painful and fitful journey along that road.

This is not to argue that the problems of Western democracies, particularly the economic ones they have faced since the early 1970s, either have been minor ones or are unlikely to recur. Economic distress, including accelerating inflation and unemployment, high interest rates, sluggish growth, and large budgetary deficits may trouble them again – not only in the 1990s but also in the next century. Although a number of Western countries have been troubled by integration problems, those confronting Canada have been more severe. To date, however, despite the simultaneity and severity of the difficulties Canada encountered during the 1970s and 1980s and the ones it currently faces, the country remains intact. Because it is, one might argue that the genius of Canadian democracy is that the system is able to adapt to and surmount the problems that periodically threaten to undo it. With equal force, however, one might contend that the Meech Lake constitutional crisis that began in the spring of 1990 is yet another illustration of the fact that although Canada long has been a state it still is not a nation.

Because both optimistic and pessimistic scenarios about the country's future are plausible and because the sociopolitical and economic problems it continues to experience can be regarded as more extreme examples of difficulties that in less acute and complex form have vexed other democracies, Canada constitutes an ideal setting for studying factors that influence political support. Thus, although our study focuses on Canada, and the great bulk of our data were collected in Canada, a systematic analysis of these data – of how Canadians have perceived themselves, their country, their political leaders, and their key political institutions and processes during an era of turmoil and travail – can help illuminate the conditions under which democracies are able to sustain themselves. Equally significant, it may help us to better comprehend the conditions under which they could founder. The purpose of this book is to conduct such an analysis.

---

3 Some scholars have disputed the "crisis of democracy" thesis. Schmitter (1981), for example, claims that arguments advanced by theorists such as Crozier, Huntington, and Wantanabi (1975) and Revel (1984) constitute unwarranted extrapolations of short-term trends or overreactions to idiosyncratic incidents that are part and parcel of the politics of Western democracies.

THE EMERGENCE OF REPRESENTATIVE DEMOCRACIES

Similar to a number of other contemporary democracies, Canada's emergence as an independent political system is coincidental with the wave of nationalism that arose in the late eighteenth century and swept Western countries during the nineteenth century.[4] The critique of a neutral state based on contractual rights and reason and the turn toward a nationalism based on mores and the spirit or genius of a people was sharply stated in the writings of Johannes Herder. Herder hated the impersonal, centralized state and held that a nation is a community based on kinship, common history, cultural affinity, and bound most strongly by language, because "without its own language, a *Volk* is an absurdity, a contradiction in terms" (Barnard, 1965:57).

For his part, Hans Kohn, one of the leading twentieth-century students of nationalism, noted that although objective factors such as common descent, language, religion, territory, and customs and traditions clearly were necessary, they were not sufficient conditions for the emergence of a nation-state. The sufficient condition, in his view, was a conscious decision on the part of a large majority of a people to be a part of such a state. In his words, "nationalism is a state of mind, permeating a large majority of a people and claiming to permeate all its members; it recognizes the nation–state as the ideal form of political organization and nationalism as the source of all creative cultural energy and of economic well-being" (Kohn, 1961:21). Like Ranke, Kohn believed there was a symbiotic relationship between nationalism and the modern state; nationalism requires the state, with its varying institutions and structures, to integrate large groups of people into political life, whereas the state requires nationalism to strengthen the bonds that sustain it.[5] Kohn observed that nationalism engenders fundamental changes in the relationship of the masses to a state. The masses come to believe that their cultural and political survival as well as their economic prosperity are inextricably linked with the fate of the state. These conditions "gave the new feeling of nationality a permanent intensity which soon made it appear as the expression of something 'natural,' of something which had always existed and always would exist" (Kohn, 1961:21).

Representative democracies, it can be argued, are a special breed of

4 The modern state developed in the late Middle Ages as a centralized administrative unit modeled on the Roman Empire and the Catholic Church. Early states such as England and France were characterized by a degree of cultural and linguistic homogeneity. Others such as Austria embraced peoples with many different languages, customs, and traditions. Even in the early modern period, however, there was a sense of the need for a more fundamental social and cultural affinity.

5 Ranke's view was that a common culture, religion, and more fundamentally, a common history were required to convert an otherwise empty state apparatus into a true nation–state that was a home for a people. See Krieger (1977:20).

political system, rooting as they do upon the concept of individual freedom. Unlike most historical political systems and many current ones, representative democracies depend upon the freely given consent of their citizens and not on systematic coercion or intensive indoctrination to sustain themselves. All states periodically have recourse to coercive measures and, in extremes, so do democracies. However, the continued use of armed force or even of institutions such as schools, churches, and the mass media to indoctrinate large segments of the population undermines the institutions that characterize representative democracies and can be regarded as a gross violation of their fundamental democratic norms.

Democracies do occasionally threaten or actually use force to maintain social and political order, and to protect their citizens from invading armies, sectarian fanatics, and even simple criminals. The maintenance of security, especially internal security, is not a requirement unique to democracies, but it does pose a significant problem for them. Other regimes can squelch internal disruptions and attendant violence with heavy-handed coercive measures but democracies that employ such means, even temporarily, abandon their essential character.

Although security is a problematic prerequisite of all regimes, the peculiar affection of citizens for democracies is not solely dependent upon the government's ability to preserve lives and property. Perhaps even more important are a host of other functions. Democratic theory prescribes that political systems are legitimate only if they guarantee citizens justice, help to secure prosperity, maintain a distinction between the concept of political regime and political authorities, provide opportunities for citizens to participate in periodic constitutionally sanctioned elections, and exercise influence over the content of public policies in the interim between elections (e.g., Mayo, 1960; Dahl, 1971; Macpherson, 1977; Barber, 1984).

Representative democratic government is understood to be fundamentally limited by the antecedent rights of the people. Indeed, a government's principal task, according to democratic theory, is to preserve those rights. Although historically there have been differences among them concerning the appropriate scope of governmental activity, all representative democracies recognize that certain areas of human activity are "off limits" to government. Democratic regimes protect rights such as freedom of speech and assembly, freedom of religion, freedom to live where one pleases, freedom of employment, and, within certain limits, freedom to acquire and dispose of personal property.

Such rights are recognized as being limited by the overriding need to preserve public peace and thus are not absolute. Indeed, democratic governments are expected to restrain those who might exercise their rights in ways that could injure others. Rights are thus both protected and limited in democratic regimes by combinations of written constitutions and bills of rights, and unwritten but powerful conventions and precedents. Public support for a democratic regime is influenced by perceptions of its record as a guarantor of citizen rights.

Support also is dependent upon citizens' perceptions that they are being treated fairly and equitably by government. Citizens expect to receive equal treatment before and from the law, and that the government will extract costs and confer benefits on them in an equitable and fair fashion. However, because democratic government is limited government, the political consequences of equity–fairness judgments are limited as well. Many decisions and actions that might lead people to think they were being either fairly or unfairly treated are made not by their governments, but rather in the economic marketplace.

The existence of a large private sector allocating goods and services by market mechanisms is widely accepted in democratic systems. However, during the past half century a broad consensus has arisen that the market cannot be allowed to operate in an unrestrained fashion, and that some degree of regulation is necessary if economies are to operate efficiently and serve the public interest. Accordingly, some two generations of candidates for elected office have tried to "sell" themselves (and asked to be judged by their constituents) on the basis of their competence as economic managers.[6] In fact, their competing claims about who can best administer economies have become the fulcrum around which interparty electoral competition typically revolves.

One of the principal reasons political candidates make claims to being effective economic managers is that a healthy and vibrant economy has become a sine qua non for funding welfare state programs that have grown almost continuously in cost and number in the post-World War II era (e.g., Flora and Heidenheimer, 1981; Dogan, 1988; Thomas, 1989). During this period public acceptance of and enthusiasm for many of these programs have grown substantially. People believe that they improve the quality of their lives, narrow economic differences, and provide a "security net" to ensure that basic needs are met. At least some such programs now are widely viewed as "rights" or "entitlements," and they have effectively added social and economic dimensions to traditional political conceptions of citizenship in representative democracies (Marshall, 1965). Social programs thus are seen as important vehicles for guaranteeing justice for all citizens; they are linked with expectations of receiving "fair shares" of economic prosperity; indeed, these are so closely linked as to virtually become two sides of the same coin.

This is not to say that the welfare state is universally popular, that its support has not varied over time, or that under certain conditions both the

---

6 For excellent reviews of empirical studies of the impact of economic conditions on support for political parties and party leaders see Asher (1983); Monroe (1984); Miller (1989). For a more general, theoretically oriented overview see Keech, Bates, and Lange (1989).

members of upper and lower socioeconomic strata will not withdraw their support for it. By way of illustration, income transfers may be unpopular among or regarded as unfair and unjust by donor groups. Also, because there is almost always a disjunction between the stated goals of a social program and its results, the welfare state also has been attacked at times from the right (e.g., Niskanen, 1971; Buchanan and Wagner, 1977; Brittan, 1978, 1983) and at times from the left (Habermas, 1973; O'Connor, 1973, 1986; Offe, 1972, 1984) as being inefficient, ineffective, too expensive, inflationary, not going far enough in dealing with basic social and economic inequalities, or going too far and posing a threat to freedom and democracy itself.

One reason for such varied criticisms is that during periods of economic boom people can lose sight of the circumstances that created the need for a welfare state (Dryzek and Goodin, 1986; Smith, Kornberg, and Nevitte, 1988). In contrast, during periods of economic decline, tax bases erode, government income contracts sharply, and the funds necessary to pay for social programs are severely diminished (Rose and Peters, 1978). Indeed, even the prospects of economic adversity can diminish support for expansion of welfare state programs.

A second, perhaps more important, criticism concerns the mechanism through which the welfare state is implemented. Although varying in specifics, the welfare state system in each country calls for the great majority of adults to contribute continuously to its funding, whereas at any point in time only a minority of persons are direct recipients of its benefits. Because there are long periods when an individual's only obvious relationship to a welfare state is as a financial contributor, the system depends upon citizens' generosity and good will, and the belief that someday they too will be beneficiaries. Such attitudes and beliefs are more likely to be manifested in good or improving economic conditions than in bad or declining ones.

The economic adversity and instability in Western countries that followed in the wake of the 1973 Arab oil embargo generated a climate of opinion receptive to proposals to halt the continuing expansion of the welfare state, and paved the way for the resurgence of ideologically conservative parties in several of them. The electoral victories of right-of-center parties in the late 1970s and early 1980s provided an opportunity for leading conservative politicians and thinkers to press their attack on specific social programs, and to reopen debate concerning the economic, social, and political goals and values served by the welfare state. Conservative electoral successes have not been paralleled by a general erosion of public support for existing social programs, however. Survey evidence shows that enthusiasm for many of these programs remains widespread (Clarke, Stewart, and Zuk, 1988; Crewe and Searing, 1988).

As noted, representative democracies are special because they emphasize the distinction between support for political authorities, on the one hand, and support for the political regime and community, on the other. According to Easton (1965:177) the members of a political *community* are a group of persons "bound together by a political division of labor." A political *regime* consists of formal structures and procedures and norms that define how both will be used (Easton, 1965:194). *Authorities* are occupants of governmental positions who have the primary responsibility and the discretion to make key binding decisions for the political system (Easton, 1965:213). Democratic theory emphasizes that authorities come and go, but the regime and community, except under extraordinary circumstances, stay on.

Democracies vary, however, in the extent to which the distinction between the "government-of-the-day," (the authorities) and "government" per se (the regime) is clear cut in the minds of their citizens. In countries with Westminster-model parliamentary systems, incumbent governments are formed on the basis of being able to secure majority support in parliament and they must retain that support to remain in office. Cabinet ministers are members of parliament and they customarily are held responsible to parliament (and hence to the people) not only for the policies and programs of their departments, but also for the actions of bureaucratic subordinates who administer them (e.g., Campbell and Szablowski, 1979:19). This fusion of executive and legislative powers enhances the probability that average citizens will blur the distinction between government qua regime and government-of-the-day. This is especially likely when one party or a coalition of parties has been in office for an extended time.

Notwithstanding this difficulty, the authorities-regime-community separation, characteristic of all democracies is a critically important one to maintain. Public grievances or criticisms which otherwise could have deleterious consequences for regime and community support are focused on the government-of-the-day, i.e., incumbent political authorities. And, because they are assumed to be merely temporary occupants of their positions, democracies have elaborate procedures for selecting, replacing, and (if necessary) removing them. Indeed, it has been argued that a genius, perhaps *the* genius, of democracies is that they have institutionalized "rules of the game" that make possible periodic peaceful transitions of power between competing groups of political elites through the mechanism of free, competitive elections. Moreover, these kinds of elections are periodic, dramatic demonstrations of the fact that the system is indeed democratic, and therefore worthy of citizen support, without which any political system, but especially a democratic one, could not be sustained.

Democracies also have developed procedures to help legitimate the actions political authorities take on behalf of citizens and to temper public unhappiness with what authorities do in the interim between elections. These include procedures that are intended to assure citizens that the policies and programs a government adopts are in the "public interest"; that individuals and organized interest groups can consult with and influence authorities; and that both individuals and groups have opportunities to be involved in the processes through which public officials are held accountable for their actions. These mechanisms of public involvement help generate feelings of trust in political leaders; make citizens feel they are capable of making both the leaders and the system respond to their needs and demands; enhance political interest and participation; and, thereby, give people a stake in and reasons to support the political regime and community.

Contemporary representative democracies are, at least formally, open systems and, in contrast to authoritarian countries, anyone who wishes to participate is ostensibly free to do so. The principal institutional vehicles of participation are political parties and interest groups. In addition to the interest articulation, aggregation, and conflict management activities that parties and interest groups are supposed to perform, the impact of parties is magnified because of the psychological attachments to them that many people develop. Party identifications have affective and cognitive components that help orient people to the political world by affecting the development of important political attitudes, beliefs, and values, and facilitating the management of a potentially overwhelming flow of information.[7] Political parties are also the principal structural means through which elections are organized; elections not only legitimize subsequent actions by public officials but, as we will demonstrate, they also provide psychically gratifying, constitutionally sanctioned opportunities for citizens to affirm and reaffirm support for the regime and its institutions and processes. In subsequent chapters we will demonstrate that citizens' judgments about elections, and the governments that result from them, are key components of one of the pillars on which public support for representative democracies rests.

Because this is both a study of political support in Canada and in democracies more generally, note that Canada is similar to other mature democracies in that it is a free society whose citizens are not subjected to either continuous coercion or systematic indoctrination. Canadians enjoy a full complement of civil rights and civil liberties. They not only are free to participate in regular, competitive, constitutionally sanctioned elections, they also can engage in various political activities that are intended to influence the content and administration of public policy in the interim between elections. They have a market-oriented economy and are subject to the economic fallout associated with such an economy. However, they also

---

7 The classic exposition of the concept of party identification is Campbell et al. (1960:chs. 5, 6). See also Campbell et al. (1966). Since its introduction numerous critiques and reformulations of the concept have been offered. Among the most important are Budge, Crewe, and Farlie (1976); Fiorina (1981).

enjoy an array of cradle-to-the-grave social programs that have helped cushion life in democratic societies for at least a half century. Although other democracies have experienced (and still experience) national integration problems, Canada differs from them because it continues to confront ones that most other democracies already have resolved or currently are experiencing in far less acute form. Moreover, unlike many other democracies whose national integration problems are or have been grounded in either sociocultural or economic particularisms, Canada's have been grounded in both. Some of the reasons for this are rooted in Canada's past; indeed, they can be traced to the country's very beginning as a formal state in the nineteenth century. It is to a brief overview of Canada's historic development that we now turn.

POLITICAL SUPPORT IN CANADA

Some of the conditions necessary for the emergence and development of a democratic state were present in 1867, when the provinces of Ontario, Quebec, New Brunswick, and Nova Scotia were united into a new Dominion of Canada by the British parliament's passage of the British North America Act. The "upside" of this event, termed "Confederation," was that it was a product of conscious decisions taken by political leaders of the four provinces and the British government-of-the-day in two conferences in Charlottetown and Quebec City. An additional plus was that in Ontario, New Brunswick, and Nova Scotia and, to a lesser extent in Quebec, forces of modernization were producing literate, secular populations and thereby working to establish the foundation for a common social and political culture.

Even more important, the cultural and structural basis for a democracy existed in the sense that within each province the institutions and processes that were to become a part of the new national government – parliament, the cabinet form of responsible government, an independent judiciary, the rule of law, a protean civil service accountable and subordinate to elected public officials, nascent political parties, free and reasonably honest and competitive elections, peaceful transitions of executive power, a loyal opposition, and the resolution of political conflict through negotiation and mutual accommodation – were largely in place and legitimized by the time the new Canadian state was established.

Canada's "Fathers of Confederation" and British colonial authorities were eager to use those instruments to integrate the populations of the four provinces, promote economic prosperity, provide for a common defense, and construct a transportation network that would link the eastern half of the country with the Western territories and British Columbia, thereby securing the latter regions against possible predatory incursions by the

United States.[8] Many leading politicians believed those goals were within reach and, thus, the new state's prospects appeared promising. Indicative of the optimistic mood, one early prime minister, Sir Wilfrid Laurier,
went so far as to express the opinion that the twentieth century would be
"Canada's Century."

The "downside" of Confederation was that it either laid or reinforced
the groundwork for many of the national integration problems that subsequently afflicted the country. First, despite the fact that Canada had been a
British colony for a century, such desiderata of nationalism as common
descent, language, religion, territory, and customs and tradition really
characterized only one of the two existing ethnolinguistic and religious
communities, the Francophone Catholics of Quebec.[9] Indeed, scholars
such as Cairns (1983) have noted that English Canada was, and continues
to be, at a disadvantage because it lacks the cultural cohesion and identity
of Francophone Quebec. Given the differences between the latter and the
Anglophone Protestant majorities in the other original provinces, it is
hardly surprising that the founders of the Canadian state opted for a federal structure, albeit one in which the provinces initially were very much the
junior partners (Cairns, 1971). In any free society, however, a federal system raises the possibility that people will divide their loyalties between
national and subnational governments. In Canada, federalism was intended to foster support for the new political regime by diminishing and
compartmentalizing Francophone–Anglophone conflict and providing a
procedural safeguard against any future arbitrary or capricious actions on
the part of the new national government. In fact, by establishing a set of
subnational governments with important and expanding constitutionally
sanctioned powers, federalism provided an institutionalized rallying point
for regionally concentrated, disaffected groups, especially in Quebec and
the Western provinces.

A second problem was that in each of the four provinces that initially
formed the new country, and particularly in the territories that later became part of it, populations were small and widely dispersed. Except for

8 Peter J. Smith (1987) claims that the Fathers of Confederation were motivated not only by
  the traditional Tory preference for a strong state that would foster commerce while being
  politically stable and defensible, but also by a shared desire to find a suitable outlet for their
  political ambitions.
9 It can be argued that the roots of the cleavage between the Anglophone and Francophone
  communities lie in the aftermath of the British conquest of Quebec in 1760. In the years
  that followed (but especially after the American Revolution) an English-speaking elite
  largely displaced or excluded its French-Canadian counterpart in commerce, the military,
  and public life. However, rather than being extinguished, Francophone culture survived
  and flourished because the French were permitted by British colonial authorities to retain
  their language, religion, civil law, customs, and educational system. As a consequence, the
  legitimacy of Francophone culture was ratified and, through the opportunities inherent in
  the socialization process, its content was transmitted to succeeding generations.

scattered bands of native peoples, the vast Western territories were largely uninhabited. Travel and communication were difficult, and this, in turn, inhibited the early development of an overarching sense of national community. The population of the thirteen colonies that became the new United States of America had faced similar problems a century earlier but had been able to overcome some of their effects because of the feelings of unity and of common identity fostered by a shared revolutionary experience. Participation in a successful revolution and the national identity that can be forged from it were not part of the Canadian inheritance.[10]

Garth Stevenson (1979, 1989) has noted a third difficulty: the several steps leading to Confederation were the product of decisions taken by a very small cadre of politicians rather than by the majority of the populations of the provinces that were to become parts of the new political system. Moreover, unlike the process by which the United States Constitution was ratified, this elite (the Fathers of Confederation) also manipulated subsequent events to ensure that only minute proportions of the populations of the four uniting provinces had the opportunity to pass judgment on what had been done.

It has been argued that Sir John A. Macdonald, the most important founding father and the first prime minister of Canada, understood that if the new state were to survive, the national government would have to establish its legitimacy and effectiveness. He undoubtedly understood that the provinces enjoyed a substantial headstart insofar as legitimacy was concerned simply because they antedated the new federal government. Because the lack of participation in the confederation process of the great majority of people in the four provinces had done little to facilitate public identity with and support for the federal government and the emerging national political community, Macdonald's efforts focused on demonstrating that the new government was more effective in dealing with the economic problems of the day than the provinces had been. He was not entirely successful in his efforts and, as a consequence, during most of the nineteenth century there probably was more support for the provincial governments than for the national one (Black and Cairns, 1966:27–44).

A fourth difficulty was that the motives of the founding fathers for establishing the Canadian state differed markedly. Some Ontario leaders viewed

---

10 On the consequences of the absence of a revolutionary experience in Canadian history see, e.g., Preston (1972); Lipset (1990). It should be noted that there were small and aborted rebellions in Upper and Lower Canada (i.e., Ontario and Quebec) in 1837 led by William Lyon Mackenzie and Louis Papineau, respectively. There also were two Metis uprisings, which would probably be termed national liberation struggles if they occurred today. These took place in Manitoba in 1870 and in Northwest Saskatchewan in 1885. Both were led by Louis Riel, a Metis of French and Indian descent. Following the quelling of the second uprising, Riel was executed, an act that prompted strong protests among French Canadians, who viewed the rebel leader as a defender of French culture.

Confederation as a way out of the political deadlock into which government in their province had fallen, whereas others anticipated that the feder
al union would shield the Western territories from possible American sei-
zure and provide an opportunity to exploit the West's mineral and other
resources for the benefit of the proposed new state. Quebec's leaders, in
contrast, were less concerned with securing the West and gaining access to
its resources than with safeguarding their cultural heritage and political
autonomy. They favored union because the proposed federal structure
appeared to be the best mechanism for achieving these goals. For their
part, New Brunswick and Nova Scotia elites anticipated that the new state,
with its greater financial resources and capacity to generate investment
capital, would permit the construction of a long-planned interprovincial
railroad on which rested many of their hopes for future economic development and prosperity.[11]

Because of their varying motives, there was no consensus then nor afterward regarding either the nature of the union that was forged or who were
the parties to it.[12] Of the several theories of Confederation one version
maintains that the new state was the product of a compact, and that the
parties to it were the governments of the four uniting provinces. A second
compact theory is that the parties to the agreement were the Anglo-Celtic
Protestant and French-Catholic ethnoreligious communities. A third is that
the contracting parties were the two levels of government (federal and provincial) themselves. The absence of consensus about the kind of state that
was being established and the failure to involve the public in the process
through which union was achieved are said to have created still other problems. For example, a number of observers have argued that the lack of
agreement about the character of the new state facilitated the ability of
British and Canadian judges to write constitutional decisions that expanded the powers of the provinces, fueled conflicts between generations
of self-interested federal and provincial politicians, and helped foster dual
loyalties and identities among many Canadians.[13]

Still another difficulty, Stevenson (1979:38) has contended, is that the
lack of popular participation in the establishment of the new state not
only deprived it of a degree of legitimacy and laid the groundwork for
future integration problems, but also encouraged an elite style of politics
that continues to this day. Elite domination of the political process sup-

11 See Kornberg and Hines's (1977) content analysis of the legislative debates of the parliament of United Canada (Ontario and Quebec) in the two years preceding the passage of
   the British North America Act in 1867 as well as their "scrapbook" report of debates in the
   new House of Commons in the years 1867–70 and 1873–6.
12 The various theories are discussed in Lower (1958); Kwavnick (1973); Mallory (1965);
   Cook (1969); Black (1975).
13 See, for example, Black and Cairns (1966); Cook (1969); Cairns (1971, 1983); Durocher
   (1978); Bell and Tepperman (1979); Smiley (1980); Stevenson (1989).

posedly is manifested both during and in the interim between elections and, as a result, the great majority of Canadians are spectators rather than players in the political arena.[14] This has had important effects on public attitudes and behavior. Canadians are said to lack political interest, knowledge, and sophistication, and to feel unable to participate efficaciously in the political process. As a result, despite numerous formal and informal opportunities open to them as citizens of a representative democracy, it is contended that a large majority confine their political activity almost entirely to voting. One of the important legacies of Confederation, then, is a political culture that supposedly does not foster the kinds of public attitudes and behavior that are conducive to the vitality of a democratic polity (Almond and Verba, 1963, 1980; Pateman, 1970; Thompson, 1970; Macpherson, 1977; Barber, 1984).

Nor are these legacies of Confederation the country's only problems. Some, it has been argued, derive from the poor "fit" between the country's geographic, social and economic realities and its political institutions and processes.[15] The geographic and social realities include an enormous land mass and a highly skewed distribution of population. Although its 3.8 million square miles make it second in land size only to the Soviet Union, the great majority of Canada's 26 million people live in a narrow band north of the American border. Two-thirds live in two provinces, Ontario and Quebec. The latter is home to 80 percent of the country's Francophones, somewhat less than 30 percent of the total Canadian population. The economic realities include, inter alia, very substantial differences in the value and character of the natural resources of the ten provinces, equally substantial variations in the extent to which they are industrialized, and a national economy that is tightly integrated with and dependent on a far richer and more powerful neighbor with some ten times the population, the United States. The political realities are a national political system that combines a decentralized federal structure with a British style parliamentary government. The bicameral national parliament consists of a popularly elected House of Commons and an appointed Senate, which, until recently, performed few significant policy and representational functions other than lobbying on behalf of the business community.[16]

14 The themes are familiar ones in analyses of the Canadian political process and Canadian political culture. See, *inter alia*, Porter (1965); Van Loon (1970); Presthus (1973, 1974); Clement (1975); Newman (1977, 1979, 1982); Campbell and Szablowski (1979); Lipset (1990).

15 Schwartz (1974:1), for example, has argued: "Nature and history have conspired to make geography central to an understanding of Canadian existence. The spatial makeup of Canada compounds every critical social and political problem the country faces."

16 Campbell (1978:147) concludes that "[t]he Senate primarily protects the interests of major business and financial concerns. To do this it regularly challenges, delays, and at times amends or deletes legislative provisions that might endanger major business and financial concerns, or might overlook 'good' business practice." In the post-1984 period, the

Over the years the combination of these social, economic, and political characteristics are said to have generated and sustained almost classic center–periphery conflicts, fueled Anglophone–Francophone sociocultural differences and disputes, exacerbated existing interprovincial and regional economic disparities, and prevented the development of a distinct and unifying national political culture. Why? Briefly, one argument is that since two-thirds of the population always have resided in Ontario and Quebec, these two provinces have been the arenas in which virtually every national election in the country's history has been decided. Further, given a Westminster-model parliamentary government and disciplined parliamentary parties, the interests of Ontario and Quebec invariably have prevailed over those of other parts of the country, or so many people in the latter areas have believed (e.g., Black and Cairns, 1966; Kornberg, 1970).

These beliefs are said to have had two principal consequences. One has been public disaffection from the national government ("Ottawa") in the peripheral regions and the tendency to rely on provincial governments, regardless of their partisan composition, to represent specifically provincial interests. The pursuit of such a provincially-oriented representational strategy was made viable by a series of judicial decisions on constitutional issues that expanded provincial powers in fields within which much of the post-World War II economic development subsequently occurred and in which public demands for social services increased the most. In turn, the growth in the size and salience of provincial governments during the post-1945 era increased their ability to compete with the federal government for the "hearts and minds" the two governments shared, while highly visible and periodically acrimonious federal–provincial conferences dramatized their struggle (Cairns, 1983; Falcone and Van Loon, 1983).

A second consequence, it is argued, of the dominant position of Ontario and Quebec in the federal system has been the periodic rise of protest parties in the Western provinces, the most enduring of which have been the right-of-center Social Credit and the left-of-enter Cooperative Commonwealth Federation (later the New Democratic Party) parties. Both Social Credit and the CCF had roots in the short-lived Progressive Party which, in turn, had originated during the first two decades of this century as an effort to amalgamate a number of Canadian Farmers parties. Both the Farmers parties and the Progressives were responses to the perceived exploitation of Western agriculture and the West more generally by the two older Eastern-oriented and Eastern-led parties, the Liberals and Conservatives.

Liberal-dominated Senate has assumed a more active role by opposing Conservative policy initiatives, the most salient examples being legislation regarding the free trade agreement with the United States and the General Services Tax (GST). Occasionally, the Senate also has concerned itself with constitutional issues and conducted investigations of a number of national social problems.

Attempts by Western MPs in these two parties to protest against discriminatory treatment were ignored or overridden by the much larger delegations of Ontario and Quebec MPs in their parliamentary caucuses (Morton, 1950; Macpherson, 1953; Irving, 1959; Lipset, 1968).

The two older parties, the Conservatives and the Liberals, developed in the two decades following Confederation (Hougham, 1972; Reid, 1972, Englemann and Schwartz, 1975:ch. 2). The Conservatives grew out of a pre-Confederation coalition of business–professional and Anglican Church elites in Ontario, and ultramontane French-Catholic and Anglo-Scottish business and financial oligarchies in Quebec. Sir John A. Macdonald, the architect of this coalition, used it to make himself Canada's first prime minister. The ancestors of the present Liberal Party were rural and small town, nonestablished church and moderate reform groups in Ontario (the so-called Grits), and antibusiness, anticlerical, relatively radical reform elements in Quebec (the "Rouges"). Under the leadership of Alexander Mackenzie, they were able to oust Macdonald and his Tory colleagues in the federal election of 1874. However, twenty-two years were to pass before the Liberal Party won its second national election. During their long period in opposition (1878–96) the Liberals gradually built strong party organizations in Ontario and Quebec. The strength of their Quebec base enabled them to achieve a seemingly endless stream of electoral successes in national elections during much of the twentieth century.

The Liberals were considerably less successful in Quebec provincial elections. Indeed, for approximately 60 percent of the post-World War II period Quebec has been governed either by the Union Nationale Party, a forceful exponent of Francophone nationalism, or the even more rabidly nationalistic Parti Québécois (Quinn, 1963; Lemieux, 1972; McRoberts, 1988). The latter party's success, and the tendency of its leaders to identify the interests of all French Canadians with those of Québécois, forced Quebec provincial Liberals to take increasingly nationalistic positions. This, in turn, widened and intensified differences between Quebec Liberals and Liberals in other provinces, and thereby made it extremely difficult for the party to perform the integrative function expected of political parties in socially and economically heterogeneous democratic systems. However, given the national integration problems the two Conservative administrations of the 1980s have experienced, it could be argued that passing such an "integrating-the-polity" test (Meisel, 1979) may well be asking too much of any party in a federal system in which the number, strength, and identities of the contesting parties vary sharply from province to province.

A second argument focuses either directly or indirectly on the "next door" presence of the United States and the consequences that presence, together with the factors cited above, have had on the development of a national political culture. Andrew Malcolm (1985:69) contends that although Canadians can agree on very few things, they can agree on what they are not, namely Americans. Notwithstanding such agreement, Canadian society has been deeply affected over the years by sharing a border with the United States. Numerous analysts (e.g., Horowitz, 1966; Clark, 1968; Bell and Tepperman, 1979; Lipset, 1990) contend that in a sense English Canada came into being as a by-product of the American Revolution and that the principal component of Canadian political culture became the counter-revolutionary ideology of Toryism transferred north. As a consequence, Canadians are supposedly more conservative, traditionalist, and deferential than are Americans, and state intervention by an administrative elite is more readily accepted because Canadians believe government is needed to foster national economic development and social well-being.

In this century the contiguity of the United States is credited with influencing the development of populism and the infusion of the social gospel into party politics which, in turn, affected the political thinking of the founders of the Social Credit and Cooperative Commonwealth Federation (CCF) parties (McNaught, 1959; Irving, 1959; Young, 1969). Arguably, the most important overall effects of the presence of the United States on Canadian political culture stem from the magnitude and power of the American mass media and the extent of American influence on the Canadian economy. George Grant (1970) has contended that the ideology of the American capitalist empire has absorbed and homogenized Canadian culture and ideological values. Others have argued that the extent of American economic ownership and control would not be tolerated by a third world country, let alone an advanced democracy (Levitt, 1970; Lumsden, 1970; Laxer, 1973). Black (1975) has described the Canadian-American relationship as a "disparate dyad" which is manifestly unequal, and Hiller (1986:65) has suggested that the realities engendered by Canada's marginal position have produced a feeling of societal inferiority that manifests itself periodically in mixed emotions of envy and admiration, hostility and friendship.

Another perspective is provided by Van Loon and Whittington (1981:ch. 2). They contend that the basic components of Canadian political culture are quite similar to those of other long-lived democracies. Canadian political values are rooted in Western tradition, especially in eighteenth- and nineteenth-century liberalism. Thus, it is hardly surprising that the principal components of Canadian political culture are similar to their American counterparts. Still others (e.g., Verney, 1986) contend that rather than having a single culture, such as an American one transferred north, Canada instead has multiple cultures delimited by regional boundaries, the most important distinction being between French- and English-speaking Canada.

To recapitulate, for a variety of reasons the seeds of many of the national integration problems that were to plague Canada during the twentieth century either already existed or were planted at Confederation. These were exacerbated by the poor fit between salient social and economic attributes and the political institutions and processes of the new state. Although the original distribution of powers between the national and provincial governments had established a highly centralized form of federalism, over time the centrifugal pressures that operate in any federal system had combined with a series of constitutional decisions, sociodemographic changes, and economic and political developments to produce a highly decentralized system in which the two levels of government appeared to be in perpetual conflict. In addition, by the end of the 1980s, prospects for a Canadian state that included Quebec were growing increasingly problematic.

SUPPORT FOR REPRESENTATIVE DEMOCRACIES

That many regimes rest in the infamous "dust-bin of history" is a stark reminder to political leaders that the task of sustaining the regimes they lead is not an easy one. The maintenance and sustenance of any state by its population entail both the discharge of routine obligations and the provision of valued personal resources. The willingness of a country's citizens to discharge such obligations and provide such services depends on a combination of three conditions: people's acceptance of the state's legitimacy in defining national goals; voluntary compliance with the state's authoritative edicts; and citizen acceptance of the state's use of coercive measures when voluntary compliance does not suffice.[17] As noted earlier, democracies differ from authoritarian systems because overt and sustained coercion and indoctrination cannot be used and, so, voluntary public conformity – presumably undergirded by a fund of positive feelings – is the main underpinning of the functioning democratic state. These supportive feelings are dynamic. They increase and decrease, are mobilized or quiescent. Mapping such variations and their causes and consequences, in our judgment, is at the core of the study of political support.

Given the fundamental importance of the problem, the study of political support has a history that goes back to the Greek city-state. Concern with understanding political support increased with the emergence of a large number of new states and the breakup of colonial empires after World War II. A number of studies of the political development of such states was informed by the work of scholars such as David Easton (1965). As noted earlier, Easton distinguished among the political community, regime, and authorities, as well as between what he termed *specific* and *diffuse* support. The essential features of diffuse support, according to Easton, is its affective character and its stability. Support is granted or withheld on the basis of powerful and relatively unchanging feelings of like or dislike. In con-

---

17 The literature on these points is vast. See, e.g., Pitkin (1967); Rawls (1971); Flathman (1980); Pateman (1979).

trast, the distinguishing features of specific support are that it is rational and labile, being based on people's judgments about the day-to-day actions of political leaders and the operation of governmental institutions and processes (Easton 1965:ch. 17). The principal objects of these two types of support are the aforementioned political community, regime, and authorities.

Easton's formulations inspired a large number of empirical inquiries.[18] However, this research generated numerous criticisms – some methodological, others conceptual or theoretical. For example, Loewenberg (1971) argued that the distinction between diffuse and specific support could not be captured empirically. In a similar vein Miller (1974a, 1974b) and Citrin (1974) pointed to the difficulty of disentangling people's evaluations of authorities from the legitimacy they ascribe to the regime, and Zimmermann (1979), echoing Loewenberg, claimed that the symbolic component of diffuse support could not be measured empirically.

Other criticisms focused on the theoretical utility of diffuse support. Wright (1976), for example, noted that even democratic systems seem to function for long periods of time without much diffuse support, and Rogowski (1974) contended that the most fervid diffuse support for a regime or community ultimately is contingent in character. Specific support, in turn, was found wanting because it rested on the problematic assumption that people can make cognitive connections between what they want from a political system and what that system actually delivers (Rogowski, 1983). According to Rogowski (1974:28) perhaps the greatest problem is what he terms the "impossible profusion of explanatory theories." As a consequence he proposed grouping the main theories of support under five headings: (a) theories that connect support with perceptions of fairness or of fair treatment; (b) theories that emphasize the subconscious and symbolic elements of support; (c) theories that relate support to the experience of participation or community; (d) theories based on the effectiveness of regimes; and (e) theories that stress people's positions in the social division of labor, and changes in that division.

Given these varying conceptions of support and the methodological problems they pose, some scholars have proposed that we employ instead analogues such as political efficacy, trust, cynicism, alienation, and legitimacy.[19] Rather than abandon the concept, we have chosen to focus *on*

---

18 See, *inter alia*, Muller (1970); Loewenberg (1971); Wahlke (1971); Boynton and Loewenberg (1973); Patterson, Wahlke, and Boynton (1973); Rogowski (1974, 1983); Patterson, Hedlund, and Boynton (1975); Jewell and Kim (1976); Muller and Jukam (1977); Kornberg, Clarke, and LeDuc (1978, 1980); Kornberg, Clarke, and Stewart (1979, 1980); Muller and Williams (1980); Muller, Jukam, and Seligson (1982); Clarke, Kornberg, and Stewart (1984); Kim et al. (1984).

19 See the studies cited in Muller and Jukam (1977:1562–4, notes 5–7). See also Gamson (1968); Finifter (1970); Citrin (1974); Miller (1974a, 1974b); Citrin et al. (1975); Shanks and Citrin (1975); Wright (1976); Muller and Williams (1980); Sniderman (1981); and Muller, Jukam, and Seligson (1982). For arguments in favor of the concept of political support see Easton (1975, 1976).

what is supported and not whether support is specific or diffuse in nature.
We regard support as an affective orientation to political objects and processes. The affect can be positive, neutral, or negative, and the objects and processes can range from the concrete and well-defined (e.g., political parties, MPs, procedures for appealing judicial decisions) to the abstract and amorphous (e.g., a political regime or community). In our view, a person's support for any political object or process has two principal sources. One is the person's socialization and resocialization experiences; the other, cost–benefit calculations, however "rough and ready," concerning the ways in which any object or process performs its ascribed functions, interacts with and affects other objects and processes, and provides for one's personal well-being and that of cherished others.

Conceptualizing political support in this way has three distinct advantages. First, it enables us to retain its core meaning while obviating some of the theoretical and methodological problems just noted. Second, it gives the support process the kind of dynamic quality it has in any political system, but especially in a democracy. In the latter, neither empirical experience nor liberal democratic theory (one of whose tenets includes the right of revolution among the conditions under which the mythical contract between rulers and ruled may be breached) are adverse to changes in even their most fundamental institutions and processes. Indeed, democracies rely on public opinion and those same institutions and processes to both initiate and implement such changes. A third advantage is that it enables us to subsume the five classes of theories delineated by Rogowski and to construct a number of empirical tests of their relative explanatory power.

For example, we can test theories viewing support as a function of citizens' perceptions of the fairness of their treatment by government and governmental authorities, as well as theories that relate support to public perceptions of whether a society's division of labor and rewards is fair and equitable by asking people whether they agree or disagree that: in a country like Canada, the laws apply to the rich and poor alike; achievement rather than ascription determines success in life; the courts and bureaucracy treat people fairly; and parliament and political parties represent general rather than particularistic interests. We can employ attitudinal variables such as how politically efficacious and trusting people are, how responsive they feel MPs are to their needs and interests, and what role elections play to test theories in which differences in support are consequences of variations in people's beliefs about whether the political system is functioning according to democratic norms. Theories that view variations in support as a product of citizen assessments of governmental performance can be tested with data on how effective people judge government to be in providing a variety of goods and services such as social welfare, health care, educational opportunities, protection of lives and property, and the maintenance of national security. Similarly, judgments about the state of the economy, one's personal financial condition, and the attributions of governmental responsibility for economic affairs can be employed to test theories that political support is a product of people's evaluations of the ability of a government to manage the economy in ways that secure and enhance their own and their country's well-being.

Finally, the specification of the relationships between support and variables such as age, gender, education, ethnicity, income, and region of residence and the delineation of the relationships between support and perceptions of the ways in which the media represent the national political community, regime, and authorities can be used to test theories focusing on the subconscious, symbolic elements underlying supportive attitudes that are products of political socialization processes. Perhaps the most difficult task is to test the latter; that is, the theoretical perspective that support for key political objects is in part a function of different socialization experiences. One of the reasons the socialization process is invariably described as complex is that rarely does exposure to a particular socializing agent produce a specific political act. Moreover, support that is the product of socialization is likely to vary with the object being judged and with the characteristics of those doing the judging. Also, socialization processes occur throughout a person's life and to clearly illuminate the ways in which they affect people over time would require a longitudinal investigation in which a random sample of children were monitored and analyzed into adulthood. Because time and money constraints make a study of this kind impossible, we have had to rely instead on the sociodemographic "proxy" variables of age, education, ethnicity, gender, income, and regional residence. The assumption is that these variables will capture some of the subtle and distal effects that family, peer groups, and social class memberships have on political socialization processes: effects that, however much they may vary cross-nationally, are likely to be manifested in any democracy.

For example, we anticipate that life-cycle or generational effects related to political socialization processes will be reflected in relationships between age and support for political objects. Income and education are convenient proxies for social class and status-related differences operative in advanced industrial democracies that bear on the development of support for political authorities, regime and community. Regional residency and ethnicity are assumed to reflect historic patterns of economic, political, and cultural development within the Canadian federal state. Ontario has been both the largest, the most economically favored and politically influential region and, thus, it is reasonable to assume that residents of that province generally will be more supportive of various political objects and processes than will people in other regions. We also expect that within Quebec the minority of non-Francophones will be more supportive of the national political system than will Francophone Quebecers. Similar to other Western democracies, women historically have been disadvantaged in a variety of ways, and we anticipate that they will be less supportive of political objects and processes than men.

Notwithstanding the difficulties involved in trying to explain variations in support with differences in political socialization experiences, it is possible to offer several hypotheses regarding the association between the two. It seems reasonable to hypothesize that the public's highest and most consistent support will be given to the national political community, in this instance, Canada, because the latter provides its citizens with an overarching political and cultural identity which everyone – Westerners, Quebecers, Maritimers, and Ontarians – can share, in addition to their regional identities. A second hypothesis is that there should be somewhat lower and less consistent support for the regime. This is because classical liberalism, which provides the most important strands in liberal democratic theory, ascribes largely instrumental value to the regime and its several institutions and processes. They are the means through which citizens can develop and fulfill themselves, not ends in themselves (e.g., Pateman, 1970; Macpherson, 1977; Barber, 1984). A public's ongoing experience with regime institutions will determine which work best and should remain unchanged, and which require modification, or even replacement. In a sense, then, the jury is always out on at least some parts of the regime, and because it is, in a democracy such as Canada, regime support should be lower and considerably more variable for it than for the national political community.

There should be even less and more mutable citizen support for political authorities. In a democracy not only are authorities assumed to be merely the temporary occupants of their positions (and subject always to dismissal by a frequently restless electorate), but also the regard in which they are held varies sharply with public judgments about their performance in office. A sense of partisanship should be an important factor. Although in any political system parties can be an integrative mechanism, in a democracy such as Canada they are part of a competitive system, and so people identifying with a particular party are likely to feel much more positively about the candidates and officeholders of their party than about those who represent other parties. More generally, as previously noted, citizens in democratic countries judge their governments on how effectively they perform in office, and how fair and equitable they are. Therefore, we can hypothesize that those who believe that the country's economy is in good shape, that they and theirs are doing well and have been well-treated, and that the government has had something to do with this happy state of affairs, should be stronger supporters of political authorities and government per se than those who, for whatever reasons, do not feel this way.

To return to the other pillar of political support, namely the socialization process, it is one component of the more general process through which people become social beings. Research indicates that in a normal course of development people move from a largely egocentric orientation to their environment to one in which they become a "social" being, in that the expectations of "significant others" assume predominant relevance in structuring their behavior.[20] Significant others, however, include various combinations and numbers of individuals and groups. Early childhood socialization, for example, occurs in the personal, interactive setting of the family, whereas many of the socializing experiences of later life take place in more impersonal settings in which relationships with socializing agents are structured by formal and informal institutional norms. Within those settings, individuals develop and change their attitudes and values, learn a variety of roles, the behavior appropriate to them, and adopt identifications with and support for numerous objects and processes – some manifestly political, others not.

It follows that the generation of support in a democracy may be two-tracked. Normally, the political and nonpolitical tracks not only intersect, they are almost inextricably, if subtly, intertwined. At times, however, the support accorded certain sociocultural objects and processes will be higher, on average, than that accorded manifestly political ones. Indeed, it can be argued that one reason democracies, in contrast to other political systems, are able to sustain themselves even during extended periods of economic or political "hard times" is that their citizens remain relatively satisfied with their personal lives and with the myriad social institutions and processes they encounter, most of which are part and parcel of everyday life. In the Canadian context, for example, even if people's overall support for the national regime and for other political objects eroded significantly during the late 1970s and early 1980s, a majority still may have had strong, positive feelings about Canada, their provinces, home towns, neighbors, and jobs: more generally, they were high on what may be termed "the Canadian way of life." This fund of positive feelings may help explain why Canadians (and citizens of other democracies as well) are willing to comply with a government's authoritative edicts, even when they are not enamored of the edicts or of the government. Simply put, they are living in a democratic society that "delivers" enough material and psychic benefits to enough people to maintain the existing social, economic, and political order.

With respect to why support – especially support for manifestly political objects – waxes and wanes, one reason is that there is a sporadic, almost haphazard quality to the socialization process, particularly political socialization in a liberal democracy such as Canada. Unlike a visibly authoritarian system such as existed until relatively recently in the Soviet Union and that still exists in the Peoples Republic of China, there are no arms of the state that systematically and continually expose people to symbols, myths, and highly favorable information about the political system

20 See Friedman (1977) for a review of relevant political socialization literature.

and its current leaders and their policies.[21] Hence citizens are not mobilized on a more or less continuing basis to support the regime, its leaders, and their policies. In democracies voluntary associations and arms of the state are agents of political socialization in the sense that they periodically provide citizens with politically relevant information and commentary about their country, its government, public officials, and the policies they do and do not pursue. However, as noted above, agents such as schools and civic groups are less extensively and intensively involved than is the case in many nondemocratic countries. Democracies normally are politically "cool" societies. Political issues rarely generate intense conflict, and the actions of political authorities, even those at the highest levels, are only infrequently matters of sustained attention and concern to average citizens. Moreover, in democracies neither the information provided by socializing agents such as schools, civic groups, and organized interests, nor the comments they make about political leaders and institutions, are invariably flattering or positive. This also is true of other important agents of political socialization such as families, peer groups, and, especially, the mass media.

Regarding the media, radical critiques of their role in representative democracies – such as that offered by the "Frankfurt School" of Adorno and Horkheimer[22] – argue that they are the most indefatigable salesmen of capitalism's ideological baggage and one of the principal pillars on which capitalist economies and democratic political regimes rest (Parenti, 1986; Bennett, 1988). In contrast, conservative critics of the media more often criticize them for a different sin – for their biases and their conceit in regarding themselves as the "real" and "permanent" opposition to a government of the day, a conceit that periodically elicits sharp criticism of them from public officials who are their frequent targets and from some social scientists who study and analyze their content. In the United States, for example, Wattenberg (1985) and others (e.g., Lefever, 1976; Robinson, 1977; Braestrup, 1978; Rothman, 1979) have argued that the media, especially television, tend to be biased, excessively negative in their selection

---

21 See, for example, Inkeles (1950); Wylie (1962); and Urban (1972). Dogan and Pelassy (1984:72) observe that "[w]hereas the modernization of societies implies the multiplication of sources of information and the development of cross-cutting messages, the totalitarian state returns to a single and indivisible Truth. The arts and sciences reflect the *Weltanschauung* of the day. Ideological slogans learned at school and repeated in youth organizations are again declared or preached in factories and delivered over the air waves. Public censorship and private cowardice contribute to make up a world where the youth, once he or she reaches adulthood, remains subject to the same socializing processes."

22 Max Horkhemier and Theodore Adorno were the central figures of the Frankfurt Institute for Social Research. Marxist in orientation, they became disillusioned by Soviet communism and the failure of the proletariat to fulfill its revolutionary role. In accounting for the latter, Horkheimer and Adorno developed a theory of "mass culture" in which the popular media served as a tool of class domination.

and presentation of politically relevant news material, and often wrong in their interpretation of the material. Since Americans obtain most of their information about politics from the mass media, they often have a distorted and negative picture of political conditions at home and abroad and what their government is doing about them. Such a picture has deleterious long- as well as short-term consequences for political support. If these criticisms are valid, and if what is true of the United States also is true of countries such as Canada, we may infer that over time both the absolute and relative levels of public support for major political objects can be adversely affected by one of the institutions their citizens value the most, a free press.

A second reason why in a democracy support for key political objects is dynamic and why there may be lower support for them than for nonpolitical ones is that people are socialized to believe that important areas of their lives are and should be outside the purview of government. Many may simply assume that the activities of government at best only marginally affect the things they care most about in their daily lives. For example, average citizens may fail to see any connection between what government does and matters such as the progress of children in school, employment opportunities and possibilities for occupational advancement, whether to purchase a new car, house, or apartment, where and when to take annual vacations, with what church to affiliate, or how often to attend religious services. This separation of what is public and what is private can have a number of effects on political support levels, some positive, others negative. By way of illustration, because the distinction between public and private spheres and responsibilities can become blurred, political authorities may be blamed or praised for conditions over which they have little or no influence. Perhaps more likely is that political authorities may fail to receive credit or be blamed for conditions over which they *do* exercise a significant degree of influence. Also, if people really feel that government and its officials have little or no effect on many of the things that are important to them, they may have little incentive to acquire political information, develop a continuing interest in politics and public affairs, and try to influence either the content or implementation of public policy in the interim between elections. They may even lack the incentive to vote.

With regard to those who actually do become politically active, it can be argued that conventional forms of political participation – like participation in social organizations more generally – tend to psychologically "implicate" people in an ongoing process and help legitimate that process for them (e.g., Ginsberg, 1982). Conventional types of political activity, such as talking about public affairs, trying to convince others how to vote, contributing money to candidates or parties, and contacting public officials about a pressing public or personal concern, can have both direct and indirect effects on political support levels. Normally, the association between conventional forms of political action and support for the community and regime (although not necessarily the authorities) should be reciprocal and positive. More extensive participation should prompt increased support, and high levels of support should prompt greater participation.

Participation in *unconventional* political activities such as street riots, illegal gatherings and demonstrations, and the attempted or actual destruction of public or private property, can be an important consequence of low levels of support at the authorities, regime or community levels. Although these kinds of activities still occur only infrequently in contemporary Western countries, their incidence has increased noticeably in the past thirty years (Barnes, Kaase et al., 1979; Jennings, Van Deth et al., 1989). In addition, public attitudes toward other, less confrontational, types of unconventional political action have changed. Activities such as signing petitions, engaging in marches and rallies, and boycotting various goods and services now are regarded by many people as legitimate forms of political expression. In contrast, activities such as unlawful demonstrations that might become violent and result in personal injury or widespread property damage are still regarded as beyond the pale.

People probably understand that the latter kinds of actions constitute serious disruptions of public order. They probably also understand that although government leaders normally are reluctant to do so, even the most indulgent and permissive will not tolerate frequent occurrences of politically inspired violence or widespread noncompliance with their authoritative edicts. They eventually will resort to coercive countermeasures because no regime can long survive extended breakdowns in public order. Consequently, the great majority of citizens in democratic polities normally refrain from engaging in actions that would elicit draconian responses from government. This kind of self-denying behavior can be thought of as a kind of citizens *quo* for their political leaders *quid* that facilitates the ability of democracies to accommodate changes that usually are incremental, but at times can be significant departures from current practice. Given these realities, it can be expected that approval of and participation in more extreme kinds of unconventional political activities among citizens of democracies such as Canada will be negatively associated with support for political authorities, regime, and community.

Not only should socialization processes in democracies affect support and some of its causes and consequences directly, they also should affect them indirectly. Socializing experiences provide cognitive and evaluative benchmarks against which people make cost–benefit calculations about their political system, its key institutions and processes, and the men and women who animate them. Of these, what has come to be viewed as the most important are public judgments about government's handling of the economy: the more satisfied people are with the condition of the economy and a government's stewardship of it, the more support they should ascribe to both a current government, and government per se. As noted, people's evaluations of their personal economic and more general welfare also may influence political support levels, but not as strongly as judgments about the economy and government's impact thereon, because citizens in democracies tend to believe that who they are, and what they have accomplished materially and otherwise, are partially or largely products of their own initiatives and efforts rather than any actions of government.

Because research indicates that people in democracies now get most of their information about politics and public affairs from the mass media, in particular, from television (e.g., Nimmo and Combs, 1983; Siegel, 1983:ch. 2; Soderlund et al., 1984:ch. 2), we may assume that global judgments about their country, its government, the state of the economy, and the ability of government to manage it, all may be strongly influenced by what they see, hear, or read in the media. In contrast, people's judgments about their own material and more general well-being may be based more heavily on personal experience. As a consequence, there may well be marked disjunctions between citizens' judgments about the condition of their society, its major social, economic, and political institutions on the one hand and their own condition, on the other.

In many ways, political life in contemporary democracies is animated by political parties, and feelings about them also should have important consequences for support. For example, as we have observed, party identifiers should like their party better than other ones, and so people identified with a governing party should be more charitable in their evaluations of its stewardship of the economy than are those identified with an opposition party. The nature and levels of interparty competition also should be relevant. For one thing, the longer a party has been in power, the more likely it is for the distinction between government-of-the-day and government as regime to be obfuscated, and for people to praise or blame the regime and not merely an incumbent government for the condition of the country. For another, the issue priorities of parties and their more general ideological positions may influence the ways in which people think about government's ability to manage public affairs. When the policy and more general ideological distance between and among parties is substantial, it is likely that people will believe that a recent or anticipated change in the governing party or party coalition will result in new policy initiatives that could have a significant impact on the country's and their own well-being. In such a circumstance, judgments about public affairs, including the condition of the economy and one's status, and how they may be affected by government, should be largely future oriented, or "prospective." In contrast, when the policies and ideologies of parties are very similar, it is likely that people may feel that a recent or prospective change in the governing party or party coalition will result in "more of the same." Consequently, public judgments will be largely "retrospective," i.e. grounded in perceptions of how well a government has done in the past. These are hypotheses, and in the analyses that follow one of our tasks will be to assess their validity in the Canadian context.

To recapitulate, we have argued that representative democracies differ in a number of ways from other political systems. Perhaps the most important is that political leaders in democracies must rely on a fund of positive feelings (support) on the part of citizens rather than on extensive and intensive coercion and indoctrination to sustain their national political communities and regimes and to keep themselves in office. The two principal sources, which we term the "twin pillars" of such support, are the political socialization experiences of citizens, and their judgments about the ability of political figures, institutions and processes to perform their ascribed functions effectively and equitably, and in so doing to provide for national and personal well-being.

Support is dynamic and can vary markedly over time because public judgments are made in a context of political and economic short- as well as long-term forces. Variations in support, in turn, affect a number of matters. Two of these – differences in levels of participation in conventional and unconventional political activities and the extent to which people are willing to comply with the authoritative edicts of government – are particularly pertinent to understanding the support process in a democracy and its consequences. In the analyses that follow we will assess the validity of these hypotheses. A schematic representation of our thinking about the causes and consequences of political support is presented in Figure 1.1.

Under the rubric "democratic norms" in the figure are matters such as people's feelings about democracy and elections, while "personal and group identifications" include psychological attachments to political parties and regions as well as identifications derived from membership in groups such as those defined by ethnicity, gender and social class. "Judgments about the system" include evaluations of the effectiveness and equitable operation of government generally and/or specific social and political institutions. As noted above, such judgments are made within the context of socialization experiences that can extend over the life space and so we have posited the existence of a reciprocal linkage between socialization experiences and judgments about the system. Both of these, in turn, affect "values, attitudes, and perspectives," including feelings of political competence, trust in political authorities and levels of political interest. Socialization experiences, judgments about the system and values, attitudes, and perspectives all influence support for political authorities. The "twin pillars" of support (i.e., socialization and judgments) also are hypothesized to have direct effects on support for the regime and the national political community. And, as noted, support has consequences. In this study we are concerned with the extent to which people are willing to comply with authoritative edicts of government and the extent to which they engage

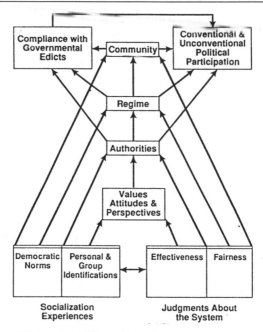

Figure 1.1. *The political support process*

in both conventional and unconventional forms of political activity. We hypothesize that compliance orientations influence the likelihood that individuals will engage in various forms of political action. Finally, we hypothesize a hierarchical ordering in which support for authorities predicts support for the regime which, in turn, predicts support for the national political community. In brief, support flows upward.

We test these several hypotheses in the chapters that follow, beginning in Chapter 2 by describing and analyzing the economic and social contexts within which public judgments are made about key political objects and processes. We use our data and those generated in other national studies of the Canadian public to address questions such as whether Canadians differentiate clearly between national economic conditions and their own; the extent to which they attribute responsibility to the government for the country's and their own economic condition; whether there is an underlying structure to their economic thinking; the extent to which they feel socially trusting and personally efficacious; the regard in which they hold major social and political institutions; and differences in the ways in which Francophones and Anglophones view one another. We conclude by offering an interpretation of why Canadians appear to hold ambivalent and frequently contradictory opinions, arguing that many of their global judgments about the country and the economy are influenced by the mass media, whereas their perspectives on their own condition and that of their local communities rest more heavily on personal experience.

In Chapter 3 we examine the political cultural context in which support judgments are made. We begin by delineating the content and structure of Canadians' beliefs about the meaning of democracy. We analyze their evaluations of Canada, the United States, and the Soviet Union as democracies and compare them with how satisfied citizens in eight European countries are with their democracies. Then, because political parties are accorded pivotal roles in support processes, we analyze the nature of Canadians' partisan attachments. We next examine judgments about the performance of the national government in several important policy areas and evaluations of the equity/fairness of major political institutions and processes. The chapter concludes by investigating four critical elements of a democratic political culture: political interest, knowledge, efficacy, and trust. We analyze variations in political efficacy and trust in political authorities over time and across levels of the Canadian federal system, as well as relationships between these attitudes and more general feelings of personal competence and social trust.

Chapter 4 traces aggregate- and individual-level variations in support for Canada's national political authorities, regime (government of Canada, parliament, civil service, judiciary), and community over a fifteen-year period. We determine if the theoretical distinctions among authorities, regime, and political community support actually correspond to the way in which people think about these entities. We then explore relationships between authorities, regime, and community support and a group of sociodemographic and attitudinal variables. The former are used to proxy the long-term effects of socialization experiences; the latter include party identification, economic and more general government effectiveness evaluations, equity/fairness judgments, as well as the extent to which people trust political authorities and feel politically efficacious.

Quebec and the West are the two regions of Canada in which political support is most problematic. In Chapter 5 we discuss the historical circumstances that have made support for the national authorities, regime, and community in these regions a problem. We describe the development of their national and provincial party systems because the party systems of two regions both reflect regional disaffection and attempts, in the case of the West, to ameliorate it, and in Quebec, to overcome it. In the former region, a noteworthy indication of this discontent has been the rapid growth of support for the new Reform Party. In the latter, the most drastic manifestation was the May 1980 Quebec sovereignty-association referendum. If approved, the referendum proposal would have given the Parti Québécois provincial government a popular mandate to negotiate Quebec independence. The referendum thus constituted a dramatic challenge to the continuing viability of the Canadian political system and a profound test of public support for it.

Although national elections are key features of democratic politics, little is known about how citizens evaluate the electoral process, or if such evaluations affect support. In Chapter 6 we delineate Canadians' evaluations of the meaning of elections and the extent to which they influence support at the authorities, regime, and community levels. Relatedly, because free and fair elections are key symbols of a bona fide democracy, we determine if the *occurrence* of national elections is associated with heightened political support. We then present case studies of the determinants of support for incumbent political authorities by examining voting behavior in Canada's two most recent national elections. The September 1984 election produced a resounding defeat for the governing Liberal Party, which had held office for nineteen of the preceding twenty years. The removal from office of a hitherto dominant party exemplifies what often has been termed the "genius of democracy," the ability of citizens to peacefully replace one set of political authorities with another, while leaving support for the regime and community intact. The November 1988 elections is a contrasting case; an incumbent government was returned to office. The major issue in this contest, free trade with the United States, like the Quebec sovereignty-association referendum, raised important questions about the continuing viability of the Canadian political community. Although the governing Conservatives argued that free trade was simply an economic arrangement that would enhance national prosperity, opposition parties claimed that closer economic ties with the Americans would endanger the country's cultural, economic, and, ultimately, its political independence.

Chapter 7 employs multivariate models to delineate the relative explanatory power of the several sociodemographic, evaluative, and attitudinal factors that we hypothesize are the principal determinants of support. The significance of economic performance judgments and election evaluations in these analyses leads us to investigate the generality of these findings. We do so by analyzing how economic conditions and salient political interventions such as election outcomes affect public satisfaction with the operation of democracy in eight European countries over a ten-year period, 1976–86. Because one of the major deficiencies of previous studies of political support is a failure to demonstrate that variations in support have important consequences for the operation of a democratic political system, we next investigate the linkages between political support, on the one hand, and its consequences, on the other. Regarding the latter we are specifically concerned with people's patterns of political participation and their willingness to comply voluntarily with the authoritative edicts of government. We demonstrate that compliance attitudes and patterns of political action are multidimensional, and that these several dimensions are affected by variations in authorities, regime, and community support as well as by attitudes and evaluations relevant to the support process.

In Chapter 8, we first review the major theoretical arguments and empirical findings of the study. We then develop a six-fold typology of political support at the authorities, regime, and community levels, examine the dynamics of membership in the six types in the several regions of Canada in the 1980s, and analyze differences in levels of compliance and participation of polar "supporter" and "alienated" types. Lastly, we consider the implications of the study for understanding the conduct of political life in Canada and other contemporary representative democracies as they reach the threshold of the twenty-first century.

2

Economy, society, self

Bourgeois society has been cast in a purely economic mold: its foundations, beams, and beacons are all made of economic material.

Joseph Schumpeter, *Capitalism, Socialism and Democracy*, p. 73

Since the late 1960s, rational choice models based on economic variables have become the dominant mode of analysis, while cultural factors have been deemphasized to an unrealistic degree.

Ronald Inglehart, *Culture Shift*, p. 16

Political support and political culture are inextricably linked. In an extended essay on the multifaceted relationship between politics and culture Samuel Barnes (1986:16) argued that "at a minimum cultural patterns are the routine, largely unexamined options followed by most people most of the time." They are derived from widely shared assumptions, meanings and values held by a group of people and provide the context and situations in which behavior occurs. As Barnes puts it, "culture comes early in the causal chain." His views about culture raise the question of how widely shared assumptions, meanings, and values have to be in order for them to be considered "cultural patterns." For example, how widely must people share views about the "meaning" of democracy or elections in order for them to be part of a cultural pattern? Also, how much political efficacy, trust, interest in politics or deference toward political authorities must people in a democracy exhibit for a culture to be considered "democratic"? Democratic theorists such as McClosky (1964:361–82) and Prothro and Grigg (1960:176–94) have argued that democratic values do not require a large measure of consensus in order for them to be a component of a democratic culture. Rather, a democratic culture can be sustained and affect the conduct of politics even if the values that lead to general democratic principles (e.g., majority rule and minority rights) are widely shared by only elite segments of a population. Although in a previous study (Kornberg, Mishler, and Clarke, 1982) we have questioned this assumption, it does suggest that any analysis of the complex relationships between political support and political culture should take into account conventional indicators of socioeconomic status such as education and income. As noted in Chapter 1, we will employ these as proxy variables to capture the effects of political socialization experiences on variations in political support.

In his essay Barnes also contended that cultural patterns, irrespective of the extent to which they are shared, are not immutable and unchanging. Instead, they are influenced and altered over time by what is going on in other areas of life. The extent to which these changes occur, however, is an empirical question that must be addressed with appropriate data. We agree, and so throughout this book we will employ cross-sectional and panel data to delineate aggregate and individual changes over time in people's social, economic, and political beliefs, and how these affect the attitudes and opinions we have hypothesized are relevant to understanding the support process.

In this chapter we will consider a variety of public beliefs about society and economy. Specifically, we will focus on whether Canadians distinguish between the condition of the national economy as opposed to their personal economic circumstances; whether they are more willing to blame government than to praise it for its impact on national and personal economic conditions; whether they are more positively disposed toward social than political institutions; whether they trust their fellow citizens and are self-confident and optimistic; and whether attitudinal and evaluative variables relevant for understanding political support are related to regional and ethnic cleavages and other sociodemographic characteristics. The analyses provide the necessary background for our subsequent investigation of support because they show that people's judgments about the economy and their own condition as well as that of other Canadians tend to be asymmetric and that variables such as ethnicity, regional residence, gender, age, education, and income that are intended to be "proxies" for the complex but elusive effects on support of multifaceted socialization processes are not generally significant predictors of variations in their attitudes and perspectives. We will also present evidence of substantively significant differences in the ways in which Francophone Quebecers, and Anglophones in the rest of the country view one another – differences that contribute to the regional disaffection chronicled in Chapter 5. We will argue that in no small part Canadians hold what seems to be ambivalent, even contradictory, opinions about these and other matters because of cultural norms, and because they rely on different sources for information when making judgments about them.

THE ECONOMY: STAGFLATION AND ASYMMETRIC NEGATIVISM

Surveys conducted by the Canadian Institute of Public Opinion (CIPO) over the past two decades document the extent to which economic problems have dominated public concerns. During this period at least two-thirds of those interviewed typically mentioned some aspect of the economy as the "most important problem" facing the country. These surveys also show that despite the perennial problem of unemployment, Canadians normally have worried about inflation or the state of the economy more generally rather than joblessness. For example, although the seasonally adjusted annual rate of unemployment was consistently high in the 1970s (7.4 percent on average) and 1980s (8.6 percent on average), in only five of thirty surveys between 1970 and 1984 did as many as 40 percent cite joblessness as the nation's most important problem. Another indication of the salience of inflation and the country's more general economic condition relative to all other major problems is that in 1980, the year of Quebec's sovereignty-association referendum, in three national surveys conducted before and after that event, 48 percent of the public, on average, stated that inflation/state of the economy was the country's most important problem, whereas not quite 7 percent awarded that dubious distinction to "national unity."

Although Canadians' high level of concern with inflation during much of the past two decades indicates a general aversion to price increases,[1] it also reflects economic reality during this period. Annual rates of inflation which averaged only 2.2 percent during the 1950s and 1960s rose sharply in the 1970s and peaked at 12.5 percent in 1981, two years after the dramatic surge in energy prices stimulated by the OPEC cartel. Contributing, undoubtedly, to the price increases of this era was the development of what may be termed an inflationary, or better, a "stagflationary" psychology. Two of the ways in which it was manifested were a widespread belief that consumer prices would continue to accelerate and, more generally, that the economic future was grim. For example, in a 1974 year-end survey majorities of varying sizes said that the coming year would be worse than the one just ending because prices and unemployment both would rise, there would be more strikes and industrial conflict, taxes would go up, and economic decline was unavoidable. The 1976, 1977, 1978, and 1979 year-end surveys were equally gloomy: inflation and unemployment would increase and economic distress would continue. These dire predictions persisted into the early 1980s but then, as the "misery index" (combining the average annual inflation and unemployment rates) declined from a high of 21.8 percent in 1982 to a low of 11.9 percent in 1988, the public mood brightened.

The improving climate of public opinion is evident in our national sur-

1 Suggestive of the relative persistence of inflation concerns is Johnston's analysis of how responses to the "most important problem" question react to inflation and unemployment rates. Using survey data gathered in quarterly Decima polls for the 1980–83 period, Johnston (1986:126–8) concluded that although Canadians are averse to both inflation and unemployment, worries about unemployment "evaporate more quickly" than those about inflation, and that there is "a standing aversion to inflation relative to unemployment."

Table 2.1. *Evaluations of the national economy and government impact, 1983, 1987, 1988 (in percent)*

		1983	1987	1988
Economy's performance relative to three or four years ago				
	Better	23	32	49
	Same	29	45	38
	Worse	48	23	13
	N	2103	1799	2182
Present performance of economy				
	Very well	2	6	13
	Fairly well	42	55	68
	Not very well	54	33	16
	Pro/con	2	7	3
	N	2162	1802	2192
Anticipated performance of economy over next three or four years				
	Better	38	22	23
	Same	52	63	63
	Worse	10	15	14
	N	2036	1760	1961
Evaluation of federal government's handling of economy				
	Very good	3	3	7
	Good	38	40	64
	Poor	36	30	19
	Very poor	15	7	3
	Pro/con	8	20	7
	N	2068	1773	2158
Government impact on anticipated performance of economy				
	Great deal	38	34	44
	Something	43	45	41
	Not much	20	21	15
	N	2080	1711	1930

Note: In this and all subsequent tables and figures, 1988 data are from the preelection survey unless otherwise indicated.

veys. In 1983, 1987, and 1988 people were questioned about the current state of the national economy, how well its past condition compared with the present, whether it would improve or deteriorate in the future, and whether the federal government had a "great deal," "something," or "not much" to do with economic performance. The 1983 survey revealed that not only were many Canadians unhappy about the economy, their displeasure extended to the federal government's handling of it. In response to the question about how the economy was doing, a majority said "not very well," and a large minority said it was worse than it had been three or four years earlier (Table 2.1). Although Canadians were somewhat more optimistic about the future, three-fifths believed the economy either would "stay the same" or "get worse" in the next few years. As for government's management of the economy, over half said the government had done either a "poor job" or a "very poor job" and less than one in twenty credited the government with doing a "very good job."

Four years later economic conditions had improved substantially, if un-

evenly, throughout most of the country and, although unbridled enthusiasm remained the exception, people took note of the change. Three-fifths
said the economy was performing well, one-third said it was performing
better than it had three or four years ago, and only one-quarter said it was
worse than it had been at that time. In 1988 Canadians were even more
optimistic about the current state of the economy – 81 percent said it was
doing either very well (13 percent) or fairly well (68 percent), and 49 percent thought it had improved. They also were more positive about the
government's ability to manage the economy than they had been in earlier
years; 71 percent stated that the government was either doing a very good
(7 percent) or good job (64 percent). And, not surprisingly in a country in
which the federal government long has been actively involved in managing
the economy, in all three surveys large majorities stated that government
would have either a great deal or some responsibility for the future state of
the nation's economic affairs.

In each of these surveys people were asked to make judgments about
their own economic circumstances – past, present, and future – and to
assess the extent to which government had an impact on their well-being.
In contrast to their measured and frequently gloomy assessments about the
national economy in 1983 and their growing, if often restrained, optimism
about its future prospects in the 1987 and 1988 surveys, large percentages
of people always stated that they were in fairly good shape financially, that
they were better off than they had been three or four years earlier, and that
they would fare even better in the future. For example, in answer to a
question concerning levels of satisfaction with their current material standard of living over 80 percent in all three surveys stated they either were
"very" or "fairly satisfied" with their condition. When asked whether they
thought they were financially better or worse off than in the past, in 1983
40 percent said they were "better off" and only 21 percent said they were
"worse off" (Table 2.2). In 1988 these opinions were essentially unchanged. Similar answers were given in all three surveys to the question of
how well off people anticipated being in the near future; on average 37
percent said they would be better off, 51 percent that they would stay the
same, and only 13 percent that they would be worse off.

The consistency of these assessments of one's material condition extended to perceptions of the extent to which those conditions were affected
by government. In every survey people believed government had less of an
impact on their personal financial condition than on that of the economy as
a whole. On average almost 40 percent anticipated that the government
would have a great deal of impact on the economy's future performance,
but only 27 percent felt government would have a similar impact on their
own standard of living. Conversely, only one in five thought government
would have very little influence on the economy, whereas about twice as
many believed government would have a negligible effect on their personal
finances.

Table 2.2. *Evaluations of personal economic condition and government impact, 1983, 1987, 1988 (in percent)*

		1983	1987	1988
Present financial condition relative to four years ago*				
	Better	40	t	41
	Same	39	t	46
	Worse	21	t	14
	N	2098		2189
Satisfaction with present material standard of living				
	Very satisfied	29	30	25
	Fairly satisfied	53	53	59
	Little dissatisfied	13	12	14
	Very dissatisfied	4	4	3
	N	2107	1853	2212
Anticipated personal material standard of living in three or four years				
	Better	35	41	34
	Same	50	49	55
	Worse	15	11	12
	N	2044	1805	2098
Government impact on financial condition over last four years*				
	Great deal	23	t	18
	Something	30	t	30
	Not much	47	t	52
	N	2078		2174
Government impact on present material standard of living				
	Great deal	28	26	25
	Something	31	35	36
	Not much	42	40	39
	N	2096	1805	2173
Government impact on anticipated material standard of living				
	Great deal	31	22	29
	Something	33	33	34
	Not much	37	45	38
	N	2003	1747	2063

Note: t - question not asked; * - "five years" in 1983 survey

Asymmetric responsibility attributions

When judgments about people's material well-being were considered in conjunction with their beliefs about the extent to which their condition was affected by government, we consistently found that the *greater* people's level of satisfaction, the *less* likely they were to attribute responsibility to government and vice versa. In 1988, for example, only 25 percent of those who said they were very satisfied with their material standard of living judged that government had a great deal to do with it (Table 2.3). The percentage rose to 38 percent among those who were a "little" dissatisfied, and to 62 percent among those who were "very" dissatisfied. The 1983 and 1987 response patterns were identical. These patterns also characterized changes in people's financial condition relative to what it had been in the past and what they anticipated it would be in the future. In 1983 only 11 percent who felt they were better off than they had been earlier attributed

Table 2.3. *Government impact on personal financial condition and national economy by personal and national economic evaluations, 1988 (in percent)*

	Government impact			
	Great Deal	Something	Not Much	N
Personal Financial Condition				
Present financial condition relative to four years ago				
Better	14a	29	57	891
Same	15	31	54	990
Worse	37	30	33	293
Satisfaction with present material standard of living				
Very satisfied	25a	28	47	537
Fairly satisfied	21	39	41	1276
Little dissatisfied	38	43	19	298
Very dissatisfied	62	13	25	62
Anticipated personal material standard of living in three or four years				
Better	19a	34	45	696
Same, pro-con	27	35	39	1121
Worse	65	24	11	246
National Economy				
Anticipated performance of the economy				
Better	49a	43	8	452
Same, pro-con	39	44	17	1218
Worse	57	25	16	260

Note: a - horizontal percentages

a great deal of influence to government for the improvement they had experienced, as opposed to 53 percent who thought that they were worse off now than previously and that it was government's fault. Similarly, only 19 percent of those who believed they would be better off in the future attributed this to government as opposed to the 62 percent who believed they would be worse off. Five years later the pattern persisted.

Regarding attributions of responsibility for the health of the national economy, Canadians again were more willing to blame the government for a projected general economic downturn than to praise it for an anticipated upswing. Thus, in 1983 one-third of those who believed the nation's economy would get better in the future judged that government would have a great deal to do with the forecast improvement, but a much larger proportion (three-fifths) of those who believed it would get worse asserted that government would play a prominent role in the anticipated decline. Similarly, 29 percent of those who saw better economic times ahead in 1987 attributed a great deal of responsibility to government, but 60 percent of those who anticipated hard times did so. In 1988 the equivalent percentages were 49 percent and 57 percent (Table 2.3). Overall, there is consistent evidence of asymmetric attributions of government responsibility for both personal and national economic conditions, with the pattern being somewhat stronger in recent years in the former than in the latter case.

There also is evidence of another kind of asymmetry in that irrespective of national economic conditions, good or bad, Canadians believed that they personally – and, in fact, their communities – were better off than most other people and communities. By way of illustration, in an October 1975 survey in which 62 percent predicted the national economy would get worse, 68 percent said they were "satisfied" with their family income. In an August 1978 survey in which 74 percent predicted that unemployment would be high for years to come, 56 percent expressed satisfaction with their own future prospects. Moreover, despite several increases in the "misery" index of combined inflation and unemployment rates, in nine national CIPO surveys conducted between September 1973 and November 1983, when asked whether their own standard of living was "going down," "staying the same," or "going up," on average, one-quarter said it was declining, an equal number said it was staying the same, but over two-fifths said it was going up. Further, repeated negative assessments of the condition of the national economy notwithstanding, in four surveys between April 1976 and June 1978, almost two-thirds stated that business conditions in their own communities either were "good" or "very good." Majorities, on average, also predicted that this happy circumstance would continue.

National surveys conducted between 1977 and 1981 also document the tendency of Canadians to distinguish between their own condition and those of others by making relatively positive judgments about themselves and negative ones about others. The 1977 Social Change in Canada survey used "ladder scales" ranging from 1–10 to measure people's present material satisfaction. Respondents also were asked to use this metric to make judgments about the best financial condition they had experienced in the past, the best they expected in the future, what they deserved right now, and to compare their own condition with that of the average Canadian. Despite significant regional differences in the volume and value of their natural resources and more general economic well-being, Canadians in every part of the country were quite satisfied with their financial condition. They also were generally optimistic about their future prospects. And, although they felt they deserved more *now*, nonetheless, they regarded themselves as significantly better off financially than the average person.[2]

2 Individual level (paired) t-tests for: (a) current financial situation v. that of ordinary Canadians; (b) current financial situation versus what is deserved now; and (c) current financial situation versus what is expected five years in the future were performed. In all cases, the results are statistically significant ($p < .001$). Three other questions employing 10-point rat-

Economic evaluations: Structure and correlates

Evidence presented above suggests that Canadians' economic evaluations and their judgments about the extent to which government is responsible for national and personal economic conditions are neither inchoate nor unidimensional. In this regard, studies of the relationship between public evaluations of government economic performance and political behavior typically have differentiated between judgments about the impact of a government's stewardship on one's personal condition as opposed to its effects on the country as a whole.[3] The former judgments have been labeled "egocentric," the latter, "sociotropic." A second dimension typically employed in research on economic judgments is temporal – a government's past performance is distinguished from its current and anticipated future performance. These three temporal categories have been labeled "retrospective," "contemporaneous," and "prospective." Taken together, these several distinctions yield six categories of the objects of evaluation and the time horizons over which evaluations can be made. To what extent do these analytic categories correspond to how Canadians structure their economic judgments?

To investigate the structure of public thinking about government's impact on economic conditions we first subjected variables corresponding to the six categories[4] to a principal components exploratory factor analysis.

---

ing scales were used in a 1979 national study to ascertain how satisfied people were with their incomes, living standards, and overall financial conditions. The questions were: (1) "How satisfied or dissatisfied are you with your family's (your) present income? Which number comes closest to how you feel?" (2) "How satisfied or dissatisfied are you with your standard of living?" (3) "All things considered, how satisfied or dissatisfied are you with your present financial situation – your income, standard of living, debts, savings, and so on?" Mean levels of satisfaction with these three aspects of one's personal economic condition were 7.4, 8.0, and 7.5, respectively. In a 1981 national survey, members of the public were again asked to assess their standard of living and general financial situation. And, again they were favorable, with means of 7.8 and 7.2, respectively.

3 See, for example, Kinder and Kiewiet (1979); Fiorina (1981); Kinder and Kiewiet (1981); Kuklinski and West (1981); Kiewiet (1983); Lewis–Beck (1986, 1988).

4 The six economic evaluation indices were constructed as follows: (1) *Past, Self:* Respondents were asked (a) "Do you think that you are financially better off now than you were five years ago, worse off, or are things about the same?" (b) "Do you think that government has had a great deal, something, or not much at all to do with this?" Responses were scored "better off" $= +1$, "same" $= 0$, and "worse off" $= -1$; "great deal" $= +2$ "something" $= +1$, "not much" $= 0$. Scores for (a) and (b) were multiplied to yield an index ranging from $+2$ to -2. (2) *Present, Self:* An index ranging from $+4$ to -4 was constructed by multiplying responses to (a) "Now let's think about the things you can buy or do, all the things which make up your material standard of living. Would you say that you are very satisfied $(+2)$, fairly satisfied $(+1)$, a little dissatisfied (-1), or very dissatisfied (-2) with the material side of your life right now?" (b) "Do you think government has a great deal $(+2)$, something $(+1)$, or not much at all (0) to do with this?" *Future, Self:* An index ranging from $+2$ to -2 was constructed by multiplying responses to (a) "Still

This procedure yielded a three-factor solution in which the first factor was dominated by evaluations of the government's past and present management of the national economy, while the second was dominated by retrospective and contemporaneous judgments about government's effect on one's personal economic condition. However, the distinction between nation and individual was blurred on the third factor because future projections about both national and personal conditions loaded heavily on it. Although an exploratory factor analysis is suggestive, the problem is that it makes unrealistic assumptions.[5] Confirmatory factor analysis (CFA), in contrast, is a much more powerful analytic tool, one that permits error terms for the indicators to be correlated and provides estimates of interfactor correlations. The technique has the additional advantage of providing a test of the overall goodness-of-fit of a hypothesized measurement model (Hayduk, 1987; Bollen, 1989).

As implemented by LISREL 7 (Joreskog and Sorbom, 1988), CFA indicated that a modified version of the three-factor model suggested by the preliminary analysis fits the data very well (Table 2.4). Canadians do distinguish between the effects of the government's stewardship of the economy on their own condition and on that of the country as a whole. However, the analysis also confirmed that when they think about future economic performance, the distinction collapses and, even though egocentric and sociotropic factors structure their thinking, so does a future. factor. Moreover, there are strong, statistically significant correlations between sociotropic evaluations, on the one hand, and egocentric and future evaluations, on the other. In 1983 they were + .55 and .50, respectively; in 1988, .65 and .60. In both 1983 and 1988 there were more modest (+ .32 and .25, respectively) relationships between the egocentric and future factors.

Having determined that there is a good fit between the data and the three-factor model of economic thinking, we used covariance structure

thinking about the material side of things and looking ahead over the next three or four years, do you think that you will be better off (+1) or worse off (−1) or will things stay about the same (0)?" (b) "Will government have a great deal (+2), something (+1), or not much at all (0) to do with this?" (4) *Past, National:* "Would you say that the federal government has done a very good job (+2), a good job (+1), a poor job (−1), or a very poor job (−2) in handling the economy?" Qualified answers, e.g., "depends" were scored 0. (5) *Present, National:* Unlike the other categories no question referring explicitly to the federal government is available. The following is used as a proxy: "Thinking generally about how the Canadian economy is doing these days, would you say it is doing very well (+2), fairly well (+1), or not very well (0)?" Qualified answers were scored +1. (6) *Future, National:* An index ranging from +2 to −2 was constructed by multiplying responses to (a) "Do you think the Canadian economy will get better (+1), worse (−1), or stay about the same (0) over the next year or so?" (b) "Will the government have a great deal (+2), something (+1), or not much at all (0) to do with this?" For all six indices "don't know" responses were scored 0.

Citizens and community

Table 2.4. *Confirmatory factor analysis of economic performance evaluations, 1988*

| Economic thinking indices | Factor Matrix (λ) | | |
	Sociotropic	Egocentric	Future
Personal economic condition:			
Past	.00	.66c	.00
Present	.00	.49c	.00
Future	.00	.00	.60c
National economic condition:			
Past	.76c	.00	.00
Present	.59c	.00	.00
Future	.00	.00	.65c

$\chi^2_5 = 9.36$, p = .096, AGFI = .990

| *Inter-factor correlations (ϕ)* | | | |
	Sociotropic	Egocentric	Future
Sociotropic	1.00		
Egocentric	.65c	1.00	
Future	.60c	.25c	1.00

Note: c-p $\leq$.05; random half-sample (N = 1108); WLS estimates

analysis (LISREL 7, Joreskog and Sorbom, 1988) to investigate relationships between the three evaluation factors and the sociodemographic characteristics of those doing the judging. There were a number of relationships, all of them quite reasonable in terms of objective economic circumstances. However, none of the sociodemographic predictors (nor, for that matter, all of them together) was strongly associated with the economic evaluation factors. In 1983 the variance explained was only 10 percent, 12 percent, and 9 percent for the sociotropic, egocentric, and future factors, respectively, and in 1988 the comparable figures were similarly small (Table 2.5). The inability of the sociodemographic characteristics to account for variations in social, economic, and political orientations relevant for understanding political support is a finding that will be replicated in many of the analyses that follow.

NONECONOMIC JUDGMENTS

The ability of Canadians to distinguish between their own financial well-being and the condition of the national economy extended to judgments about a variety of noneconomic matters. For example, in January 1979 when CIPO interviewers asked people whether they were satisfied with the general direction the country was taking, two-fifths said "yes," but almost the same proportion said "no." In March of the same year the size of the

Table 2.5. *Covariance structure analysis of economic performance
evaluation factors by sociodemographic characteristics, 1988*

	Economic Performance Evaluations Factors		
	Sociotropic	Egocentric	Future
Sociodemographic variables			
Age	-.05a	.17a	-.05
Education	.04	.04	-.02
Gender	-.21a	-.01	-.10c
Income	.09c	.15b	-.04
Region-ethnicity			
Atlantic	-.05	-.07	.18a
Quebec-French	-.12b	-.15b	.19a
Quebec-Non-French	-.08	-.00	.07
Prairies	-.25a	-.15b	.10c
British Columbia	-.19a	-.17a	-.02
$R^2=$	.16	.10	.07

Note: a-p $\leq$.001; b-p $\leq$.01; c-p $\leq$.05; two-tailed test; random half-sample (N = 1108);
ML estimates

dissatisfied group had risen to 62 percent and it climbed to 80 percent in
July 1982. Similarly, when asked in June 1974 whether they were satisfied
with the "honesty" of other Canadians, a majority said they were not.
When asked in 1977 about the morality and honesty of the public, majorities again were dissatisfied. Three years later, even larger majorities felt
that the morality and honesty of their fellow citizens were deteriorating.

In two other CIPO surveys conducted five years apart (June 1974 and
June 1979) Canadians were asked to evaluate a number of their major
social and political institutions. In the 1974 survey they were asked how
much "confidence" they had in the churches, public schools, the Supreme
Court, the House of Commons, large corporations, labor unions, and
newspapers. Over 50 percent had a "great deal" or "quite a lot" of confidence in churches, public schools, and the Supreme Court. However, the
same degree of confidence in the country's premier political institution, the
House of Commons, was expressed by only 42 percent. For the other three
institutions (newspapers, large corporations, labor unions), the proportions were even smaller. Five years later when asked how much "respect"
they had for churches, newspapers, large corporations, political parties and
labor unions, not much had changed. Small majorities expressed a great
deal or quite a lot of respect for the first three (churches, the Supreme
Court, public schools), but again, only minorities expressed similar respect
for the others (House of Commons, newspapers, large corporations, political parties, and labor unions). When asked in 1976 to make judgments
about the ethics and honesty of people engaged in different occupations,

Canadians gave high grades only to physicians; fully three-fifths believed that the honesty and ethical standards of doctors were either high or very high. At the other end of the scale over half thought that the honesty and ethical standards of union leaders were low or very low.

In contrast to the negative views Canadians expressed about the condition of their society, its major institutions and various occupational groups, were the generally positive judgments made about their *own* condition and that of their families and local communities. Thus, in the October 1975 survey in which 44 percent of the interviewees expressed dissatisfaction with the honesty of fellow Canadians, 58 percent said they were satisfied with the future facing their families. High levels of satisfaction with one's present life and future prospects are also apparent in other surveys. The 1981 Social Change in Canada data are illustrative.[6] The pattern of judgments about life satisfaction in this survey was very similar to that expressed about one's personal financial condition. On average, Canadians in every region were quite satisfied with their present lives.[7] There was relatively little difference between the best life they felt they had experienced in the past and their current condition. They were optimistic about the future, they felt they deserved better right now, but, the "other guy" – the average Canadian – was not, in their view, enjoying as good a life as they were. This also was the case when the same questions were asked in Social Change surveys conducted in 1977 and 1979.[8] It appears, therefore, that rather than experiencing feelings of *relative deprivation*, individual Canadians in every region instead felt *relatively advantaged*.

5 EFA assumes that the error terms of the indicator variables are uncorrelated and, when a varimax rotation is used, that the factors are uncorrelated (Long, 1983:11–15).

6 Respondents were told, "Here is a picture of a ladder. At the top of the ladder is the best life you can imagine – the ideal life. At the bottom of the ladder is the worst life you can imagine – a life that is terrible. Using a number on this card, where on the ladder would you place your life at this time?"

7 Regression analyses employing age, gender, education, and income as well as region as predictors indicated, as was the case with the correlates of the structure of their economic thinking, that one or two of these variables would achieve statistical significance in a particular equation. However, none was consistently significant, and the proportion of variance explained in this and other analyses was very modest – from 2–6 percent. These findings are consistent with data derived from other studies (Campbell, Converse, and Rodgers 1976; Allardt 1978; Barnes et al., 1979; Inglehart 1990) that indicate that in Western democracies differences in life satisfaction among people in different social and economic categories tend to be very small. Also, Euro-Barometer data for eight Western European countries (Belgium, Denmark, France, Great Britain, Ireland, Italy, the Netherlands, West Germany) for the 1976–86 period indicate that, on average, substantial majorities (ranging from a low of 65 percent in Italy to a high of 96 percent in Denmark) said they were either "very" or "fairly" satisfied with their lives.

8 Three paired t-tests were performed: (a) present life versus life of average Canadians; (b) present life v. what is deserved now; and (c) present life versus two years ago. All three were significant at < .001 level.

Table 2.6. *Life satisfaction and government impact, 1983, 1988 (in percent)*

		1983	1988
Life satisfaction relative to four years ago*			
	Better	40	41
	Same	47	52
	Worse	13	7
	N	2096	2194
Government impact on life satisfaction over last four years*			
	Great deal	17	13
	Something	31	29
	Not much	51	58
	N	2095	2176
Satisfaction with present life as a whole			
	Very satisfied	34	35
	Fairly satisfied	53	56
	Little dissatisfied	10	8
	Very dissatisfied	3	1
	N	2103	2194
Government impact on present life satisfaction			
	Great deal	15	10
	Something	36	33
	Not much	48	57
	N	2087	2177

Note: * - "five years" in 1983 survey

The 1979 Social Change survey provides additional evidence. Here, 100–point thermometer scales were used to measure people's opinions about a variety of matters such as their house or apartment, neighborhood, community, country, job, and leisure time. With few exceptions, people were most pleased with their marriages, children, friends, and life as a whole. They were somewhat less gratified, but still very positive about their health, their house or apartment, their neighborhood and community, their jobs, family financial situation, and life in general in Canada. The unmarried among them were less pleased with their romantic relationships, and both married and unmarried alike wanted to have more leisure time. Even in these two areas, however, many people expressed satisfaction.

In our 1983 and 1998 national studies we also asked people about their general life satisfaction currently and relative to what it was in the past, as well as what impact government currently has had on their lives. As Table 2.6 indicates, despite a five-year hiatus, their responses were very similar. Throughout the 1980s overwhelming majorities either were very or fairly satisfied with their lives as a whole. Further, in both surveys only small minorities judged that they were living worse lives than they had in the past.

Recall that in both 1983 and 1988 Canadians tended to believe that government had a greater impact on the national economy than on their own financial condition. They felt government had even less of an impact on their lives generally. However, as was the case with their financial condition, when the perceived impact of government was cross-tabulated with judgments about the quality of their lives, the same asymmetric patterns of relationships appeared; people who were satisfied with their lives were less likely to think government had any effect on them than were those who were dissatisfied. Similarly, those who felt their lives were better than what they had been in the past were less likely to judge that government bore responsibility than were those who believed their lives had deteriorated.

Trust, optimism, competence

We also ascertained how optimistic, competent and socially trusting Canadians felt, hypothesizing that these feelings not only affect social interactions, but also spill over to influence feelings about political authorities and the institutions and processes of government. In our 1988 study respondents were asked to reply to three statements about trusting others.[9] Three-fifths stated that most people can be trusted, slightly more believed others try to be helpful, and over two-thirds believed that most people try to be fair in their dealings with others. Francophone Quebecers, indeed all Quebec residents, were substantially less trusting of their fellow citizens than were other Canadians.

In the 1988 survey we also asked a series of questions intended to measure people's feelings of personal competence.[10] This battery of questions permitted us to test the hypothesis that feelings of social competence are related to feelings of political efficacy which, in turn, influence political support. Canadians most often (85 percent) felt they could run their own lives and least often (41 percent) that things in life work out as anticipated. Nonetheless, two-thirds felt it was better to plan ahead than leave things to

9 The social trust questions are: (a) "Generally speaking, would you say that most people can be trusted or that you can't be too careful in dealing with people?" (b) "Would you say that most of the time people try to be helpful or that they are mostly just looking out for themselves?" (c) "Do you feel that most people would try to take advantage of you if they had the chance or would they try to be fair?" The social trust index is the sum of the number of "trusting" responses to (a), (b), and (c).

10 The personal competence questions are: (a) "Do you think it's better to plan your life a good way ahead, or would you say life is too much a matter of luck to plan ahead very far?" (b) "When you do make plans ahead, do you usually get to carry out things the way you expected, or do things usually come up to make you change your plans?" (c) "Have you usually felt pretty sure your life would work out the way you want it to, or have there been times when you haven't been sure about it?" (d) "Some people feel they can run their lives pretty much the way they want to; others feel the problems of life are sometimes too big for them. Which are you most like?" The personal competence index is the sum of the number of "competent" responses to (a), (b), (c), and (d).

chance, and 53 percent believed that usually their plans worked out. These feelings were relatively evenly distributed across the country. The only notable regional difference was between Francophone residents of Quebec and other Canadians. As with social trust, Québécois expressed lower levels of personal competence.

Regarding optimism, in 1979 people were asked to agree or disagree with five statements intended to shed light on the question of whether the proverbial glass of water was half empty or half full.[11] An overwhelming majority strongly agreed or agreed that in the long run everything will work out right, two-thirds agreed that good things can come from bad situations, and two-thirds saw the silver that supposedly lines every cloud. Conversely, one-fifth and one-third, respectively, felt that society and civilization were falling apart and that even when things look good, bad things are likely to happen. Overall, then, although many Canadians felt optimistic and personally self-confident and trusted their fellow citizens to "do the right thing," sizable minorities did not share these sentiments. Relationships between these feelings and their political analogues will be investigated in the next chapter.

I'M ALRIGHT, BUT . . .

It is worth remembering that during the mid-1970s and early 1980s many Canadians continuously complained about the national economy and its less than satisfactory management by the federal government. Moreover, their judgments about key social and political institutions and the honesty, ethics, and trustworthiness of fellow citizens were at best mixed. Despite such negativism most people were more than satisfied with their own and their families current lives and quite optimistic about the future. And, their aforementioned unhappiness about the deterioration of Canadian society notwithstanding, they wanted to live in Canada, and *only* in Canada. For example, when asked in March 1972 whether they would like to live in another country, 81 percent said "no," only in Canada. It could be argued that such positive feelings would erode as economic conditions worsened. However, five years later (November 1977) when asked which country they would most like to be a citizen of, an even larger percentage said "only Canada." Asked what they liked most about their country, they provided many answers. By far the largest proportion (61 percent), however, said that what they liked most was the freedom they enjoyed and that Canada simply was the "best country in the world."

Responses to two other questions further reflect very positive feelings

11 The statements were: (a) "No matter how hopeless things seem, in the long run everything will work out right"; (b) "Good things often come from the worst situations"; (c) "Our society and civilization are falling to pieces"; (d) "Every cloud has a silver lining."

about Canada. In December 1979 people were asked which country afforded its citizens the highest standard of living and which had the most to offer for personal happiness. Although 39 percent said Canada offered the highest standard of living, 28 percent said it was the United States. In response to the happiness question, however, Canada was the "hands down" winner; 61 percent picked Canada and only 10 percent the United States. In addition, such warm feelings extended to the provinces, communities, and the neighborhoods in which they lived.

We must ask why? Why do Canadians seem to hold such contradictory opinions about their country and their fellow citizens? Why, for example, do they state that it is the greatest country in the world and that they are satisfied with virtually every aspect of their daily lives and at the same time complain that life in Canada is getting worse and that standards of honesty and public morality are deteriorating? Why, also, do they judge, on the one hand, that the national economy is in bad shape and getting worse and, on the other, that business conditions in their own community are good and will remain so? Why are their judgments about the impact of government on their financial and more general condition so asymmetric, and why do those judgments as well as other attitudes and perspectives vary little across social groups and regions? Finally, if most people were satisfied with their lives, confident about their own and their families' futures, and enamored of their communities, provinces, and country, then why has there been so much regional discontent – culturally based in Quebec and economically grounded in the Western provinces?

We cannot answer all of these questions here but we can begin to illuminate them in this and the next chapter. A study consisting of three waves of interviews with approximately 300 people in each of three medium-sized cities (Trois Rivières, Quebec; Peterborough, Ontario; Lethbridge, Alberta)[12] before and after the May 1980 sovereignty-association referendum contains pertinent data. For each of fourteen pairs of alternatives, respondents were asked which most clearly matched their feelings when "Canada" was mentioned. Except for very small groups of strident, dissatisfied people, the images held of Canada were largely positive and built, in various combinations, around themes of social justice and energetic dynamism.[13] In addition to the positive view of Canada were the generally positive images held of the federal government, especially those held by Quebecers. Somewhat more often than in the other two communities,

---

12 The reasons for the selection of these three sites are given in Smith and Kornberg (1983:357–8).

13 The fourteen pairs that were poles of a seven-point scale were: "united–divided," "like–dislike," "weak–powerful," "democratic–undemocratic," "just–unjust," "favoritism–equality," "dynamic–stagnant," "progressive–conservative," "aggressive–passive," "restricted-free," "pound-humble," "lazy-energetic," "humanitarian-calloused," and "prejudiced-unprejudiced."

Ottawa, the symbolic protagonist in the 1980 referendum campaign, was characterized by Trois Rivières residents using words such as "like," "effective," "necessary," "in the public interest," "strong," and "near."

If people in different parts of the country perceived Canada and its style of governmental organization so positively, where, it may be asked, were the seeds of national discord and disunity that had culminated in the referendum? Data from our 1988 study can begin to shed light on this question. They indicate that Francophone Quebecers are something of an island unto themselves – or they certainly seem so in comparison to other Canadians. For example, to investigate the extent of social ties among Canadians living in different areas of the country, people were asked how many had ever *lived* in another province, how many had ever *visited* another province, and how many had *relatives living* in another province. Large minorities (ranging from 30 percent to 49 percent) of Anglophone Quebecers and residents of regions other than Quebec had lived in other provinces, but only 14 percent of the Francophone Quebecers had done so. And, whereas 82 percent of the Quebec Francophones at least had visited another province, this was true of well over 90 percent of other Canadians. Further, only 57 percent of Quebec Francophones as compared to upward of 90 percent of Canadians in other regions had relatives living outside of their province.

Data in the three-cities referendum surveys suggest that the divisions between Quebecers and other Canadians also are rooted in negative perceptions of the attitudes of persons living in different regions. For example, each city's residents tended to see their own province as a "giver" and the other two as "takers," and each tended to see its province as "altruistic" and the other two as "self-centered." The same pattern applied to the "only care about themselves – care about the country" dimension. Quebecers saw Ontario and Alberta as much more powerful than the residents of those two provinces saw themselves or one another. In contrast, Ontarians and Albertans saw Quebec as less productive, more uncooperative with Ottawa, much more of a taker, less wealthy, and much less concerned with the welfare of the country than people in their own provinces. In brief, the results suggested that at a general level residents of each city had the same Canada and federal government in mind. However, there were sharp differences in their conceptions of each other's provinces, images associated with strong feelings of like and dislike that reflected a genuine sense of inequity and distrust.[14]

---

14 Our 1983 study indicated that three years after the referendum proposal had been defeated the residents of the three provinces regarded their own provinces much more favorably than they did the other two. The magnitude of the differences between each group's support for their own province and that which they ascribed to the other two provinces remained substantial – in each case, approximately 20 points.

A second perspective on the issue of why relations between Anglophone and Francophone Canadians often have been strained is provided by responses to other questions asked in the three cities study. It was clear that although virtually all of the residents of Trois Rivières used French as a first language and almost all of the residents of the latter two communities used English, Francophones clearly had a better working knowledge of English than Anglophones had of French.[15] Moreover, in each of the communities only a small minority came into regular contact with people who spoke the "other" language. When they did, it was most often with "friends and neighbors." Francophones also had somewhat warmer feelings toward English Canadians than the latter had toward French Canadians. Whereas 70 percent of the residents of Trois Rivières said they liked English Canadians, only 41 percent and 44 percent of the Peterborough and Lethbridge population said this of French Canadians.

In other questions respondents in each city were asked whether they believed English- or French-Canadians had fared better; which group was wealthier; which had the best prospects for jobs and promotions in the public and private sectors; and which held the highest and most important places in the world of business and finance. Both groups more or less agreed that English Canadians generally are wealthier and have better prospects than French-Canadians for jobs and promotions in the private sector (Table 2.7). However, the residents of the two English-speaking communities were more likely to condition their judgments regarding the private sector prospects of the two groups with responses such as "depends upon what the position is," "depends upon with whom it is," or "depends upon where the job is located." Both groups judged that French-Canadians had considerably better prospects in the public sector, with one-third of the members of each ethnolinguistic group stating that both Anglophones and Francophones had the same opportunity to acquire jobs and to be promoted. However, French-Canadians felt that even here their English-speaking counterparts had better prospects than they did, whereas the opposite view was held by Ontarians and Albertans. Perhaps because of the prominence and visibility of a very small number of French-Canadian business leaders (and notwithstanding the agreement of both groups that English-speaking Canadians have a distinct advantage in the private sector) the two groups disagreed most sharply over which held the most important positions in business and finance. Ontarians and Albertans said it was French-Canadians, the latter said the opposite (Table 2.7).

These data, like those on the images of their own and the others' prov-

---

15 Fifteen percent of the Trois Rivières sample said they spoke English "fluently" or "quite well" and 32 percent said they spoke it "with difficulty," whereas only 6 percent and 5 percent, respectively, of the Peterborough and Lethbridge samples spoke French "fluently" or "quite well," and 36 percent and 20 percent, respectively, spoke it "with difficulty."

Table 2.7. *Perceptions of whether French or English Canadians are the more economically advantaged group in Canadian society, 1980 (in percent)*

Which of the two groups do you think is generally wealthier?

	Trois Rivieres	Peterborough	Lethbridge
French Canadians	4	3	4
English Canadians	54	64	45
Neither, they are equal	24	16	28
Depends	7	6	6
DK/NA	9	9	16

Which group has the better chance at jobs and positions in the government?

	Trois Rivieres	Peterborough	Lethbridge
French Canadians	3	25	19
English Canadians	40	11	9
Both have same chance	32	33	32
Depends	19	23	31
DK/NA, other	6	8	9

Which group has the better chance at jobs and promotions in private business?

	Trois Rivieres	Peterborough	Lethbridge
French Canadians	3	7	1
English Canadians	41	21	21
Both have same chance	31	32	28
Depends	19	33	42
DK/NA, other	6	7	8

Which group has the most important place in the world of business and finance?

	Trois Rivieres	Peterborough	Lethbridge
French Canadians	6	37	41
English Canadians	60	27	26
Both have same chance	24	7	10
DK/NA	10	28	22

Note: Trois Rivieres – N = 350; Peterborough – N = 308; Lethbridge – N = 303

inces, suggest that the two principal ethnolinguistic groups saw important aspects of their society and their place within it in a quite different light. The French thought they were significantly disadvantaged economically, the English did not view them in this way. The French saw the English enjoying more of the economic fruits of society than they did, the English tended to feel that neither group was particularly advantaged or disadvantaged. In part this is because the great majority of each group literally did not speak the other's language, or did so only with great difficulty. Nor did they interact much with one another. It may be an exaggeration to characterize their current relationship as one of "two solitudes," but it appears that on the eve of what was a watershed event in their country's history, Francophones and Anglophones were a long way from either knowing about or empathizing with one another's condition.

That they did not really know one another is, in one sense, an anomaly because in a democracy information (although it is not without some opportunity costs) is a commodity that is readily, and oftentimes almost instantly available to most people. Much of that information is acquired from the mass media, particularly television, and is the basis for many of the global kinds of economic judgments people make and for the social and political opinions they hold. Our 1983 survey provides ample evidence that Canadians spend substantial amounts of time monitoring media; 54 percent indicated that they watched up to two hours of television a day and another 36 percent said they watched between three and five hours daily. The figures for radio listening were similar. Sixty percent also stated they read a newspaper every day, and another 24 percent said they read one "sometimes" or on "weekends." Moreover, some of what they read, heard, and saw apparently was politically relevant and appeared related to their political attitudes and opinions. By way of illustration, three-quarters of those who read newspapers, three-fifths who watched television, and two-fifths who listened to radio, said they "often" or "sometimes" read, looked at, and listened to information about politics in the media. Further, 21 percent stated their feelings were influenced "a great deal," 38 percent said the media had "some influence" on them, and although 30 percent said they had "not much" influence, only 2 percent said the media had "no" influence.

As to the content of their media-based images of the Canadian political community, regime, and authorities, in the minds of Canadians their country came off considerably better in the media than their government and politicians. A substantial majority (61 percent) stated that the images the media projected of Canada were "good." In contrast 47 percent said this of the federal government, and 43 percent of the media images of federal politicians. Only one-third felt the images of the country either were "bad" or "not so good," while nearly half said this of media representations of the federal government and politicians.

Although their personal experiences with public officials such as MPs and civil servants obviously play a part, in our view most Canadians (and most citizens of other democracies) make global judgments about the performance of important political institutions such as parliament and the bureaucracy largely on the basis of information they acquire from the mass media. The situation regarding the economy is more complex, but the media are important here as well. Recall that judgments about government's impact on personal economic conditions have strong correlations with evaluations of government's handling of the national economy, and smaller, but still significant, correlations with projections about government's influence on personal and national economic conditions in the future. These correlations suggest that people's judgments about the present and future state of the national economy and government's management thereof are partially rooted in their own economic circumstances.[16] Such relationships are far from perfect, however, a situation that reflects the constant flow of information and interpretation concerning the national economy and government's economic performance provided by the mass media. If our argument is correct, it is hardly surprising that large numbers of Canadians, especially during the 1974–84 decade, believed their country and, in particular, the economy, was in trouble and that government attempts to solve economic and other related problems largely were ineffective. This was because unemployment and inflation levels increased steadily during most of this period and the media constantly reported and, indeed, harped on these developments.

In democracies the media not only report on economic and political events, they also continuously and routinely comment on social pathologies such as robbery, arson, murder, rape, and child abuse, on natural disasters such as floods and earthquakes, and on man-made ones such as industrial pollution and automobile and airline accidents. In the Canadian context, those reports may have led people to assume that life in their country was getting worse, that there was less peace of mind, that many fellow citizens were dishonest, immoral, and lacked integrity. Add to this the homogenizing effects on their attitudes of national television and radio networks, the fact that their newscasts, documentaries, and other programs are fed to the entire country by their affiliates, and that much of the hard news that large newspaper chains print comes from a small number of wire services (Siegel, 1983:ch. 7). This may partially explain why, irrespective of variables such as age, gender, residence, education, and income, there was little variance in their global views about societal conditions, the condition of the economy, or the government's effectiveness in managing it.

In contrast to their reliance on the media for information about the country, its major social and political institutions and processes, people in democracies such as Canada, we would argue, rely largely on personal experiences in forming opinions and making judgments about their own condition, those of their family, friends, and neighbors, and that of their community. *Pace* the old chestnut about far away pastures looking greener, for most people the opposite is the case; the closer to home, the better things look. And, irrespective of what they may hear, read, and see about unfortunate things that are happening to other people in other places, as individuals, most people also are unaffected by such events. For example, even during the 1979–84 period when economic conditions were at their worst, the great majority of Canadians were gainfully employed. If prices

16 More detailed analyses show that these relationships are not spurious artifacts of the impact of identification with governing versus opposition parties on assessments of government's impact on both personal and national economic conditions. See Clarke and Kornberg (1989:266–8).

rose, so too did their salaries and wages. If acts of violence were committed and the tragic accidents occurred, they happened in other places and to other people, not in their communities, to themselves, or to their family, friends, and neighbors. This is perhaps best illustrated in cases where people actually have experienced a tragedy or calamity of some kind. In television interviews it is common for them to acknowledge that they know this kind of thing happens to other people in other places, but they never dreamed it could happen to them or their home town. This tendency to rely on both personal experience and the media in forming opinions and making judgments helps explain why people are able to make such seemingly contradictory evaluations of national conditions, on the one hand, and their lives, on the other.[17]

Democratic cultural values learned through socialization are a second reason why Canadians hold differing opinions about matters such as the relative effects that government and their own efforts have on their economic well-being. They also may help explain why, rather than experiencing feelings of deprivation and envy of others, people instead felt they were better off – generally and economically – than their fellow citizens. Recall that the liberal elements of a democratic culture focus on the individual, ascribe great value to qualities such as independence, initiative, autonomy, and industry, and hold out the prospect of progress and improvement through personal effort (Almond and Verba, 1963, 1980; Nisbet, 1980; Dahl, 1982; Powell, 1982). Recall, as well, that the Judeo-Christian heritage that is a part of Western culture constantly admonishes people to "give thanks" and to "count your blessings" – admonitions which, over an extended time period, can have a powerful effect on the way people evaluate their own lives and those of others. Because of such socialization-derived and -perpetuated cultural values, many people believe that they can and will prosper economically, and that they can and will rise through the social system because of their initiative, industry, hard work, and good fortune.

In the Canadian context an additional factor is that social class is not a salient cleavage, and its effects on political attitudes and behavior are relatively inconsequential (e.g., Alford, 1963; Pammett, 1987). Surveys conducted since the mid-1960s reveal that about 50 percent of Canadians report that they do not normally think of themselves in class terms. Data from the 1974–79 panel survey provide further evidence of the weakness of class consciousness. Over the five-year period only 22 percent of the respondents consistently stated that they thought of themselves in class

---

17 The argument that evaluations of personal and national economic conditions are based on different mixes of information does not imply that one or the other type of evaluation is more important for explaining political support. The latter topic has occasioned considerable debate in the voting behavior literature. Compare, e.g., Kinder and Kiewiet (1979, 1981) and Kramer (1983). Our analyses of the impact of economic evaluations on political support are presented in Chapters 4 and 7.

terms. Of these more than four times as many (18 percent versus 4 percent) thought of themselves as middle rather than working class. The predominantly middle class orientation of most Canadians also was revealed when they were forced to "choose" a class. In several surveys an average of 10 percent thought of themselves as members of the upper and upper-middle class, 50 percent as middle class, about 35 percent as working class, and 3 percent as "lower class." Also, people in manual occupations were slightly more likely to have a middle or even an upper-middle rather than a working class identity, and nearly three-fifths of them had no spontaneous class consciousness whatsoever. Further, in his analysis of these data, Pammett reports that the most class conscious element in the population was "slightly more middle class in identity and more likely to think that the middle rather than the working class pays an undue amount of taxes" (Pammett, 1987:227–8). We may conclude that a search for a militant working class in Canada would find it to be a very small one.

As noted, the political culture of a democracy such as Canada contains a liberal element emphasizing the intrinsic and instrumental value of hard work and the virtue of self-reliance as well as an element emphasizing the legitimacy of an interventionist role for government. The justification for intervention is that government can remove constraints that prevent individuals from realizing their full potential and also narrow economic differences among them, thereby contributing to their greater freedom and equality. The interaction of these two cultural components, we would argue, partially explains the asymmetries that characterize Canadians' judgments about the government's and their own contribution to their financial and more general well-being. The liberal component makes it easier for those who feel they are in good shape financially and otherwise to attribute their circumstances to their own hard work. But it makes it harder for those who are doing less well to blame themselves for their condition. However the interventionist element in the culture provides them with an out; they can blame the government not only for their own lot, but for the parlous state of the economy as well.[18]

18 The idea that the classical liberal and interventionist elements in political culture interact in complex ways to condition political demand in contemporary democracies is illustrated in Scholzman and Verba's (1979) study of unemployed persons in the United States. They conclude that whereas the unemployed "took it upon themselves to cope with unemployment by finding new jobs . . . almost unanimously our jobless respondents agreed not only that the government should be responsible for creating jobs and helping those in economic need, but also that the government is not doing enough in this regard. And, in general, they saw this intervention as their right, not as a matter of governmental beneficence" (ibid., 348) We argue that this is true, a fortiori, in countries such as Canada where the classical liberal strain in political culture is relatively weaker and the interventionist strain relatively stronger than the United States. Sniderman and Brody (1977:520), for example, conclude that "the idea that one should cope with one's problems on one's own in America, is a major restraint on the production of political demand."

No one would dispute the fact that in addition to rising inflation and unemployment, Western democracies encountered a variety of complex social and political problems during the decade following the Arab oil embargo in 1973. We have noted that in addition to these difficulties Canada encountered national integration problems that the others either did not face, or else confronted in far less serious form. Their manifold problems notwithstanding, democratic countries also possessed some very formidable assets during that period. Canada is a prime example. Unemployed Canadians, for instance, received sustained and generous unemployment benefits. The rearing of their children was eased by the federal government's monthly family allowance checks, and the ability of parents with small children to hold jobs was increasingly facilitated by day-care centers. Massive expenditures on public education provided training for technical service and clerical jobs and generous scholarships and loans enabled the academically talented among them to attend institutions of higher learning preparatory to securing well-paying professional and managerial positions. Taken together, during the 1970s and early 1980s the several programs of the Canadian welfare state – regardless of how significant their actual distributional effects may have been – undergirded a standard of living for average people that was the envy of the great majority of people in most non-Western countries. Indeed, it would have excited the imagination and envy of previous generations of Canadians. In sum, the contradictions in the opinions and judgments of people during this period were real, understandable, and rooted in the complexities of life in a modern liberal democracy.

SUMMARY

In this chapter we have tried to shed light on some of the hypotheses posited in the first chapter. The data we have examined support some, but not all, of them. By way of illustration, we hypothesized that Canadians may be more positively disposed toward their social institutions than to their political institutions and processes. The evidence for this hypothesis is that the two institutions in which they expressed the greatest confidence, and for which they had the most respect, were churches and public schools. However, churches and schools were the only two social institutions that were held in reasonably high regard by a majority. Consequently, a more appropriate hypothesis would seem to be that they do not feel strongly favorable about any of their major institutions. Nor, other than doctors, do they have many complimentary things to say about the people who give life to such institutions.

We also found that Canadians' judgments about government's economic performance were multidimensional and asymmetric. When thinking about the past and present they distinguished government's impact on the national economy from its impact on their personal circumstances. When thinking about the future, however, this distinction collapses. Furthermore, those who were satisfied with their financial condition ascribed their good fortune to their own efforts, whereas the dissatisfied tended to blame government rather than themselves. People also were more willing to blame government for its perceived mishandling of the national economy than to praise it when things were seen as going well. More generally, people tended to distinguish between national conditions and their own, their family's, and their community's circumstances. Thus, despite the (at best) mixed reviews they gave key institutions, and the doubts they harbored about the honesty, ethics, and trustworthiness of fellow citizens, most people were satisfied with their own and their family's current lives and optimistic about the future.

We asked why Canadians seem to hold ambivalent and frequently contradictory opinions. Why also, if they have such an economic- and culturally-based high regard for their country, have there been so many strong regional and ethnolinguistic cleavages? Regarding the latter question, we found there were sharp differences in people's conceptions of other provinces and regions, images that reflected a genuine sense of inequity and distrust. As for the ambivalent and often contradictory attitudes expressed about societal conditions and their own lives, we contended that their global attitudes, perspectives, and evaluations are based in large part on information they acquire from the mass media. In Canada, as in other democracies, the media not only report fully and continuously on economic and political conditions – warts and all – they also routinely focus on a variety of social pathologies. Consequently, it is hardly surprising that at times it appeared to people that their political system and society more generally were going to hell in a hand basket. The situation with regard to the economy is more complex – evaluations of national economic conditions are related to personal economic circumstances, but the relationships are far from overwhelming, a situation that reflects the continuous flow of information about the economy and government economic policies and interpretations thereof provided by the media.

In contrast to citizens' reliance on the media for information about national conditions, we have argued that they rely heavily on personal experience in forming opinions and making judgments about their own economic and more general condition, as well as those of their family, friends, and community. We also contended that two other factors that contributed to people's ambivalent and often contradictory opinions, as well as the lack of variation therein, were democratic cultural values and the leavening effects of almost a half century of welfare state programs.

For now we may note that the positive feelings about country, province of residence, home town, and material and more general life circumstances that so many Canadians display constitute a syndrome of attitudes that is conducive to support for key political objects. So, also, are relatively widespread feelings of social trust, individual competence, and being relatively advantaged vis-à-vis one's fellow citizens. Conversely, the asymmetric judgments Canadians make about the condition of the economy and their own lives and the relative responsibility for these conditions they assign to government and themselves are not conducive to supportive feelings. Nor is support facilitated by the kind of general "sourness" that Canadians displayed during the 1970s and early 1980s toward key social institutions and the several professions. We may speculate that citizens of other democratic countries are not significantly different in these regards. Where Canadians may well differ from citizens of most other democracies, however, is in the relative lack of salience social class has for them. It belabors the obvious to note that social class identifications, under certain conditions, can transcend or cut across cleavages structured in sociocultural terms such as the ones that historically have defined interactions between the Anglophone and Francophone communities, and which have led them to be described as "two solitudes."

3

Democracy, political system, self

It is thought that once a society becomes an electoral democracy based on universal suffrage power becomes diffused throughout the general population.

John Porter, *The Vertical Mosaic*, p. 6

Citizens' beliefs, attitudes and opinions lie at the heart of democratic theory and practice. How people perceive and evaluate the political system and their roles therein affect support for political authorities and the institutions and processes that constitute a democratic political order. In this chapter we will examine a variety of psychological orientations relevant to political support processes in a representative democratic polity. We begin with the concept of democracy itself.

It is reasonable to assume that until the defeat of the Axis powers in World War II, the Cold War and the division of Europe, the end of colonialism, and the emergence of dozens of new states in Asia and Africa that most Canadians would have understood and agreed on what a democratic political order entailed. However, given events since that time – the creation of a number of "peoples' republics" with command economies, the appropriation of the label "socialist" by communist and other authoritarian political regimes of both the right and left, the increasing emphasis on economic as well as political equality in Western countries and, more recently, the collapse of communism in the Soviet Union, of communist regimes in Eastern Europe, and the economic and political restructuring of those countries – this may be too easy an assumption. As a consequence, we are interested in delineating Canadians views of the meaning of democracy, and the extent to which they believe their country and two premier examples of liberal and nonliberal political systems, the United States and Soviet Union, approximate an ideal democratic polity. We will demonstrate that ordinary citizens, no less than political philosophers, differ in their conceptions of democracy and that some of those differences influence their judgments about the extent to which Canada approximates the democratic ideal.

Political parties are one of the distinguishing features of a democracy, and they play a variety of important roles in the support process by representing public needs and demands and mobilizing citizens to participate politically. Regarding political culture, parties are important because people develop psychological identifications with them. Depending upon the intensity of their partisan feelings, party identifiers will ascribe significantly greater support to their party and its leaders than to the opposition. However, maintaining a viable democracy does not require citizens to ascribe as much affection to every party and its leaders as they do to their own. Rather, democratic theory requires that citizens recognize that parties other than the one they prefer have a legitimate role to play in the system, and that moderate evaluations of such "other" parties are critical for permitting peaceful transfers of power after an election. Whether people actually subscribe to this theoretical requirement is an empirical question that we will examine in the next chapter.

A complicating factor in parliamentary systems is that the distinction between a party in power and the regime can become obfuscated when, as in Great Britain, the head of state opens every session of Parliament with a Throne speech in which she continually describes the policy proposals of the prime minister and the cabinet as those of "the" or even "my" government. The tendency to blur the distinction between party in power and regime is likely to be exacerbated when, as in Canada, a particular party governs for a lengthy period of time. Under a condition of one-party dominance partisan identification may strongly influence regime as well as authorities support directly and even community support indirectly. To test these hypotheses we first focus on the direction and intensity of party identifications among members of the Canadian public. In subsequent chapters, partisanship will be employed in multivariate models of the support process and to illuminate the historic disaffection of Quebec and the Western provinces.

We also will examine attitudes toward federalism, one of the key structural components of Canada's political system, and one which has done much to define the contours of conflict engendered by the deep, reinforcing regional and ethnolinguistic cleavages that characterize Canadian society. Because the concepts of "effectiveness" and "equity–fairness" establish crucial normative standards for evaluating the legitimacy of contemporary democracies, we examine the extent to which citizens perceive their national government and the larger political system operate in accordance with these standards. Finally, we investigate the distribution and correlates of four critical elements of a democratic culture; namely, political efficacy, political interest, political knowledge, and trust in political authorities because we assume they have both direct and indirect effects on support for key political objects.

PERSPECTIVES ON DEMOCRACY

To ascertain Canadians' beliefs about democracy, our 1989 survey included 10 agree–disagree statements intended to reflect the historic tensions that grow out of the need in a liberal democratic state to balance liberty with equality and the rights of the individual with those of the community. The tension between liberty and equality reflects the initial liberal commitment to provide individuals with an environment in which everyone is free to fully realize their potential (e.g., Pateman, 1970; Macpherson, 1977). The question is how to accomplish this goal. How may government acting for one person or group create such an environment without violating the rights of other individuals or groups? Philosophical analyses by scholars such as John Rawls (1971, 1980) and Robert Nozick (1974) illustrate the complexity of the problem of balancing liberty with equality and help provide theoretical justifications for competing claims such as, on the one hand, that genuine freedom in a democracy requires a relatively equal distribution of wealth and resources, and on the other, that such a condition not only is utopian in that it never can be achieved, but of necessity, is also destructive of that same freedom.

The tension between individual and community rights is grounded in the assumption that the epicenter of liberalism is individualism. The liberal democratic state is the modern structural expression of liberalism, and the social and economic conflicts within it reflect varying perspectives on individualism ranging from libertarianism to various forms of absolutism.[1] Related aspects of the strains between liberty and equality and individual and community rights involve, in the first instance, opposing perspectives on the effectiveness of state intervention in the economy. Do economic exchanges, of whatever magnitude, fall solely within the private realm or does the state, acting on behalf of its citizens, have a legitimate interest in them? In the second instance the debate concerns the efficacy and utility of citizen participation in a democratic society's institutions and processes. Does it matter that the great majority of citizens confine their participation in public affairs to voting in periodic elections? What, if any, difference does it make to the good health of a democracy that people do participate extensively in making decisions in its social and economic as well as its expressly political institutions and processes?

The 10 statements designed to ascertain public beliefs about democracy are listed in Table 3.1. Statements "D" (democracy is about political not

---

1 For a series of discussions and critiques of liberalism, democratic theory and its political expression, the liberal democratic state, that we cannot begin to summarize here, see, *inter alia*, Buchanan and Tullock (1962); Bachrach (1967); Macpherson (1962, 1977); Pateman (1970); Pennock (1979); Nisbet (1980); Arblaster (1984); Flathman (1980); Spragens (1981); Held (1987).

Table 3.1. *The meaning of democracy, 1989 (in percent)*

Democracy statement	Agree	Disagree	Don't know
A. A democracy has the right to protect itself from violent political groups, even if it means taking away certain people's rights	54a	30	15
B. All democracy really means is giving people the right to choose their leaders in free elections	57	29	14
C. A democracy has the right to make people serve in the armed forces in times of national emergency	53	34	14
D. Democracy is about political equality, not economic equality	45	30	25
E. For the benefit of all, a democracy has to put limits on people's rights to do what they want	57	30	13
F. In a democracy, even people who want to destroy democracy have the right to state their political opinions	78	11	10
G. Democracy is much more than people voting in elections, it's participating actively in making important decisions in their community and workplace	85	3	12
H. Democracy gives everyone the same opportunity to get ahead economically but doesn't try to make everyone economically equal	70	16	15
I. Democracy does not mean that all groups have the same amount of influence	65	17	18
J. Democracy and capitalism always go together	26	51	24

Note: a - horizontal percentages; N = 1842 for items A-D; N = 1841 for items E-J

economic equality); "H" (democracy is about equality of opportunity not equality of condition); "I" (democracy doesn't ensure equal influence); and "J" (democracy and a capitalist economic system always go together) are designed to capture people's views on and to delineate the potential for conflict between freedom and equality. Similarly, statements "A" (a democracy has a right to protect itself even if it means depriving people of rights); "C" (a democracy has a right to make people serve in the armed forces); "E" (a democracy can constrain individual behavior for the benefit of the community) and "F" (a democracy must ensure that even its enemies are able to express their opinions) are employed to shed light on the conflict between the rights of the individual and those of the community. Finally, statements "B" (all democracy really means is elections); and "G" (democracies are much more than elections) are used to ascertain people's views on what might be termed the "Schumpeterian" (1942) and the "Patemanesque" (1970) conceptions of democracy. We judged that people who *disagreed* with statements A, B, C, D, E, H, I, and J and *agreed* with statements F and G had a more expansive and egalitarian view of democracy whereas those who expressed the opposite views conceived of democracy in more restrictive and less egalitarian terms.

Empirically, Canadians have what might be designated as "mixed beliefs" about democracy. In some cases their responses were oriented primarily in terms of an expansive view of democracy. This was particularly true of the statements that freedom of speech should be extended even to those who wish to destroy democracy, and that democracy as a political process entails more than voting in elections (Table 3.1). Also, a majority did not agree with the statement that democracy and a capitalist economic system (that brings with it inevitable economic inequalities) invariably go together. Elements of a more restrictive view of democracy on which there were the greatest agreement were that democracy provides for equality of economic opportunity but not for equality of outcome and that democracy does not entail equality of group influence. Additionally, majorities agreed that a democracy has the right to protect itself from violent political groups, and to limit group and individual rights for the benefit of the whole community. Opinions on the proposition that democracy is about political not economic equality were divided – while a plurality agreed, nearly one-third disagreed, and one-quarter had no opinion.

We next determined whether there was an underlying structure to expansive and egalitarian versus more restrictive and less egalitarian beliefs about the meaning of democracy. A preliminary exploratory factor analysis suggested the existence of three factors and, with some modification, this structure was validated by confirmatory factor analysis.[2] Inspection of the pattern of factor loadings suggests that the first factor might be labeled "participation-equality," the second, "rights-order," and third, "inequality-rights" (Table 3.2). Suggesting that the overall structure of beliefs was only loosely articulated, most of the factor loadings were modest and the first factor was only very weakly related to the second ($\phi = .06$). The correlations between the first and third, and second and third factors were stronger but hardly overwhelming (ϕ's = .44 and .38, respectively).

The complexity of the first factor is suggested by the fact that items loading on it include the beliefs that democracy is more than simply voting in periodic elections (statements G and B), and that freedom of speech should be extended even to enemies of democracy (statement F). However, items J (democracy is about economic as well as political equality) and D (capitalism and democracy do not necessarily go in tandem) also load on this factor. Taken together, the set of items loading on factor one

---

2 In accordance with the discussion above, for items A, B, C, D, E, H, I, and J, "disagree" responses are scored 1; "agree" responses, −1; and "don't know" responses, 0. For items F and G, "agree" responses are scored 1; "disagree" responses, −1; and "don't know" responses, 0.

Table 3.2. *Confirmatory factor analysis of meaning of democracy statements, 1989*

	Factor Matrix (λ)		
Meaning of democracy statements	F1	F2	F3
A. Take away rights to protect democracy	.00	.32c	.38c
B. Democracy only means elections	.64c	.00	.00
C. Force people to serve in armed forces	.00	.17c	.40c
D. Political, not economic equality	.26c	.00	.34c
E. Limit rights for benefit of all	.00	.69c	.00
F. Free speech for opponents of democracy	.69c	.00	.00
G. Community and workplace participation	.97c	.00	.00
H. Economic opportunity not equality	.00	.00	.33c
I. Unequal group influence	.00	.00	.45c
J. Democracy and capitalism go together	.41c	.00	.15c

$$\chi^2_{25} = 32.17, \ p = .153, \ AGFI = .997$$

Inter-factor correlations (ϕ)

	F1	F2	F3
F1	1.00		
F2	.06	1.00	
F3	.44c	.38c	1.00

Note: c-p $\leq$.05; N = 1840; WLS estimates

indicate that beliefs about political and economic equality are interrelated aspects of what might be broadly termed varying conceptions of democratic citizenship (Marshall, 1965).

The second, "rights-order" factor is less complex in that the items loading on it (A, C, E) clearly focus on individual rights and whether they should be constrained to maintain public order and protect a democratic polity from internal subversion and external aggression. The third factor is an amalgam of beliefs that define factors one and two. Some of the items loading on it focus on the extent to which inequality characterizes a democratic society (D, H, I, J), but others (A, C) concern actions inhibiting individual rights that might be entertained to preserve democracy from its foes.

To gain further insights on public beliefs about the meaning of democracy we also asked people to rate Canada, the United States, and the Soviet Union on a 10-point scale with the end points defined as "a perfect democracy" (10) and "not a democracy" (1). Most Canadians gave their country fairly high marks ($\bar{X} = 6.9$), but few were willing to give it either an extremely positive or, especially, an extremely negative score (Figure 3.1). Most also held their giant neighbor to the South in reasonably high regard ($\bar{X} = 6.6$). In sharp contrast, Gorbachev, Yeltsin, Perestroika, and Glasnost notwithstanding, a vast majority indicated that they thought the Soviet Union is still a long way from being a democracy ($\bar{X} = 2.6$).

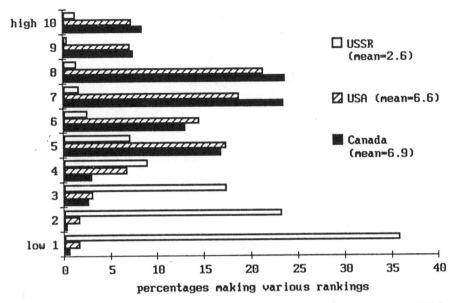

Figure 3.1. *Ratings of Canada, U.S.A. and U.S.S.R. as democracies, 1988*

Do these ratings vary according to sociodemographic and political cleavages in the Canadian population? How are the ratings related to people's understanding of the meaning of democracy? Are Canadians' ratings of democracy in their country stable over time? And how do they compare with those offered by citizens of other democracies? The latter two questions cannot be answered directly because the rating of democracy items is available only in the 1989 Canadian survey. However, data from the semi-annual Euro-Barometer surveys enable us to address these questions indirectly. The Euro-Barometers regularly have asked a question that taps people's satisfaction with democracy as it is practiced in their country.[3] Here, we examine these feelings using data gathered between 1976 and 1986 in Belgium, Denmark, France, Great Britain, Ireland, Italy, the Netherlands, and West Germany. Satisfaction with democracy varied widely across these countries. At one extreme, an average of fully 76 percent of West Germans stated that they were either "very" or "fairly" satisfied and, at the other, only 21 percent of Italians expressed similar sentiments (Figure 3.2). In all other cases but France, majorities of varying size expressed *some* degree of satisfaction, and in France 48 percent did so. However, the operation of democracy was not enthusiastically endorsed in

---

3 The question is "On the whole, are you very satisfied, fairly satisfied, not very satisfied, or not at all satisfied with the way democracy works [in your country]?"

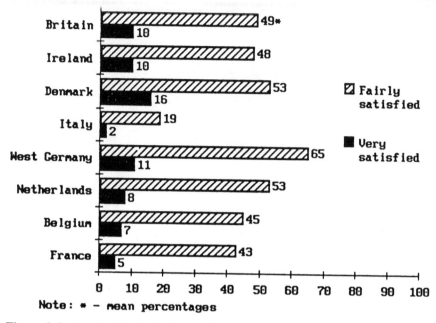

Figure 3.2. *Levels of satisfaction with democracy, eight Western European countries, 1976–86*

any country; the average percentages stating they were *very* satisfied ranged from a low of 2 percent in Italy to a high of 16 percent in Denmark. Overall, then, it appears that Canadians' feelings about how democracy works in their country are not atypical of those of citizens of other Western democracies. In most of these countries, positive evaluations are the norm, but ringing endorsements are the exception.

Although the lack of longitudinal data prevents us from determining whether levels of satisfaction with democracy vary over time in Canada, in several instances the European data do reveal sizable over-time change. For example, democracy satisfaction decreased substantially in Belgium, France, Great Britain, and West Germany in the late 1970s. Also, as Figure 3.3 shows, public appraisals of democracy did not simply trend upward or downward, but rather fluctuated sharply over short periods of time. In France, for example, the percentage satisfied climbed sharply in 1981, a presidential election year in which the Socialists swept to power. In Great Britain, satisfaction rose considerably in 1982, coincident with that country's victory over Argentina in the Falklands war. In both cases, the increase in satisfaction was short-lived; in France the percentage satisfied declined sharply the following year, whereas in Britain it did so after a two-year lag. The French and British data, therefore, suggest that satis-

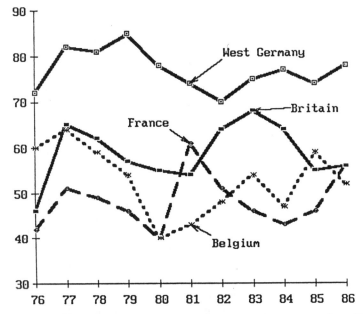

Figure 3.3. *Percentages very or fairly satisfied with democracy, four Western European countries, 1976–86*

faction with the operation of a democratic regime is related not only to longstanding political cultural or structural factors, or levels and trends in economic well-being, but also to transitory events and conditions such as election outcomes or the successful prosecution of a highly salient international conflict.

Regarding differences in the ratings of Canada and other countries as democracies, the Canadian data reveal that the ratings were only very loosely associated with sociodemographic and partisan divisions in the population. Of the relationships that were statistically significant, older persons, the better educated, men and Quebec Francophones gave Canada a higher score than did others. This was also true of all groups of party identifiers as compared to nonidentifiers. Older persons, Francophone Quebecers and PC party identifiers also rated the United States more highly, whereas younger people, those with lower incomes and, especially, NDP partisans accorded higher scores to the Soviet Union.

More important theoretically, perhaps, is that variations in ratings of Canada as a democracy were related to differences in what people felt democracy entails. Specifically, persons rating Canada highly tended to believe that a democracy has the right to protect itself at the expense of individual and group rights, to force people to serve in the armed forces in times of national emergency, to limit individual rights for the benefit of all, and to limit the freedom of speech of opponents of democracy. They also were significantly more likely to agree that capitalism and democracy go together, that democracy means equality of economic opportunity, not equality of economic condition, and that democracy means political, not economic, equality. In short, they had what we have termed a more restrictive and traditional view of democracy.

More generally, the data on Canadians' views of democracy accord well with most other assessments of political belief systems in mass publics. In a recent essay, Cooper, Kornberg, and Mishler (1988:22) note that "in democracies such as Britain, Canada and the United States, conservatism and liberalism or socialism are movements of opinion that cohere not as largely integrated doctrines but as pragmatic equilibria. They work, more or less well, as guides for public policies despite the internal intellectual tension that seems to be inevitable when the reflective capacities of human beings abstract the world in order to see it as it is." The same can be said of Canadians' opinions about democracy. Most have opinions about what democracy entails, but these do not cohere in a closely knit fashion. To employ Converse's (1964) terminology, beliefs about the meaning of democracy are not *tightly* constrained by a small set of underlying, general factors. This is not say that the beliefs are wholly unstructured, but rather that they are associated in complex ways, and that the underlying structure is only loosely articulated. Thus, Canadians' views on political and economic equality are imperfectly related, and these, in turn, are correlated only very weakly with beliefs about the rights of the individual as opposed to those concerning the need for a democratic polity to maintain public order and counter external threats.

The nuances of the content and structure of their beliefs about democracy notwithstanding, Canadians do share a broad consensus about what the concept means in practice. Thus, disagreements about what democracy means in the abstract do not extend to how they rate real-world political systems claiming to be democracies. A large majority of Canadians believe that their country and the United States come much closer to the democratic ideal than does a country like the Soviet Union. In this regard, the data on satisfaction with democracy in Western European countries indicate that Canadians views of democracy generally resemble those of citizens in several such countries. Democracy may not be fully realized in their political system, but it essentially means politics as it is practiced in that system. The European data also indicate, however, that levels of satisfaction with democracy differ from one country to the next and can change quickly over brief periods of time. In Chapter 7 we consider how these findings help us to understand the determinants of support for democratic political systems. Because political parties play critical roles in the support processes that undergird such systems, we next focus on Canadians' partisan attachments.

PARTISANSHIP

The significance of political parties in contemporary democracies is indisputable. They are crucial mechanisms for organizing and channeling societal conflicts and for linking citizens to their government. As noted in Chapter 2, one of the factors affecting the ability of Canadian parties to perform these functions is that, unlike many other advanced industrial societies, social class historically has not been an important dimension for organizing the party system. A second, related factor is that many Canadians do not employ a "left–right" continuum as a means of organizing and interpreting information about parties and the political world more generally. In many Western European democracies such a continuum has served as the functional equivalent of political ideology. As such, it has enabled people to comprehend and evaluate political phenomena ranging from relatively concrete matters, such as a party's electoral platform and position on salient issues of the day, to more abstract subjects, such as how the party system functions to represent the needs and demands of social groups.

In studies conducted in the 1960s John Meisel found that many Canadians saw almost no class differences between the two major centrist parties, the Liberals and Progressive–Conservatives (Meisel, 1975:70). Moreover, many also perceived only very modest differences between the two larger parties and the social democratic New Democratic Party (NDP). In addition, Meisel found that many people were unable to place the parties on the left–right scale. He reasoned that "this was probably so because respondents did not understand its meaning or because they thought the dimension was not compatible with the politics they know" (Meisel, 1975:69). Another study (Kornberg, Mishler, and Smith, 1975) found that although Canadians did employ a left–right scale to structure some of their own policy positions and those ascribed to parties, they also employed other dimensions such as "government party–opposition parties," "major–minor parties" and "national–regional parties" as well. More recent data tell a similar story. In 1984 fully 40 percent of Canadians were unable to place either themselves or the parties on a left–right scale. Of those who could use the scale, about one-quarter placed themselves exactly at the center and another 20 percent within one point of it. Similarly, many placed the parties at or very near to the mid-point and, although the image of the NDP was relatively clearly defined in left–right terms among those using the scale, only one-third located the New Democrats as a left-of-center party.

We may infer from these studies that class-related ideologies and ideological surrogates, like social class itself, do not play a major role in defining relationships between citizens and parties in Canada. However, the weakness of class and associated ideological constraints on Canadians' thinking about political parties does not mean that psychological orientations to-

ward them are absent. In this regard perhaps nothing is more important
than a sense of party identification. The concept of party identification was
introduced in studies of mass political behavior in the United States in the
1950s (Belknap and Campbell, 1952; Campbell et al., 1954, 1960). In these
studies party identification was viewed as an affective bond between
citizens and parties having the potential to influence beliefs, attitudes,
opinions, and actions relevant to political support.

The theoretical importance of party identification was magnified by its
presumed stability across and within generations. Early research suggested
that most people acquired a sense of party identification during childhood
or adolescence, largely as a result of familial socialization processes (e.g.,
Campbell et al., 1960:ch. 7; Greenstein, 1965:71–75). Moreover, except in
the face of major upheavals such as those precipitated by wars and depres-
sions, a party identification tended to remain unchanged throughout the
life cycle, and acted as a long-term force in the set of psychological forces
influencing political behavior. In addition to its direct impact it exerted
indirect effects by serving as a "perceptual screen through which the individual tends to see what is favorable to his [her] partisan orientation"
(Campbell, et al., 1960:133). Short-term forces on electoral choice such as
issue perceptions and evaluations of the performance of parties and their
leaders, although not completely determined by party identification, were
subject to its screening effects. Party identification thus was accorded the
status of a crucial variable in individual-level explanations of voting behavior and aggregate-level theories of political stability and change.

In the Canadian case, measures of party identification have been included in national surveys over the past quarter century. These surveys
present a picture of partisan attachments that have important implications
for explanations of political support. This can be appreciated by considering several properties of party identification, namely: direction, strength,
distribution, consistency across levels of the federal system, and stability
over time.

Direction and intensity

Figure 3.4 depicts the direction of identification with national political parties derived from fourteen national surveys conducted between 1965 and
1989.[4] The figure shows that a large majority of Canadians hold a federal

4 For all of the surveys employed in this chapter, except those by Meisel et al., the sequence
  of questions used to measure federal party identification is as follows: (a) "Thinking of
  federal politics, do you usually think of yourself as Liberal, Conservative, NDP, Social
  Credit, or what?" (b) "How strongly [party named] do you feel; very strongly, fairly strongly, or not very strongly?" (c) [If "refused," "don't know," "independent," or "none" in (a)]
  "Still thinking of *federal* politics, do you generally think of yourself as being a little closer to
  one of the parties than to the others?" (d) [If "yes"] "Which party is that?" All respondents

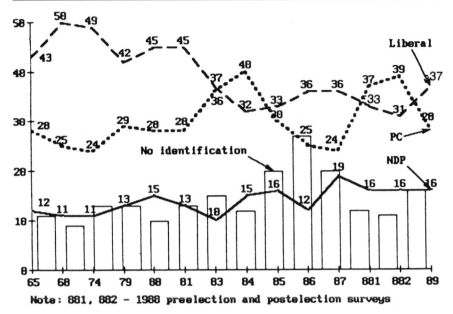

Note: 881, 882 - 1988 preelection and postelection surveys

Figure 3.4. *Federal party identification, 1965–89 (in percent)*

party identification and, until the early 1980s, the aggregate distribution of these identifications was quite stable. During the 1965–81 period the Liberals consistently enjoyed the support of a large plurality of the electorate (45 percent on average), whereas identification with the Progressive Conservatives and NDP averaged 27 percent and 13 percent, respectively. In the 1980s aggregate support for the federal parties became more volatile. The PCs' share of identifiers climbed to 41 percent in 1984, but fell precipitously, before rebounding to 39 percent at the time of the 1988 election. Afterward, the PC share of federal identifiers again diminished rapidly. The Liberal pattern is a pale mirror image of the Tory one. After the 1984 election the Liberals partially recovered their losses of the early 1980s, but their share of identifiers remained well below what it had been when the

---

supplying a party label to questions (a) or (c) were considered to have some degree of party identification. Persons declining to provide a party label in (a) but doing so in (c) were classified as "not very strong" identifiers. The summary index of strength of party identification is obtained by scoring very strong identifiers = + 3, fairly strong identifiers = + 2, not very strong identifiers = + 1, and nonidentifiers = 0. A parallel sequence of questions and procedures was used to measure provincial party identification. The 1965 and 1968 party identification questions are similar, except that the federal and provincial questions are integrated into one sequence.

decade began. In 1988 the cohort of Liberal partisans shrunk to its lowest level (31 percent) in over twenty years before expanding modestly in 1989. Compared to the two larger parties, the size of the group of NDP partisans has been relatively stable. Although the party enjoyed a brief surge in partisanship in 1987, this quickly dissipated in the run-up to the 1988 election. In 1989 the percentage of federal New Democrats was 16 percent, only marginally above what it had been twenty-five years earlier.

A significant recent trend has been the weakening of identification with the national parties. Although the incidence of nonidentification was quite stable prior to 1984 (averaging 12 percent), it subsequently increased such that in 1986 one Canadian in four refused a party label. Relatedly, the percentage identifying "very strongly" with a party declined. In 1984 25 percent stated they had a "very strong" identification; between 1985 and 1987, an average of only 17 percent did so. One interpretation of the 1984–87 decline is that it reflects the absence of the mobilizing stimuli provided by a national election. Such an interpretation appears to have some validity in that the percentage of federal nonidentifiers declined to only 12 percent at the time of the 1988 election and then increased to 16 percent in 1989. However, an "election-mobilization" explanation cannot account fully for the stronger levels of partisanship evident in earlier surveys conducted in nonelection years. In 1981, for example, only 13 percent stated that they did not have a party identification and in 1983 15 percent did so. Although we lack the requisite panel data to establish the point at the individual level, political events and conditions in the post-1984 period suggest that the weakening of federal partisan attachments in the 1984–87 period was largely a product of widespread public unhappiness with the performance of the Mulroney Conservative government coupled with a lack of enthusiasm for a Liberal alternative led by the decidedly unpopular John Turner.[5] Whether this period effect will be translated into a long-term ratcheting down of the strength of Canadians' feelings about their national parties remains to be seen.

5 Collateral support for this interpretation is provided by the results of time series analyses of CIPO and Canadian Facts monthly vote intention data. These show that neither inflation nor unemployment levels had significant effects on the Conservative government's popularity between 1984 and 1988. Rather, the marked decrease in Conservative support was strongly associated with various political interventions, most notably a seemingly endless series of scandals involving high-ranking Conservative cabinet ministers (see Gratton, 1988). Conservative support also was eroded by the Mulroney government decision to place a major Air Canada maintenance facility in Montreal, Quebec, rather than in Winnipeg, Manitoba – a decision that angered and disappointed Conservative partisans in Western Canada. In contrast, and consistent with our interpretation, analyses show that the Conservatives benefitted from periodic attempts by disaffected Liberals to oust their then national leader, John Turner.

Party and society

Even a cursory inspection of federal election returns reveals that a party's vote share normally varies sharply by region. It is not surprising, therefore, that party identifications do the same. From the starting point of our survey data in the mid-1960s through the early 1980s the pattern was one of Liberal dominance in Quebec, coupled with Conservative strength in the Prairies. Since then, however, Liberal strength in Quebec has declined and Quebecers have shown great volatility in their partisan attachments. When the 1984 and 1988 elections were held sizable percentages of persons in the latter province accepted a PC party label. In the interval between these contests the percentage of Conservatives decreased markedly, but the percentage of Liberals, although increased, did not return to pre-1984 levels. Like the PCs, the NDP traditionally has had its largest cohort of identifiers in the Western provinces. Unlike the Tories, however, the New Democratic group of identifiers always has been minuscule in the Atlantic provinces and Quebec. Regional differences in patterns of federal party identification are not absolute, however; sizable groups in most areas of the country identify with one of the two major parties, and this mutes the strength of region as a correlate of party support.

The strength of relationships between federal party identification, on the one hand, and region and other sociodemographic cleavages, on the other, may be assessed by probit analyses[6] employing measures of region-ethnicity, gender, age, income and education as predictors of identification with the Liberals, PCs, and NDP. Two such analyses are reported in Table 3.3. The 1974 results are typical of those for any survey conducted before 1984, i.e., the Quebec–Francophone and Quebec–Anglophone region-ethnicity variables were positively associated with Liberal identification and negatively with Conservative and NDP identification. In contrast, residence in the Prairies was related positively to Conservative identification and negatively to Liberal identification. Regarding other predictors, NDP identifiers tended to be men and to have lower incomes and higher levels of formal education, whereas Liberal identifiers tended to be women and PC identifiers, older persons. However, none of the predictors, nor all of them together, had much explanatory power.

In 1988 some of the relationships between federal party identification and sociodemographic characteristics of the Canadian electorate had changed. Most notably, net of other considerations, being a Quebec Francophone was *positively* associated with being a Conservative, and *negatively* associated with being a Liberal identifier in a province that for most of

6 Probit is chosen because the dependent variable, party identification is scored as a series of dichotomies (e.g., Liberal identification = 1, other identification and no identification = 0). The R^2 statistic is that proposed by McKelvey and Zavoina (1975).

Table 3.3. *Probit analyses of federal party identification by sociodemographic characteristics, 1974, 1988*

	1974			1988		
	Liberal	PC	NDP	Liberal	PC	NDP
Predictor variables	b	b	b	b	b	b
Region-ethnicity						
Atlantic	.16	.12	-.44a	.07	.11	-.15
Quebec-French	.36a	-.91a	-.51a	-.24a	.19a	-.19c
Quebec-Non-French	.49a	-.57a	-.53b	.70a	-.82a	-.22
Prairies	-.35a	.31a	.02	-.52a	.44a	.04
British Columbia	-.16	-.09	.16	-.52a	.01	.57a
Age	.00	.01a	-.01a	.00	.01a	-.01a
Education	.02	-.01	.09a	.06c	-.05	.04
Gender	.15a	-.01	-.15b	.12b	-.14a	-.03
Income	.03	.01	-.04b	-.00	.08a	-.08a
Constant	-.54a	-1.04a	-.40	-.75a	-.65a	-.37
Estimated R² =	.11	.22	.15	.08	.07	.09
% correctly classified	58	76	89	68	64	84

Note: a-p ≤.001; b-p ≤.01; c-p ≤.05; two-tailed test

this century has been the rock on which Liberal party hegemony in national politics has rested. The changing patterns of support for the national Liberal and Conservative parties in the 1980s in Quebec and other parts of Canada is a topic to which we return in Chapters 5 and 6.

The 1988 analyses also show that, unlike 1974, well-educated persons tended to be Liberals and those with higher incomes tended to be PCs, whereas women were less likely than men to identify with the latter party. However, perhaps the most important finding in these analyses is that the overall strength of the relationships between sociodemographic characteristics and federal party identification remained very weak. In contrast to many other Western democracies, in Canada support for national parties long has been substantially decoupled from the societal cleavages that are commonly assumed to define the parameters of partisan conflict.[7]

Consistency

The federal nature of the Canadian polity raises the possibility that citizens may develop dual partisan allegiances at the national and provincial levels of government. The historic importance of regional cleavages and federal–provincial conflicts, together with marked differences in party vote shares

---

7 Nor is it the case that societal cleavages have strong relationships with provincial party identifications. The strength and direction of relationships varies from one province to the next, but nowhere are they particularly strong. On provincial party support see Kornberg, Mishler, and Clarke (1982:114–22).

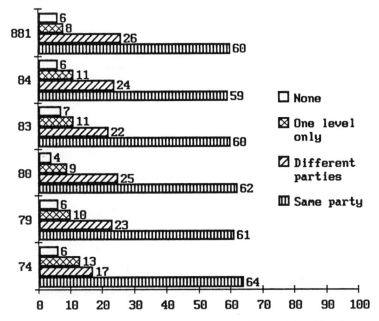

Figure 3.5. *Consistency of federal and provincial party identifications, 1974–88 (in percent)*

in national and provincial elections in several provinces suggest that many people fail to identify with the same party at both levels of government. This is, in fact, the case. Across the 1974–88 period an average of only three voters in five identified with the same federal and provincial party, one in ten identified with a party at only one level of government, and more than one in five actually identified with *different* federal and provincial parties (Figure 3.5). Inconsistency in federal and provincial party identifications is an enduring feature of Canadian political psychology,[8] with the percentage of persons holding different federal and provincial party ties increasing from 17 percent in 1974 to 26 percent in 1988. The incidence of "split" partisanship is not confined to provinces such as Quebec or British Columbia where differences between the federal and provincial party systems are most pronounced. Although levels of split party identification are considerably higher in those provinces than elsewhere, dual identifiers can be found in every province. The continuing presence of a sizable cohort of inconsistent partisans and their differential regional distribution is indica-

8 The term "inconsistency" denotes that a respondent does not identify with the same party at both levels of government. Whether it is ideologically inconsistent or irrational to identify with different parties in federal and provincial politics is a separate matter. See Blake (1982) and Clarke and Stewart (1987).

Table 3.4. *Stability of federal party identification, 1974–88 national panels (in percent)*

Pattern	National panels							
	74–79	79–80	80–83	83–84	80–84	84–88I	88I–88II	84–88II
Stable identification	62	72	67	64	63	66	73	64
Switched parties	16	12	16	18	21	19	12	20
To/from nonidentification	16	12	14	13	12	11	11	11
Stable nonidentification	5	4	4	6	4	5	5	5
N	1299	1690	834	1294	600	794	1429	675

Note: 88I-1988 preelection survey; 88II-1988 postelection survey

tive of the complexity of Canadians' feelings about the national parties, a conclusion that is reinforced by an analysis of the stability of party attachments over time.

Stability

As noted, it was originally assumed that, except in exceptional circumstances, party identification was an "unmoved mover" that structured other political attitudes and exerted powerful direct and indirect stabilizing effects on voting choice and party support more generally. Such effects suggested, in turn, that party identification had important system-level consequences – it contributed to the continuity of the party system and the larger political order (Campbell et al., 1966). The constancy of party identification is, however, an empirical question, and findings from the Canadian surveys are strongly at odds with such an "unmoved mover" characterization. Panel data reveal substantial individual-level mutability in partisan attachments between adjacent waves of interviewing (Table 3.4). Between 1984 and 1988, for example, three persons in ten either reported switching their federal party identification (19 percent), or moving to or from the status of nonidentifier (11 percent). Nor is partisan instability a recent development; across the 1974–9 panel 32 percent changed their party identifications. Similarly, recall data from the 1965 and 1968 cross-sectional surveys reveal equally impressive levels of change, as does evidence from political socialization studies (Kornberg, Smith, and Clarke, 1979:48). Partisan instability, then, is not a novel product of the highly charged political atmosphere of the past decade. Rather, it is a longstanding phenomenon.

The instability of federal partisanship suggests it is affected by various attitudes and beliefs pertinent to the political support process. This is the case; multivariate analyses of our national panel data reveal that changes in voter evaluations of party performance on salient issues and changes in their feelings about party leaders enhance the likelihood of partisan instability. Partisan inconsistency is relevant as well – instability in federal and provincial party identification is greater among voters who fail to identify with the same party at both levels of government. Analyses also show that party identification is affected by voters' sociotropic economic evaluations and, in the case of NDP identification, by future-oriented economic evaluations as well (Clarke and Stewart, 1987; Kornberg and Clarke, 1988; Martinez, 1989).

Finally, the instability of party identification in Canada is pronounced, but not pervasive. Although very long-term panel studies would be required to prove the point conclusively, existing research indicates that many people form their initial party identifications during childhood or adolescence, and that upwards of 50 percent do not change them in later life. Party identification in Canada is thus a complex phenomenon. For some persons, it seems to be little more than a convenient "score card" for recording (possibly highly mutable) issue and leader evaluations. For others, it is laden with durable affective components generated by powerful early-life socialization processes. The implication of this complexity for models of the support process is that party identification is both cause and consequence of other significant political attitudes.

FEDERALISM

In Canada political participation and representation are structured by a federal system of government. Indeed, it is often argued that Canadian politics is the politics of federalism, and analyses of the problematic nature of political support often focus squarely on conflicts between Ottawa and the provinces (e.g., Simeon, 1977; Smiley, 1980; Milne, 1986; Stevenson, 1979, 1989). The presence of a federal system means that people have opportunities to participate in politics at multiple levels of government and to develop multifaceted, even contradictory attitudes toward political parties, institutions and processes. Perhaps most importantly, the federal system provides the structural basis for creating and sustaining "divided loyalties" (Black, 1975) that may have profound consequences for political support. In the next chapter we will test these pieces of conventional wisdom; here we simply will document orientations toward the federal system.

National survey data indicate that feelings about the national and provincial levels of government and evaluations of the operation of the federal system vary widely. For many Canadians provincial governments are at least as salient as the federal one. When asked which level of government they "pay more attention to" 27 percent in our 1983 study chose the federal, but nearly as many (22 percent) chose the provincial, and an additional 26 percent stated that they pay the same attention to both. Some also believe that their provincial government has an equal or greater impact on their own and their families' well-being. To illustrate, in 1983 40 percent said their provincial government had a greater effect, and the same number cited the federal. In 1988 31 percent chose the national government, and fully 46 percent, their provincial one. And, when those in the 1983 survey were asked "[w]hen you think of *your* government, which government comes to mind, the government of Canada or the government of [province of residence]?" fully one-third chose the provincial alternative. Other surveys also strongly confirm the strength of provincial sentiments.

These orientations are not randomly distributed. Regressing a federal–provincial orientation index[9] based on responses to the three questions discussed above on our standard set of sociodemographic characteristics (age, education, gender, income, region-ethnicity) revealed that only the latter has strong effects. Compared to Ontarians, Francophone Quebecers, British Columbians and, to a lesser extent, residents of the Prairies and the Atlantic provinces were all more likely to exhibit a provincial orientation. Anglophone Quebecers resembled Ontarians in their strong federal feelings, but even they were more "provincial" than residents of Ontario. Of the other sociodemographic variables, only age was a significant predictor, with older persons being slightly more favorably disposed toward the national level of the political system.

It also is clear that a large majority believe that some provinces are more equal than others. In 1979 the provinces viewed as most influential were Ontario (by 62 percent), Alberta (by 57 percent) and Quebec (47 percent). Only 15 percent chose British Columbia and no other province was mentioned by more than one person in twenty. These perceptions accord well with scholarly accounts of the distribution of power in the federal system, and the roles played by various provinces in the protracted and oftentimes acrimonious federal–provincial conflicts of the past two decades. The 1981 survey also revealed substantial sentiment in favor of more provincial power. When asked whether the federal or provincial governments should be accorded more power, although 42 percent of the public favored the status quo, nearly as many (40 percent) opted for more power to the provinces. Only 18 percent wanted to give Ottawa more power. Opinions

---

9 The federal–provincial orientation index is constructed using responses to the following three questions: (a) "Would you say that you pay more attention to federal politics, provincial politics, or local politics?" (b) "As far as you are concerned personally, which government is more important in affecting how you and your family get on, the one in Ottawa, the provincial government here in [province], or the local government?" (c) When you think of *your* government, which government comes to mind, the government of Canada or the government of [province]?" Federal answers are scored +1, provincial answers are scored −1, and all other answers are scored 0. The scores are summed to yield an index ranging from +3 (federal orientation) to −3 (provincial orientation).

about the potential redistribution of power also were strongly related to region/ethnicity. In every region other than Ontario, which historically has been the most populous and powerful province, majorities or large pluralities favored more provincial power. Ontarians were most in favor of the status quo, and the only group opting for a stronger central government were non-Francophone Quebecers.

A substantial percentage not only wanted to change the distribution of power between Ottawa and the provinces, but also wanted a more equitable distribution of power, influence and resources among the latter. When asked: "In your opinion, are some of the provinces bearing more than their fair share of the costs of governing Canada?" nearly half of those interviewed in 1983 answered "yes" and two-thirds of these persons believed that it was *their* province that bore unfair costs. Some provinces also were seen as receiving unfair benefits. When queried "What about benefits? Are some provinces receiving more than their fair share?" 45 percent agreed and an overwhelming majority of them stated that provinces *other than theirs* were the recipients.

As might be expected given the data presented in the last chapter, the "my costs" and "your benefits" responses varied by region. Although perceptions of unfair benefits going to others were widespread, feelings that one's own province was bearing unfair costs were concentrated in the five Western provinces and Ontario (Figure 3.6). Quebecers – whose long-time discontent with the federal system has threatened the integrity of the national political regime and community – were not atypically unhappy about what that system was costing them. Nor were they especially likely to complain about unfair benefits going elsewhere. Unlike Westerners, the roots of Quebecers' discontent with federalism are primarily cultural rather than economic.[10] Similarly, an analysis of how many Canadians believe that their province both pays unfair costs and that other provinces receive undue benefits showed that a large majority of people with this combination of negative evaluations were concentrated in the West and Ontario.

These data are from the 1983 survey, which was administered a year after a new constitution had been put in place. The pattern of regional differentiation in perceptions, therefore, might simply reflect unhappiness with a province's prospects under the new constitution, rather than discontent with the federal system as it had operated previously. Evidence from the 1979 study suggests this is not the case. Although the questions were not identical to those asked in 1983, the response patterns were similar. In 1979 38 percent believed that their province bore unfair costs, 48 percent believed that other provinces received unfair benefits, and 26 percent held

10 See, for example, Bernard (1978:46–7). This is not to say that the emphasis in contemporary Quebec nationalism is a defense of traditional cultural values. As McRoberts (1988:435–6) argues, since the "Quiet Revolution" of the early 1960s these values have been rejected in favor of an aggressive attempt to realize the full potential of Québécois culture in an advanced industrial, urbanized society.

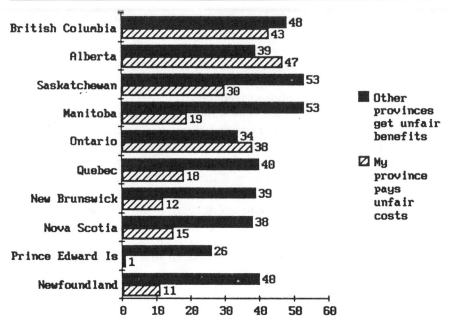

Figure 3.6. *Perceived inequities in the federal system, 1983 (in percent)*

both beliefs. Also, as in 1983, unhappiness with the costs and benefits of federalism was concentrated in the West and Ontario.

That discontent in 1979 was somewhat greater than in 1983 is consistent with the hypothesis that federal–provincial and interprovincial tensions receded after the constitutional accord had been reached. Nevertheless, it certainly did not end unhappiness with the operation of the federal system. In terms of intensity of dissatisfaction, it appears that residents of Alberta, the province that has made the political economy of federalism the raison d'être of its struggle for constitutional change, were particularly unhappy. Albertans were not alone, however; in 1983 people in all parts of the country continued to complain about federal arrangements. Nor have these complaints subsequently abated. In 1988 the percentage dissatisfied with the costs of federalism ranged from a low of 53 percent in Ontario to a high of 61 percent in British Columbia; the percentage unhappy with benefits, from a low of 51 percent in the former region to a high of 73 percent in the latter.[11] And, in 1990 controversy over the "special status" of Quebec in

11 The 1988 question sequence inquired only about perceived inequities in the costs and benefits of federalism, i.e., "In your opinion, are some of the provinces bearing more than their fair share of the costs of governing Canada?" "What about benefits? Are some provinces receiving more than their fair share?" In 1979 and 1983, follow-up questions were asked about which provinces the respondent had in mind.

the federal system envisaged by the Meech Lake Accord again threatened to tear that system apart.

EVALUATIONS OF GOVERNMENT PERFORMANCE

Although federalism is a highly salient feature of Canadian political life, judgments about the costs and benefits the system confers are only one part of a much larger array of public evaluations of governmental performance. In Canada, as in other political systems, the key functions of government historically have entailed securing people's lives and property and their freedom from both domestic and foreign threats. In the twentieth century, and more particularly in the wake of the great depression of the 1930s and the mobilization of societal resources occasioned by World War II, the scope of governmental activity expanded greatly. Especially notable was the growth of the welfare state with its many social programs. Some of these, such as health care and medical insurance, pensions for senior citizens and handicapped persons, financial aid to families with children under eighteen ("baby bonuses"), and unemployment insurance, touch virtually everyone at some point in their lives. More recent additions to the menu of government programs with broad impact include initiatives in fields such as higher education, culture and the arts, and environmental protection.

Equally striking (as reflected above in responses to our questions regarding the meaning of democracy) has been the expansion of governmental involvement in and oversight of the economy. In response to the economic trauma of the 1930s, the governments of Western countries abandoned classical laissez-faire economic doctrines and adopted activist policies designed to stimulate economic growth and renew prosperity. Although many of those policies were essentially ad hoc responses, they were given intellectual justification by J. M. Keynes's pathbreaking macroeconomic theories. Keynes's *General Theory* (1936) was written in response to the world economic crisis of the 1930s and, more particularly, to the massive unemployment that was plaguing Western countries at the time (Stewart, 1986; Hall, 1989). In the postwar era Keynes's argument that governments could use fiscal policy to influence aggregate demand and, hence, levels of unemployment, became the cornerstone of a new macroeconomic orthodoxy. By the 1960s it was widely believed that political leaders and their Keynesian economic advisors could use fiscal instruments to "fine tune" a country's economy. The now familiar "Phillips curve" (Phillips, 1958) seemingly demonstrated that governments could trade off increments of inflation and unemployment and thereby maximize national economic well-being.

Keynesian demand-management techniques proved highly seductive to governments of all ideological hues because the ability to use them to control a capitalist economy held out the promise of countering its "boom and bust" cycles, and, thereby, of vitiating the twin evils of inflation and unemployment. Equally important, the resulting economic prosperity would provide the fiscal resources needed to finance both current welfare state programs and to initiate new ones. "Selling the welfare state" was seen as both a responsible and a profitable political strategy. In periodic elections party leaders competed with one another in efforts to convince voters that not only did they have the best new social policies, but also that they were most qualified to administer ongoing ones and the economic engine that fueled them. In the affluent 1950s and 1960s a broad consensus emerged regarding the desirability of governmental intervention in many areas of social and economic life. This consensus encompassed both political elites and the general publics of Canada and other Western countries.

In the 1970s the assumptions that economies would continue to expand and that governments could use Keynesian macroeconomic prescriptions to promote this expansion were severely challenged. The inflationary stimulus provided by President Johnson's "guns and butter" policies during the early years of America's involvement in the Vietnam war (Stein, 1988), and the dramatic increases in world energy prices following the 1973 Arab oil embargo and the emergence of OPEC as a major force, sent the economies of all Western countries, including Canada's, into a tailspin. Skyrocketing inflation, sharp upturns in unemployment, and sluggish growth were ailments that proved highly resistant to traditional demand-management prescriptions. The new, persistent reality of stagflation and the failure of Keynesian remedies to cure the maladies of inflation and unemployment prompted a breakdown of elite consensus on economic and social policy, and a loss of public confidence and trust in government. Neoconservative (neoliberal) economists and political thinkers mounted a frontal attack on the welfare state and the economic policies that had undergirded it. In several countries conservative political leaders such as Margaret Thatcher and Ronald Reagan came to power promising renewed prosperity through the application of monetarist, or supply-side, economic doctrines and deep cuts in social spending.

It might be assumed that the success of "new right" politicians such as Thatcher and Reagan indicated that the economic hardships of the 1970s and early 1980s were enough to induce electorates to abandon their belief in the desirability of the welfare state and the programs governments had assumed in the high tide of postwar prosperity. There is, however, mounting evidence that this did not happen. Among average citizens the cultural basis of the political economy of political support remained much as it was before the stagflation era (e.g., Crewe and Searing, 1988; Clarke, Stewart, and Zuk, 1988).

As indicated in the previous chapter, Canada suffered as much as or more from stagflation than most Western countries. It is, however, an excellent example of a country in which the general public has continued to demand government involvement in many aspects of social and economic life. This is true not only for such longstanding and fundamental activities as maintaining the armed forces, protecting lives and property and securing rights and liberties, but also for social programs such as health, welfare, and education. In every case, overwhelming majorities of those participating in surveys conducted since 1979 have stated that government involvement in areas such as these is highly desirable. In 1983, for example, 85 percent believed the federal government should "provide welfare services for anyone who needs them," 86 percent wanted national government action to "ensure that people get all the education they are capable of," and fully 94 percent believed that Ottawa should "ensure that everyone has their health needs looked after."[12] Moreover, there continues to be almost universal agreement that the federal government should try to control inflation and promote high levels of employment, suggesting that neoconservative economic doctrines have had little resonance. Canadians also are strongly in favor of governmental efforts to protect the environment and to enhance culture and the arts – activities central to what some have labeled "postmaterialist" value orientations (e.g., Inglehart, 1977, 1990; Dalton, 1988).

Not only do Canadians believe government should be concerned with these matters, they also believe the activities are very important. For example, in the 1983 study large majorities (75 percent or more) expressed this opinion about health services, inflation, unemployment, environmental protection, and protection of lives and property. Conversely, only support for culture and the arts and the provision of welfare services were deemed unimportant by as many as 15 percent. On average, two-thirds believed the several areas of possible government activity were "very" important and nearly a third more believed they were "fairly" important.

The widely shared view that a government should and can have a significant impact on the social and economic lives of its citizens is, then, a major component of the political culture of Canada and other Western democracies. However, another core element of the liberal democratic creed is the aforementioned distinction between public and private realms and the prescription that democratic citizens should shoulder considerable

---

12 Similar attitudes were expressed in the 1977, 1979, and 1981 Social Change in Canada surveys. Respondents were asked if they favored "more," "the same," or "less" governmental involvement in a wide range of policy areas. There was strong support for maintaining current levels of activity and, in several areas, large majorities wanted more governmental involvement. The 1981 data are illustrative. Here, majorities (ranging from 50 percent to 75 percent) wanted more governmental effort in policy areas such as education, environment, women's issues, crime, poverty, and health care. On average, fully 52 percent wanted more governmental action, 38 percent wanted at least the present level of activity, and only 11 percent favored less governmental action.

responsibility for their own lives and rise through their own efforts. This tension is reflected in the survey data presented in this and the previous chapter.

Given the belief, then, that the activities of government are important, it is not surprising that citizens in a democracy make judgments about how successful governments are in carrying out these activities and that the latter, in turn, have significant consequences for support. Indeed, one of the primary theoretical justifications for democracies is that they derive their legitimacy from and establish governments for the people. However, for at least a half century effectiveness in "delivering the goods" has not been enough. Governments must do so in ways that meet prevailing conceptions of *equity* and *fairness*, not only in determining the "whens" and "hows" of their policies and programs, but also the "who gets what." In the language of Easton (1965), both political inputs and outputs are subject to equity/fairness tests.

Accordingly, in the 1979, 1983, and 1988 surveys we invited respondents to offer judgments about both the effectiveness and equitable operation of their national government. At best they gave it only mixed grades for being effective.[13] The highest marks in 1983 were reserved for health and educational activities – 32 percent and 22 percent, respectively, said the federal government was performing "very well" in those two areas (Table 3.5). However, in three other areas – the environment, inflation, and unemployment – fewer than one in ten gave it a high rating. Judgments about Ottawa's handling of the economy were especially harsh, with 42 percent and 60 percent stating that it had performed poorly in coping with inflation and unemployment, respectively. Bad marks also were given for defense and environmental protection, over half believed the federal government had not done very well in the former area, and over a third, in the latter. The 1988 evaluations were generally quite similar, with the biggest differences being a willingness to award somewhat higher marks for managing the economy, and increasing negativity concerning efforts to protect the environment. In the earlier 1979 survey responses also were lukewarm at best, with Ottawa coming in for scathing criticism regarding its handling of the economy. More generally, no more than slightly over one-third of those

13 The 1983 government effectiveness statements were: (a) "Provide welfare services for anyone who needs them"; (b) "Keep our armed forces strong enough to protect us from a possible attack from any source"; (c) "Make sure that everyone who wants to work has the opportunity to do so"; (d) "Protect people's lives and property"; (e) "Ensure that the personal liberties and rights of people never are endangered by the police, the courts, or the civil service"; (f) "Ensure that inflation is kept under control"; (g) "Ensure that everyone has their health needs looked after"; (h) "Ensure that people get all the education they are capable of"; (i) "Clean up and protect the environment"; (j) "Provide money for and generally support culture and the arts." In each case respondents were invited to give a "very well," "fairly well," or "not very well" evaluation. The 1988 sequence is the same except the items (b) and (j) were not asked.

Table 3.5. Evaluations of federal government performance, 1983, 1988 (in percent)

Performance Area	1983				1988			
	Very well	Fairly well	Not very well	N	Very well	Fairly well	Not very well	N
Provide welfare service	13a	58	29	1708	25a	56	19	2056
Provide employment opportunities	4	36	60	1844	12	52	36	2132
Protect lives and property	16	65	19	1745	17	67	16	2057
Protect rights and liberties	15	64	21	1749	19	61	20	2049
Control inflation	6	52	42	1964	11	60	29	2091
Provide health care	32	56	12	1993	37	49	14	2141
Protect environment	9	55	36	1965	6	32	62	2157
Provide educational opportunities	22	58	20	1728	20	54	26	2105
Maintain armed forces	10	37	53	1533	t	t	t	
Foster culture and the arts	14	67	19	1359	t	t	t	

Note: t - question not asked in 1988; a - horizontal percentages

interviewed in any survey believed that the federal government was performing "very well" in *any* policy area.

One may appreciate the negative tenor of these judgments better by
juxtaposing them with the importance the public ascribed to them. A comparison of "importance" and "effectiveness" index scores[14] shows dramatic
differences. Four of five respondents in our 1983 survey had positive scores
concerning the importance of various activities, but only one in five gave
the federal government a positive "effectiveness" score. Nor, as we have
seen, were Canadians in an unusually sour mood in 1983 – the 1988 data on
governmental effectiveness argue otherwise, as do responses in the earlier
1979 survey. The similarity in responses in three surveys conducted over
nearly a decade suggests that Canadians' propensities to make unfavorable
judgments of federal government effectiveness are not idiosyncratic to a
specific and, possibly, transitory political context. Instead, they represent
ongoing discontents with Ottawa's performance in a wide range of policy
areas where expectations concerning government involvement are deeply
embedded aspects of public political culture.

Evidence consistent with the conclusion that discontent is widespread
and enduring also is provided by survey responses concerning the equity
and fairness of government activity and the broader political system. Because the issues of equity and fairness pertain to the processes by which
political decisions are made as well as their outcomes, the range of relevant
equity–fairness judgments is broad. Accordingly, in our 1983 and 1988 surveys we included items about the fairness of the system, whether it is
achievement based on merit or "connections" that enables people to advance themselves, whether institutions such as the civil service, courts and
the federal government generally function fairly, and whether parties and
parliament provide unbiased representation to individuals and groups.[15]

14 To provide a summary comparison, each of the "importance" judgments are scored "very
    important" = + 1, "somewhat important" = 0, "not very important" = – 1. Similarly, each
    of the effectiveness evaluations are scored "very well" = + 1, "fairly well" = 0, and "not
    very well" = – 1. The importance index ranges from –10 (unimportant) to 10 (important),
    and the effectiveness index (1983) ranges from –10 (ineffective) to +10 (effective). Since
    two effectiveness items were not asked in 1988, the 1988 effectiveness index ranges from
    –8 to +8.

15 The equity–fairness question sequence included the following "agree–disagree" state-
    ments: (a) "In Canada some people don't pay enough taxes whereas others pay too
    many"; (b) "In Canada what people become depends on what they can do, and not on who
    they are or who they know"; (c) "In Canada the federal government treats some groups
    much better than others"; (d) "Over the years the federal civil service in Ottawa has
    treated all Canadians equally"; (e) "Over the years political parties generally have tried to
    look after the best interests of all Canadians, not just the interests of those who vote for
    them"; (f) "In Canada some groups get too much and others get too little"; (g) "Over the
    years the federal courts generally have acted speedily and treated people fairly"; (h)
    "Parliament in Canada does not represent everyone fairly"; (i) "In some countries there
    may be one law for the rich and another for the poor, but that's not the way the federal
    government works in Canada."

Table 3.6. *Equity-fairness evaluations, 1983, 1988 (in percent)*

	1983		1988	
Equity-fairness statement	Agree	Disagree	Agree	Disagree
Taxation unfair	80a	20	91a	9
Achievement not ascription	56	44	63	37
Government treats some groups unfairly	77	23	82	18
Civil service treats everyone equally	28	72	28	72
Parties look after everyone's interests	48	52	48	52
Some groups get too much; others, too little	82	18	87	13
Courts act speedily and fairly	52	48	52	48
Parliament does not represent everyone fairly	65	35	65	35
Laws apply equally to everyone	49	51	48	52

Note: Italicized percentages indicate negative evaluations; a - horizontal percentages

Many of those interviewed stated that their political system does not operate equitably or fairly. Indeed, in seven of nine instances in both studies, majorities made negative judgments, and in the remaining two cases over one-third did so. More specifically, the federal government was castigated for its distribution of resources to and treatment of various social groups. In 1983 82 percent believed that "in Canada some groups get too much and others get too little" and 77 percent thought that the laws apply differently to rich and poor (Table 3.6). In 1988 these percentages had grown even larger. Similarly, the taxation system was strongly criticized, with 80 percent in 1983 and 91 percent in 1988 agreeing that "in Canada some people don't pay enough taxes, whereas others pay too many." The public also was sharply critical of the kind of representation that political parties and parliament, the country's premier political institution, afford. In both studies slightly over two-thirds agreed that "parliament does not represent everyone fairly," and over half disagreed with the proposition that "parties try to represent the interests of everyone and not merely those who voted for them." Nor did the judicial system escape unscathed; majorities did not believe that the laws were applied equally, and large minorities did not think that the courts acted speedily and fairly.

Governmental effectiveness and equity–fairness judgments constitute logically distinct criteria for evaluating the performance of a political order. However, it is reasonable to hypothesize that these two types of judgments are interrelated. Empirically, this is the case – the correlation between summary effectiveness and equity–fairness indices[16] is .35 in 1983 and .44 in 1988. It also seems sensible that positive or negative combinations of judgments based on these criteria might have an especially strong

16 The summary effectiveness index is described in note 14 above. The summary equity–fairness index is constructed by summing "agree" responses to items (b), (d), (e), (g), (h), and (i) together with "disagree" responses to items (a), (c), and (f) in note 15 above. The resulting index ranges from 0 (inequitable and unfair) to 9 (equitable and fair).

influence on support for key political objects. This hypothesis is tested in the next chapter. For the present we note that few Canadians (less than one in five in 1983) accorded their political system and its officials above average scores on both effectiveness and equity–fairness dimensions, whereas nearly half conferred average or below average scores. The remainder (slightly over one in three) gave above average scores for either effectiveness or equity–fairness, but not both.

The conclusion that negative judgments about the performance of the political system are widespread is reinforced by analyses in which the effectiveness and equity–fairness indices were regressed on our standard set of sociodemographic variables. Age, level of formal education, annual family income, gender, and region-ethnicity *together* were able to explain only small fractions of the variance in effectiveness or equity–fairness evaluations and their individual effects were either extremely modest or, more often, statistically insignificant. Moreover, despite the extent to which explanations of Canada's problems of political support have focused on regional and ethnic discontent, negative effectiveness and equity–fairness judgments were not confined to residents of Quebec and the West who have complained the loudest and been disaffected the longest. Residents of those regions were significantly less satisfied with the operation of the federal system, but when other performance criteria were considered their judgments were not appreciably harsher than those of other Canadians.

Nor were such judgments correlated with conventional indicators of social class. Wealthier persons were only slightly more likely than the less well-off to express satisfaction and well educated individuals were neither more nor less likely to do so. Similarly, although much has been written about age cohort differences in political attitudes and values and the consequences these may have for understanding political conflict and change in contemporary Western countries (e.g., Inglehart, 1977, 1990), younger Canadians were only slightly more critical of their political system than were older persons. Further, despite their historically disadvantaged position, women were no more likely than men to make negative judgments. In Canada, then, discontent with the operation and outputs of the political system transcends societal cleavages that are commonly assumed to structure political conflict in contemporary democracies.

DEMOCRATIC CITIZENSHIP

In democracies citizens' perceptions of themselves and others as political actors are important factors in the support process. In Chapter 1 we noted that a democracy is a special kind of political system because citizens voluntarily comply with the constitutional order and the authoritative edicts of government rather than having to be continually coerced to do so. On the one hand, people are free to participate in the periodic election of public officials and to try to influence the decisions of elected and appointed political authorities in the interim between elections. On the other hand, those authorities are expected to respond to citizen needs and demands. If they fail to do so – in the case of elected officials – people are justified in "throwing the rascals out," and regardless of whether public officials are elected or appointed, democratic theory asserts the public's right to modify existing institutional and procedural arrangements to make them more accountable. Citizens' opinions, attitudes, and behavior are, then, the fulcrum of the support process in a democracy. Because they are, public levels of political interest, efficacy, knowledge, and trust in political authorities are crucial factors that influence how that process works in practice.

Political interest and knowledge

The cognitive processes that people employ in arriving at decisions that ultimately result in political behavior do not yield easily to empirical analysis. Knowing how politically interested in and knowledgeable people are is a valuable beginning because it provides a convenient window for viewing the psychological linkages between citizens and their government. Data on the level of general political interest in Canada are consistent; in every survey conducted between 1974 and 1988 only small percentages (15 percent on average) reported that they followed politics very closely, and more than twice as many (34 percent on average) stated that they did not follow them much at all. However, elections appear to stimulate interest in the world of public affairs; one-third to one-half stated that they were very interested in the six national elections held between 1968 and 1988. One reason for this may be that in a liberal democracy such as Canada elections not only are mechanisms by which people can hold public officials accountable for actions taken on their behalf, they also provide citizens with periodic opportunities to affirm the legitimacy of, and their support for, what is arguably a democratic regime's most important political process. This is a possibility we will explore in Chapter 6.

The heightened interest that elections stimulate appears short-lived. Evidence suggesting this conclusion comes from a comparison of the results of the two national surveys conducted after the 1984 election. The two sets of election interest figures generated by the surveys are quite different; in our political support study 50 percent indicated they were "very interested," as opposed to 34 percent in the national election study. The former survey was conducted using telephone interviews, the large majority of which were completed very shortly after the election had occurred. The latter, in contrast, employed in-person interviews begun several weeks afterward (in October 1984), with many respondents not being interviewed until three or four months later, when the salience of the election may well have faded.

More direct evidence is available from an analysis of reported election interest among respondents in the *same* survey. In our 1988 political support
study the percentage stating they were "very interested" in the federal election declined from 56 percent among persons interviewed immediately
after the contest to 39 percent among those interviewed six weeks to two
months later. Even among "late interview" respondents, however, election
interest remained much higher than general interest (39 percent versus 18
percent in 1988) – again suggesting the importance of elections for focusing, if only temporarily, public attention on political affairs.[17]

One may ask whether Canadians are significantly less interested in politics than are people in other Western democracies. The Barnes, Kaase et
al. Eight Nations Study (Austria, Finland, Great Britain, Italy, the Netherlands, Switzerland, the United States, West Germany) reveals that, as is
the case in Canada, only small minorities (ranging from a low of 4 percent
in Italy to a high of 24 percent in the United States) are generally very
interested in politics. The percentages expressing little or no interest vary
more widely with the countries dividing into two groups. For Austria, the
Netherlands, the United States, and West Germany the size of the un-
interested group ranges from 32 to 46 percent, and in Britain, Finland,
Italy, and Switzerland, from 55 to 80 percent. Our data indicate that Canada belongs in the first group of countries that have a relatively larger cohort
of politically interested citizens.

Our several surveys contain precious few items that would allow us to
measure directly the quantity of political information citizens possess. Data
on media consumption provide a convenient, if admittedly imperfect,
proxy. As noted in the previous chapter, persons interviewed in 1983
were asked not only about media consumption generally, but also about
the extent to which they monitored newspapers and radio and television
broadcasts for political news and information. The responses suggest that
many Canadians are exposed to political information on a fairly regular
basis, most frequently by reading a daily newspaper. Although radio and
television are less frequently monitored for political content, they too constitute sources of relevant information. Overall, few people totally ignore
political news in the two most popular media; only 10 percent and 14 percent, respectively, stated that they never read about politics in newspapers,
or never watched programs about politics on TV. Although the quality and
quantity of information derived from the mass media may fall short of the
standards to which democratic theory aspires, many Canadians do avail
themselves of at least some of what the media makes available.

17 The analysis might be confounded by a tendency for reluctant, low-interest respondents to
   avoid being interviewed as long as possible. This possibility seems reasonable, but we may
   discount it because the percentage answering "very closely" to the general political interest question among late interviewees was nearly as great (18 percent) as that among the
   early interviewees (20 percent).

Political efficacy

In the context of a democratic culture a sense of political efficacy, a citizen's belief that he or she can influence the political process, should be especially relevant for political support. Two types of efficacy may be distinguished. *Internal* efficacy refers to the belief that one has the personal resources needed to be an effective political actor. *External* efficacy, in contrast, refers to perceptions that one's attempts to exercise influence will prove successful (Lane, 1959; Converse, 1972). Although the two types of efficacy are conceptually distinct, research based on surveys conducted in several Western countries indicates that they are strongly interrelated. Persons who believe that they have the resources needed for effective action also are disposed to feel that the political system is responsive, and those who regard the system as responsive are likely to believe they have the resources required to affect the political process. The relationship is imperfect, however, and the two forms of efficacy may have different sources and varying effects on behavior and support.

Large numbers of Canadians lack internally efficacious feelings.[18] In the 1965–88 national surveys about one-half of the respondents agreed that "people like me have no say" (Figure 3.7, Panel A). Well over half also consistently agreed that politics and government were "too complicated to understand." There is little variation over time in the distribution of internally efficacious feelings, particularly in the case of the latter measure. Nor is there consistent evidence to suggest that elections affect internal efficacy. Although the percentage of efficacious responses to the "people like me – no say" item was lowest in a nonelection year (1983), in other nonelection years (1977, 1981) the percentages of efficacious responses to this item were not especially low. This also is true of the nonelection year percentages for the "politics complicated". The relative stability of the internal efficacy responses and their general insensitivity to election-year contexts is consonant with the conception of internal efficacy as a self-perception. As such, it presumably is anchored by more general feelings of ego strength and self-esteem.

Responses to the external efficacy statements resemble those for internal efficacy in some respects, but not in others. They are similar in that many people give inefficacious answers. They differ in that there is evidence of a modest downward trend over the past two decades (Figure 3.7, Panel B).

18 The federal political efficacy questions are: (a) "Generally, those elected to parliament in Ottawa soon lose touch with the people"; (b) "I don't think that the federal government cares much what people like me think"; (c) "Sometimes, politics and government in Ottawa seem so complicated that a person like me can't really understand what's going on"; (d) "People like me don't have any say about what the federal government does." Items (a) and (b) are used to measure external efficacy, and items (c) and (d), internal efficacy. The provincial efficacy sequence is identical except for references to the provincial government.

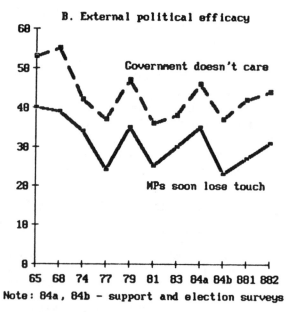

Figure 3.7. *Internal and external political efficacy, federal politics, 1965–88 (percentages disagreeing with statements)*

There are, however, two deviations, 1979 and 1984 – years in which the Conservatives won national elections. Because the PCs spent most of the post-World War II era in the political wilderness, these two increases in external efficacy may reflect the expectations of Conservative partisans that their voices finally would be heard. If so, such election outcome effects are short-lived. The 1984 national election survey which, as noted, contained a large number of interviews conducted several months after the election, reveals much lower levels of external efficacy than do the 1984 political support data derived from interviews completed shortly after the contest. More generally, the finding that external efficacy is more volatile than internal efficacy is consistent with the conception of the former as perceived system responsiveness which can change as a result of significant events and conditions such as the outcome of an election.

To learn more about how responsive Canadians believe public officials are to their needs and concerns, the 1979, 1983, and 1988 surveys contained additional questions about the perceived responsiveness of federal Members of Parliament.[19] Answers indicate that many people do not believe MPs perform their representational roles adequately. In 1988, for example, only about one person in six stated that MPs were "very likely" to consider their opinions when making decisions on important issues, or would try to help if approached about an important personal problem, and from two-fifths to one-half felt that MPs were "not very likely" to do either. Somewhat more (but still only one in four) believed that MPs were likely to try to help get something for their riding if asked to do so, or that MPs would make themselves available in Ottawa, or in their local offices to speak with constituents. These responses again indicate the weakness of external political efficacy.

To recapitulate, it is clear that many Canadians lack internally and externally efficacious feelings. But are Canadians different in this regard from citizens in other democracies? The Barnes, Kaase et al. Eight Nations Study data reveal that they are not. In fact, a comparison with the eight countries shows that in the mid-1970s Canadians had the highest percentages stating politics was "too complicated" and "MPs lose touch," but ranked fourth and sixth, respectively, in the percentages giving the "government doesn't care" and "people like me have no say" answers. Thus, widespread feelings of political *inefficacy* appear to characterize the publics of most democracies and Canadians are not outliers on one of the attitudinal building blocks of a democratic polity.

19 The question sequence is "Do you think it is very likely, somewhat likely, or not very likely, that a Member of Parliament would do each of the following: (a) Take into consideration the opinions of people like yourself when making up their mind on an important issue, if they know your feelings on it; (b) Try hard to do or get something for their riding if people like yourself asked them for it; (c) Try hard to do something about a specific personal or family problem that a person like yourself approached them with; (d) Make themselves available in their constituency office and in Ottawa to people like yourself."

In Canada's federal system citizens can try to exert influence at multiple levels of government. We previously observed that large numbers of people are oriented primarily toward provincial rather than federal politics, and they are dissatisfied with the performance of the national government. This suggests that many Canadians may feel more competent to affect provincial politics and believe that provincial officials are more responsive to their needs and interests. During the past two decades the argument for provincial responsiveness has been a staple element of the rhetoric of provincial premiers who have maintained that their governments are the "real" representatives of residents of their provinces and that the federal government in Ottawa is both distanced from and unresponsive to the concerns of ordinary Canadians (e.g., Cairns, 1983).

Although most surveys do not contain provincial-level efficacy measures they were included in two studies conducted in 1983 and 1984. These studies show that efficacious responses are somewhat more frequent at the provincial than the federal level, but that the lack of efficacy is the rule at both levels. In 1984, for example, 78 percent agreed that federal MPs "soon lose touch with the people" and 73 percent felt this way about provincial MLAs (Table 3.7). Similarly small differences obtain for the "government doesn't care," "politics too complicated" and "no say" items and, in every case, inefficacious responses were the norm at both levels of government.

We have presented evidence that many Canadians form identifications with federal and provincial political parties which differ in direction or intensity. Are other important attitudes such as political efficacy structured by level of government? Confirmatory factor analysis can help answer this question. Empirically, a CFA of a four-factor federal–internal, federal–external, provincial–internal, provincial–external efficacy model has an extremely good fit with the 1984 data ($\chi^2_{12} = 8.12$, p = .776), whereas several alternative models, including a two-factor one that does not make the federal–provincial distinction, prove totally unsatisfactory. This is not to say that feelings of efficacy at the two levels of government are uncorrelated. On the contrary, federal external efficacy has a correlation of .63 with provincial external efficacy, whereas the correlation between federal internal efficacy and its provincial counterpart is .83 (Table 3.7).

Although both correlations are strong, the greater magnitude of that for federal and provincial internal efficacy accords well with its definition as a self-perception. The somewhat weaker correlation for external efficacy at the two levels of government is consistent with the definition of this form of efficacy as involving perceptions of the responsiveness of political actors, processes and institutions, perceptions that can vary markedly in response to differences between federal and provincial politics in the several provinces. Consonant with this hypothesis, regional analyses of the structure of efficacious feelings at the two levels of government show that the strength of the correlation between the two external efficacy factors varies

Table 3.7. *Federal and provincial efficacy, 1984 (in percent)*

Responses to federal and provincial political efficacy statements

Federal level	Agree Strongly	Agree Somewhat	Disagree Somewhat	Disagree Strongly	N
MPs soon lose touch with people	29a	49	17	5	3107
Government doesn't care	28	36	27	10	3153
Politics too complicated	30	35	21	14	3236
Respondent has no say	33	30	21	15	3240

Provincial level

	Agree Strongly	Agree Somewhat	Disagree Somewhat	Disagree Strongly	N
MLAs soon lose touch with people	26a	47	21	6	3081
Government doesn't care	25	35	31	9	3153
Politics too complicated	26	38	20	15	3213
Respondent has no say	27	31	26	16	3179

Correlations between federal and provincial political efficacy factors*

	Federal Internal	Federal External	Provincial Internal	Provincial External
Federal internal	1.00			
Federal external	.71	1.00		
Provincial internal	.83	.62	1.00	
Provincial external	.56	.63	.83	1.00

Note: * - ϕ correlations from confirmatory factor analysis using polychoric inter-item correlations and weighted least squares estimation; a - horizontal percentages

Source: 1984 national election survey

extremely strongly and inversely ($r = -.97$) with the degree of discontinuity between the federal and provincial party systems in different regions (Acock et al., 1989). Party system dissimilarity also is related to regional differences in the strength of the federal–provincial internal efficacy correlations but, as anticipated, the correlation is somewhat weaker ($r = -.82$). The strength of these relationships clearly indicates that the structure of public political attitudes is related to the nature of the party systems at the two levels of government. More generally, this finding helps us to comprehend forces affecting the "nature of belief systems" in a democratic polity. Governmental structures, in this case federalism, *matter.* They provide the context in which political beliefs and attitudes form and develop.

Political trust

Trust in political authorities is the belief that public officials have the capacity and inclination to perform their tasks effectively and in accord with prevailing ethical standards. Democracies, like other real-world systems of governance, rely upon a division of labor between rulers and ruled. Trust in the former by the latter is an important condition for continuing public support for political authorities and the systems they lead. In democratic theory the role of trust is complex, however, because citizens are exhorted not to exhibit "blind faith" in the character and competence of public officeholders, or to always follow orders, regardless of their content (Sniderman, 1981). Instead, they are enjoined to maintain a degree of skepticism about the motives and promises of public officials as well as to monitor their behavior in office. Although some skepticism concerning the motives and behavior of public officials may well be an important requisite for the successful functioning of a democratic polity, at the aggregate level it is difficult to specify exactly how much trust is optimal, or how it should be distributed. At the *individual level*, however, the situation is clearer. Trust in political authorities should be related to support for them, and either directly or indirectly, to support for the regime and community (Citrin, 1974; Miller, 1974a, 1974b). A paucity of trust should be related to diminished support at all levels.

In several national surveys four "agree–disagree" statements were employed to measure trust in federal political authorities, with the 1983 and 1984 surveys also including equivalent questions about provincial authorities.[20] The data show that Canadians are ambivalent about the probity and wisdom of public officials. About three persons in five stated that "people in the federal government" were smart and trustworthy, and from one-half to three-fifths felt they were honest (Table 3.8). In sharp contrast, overwhelming majorities were convinced that federal officials "waste a lot" of the public's tax dollars. Also, similar to feelings of federal and provincial political efficacy, Canadians were not markedly more trusting of provincial officials. Compared to their federal counterparts, provincial authorities were seen as slightly more likely to be honest and thrifty with the public purse, but they were not regarded as either smarter or more trustworthy than their federal counterparts.

Correlates of citizen political involvement

If we are to understand the impact of public beliefs and attitudes on political support, we need to know how these beliefs and attitudes are distributed in the population. In the Canadian context one might anticipate that feelings of inefficacy and mistrust are concentrated in Quebec and the West – regions where dissatisfaction with the operation of the federal system has been particularly pronounced. It also is possible, although less probable, given that many Canadians lack a sense of class consciousness, that political orientations differ according to social class. It could be argued that the orientations of working-class persons would be considerably more negative

20 The federal political trust questions are: (a) "Many people in the federal government are dishonest"; (b) "People in the federal government waste a lot of the money we pay in taxes"; (c) "Most of the time we can trust people in the federal government to do what is right"; (d) "Most of the people running the government in Ottawa are smart people who usually know what they are doing." The provincial political trust sequence is identical except for references to the provincial government.

Table 3.8. *Trust in federal and provincial political authorities, 1984 (in percent)*

	Agree strongly	Agree somewhat	Disagree somewhat	Disagree strongly	N
Federal level					
Many people in federal government are dishonest	14a	31	31	25	2670
People in federal government waste tax money	49	37	10	4	3110
Can trust people in federal government	12	51	26	11	3042
People in federal government are smart	17	51	23	9	3076
Provincial level					
Many people in provincial government are dishonest	13a	29	34	24	2603
People in provincial government waste tax money	40	43	13	4	3008
Can trust people in provincial government	12	54	21	13	2974
People in provincial government are smart	16	55	21	9	2974

Note: a - horizontal percentages

Source: 1984 National Election Survey

than those of middle- and upper-class individuals, a condition that would accord with the Marxist arguments concerning class differences in political representation and the manner in which a liberal democratic political system affects the distribution of goods and services in capitalist societies. It also is possible that differences in key political attitudes are related to age. Age differences might be products of socialization processes that operate across the life-cycle or, as noted above, they might reflect generational discontinuities in socialization in affluent industrial societies analogous to those hypothesized in research on the emergence of postmaterialist values in such countries.

To investigate relationships between political orientations and sociodemographic characteristics we employed our 1983 survey data and regressed measures of general political and election interest, internal and external political efficacy, perceptions of MPs responsiveness, and trust in federal political authorities[21] on region/ethnicity, gender, age, income, and education. With few exceptions, regional–ethnicity effects were inconsequential. The most consistently significant predictors were annual family income and, especially, level of formal education. Better-educated persons and those in higher income brackets manifested greater general political and specific election interest, stronger internal and external efficacy, more faith in the responsiveness of MPs, and greater trust in political authorities. However, all of these relationships were quite weak, and the overall variance explained by the several sociodemographic variables ranged from 3 percent (trust) to 15 percent (interest). Nor are the 1983 results atypical. Comparable analyses using data gathered in other surveys yielded very similar results. Once more, it is evident that important political orientations in the population are only very loosely grounded in societal cleavages such as region, ethnicity and social class that often are given "pride of place" in discussions of political support in Canada.

Self, society, polity

The failure of sociodemographic variables to explain key political orientations suggests that other factors need to be investigated. Previous studies (e.g., Lane, 1959; Almond and Verba, 1963; see also Milbrath and Goel,

---

21 General political interest is scored: follow politics "very closely" = 2, "fairly closely" = 1, "not much at all" = 0; election interest is scored: "very interested" = 3, "fairly interested" = 2, "slightly interested" = 1, "not at all interested" = 0. The federal internal political efficacy index is the number of "disagree" responses to items (c) and (d) in note 18; the federal external political efficacy index is the number of "disagree" responses to items (a) and (b) in note 18. The trust in federal political authorities index is the sum of the number of "disagree" responses to items (a) and (b) in note 20 above plus the sum of the number of "agree" responses to items (c) and (d). The MPs responsiveness index is the sum of responses to items (a), (b), (c) and (d) in note 19 above. They are scored "very likely" = + 2, "somewhat likely" = + 1, "not very likely" = 0.

1977) have argued that orientations such as political efficacy and trust are linked to psychological characteristics such as self-esteem, ego strength, and social trust. If democratic theorists (e.g., Pateman, 1970; Macpherson, 1977) are correct, there is a reciprocal causal flow between these characteristics and political efficacy and trust. Feelings of general personal competence and social trust affect political efficacy and trust, but the latter attitudes also influence the former.

To investigate these relationships we employed the 1988 political support study which contains batteries of social trust and personal competence measures[22] as well as the standard political efficacy and trust variables. We began by hypothesizing a five-factor measurement model – internal and external political efficacy, political trust, social trust, and personal competence. The fit of this model was tested by performing a confirmatory factor analysis on a random half-sample of the 1988 data. An initial CFA indicated that the fit was not entirely satisfactory. Inspection of LISREL modification indices indicated, however, that the fit might be improved substantially by correlating selected error terms for the indicators. The revised model had an excellent fit ($\chi^2_{74} = 77.95$, p = .35), and LISREL diagnostics were satisfactory. As an additional test of the revised model, we replicated the analysis using the second half-sample. The fit remained excellent and, again, all diagnostics were acceptable.

The satisfactory fit of the five-factor model indicates that political efficacy and trust are not coterminous with more general feelings of social trust and personal competence. However, the correlations between the political and social factors are substantial. As expected, feelings of general personal competence are related to political efficacy, with the relationship with internal efficacy ($\phi = .53$) being considerably stronger than with external efficacy ($\phi = .38$). Similarly, social trust was associated with trust in political authorities ($\phi = .49$), and its relationship with external efficacy ($\phi = .38$) was somewhat stronger than that with internal efficacy ($\phi = .28$). The relative magnitude of these latter two correlations is exactly what one would expect given that external efficacy focuses on the perceived behavior of others, whereas internal efficacy is concerned with self-perceptions. Similarly, political trust was much more strongly associated with external than internal efficacy, the ϕ's being .71 and .38, respectively. These several statistically significant relationships accord well with conceptual definitions of political efficacy and trust and their nonpolitical analogues. Moreover, the strength of the relationships is consonant with the argument that important political attitudes such as efficacy and trust are related to more general personality characteristics.

---

22 The social trust and personal competence questions are cited in Chapter 2, notes 9 and 10, respectively. For purposes of the confirmatory factor analysis, each response indicating social trust or personal competence is scored +1; other responses are scored 0.

SUMMARY

We have investigated political cultural orientations central to theories of support processes in representative democracies. We first delineated public beliefs about the meaning of democracy. Those who held what might be termed an expansive view of democracy agreed that the right to speak freely must be extended to even democracy's enemies and that, as a process, democracy entails more than voting in periodic elections. The strongest consensus among those taking a more traditional, restrictive view of democracy was that democracies make provision for equality of economic opportunity but do not try to ensure equal economic outcomes. Nor do they try to ensure equal political influence. Views about democracy were structured in terms of three underlying factors, but these factors were complex and the correlations among them were modest at best. Canadians thus do not have a tightly constrained set of beliefs that merits the label an "ideology of democracy." However, beliefs about the meaning of democracy in practice were clear-cut – Canada and the United States come much closer to the democratic ideal than does the Soviet Union. For Canadians, democracy means representative democracy and those with more traditional views of what democracy entails also are more likely to feel that Canada closely approximates a democratic ideal.

An identification with a political party is one of the ties that bind people to a democratic political system and most Canadians have party identifications at both levels of government. Until 1980 the aggregate distribution of identifications with federal parties was quite stable. Since that time, however, percentages identifying with the two major parties, the Liberals and the Conservatives, have fluctuated sharply, and the overall strength of attachments to the national parties has weakened somewhat. Although the 1980s witnessed a modest "dealignment of degree," it is important to emphasize that partisan attachments long have exhibited substantial flexibility. Panel surveys conducted since the mid-1970s consistently show considerable *individual-level* instability in party identification at both the national and provincial levels. This pattern continued in the 1980s, but the incidence of directional instability has not increased. Noteworthy also is the inconsistency of party identifications across levels of the federal system. A sizable minority of Canadians have different party identifications at the two levels of government, and again this is a long-standing pattern. The ways in which these patterns affect support for key political objects, especially in Quebec and the West, are discussed in Chapter 5.

Canadian politics is often described as the politics of federalism, and conflict between federal and provincial governments has dominated the political agenda during much of the past two decades. During that time so-called executive federalism has given the system an open-ended quality – that anything and everything are subject to change pending the outcome of the most recent, highly publicized First Minsters Conference. At these conferences the principal actors, the prime minister and the premiers of the ten provinces, habitually represent themselves as "their" governments. Formal opening statements are followed by several days of frequently acrimonious exchanges over the issues under consideration. Invariably, however, and regardless of which party controls either the national or provincial governments, the prime minister and the several provincial premiers are cast in adversary roles. For example, the prime minister asserts that a subsidy to the provinces cannot be increased, or he asks that the provinces pay a larger proportion of the costs of some shared program. The premiers take the opposite position in a stylized ritual that has come to symbolize the largely nonpartisan, government-to-government character of such conferences.

It could be argued that other democracies that are federal systems also are subject to periodic intergovernmental conflicts. In Canada, however, the incidence of conflict is far greater. Indeed, it would be no exaggeration to assert that rather than being episodic, such conflicts have become regularized, even institutionalized. The "upside" of this development is that it serves electoral interests of the prime minister and provincial premiers, as well as the organizational needs of their respective bureaucracies.[23] The "downside" is that it injects a kind of extra-partisan tension into the system that is conducive to transforming genuinely partisan issues into constitutional ones, and constitutional issues into constitutional crises.

Citizen attitudes reflect this intergovernmental conflict. We find that whereas some Canadians are more strongly oriented toward national politics, many others have strong provincial orientations. Moreover, surveys conducted during the 1980s show that unhappiness with the federal system did not end with the implementation of a new constitution in 1982. Rather, in the late 1980s discontent with the costs and benefits of federalism remained widespread in every region of the country.

In Canada, as in other contemporary democracies, perhaps the most widely shared perspective on government is that it should do a great deal. However, although Canadians expect a great deal from government, many do not think it is very effective in delivering services. In the late 1970s, the federal government's handling of the economy came in for especially harsh criticism. These evaluations moderated in the mid-1980s and after, but many people continued to give government low marks for economic

23 Interspersed with the acrimony and public posturing on the part of the prime minister and his provincial counterparts are a series of informal, behind-the-scenes interactions. The conference then adjourns, and the real and detailed business of addressing current issues is left to appropriate sectors of the federal and provincial bureaucracies. The positive effect these interactions could have on support for both political authorities and the federal system is vitiated because the public is not privy to this informal dimension of executive federalism.

management. Nor is the economy the only cause for complaint. Many
Canadians judge that government is ineffective in a variety of other areas
as well. They also express dissatisfaction with the equity–fairness of their
political system. Indeed, the belief that the system is not operating equitably and fairly has become more widespread in recent years.

A hallmark of a democratic polity is the provision of institutionalized
opportunities for citizens to select their political decision-makers through
elections. Most Canadians have only modest levels of interest in politics,
but their interest is piqued by periodic national elections. However, this
heightened interest erodes in the following months. Feelings of external
political efficacy also appear to rise during election periods, particularly if a
former opposition party is successful in capturing the reins of power. In
contrast, internally efficacious feelings remain relatively undisturbed.
More generally, large numbers of Canadians do not believe that they are
effective political actors. Nor is this a recent phenomenon; rather it is evident throughout the past quarter century. Also, low political efficacy is not
confined to reactions to the national political system. Although Canadians
develop separate feelings of internal and external efficacy at the federal
and provincial levels of government, inefficacious feelings are common at
both levels among all age, gender, income and region–ethnicity categories.
However, comparisons with a number of European democracies reveals
that Canadians are not "outliers" in these regards. Relatively low levels of
such feelings characterize people in European countries with different
historical experience with democratic government.

Canadians also exhibit only modest amounts of trust in political authorities. One could argue that this condition is consonant with the notion that
the proper functioning of a democratic polity requires a healthy skepticism
on the part of the citizenry. However, it also can be argued that distrust in
authorities is an important source of diminished levels of support for a
political system. Like efficacy, negative feelings about public officials are
not confined to the national political arena but extend to provincial officials
as well.

Negative attitudes about political authorities and the operation of key
political institutions and processes are related to psychological orientations
such as social trust and personal competence. But they are not tightly tied
to the regional and ethnolinguistic cleavages that have defined the way in
which questions of political support historically have been addressed in
Canada. Nor are they closely associated with factors such as age, gender,
or social class that typically are held to affect support in advanced industrial countries. The implications of the content and patterning of Canadian
political culture for understanding support processes will be addressed in
the following chapters.

4

Political support and its correlates

National unity is an expression that evokes a variety of issues, ideas, feelings: the absence of conflict; loyalty to the national government; harmony or positive feelings among people in different parts of the country; pride and other good feelings about being Canadians; cooperation rather than tension between levels of government; giving precedence to one's Canadian identity over one's regional identity; the feeling of getting a good or bad deal from being part of the country, and so on.

Breton, Reitz, and Valentine, *Cultural Boundaries and the Cohesion of Canada*, p. 1

The same can be said of the concept of political support. Feelings of loyalty toward and an identification with a national political regime and the political community of which it is a part, the belief that the regime is both effective and fair in its dealings with citizens, the latter's sensitivity toward, and even affection for, people and regions of the country other than their own – all of these should be correlates of political support as well as national unity. Indeed, because the two concepts are closely intertwined, in earlier chapters we have examined some of the images Canadians have of themselves, of their society and polity and their relationship to both. Those data provide the context in which we analyze the distribution, structure and correlates of the correlates of support for Canada's national political community, regime, and authorities.

POLITICAL SUPPORT: 1974–1988

In Chapter 1 we argued that in representative democracies such as Canada public support for key political objects is likely to be hierarchically ordered and to vary in stability over time. Support for the national political community should be the highest and most stable. Support for the national regime should be lower and somewhat more mutable, and that for political authorities should be even lower and more variable. This ordering of the levels and stability of support should obtain because democratic political cultures emphasize the distinction between political authorities, on the one hand, and the structure and processes of government (the regime) and the political community, on the other. Elected public officials both receive their "authority" from the public and are held accountable to them in periodic, constitutionally sanctioned elections. Their tenure of office is, by definition, a limited one, being governed by public judgments about what they have and have not done in the past, and what they are likely to do in the future. The political community, in contrast, is a collective expression of the country's past achievements, the ties that bind its current members, as well as the latter's hopes for and expectations about the future. The regime, occupies an intermediate position between the community and authorities in that it constitutes the structural framework for political action. Although normally viewed as an enduring feature of the polity, this framework is not immutable. Specific institutions and processes may be changed periodically or even replaced if the maintenance or enhancement of a more democratic, effective and equitable political order is thought to require it.

We also have observed that democracies will vary in the extent to which their publics are able to distinguish clearly between the regime and the authorities. Making this distinction should be more difficult in parliamentary than in presidential systems, especially if, in the former, a particular party or coalition of parties has been in office for an extended period of time. This has been the case in Canada. Other than for a nine-month period in 1979 and an earlier six-year hiatus (1957–63) – a single party, the Liberal Party, formed the incumbent government from 1935 until its spectacular defeat in the September 1984 federal election.

Measuring support

Support for the political community, regime and authorities is measured using 100-point thermometer scales. Survey respondents either were presented with a picture of a thermometer scaled from 1–100, with 50 explicitly designated as the *neutral* point or, in telephone interviews, asked to think of such a thermometer. They were told that the warmer they felt about an object or person named, the higher the score that should be given the object or person, and the cooler their feeling, the lower the score. Support for the national political community was measured by asking interviewees, "How do you feel in general about Canada?" Regime support was measured by asking the feelings question about the "government of Canada" and the national parliament, civil service, and judiciary. Support for political authorities was operationalized in terms of feelings about the national Liberal, Progressive Conservative, and New Democratic parties and their leaders.

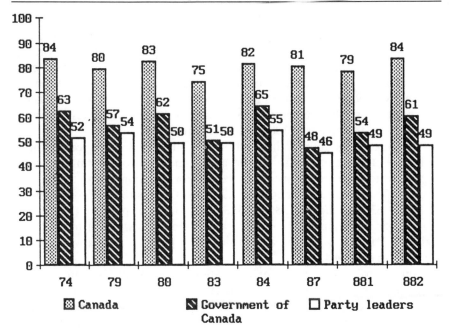

Figure 4.1. *Mean support: Canada, government of Canada and national party leaders, 1974–88*

Community, regime, and authorities support

As anticipated, support for the national political community, the government of Canada and authorities was hierarchically ordered. In each of the several surveys it was substantially higher for the community than for either the government or the authorities (Figure 4.1). Support for the regime also was higher than for the authorities, although the regime–authorities differences were minuscule in comparison to those between the community and the regime. The compression of the levels of regime and authorities support was anticipated given Canada's Westminster-model parliamentary system and long periods of one-party dominance at the federal and provincial levels of government.

People's relatively strong, positive feelings about the community, in comparison to those about the regime and authorities, also were evident in the distributions of the thermometer scores. The percentage ascribing a score of 75 or more to the political community ranged from a high of 76 percent in 1974 to a low of 52 percent in 1983. In contrast, the range of highly positive scores for the regime (as reflected in the government of Canada scores) were 31 percent in 1974 and 12 percent in 1983. Support scores of 75 or more for the authorities (as measured by average scores for the leaders of the three national parties) were rare, ranging from 6 percent in 1979 to 1 percent in 1987. In sharp contrast, the percentage according the community negative scores (less than 50) exceeded 5 percent only once, in 1983. The percentage of negative scores given the regime ranged from a low of 9 percent in 1984 to a high of 36 percent in 1983, whereas for the authorities, the percentages assigning them scores of less than 50 ranged from 28 percent in 1984 to 51 percent in 1987.

The differences in the distributions of support for the community, regime, and authorities also can be appreciated by considering the ratio of positive to negative thermometer scores. For the community, the ratio of positive (51 or greater) to negative (49 or less) scores ranged from a low of 10:1 in 1983 to a high of 38.1 in 1984. The ratio of positive to negative support for the regime, in contrast, ranged from a low of 1:1 in 1987 to a high of 8:1 in 1984. For the authorities the equivalent ratios were .7:1 in 1987 and 2:1 in 1984.

Overall levels of support for the national community and the federal government were lowest in 1983 and 1987, respectively (Figure 4.1), the two nonelection years for which we have data. As we will demonstrate in greater detail in Chapter 6 this finding is consistent with, and evidence for, the idea that by providing regular, institutionalized opportunities for citizens in democratic countries to participate in the political process, elections encourage citizens to demonstrate their loyalty to and support for their political systems. Even if elections do not function in strict accordance with the precepts of democratic theory, by permitting citizens to authorize representatives to act on the public's behalf and to hold those representatives accountable for their behavior in office, elections periodically demonstrate that the political order is one in which the people's voices are heard. By so doing, elections help, if only temporarily, to bolster political support.

Figure 4.1 indicates that regime support, measured in terms of government of Canada thermometer scores, not only is more variable than support for the national political community, but also that it seems less stable than that ascribed national party leaders. However, a more detailed analysis reveals that support varied substantially among the leaders at any particular time, as well as for the same leader over time. For example, in 1968, 1974, 1979, and 1980 there was more support for the Liberal leader, Pierre Trudeau, than for Tommy Douglas, David Lewis, and Ed Broadbent, the NDP leaders, or Robert Stanfield and his successor, Joe Clark, the Progressive Conservative leaders. But in 1983 support for Trudeau and Broadbent dropped, whereas that for Brian Mulroney (1983–present), the new Conservative leader, rose sharply. Mulroney's support continued to increase the next year, and Broadbent's also rose, but support for John Turner, Trudeau's successor as Liberal leader and short-lived prime minister, did not. By 1988 support for all three leaders had decreased, with the decline in affection for Mr. Mulroney being especially pronounced.

More generally, support for the Conservative and New Democratic leaders both surged and declined over a twenty-year period, as did support for the Conservative Party. In contrast, support for the Liberals and their long-time leader, Pierre Trudeau, declined almost monotonically, and support for the NDP was consistently negative. Trudeau's national scores mask regional variations that increased substantially over time. In Western Canada he came to be regarded as a virtual "prince of darkness" during the late 1970s and early 1980s, largely because his government's economic policies were seen to work strongly to the disadvantage of the Western provinces, his unyielding defense of the powers of the central government, and his penchant for making controversial and, at times, outrageous statements.

Panel data reinforce the cross-sectional findings that support for the national political community is both higher and more stable than that for the regime or authorities. In Table 4.1 we report the extent of positive–negative turnover in community, regime, and authorities support using responses made by the same persons at different points in time. In successive surveys approximately eight Canadians in ten gave consistently positive support to the political community whereas only about one-third to two-fifths did so for the national government and authorities. Moreover, support for the latter two objects was more unstable; in every panel large percentages of respondents moved from positive to negative government or authorities support and vice versa. The greater stability of community support also is reflected in the gamma coefficients that summarize the strength of the relationships between levels of support measured in adjacent waves of a panel. In every case these coefficients are considerably larger for the community than for the regime or authorities. And, in keeping with the hypothesis that feelings about the national regime are influenced by affect for an incumbent government, the gamma for regime support was strongest for the 1984–88 and, especially, the 1980–83 panels, the two instances during which time the same party (the Liberals – 1980–83; the PCs – 1984–88) held the reins of power in Ottawa.

Partisanship. In a democratic political system public support for parties and their leaders varies over time in response to evaluations of their performance in office and/or their policy proposals and stands on important issues. Because competition among the parties is open and often intense, partisans of different parties should accord greater support to their party leaders and their parties than to other parties and leaders. For similar reasons, identifiers with the party that forms the government at any particular time should ascribe more support to the regime, especially insofar as it is reflected in support for the government of Canada, than should

Table 4.1 *The dynamics of support for national political community and regime, 1974–88 national panels*

	Community	Regime	Authorities
1974-79 Panel			
Positive and remained positivea	82.3	35.1	39.3
Negative and remained negativeb	.4	4.2	1.0
Neutral and remained neutralc	1.9	6.6	18.9
Changed from positive to negative or neutral, or vice versa	15.4	54.1	40.8
Gamma =	.71	.13	.52
1979-80 Panel			
Positive and remained positive	81.5	33.2	37.6
Negative and remained negative	.8	4.4	21.0
Neutral and remained neutral	2.1	6.2	1.9
Changed from positive to negative or neutral, or vice versa	15.6	56.2	39.5
Gamma =	.75	.06	.59
1980-83 Panel			
Positive and remained positive	79.1	35.0	34.2
Negative and remained negative	1.1	15.4	25.4
Neutral and remained neutral	2.8	6.5	.8
Changed from positive to negative or neutral, or vice versa	17.0	43.1	39.6
Gamma =	.76	.4	.58
1983-84 Panel			
Positive and remained positive	77.0	35.2	36.1
Negative and remained negative	.8	6.1	14.7
Neutral and remained neutral	1.6	4.5	11.7
Changed from positive to negative or neutral, or vice versa	20.6	54.2	37.5
Gamma =	.60	.31	.30
1984-88 Panel			
Positive and remained positive	84.0	42.1	37.2
Negative and remained negative	.1	5.0	15.4
Neutral and remained neutral	1.6	4.3	.6
Changed from positive to negative or neutral, or vice versa	14.3	48.6	46.8
Gamma =	.73	.38	.34

Note: a positive support = 51-99
       b negative support = 1-49
       c neutral support = 50

either identifiers with opposition parties or nonidentifiers. In 1974, 1980, and 1983 the Liberal Party governed, as it had for most of this century. Accordingly, if our hypotheses are valid, the highest support for the regime in these years should come from federal Liberal identifiers, whereas in 1979, 1984, and 1988 it should come from federal Conservatives.

However, partisanship in a democracy cannot be a "zero-sum" game, because periodic peaceful transfers of power from an outgoing administration to its successor would be impossible if opposing parties and their leaders were not trusted with the reins of office. To the extent this feeling of trust in the opposition is widely shared, party identifiers should give their own party and a government formed by it strong support and accord other parties and governmental leaders moderately negative, but not extremely low, support. Lastly, unlike the regime and its authorities, support for Canada should be, in a sense, above partisan politics, and thus should not be subject to the kind of sharp fluctuations that characterize regime and authorities support.

In fact, these hypotheses are well-grounded. First, identifiers with each of the three national parties[1] generally gave their own leaders and parties scores in the sixties and seventies while giving scores in the forties to the opposition. As noted above, although support for the Conservative and New Democratic leaders and the Conservative Party rose and fell over time, that for the Liberals generally declined. Even among Liberal identifiers there was a monotonic decline in support for the national party and its longtime leader, Mr. Trudeau. After Trudeau resigned in 1984 support for the party and its new leader, John Turner, remained well below what it had been a decade earlier. Indeed, in 1984 Liberal identifiers were almost as positive about the PC and NDP leaders, Mulroney and Broadbent, respectively, as they were about their own party's leader. By 1987 their support for Mulroney had declined markedly but their enthusiasm for Broadbent continued to approximate that for the still unpopular Turner.

Second, the impact of partisanship on regime support, as measured by thermometer scores for the government of Canada, is apparent in Figure 4.2. On average federal Liberal identifiers were more supportive of the government of Canada in 1974 and 1980 – when the Liberal Party was in office – than in 1979, 1987, and 1988, when the Conservative Party was at the helm. Similarly, when the Conservatives were elected in 1979, the government of Canada support scores of Conservative identifiers were ten points higher than they had been in 1974. They were fully thirty points higher in 1984, shortly after Mr. Mulroney became prime minister of another Conservative government than they had been a year earlier when the Trudeau-led Liberals were approaching the end of their lengthy tenure. Similarly, in 1987 and 1988 the support scores for the government of Canada among PC identifiers were well above what they had been five years earlier, when the Liberals were in office.

The data for NDP identifiers and nonidentifiers also were consistent with the idea that partisanship influences regime support. In neither case, however, did these scores show the regular fluctuations characteristic of Liberal and Conservative identifiers, the two groups of partisans whose parties have been both the government-of-the-day and the official opposition (Figure 4.2). Finally, national community support was "above party" in that it was essentially uncorrelated with differences in partisan identification. As Figure 4.2 shows, support for Canada was strongly and consistently positive among all groups of partisans as well as among persons without a federal party identification.

1 The questions measuring party identification are described in Chapter 3, note 4.

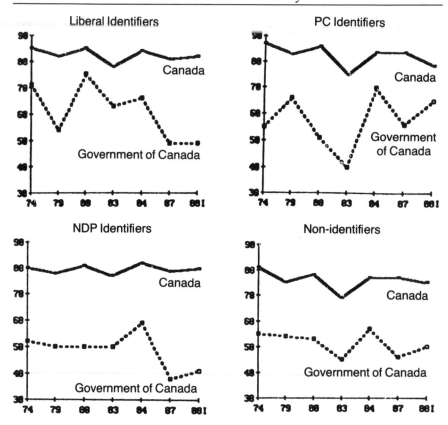

Figure 4.2. *Mean support for Canada and government of Canada by federal party identification, 1974–88*

National political institutions. The observation that party identification correlates with support for the government of Canada thermometer scores is not an argument that partisanship accounts for all or even the majority of the variance in regime support. For example, in 1974 measures of the direction and intensity of partisanship explained only 17 percent of such variance; fourteen years later, in 1988, the percentage explained was 20 percent. However, because partisanship does affect how respondents answer the government of Canada question, and since the national regime encompasses a variety of institutions about which the public may have quite different feelings, we ascertained those feelings directly. We used the feeling thermometer to measure support for parliament, the most visible, and, arguably, the most important institutional component of a democratic regime, as well as two other major national institutions: the civil service and the judiciary.

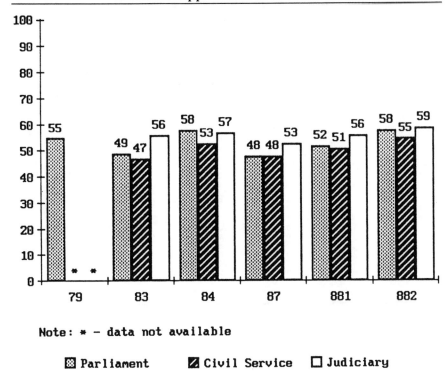

Note: * — data not available

⊠ Parliament   ▨ Civil Service   ☐ Judiciary

Figure 4.3. *Mean support for national parliament, civil service, and judiciary, 1979–88*

Figure 4.3 shows that Canadians offered somewhat more support for the judiciary than for either parliament or the civil service in four of the five instances (i.e., in 1983, 1987, and the 1988 preelection and postelection surveys) where all three measures were employed. These and the 1984 differences were small, however, and the dominant picture is similar to that for the government of Canada – one of lukewarm support. However, support scores for parliament, the civil service, and judiciary generally were lowest in two nonelection years. This constitutes additional evidence that elections in democracies encourage citizens to reaffirm their support for key political institutions and processes. Because elections do have this effect, they may inflate support over what may well be "normal" levels. It seems reasonable, therefore, to base our more detailed analyses of political support on data gathered in both an election and a nonelection year. Given the greater range of information available in the 1983 and 1988 surveys, we used these data to investigate the correlates of community, regime, and authorities support.

Table 4.2. *Confirmatory factor analyses of the structure of political support, 1983, 1988*

Thermometer Ratings	Factor Matrix (λ)			
	Community	Parliament- Civil Service	Judiciary	Incumbent Authorities
1983				
Canada	1.00	.00	.00	.00
Parliament	.00	.86a	.00	.00
Civil Service	.00	.76a	.00	.00
Judiciary	.00	.00	1.00	.00
Liberal leader	.00	.00	.00	.88a
Liberal party	.00	.00	.00	.94a

$$\chi^2_7 = .74, \ p = .998, \ \text{AGFI} = 1.00$$

1988				
Canada	1.00	.00	.00	.00
Parliament	.00	.84a	.00	.00
Civil Service	.00	.67a	.00	.00
Judiciary	.00	.00	1.00	.00
PC leader	.00	.00	.00	.92a
PC party	.00	.00	.00	.90a

$$\chi^2_7 = 1.18, \ p = .991, \ \text{AGFI} = 1.00$$

Note: a-p $\leq$.001; 1983 N = 1461, 1988 N = 1675; WLS estimates

Structure.   Do the conceptual distinctions among authorities, regime, and community correspond to how Canadians organize their feelings about their political system? The data presented above showing that levels of support for the national political community are consistently much greater than those for regime institutions and political authorities and that feelings about authorities wax and wane over time suggest that Canadians do, in fact, make these kinds of distinctions. As a more rigorous test of this hypothesis, we performed confirmatory factor analyses using the 1983 and 1988 thermometer score measures of feelings about Canada, the three regime institutions (the civil service, judiciary, and parliament), and incumbent political authorities (the governing party and its leader). To establish a baseline for interpreting our findings, we first used the 1983 data to test a single factor that specifies that, unlike political theorists, the Canadian public does not differentiate support at the community, regime, and authorities levels. As anticipated, this model had a totally unsatisfactory fit ($\chi^2_9 = 352.00$, p = .00). In sharp contrast, a three-factor community, regime and authorities support model performed very well ($\chi^2_8 = 16.87$, p = .03), although the loading of the judiciary item on the regime factor was relatively weak (.44) compared to those for the civil service (.76) and parliament (.87). This, and recognition of the historic "encapsulated" political status of the judiciary in Canada (Baar, 1977:272–4), suggested that

Table 4.3. *Correlations between political support factors, 1983, 1988*

	Community	Parliament– Civil Service	Judiciary	Incumbent Authorities
		Inter-factor correlations (ϕ)		
1983				
Community	1.00			
Parliament-Civil Service	.48c	1.00		
Judiciary	.32c	.46c	1.00	
Incumbent authorities	.32c	.69c	.26c	1.00
1988				
Community	1.00			
Parliament-Civil Service	.35c	1.00		
Judiciary	.30c	.51c	1.00	
Incumbent authorities	.11c	.47c	.18c	1.00

Note: c-p $\leq$.05; WLS estimates

there are two national regime factors, one for parliament and the civil service, and one for the judiciary. Empirically, this four-factor model had an extraordinarily good fit ($\chi^2_7 = .74$, p = .998) (Table 4.2). The four-factor model also had an outstanding fit with the 1988 data and, again, the three-factor model performed somewhat worse, and the one-factor model was clearly unacceptable.

The correlations among the four support factors deserve comment. In both 1983 and 1988 none of them was overwhelmingly strong, a finding that provides additional evidence that Canadians do distinguish among community, regime, and authorities (Table 4.3). However, as anticipated by our hypothesis regarding the likely "blurring" of authorities and regime images in a Westminster-model parliamentary system, there was a relatively strong correlation between the authorities factor and that for parliament/ civil service. This relationship was stronger in 1983 ($\varphi = .69$) than in 1988 ($\varphi = .48$) – exactly what one would predict given the political changes that had occurred between the two surveys. In 1983 the Liberals were the government-of-the-day in Ottawa, as they had been for much of the post-World War II era. In a situation of one-party dominance, the authorities–regime nexus should be – and, in fact, *was* – considerably stronger than in 1988 when the governing party had been in power for only four years. The authorities-community and parliament/civil service-community correlations also were stronger in 1983 and in 1988. This makes sense given the federal Liberals widely publicized emphasis on national unity, their protracted struggle against separatist forces in Quebec, and the highly salient role that their leader, Pierre Trudeau, had played as the principal advocate and architect of the new constitution. Finally, the weak correlation between the authorities and judiciary factors in both years is consonant with the relative isolation of the latter from the overtly partisan aspects of Canadian politics.

CORRELATES OF POLITICAL SUPPORT: AN INITIAL ANALYSIS

In Chapter 1 we argued that a person's support for any political object or process has two principal sources: (A) political socialization experiences and (B) judgments of how a political object or process functions generally and the way it affects the person making the judgments in particular. Unfortunately, the protracted and dynamic qualities of socialization processes mean that we have been unable to observe their operation and effects directly. Indeed, a proper analysis of the impact of socialization experiences would require monitoring individuals throughout much of their lives. Thus, we have been forced to rely on proxy variables that are assumed to capture and reflect a variety of such experiences. As in earlier chapters, the variables are gender, age, level of formal education, annual family income, and region–ethnicity. And because the mass media in Western democracies play important roles in the socialization process by providing much of the information on which many of the attitudes and values of their publics are based, we also have employed measures of public perceptions of how the media represent politicians, the national government, and the country as a whole to predict variations in support.

We were sensitive to the fact that sociodemographic factors not only may proxy group differences in judgments about the operation of the political system, but also may help establish standards that form the bases of instrumental judgments about a political order. The former effects can be observed directly; the latter, unfortunately, are obscured, being the products of possibly protracted socialization processes. Nonetheless, in subsequent chapters we will employ multivariate analyses to try to estimate such residual socialization effects. For the present, we will confine ourselves to cataloguing group differences in community, regime, and authorities support.

It seems reasonable to hypothesize that the effects of political socialization will be manifested in higher levels of support being ascribed to key political objects by older, better educated, higher income-generating men who are residents of Ontario, historically Canada's wealthiest and most politically powerful province. And because part of the conventional wisdom about Canadian politics is that the most fundamental and enduring societal cleavage is that which divides Francophone residents of Quebec from other citizens, it also is hypothesized that French Quebecers will be less supportive of the community and regime, and possibly the authorities as well, than other Canadians. Regarding perceptions of how federal politicians, the federal government, and Canada are represented by the media, we expect higher levels of support to be associated with perceptions that the media are portraying these persons and the political system favorably. This is because, as we hypothesized in Chapter 2, global judgments about matters such as the political system and the economy that average citizens make are influenced by information and interpretations of national conditions and events provided by the media. The impact of such information on support may well be substantial because, as shown in Chapter 3, many Canadians report that they monitor the media for information about government and politics.

We have used three categories of variables to assess the impact on support of people's judgments about the performance of the federal government and the political system more generally. The first category includes variables intended to index evaluations of how effectively the federal government performs its functions, with special attention paid to its management of the economy. The second taps public judgments of how fairly and equitably the federal government and the political and social systems function. The third includes several measures of people's orientations toward the political system, with emphasis on how responsive they feel it is to their needs and demands, and feelings of how much they trust the public officials who operate it.

We hypothesize that people who believe that the federal government operates effectively and fairly will be more supportive of that government and other political objects than will be those who do not share such views. Similarly, we anticipate that those who are satisfied with their own and the country's condition, and who judge that the well-being of both have been positively affected by governmental actions, will be stronger supporters than persons who are dissatisfied and hold government accountable for their own and the country's condition. In addition, given the historic importance of federalism in Canadian political life, we expect that those who believe the costs and benefits of federalism are balanced and fair will be more supportive than those who think the federal system operates unfairly. We also anticipate that people who are interested in politics, feel politically efficacious, believe that Members of Parliament are responsive to their needs and demands, trust government officials, and are oriented toward the federal rather than the provincial level of government will be more supportive of the national political community, regime, and authorities than those who believe differently, or who take opposite positions.

Regarding the economic evaluations and political support, as noted previously, existing studies on economy-political support linkages have focused almost exclusively on *incumbent* parties and their leaders, and have emphasized the importance of *retrospective* judgments about the state of the *national* economy. In our view, however, the impact of economic judgments may extend both to the regime and the community. Also, depending upon the kinds of economic issues that are most salient at a particular time, the effect of prospective judgments on support may be as great or greater than retrospective ones.[2] For example, in 1983 the chief Canadian economic concern was unemployment, which had increased sharply since the 1980 election. This was a context in which the importance of retrospective and contemporaneous judgments about the government's management of the economy should have been manifested. In 1988, in contrast, the principal issue was the desirability of a proposed free trade agreement with the United States.[3] Given the many uncertain effects of free trade on the future of Canada's economy, polity and society raised by the debate on the issue, 1988 should have been a year in which prospective judgments should have had a relatively strong influence. Our 1983 and 1988 data enable us to test the hypothesis that varying contexts of political debate affect the type of economic judgments having the greatest impact on political support.

Political socialization

With respect to the impact of socioeconomic and demographic characteristics that were intended to be surrogate measures of empirically elusive socialization processes, many of the variables did not achieve statistical significance. Those that did largely involved support for the national political community. As anticipated, men, older persons, and those with higher incomes and better educations tended to be more supportive of the political community than were other Canadians. The strongest of these relationships involved variables that tap regional and ethnolinguistic divisions in the population. As expected, Quebec Francophones were not as strong supporters of the national political community as were Anglophone Quebecers and residents of other regions (Table 4.4). However, Québécois were not notably less supportive of either the political regime (as measured by the government of Canada, parliament, civil service, and judiciary) or the authorities (as measured by the mean score for national party leaders) than were Canadians living in other parts of the country.

Somewhat better predictors of support (other than support for the political community) were people's perceptions of how the media represent the country, the federal government and federal politicians (data not shown).[4]

2 Also relevant are the issue priorities of the competing parties, a point we return to in Chapters 6 and 7. Parties' issue priorities may vary across political systems and within them over time. See Budge and Farlie (1983). The Canadian case in the late 1970s and early 1980s is discussed in Clarke, Stewart, and Zuk (1986) and Clarke and Zuk (1987).

3 The differing contexts of the 1984 and 1988 federal elections are discussed in Chapter 6.

4 The questions are: (a) "Do you think that television, radio, and newspapers generally make Canada look very good, good, not so good, or bad?" (b) "What about the government of Canada, that is, the *federal* government generally and not just a particular party government? Do you think that TV, radio, and newspapers make it look very good, good, not so good, or bad?" (c) "How about federal politicians generally, do TV, radio, and newspapers make them look very good, good, not so good, or bad?"

Table 4.4. *Mean support for national political community, regime and authorities by region-ethnicity, 1983, 1988*

	Canada	Government of Canada	Parliament	Civil Service	Judiciary	Party Leaders
1983						
Atlantic	76	54	50	50	57	51
Quebec-French	64	54	52	50	54	50
Quebec-non-French	81	62	59	53	62	57
Ontario	76	52	50	46	57	51
Prairies	77	42	43	41	55	46
British Columbia		48	47	45	56	49
eta=	.31a	.20a	.17a	.16a	.07	.15a
N	2085	2047	1923	1692	1866	1733
1988						
Atlantic	84	54	55	54	58	51
Quebec-French	67	57	53	52	56	51
Quebec-non-French	86	58	56	53	60	49
Ontario	83	53	53	51	56	50
Prairies	80	52	50	46	56	47
British Columbia	82	51	49	50	55	47
eta=	.34a	.11a	.10a	.12a	.04	.11a
N	2183	2166	2043	1791	2092	2143

Note: a-p ≤.001; b-p ≤.01; c-p ≤.05

People who reported political objects were favorably represented in the media tended to have higher levels of support for such objects. In fact, in virtually every instance mean support scores increased monotonically as judgments about the media images of the country, government and politicians went from "very bad" to "very good." For example, average support for the government of Canada progressed from 45 to 55 as images of the federal government changed from highly negative to highly positive. Similarly, average support for parliament in that year went from 41 to 54 as perceptions of media representations of the country became more sanguine.

In sum, although many of the relationships involving sociodemographic variables and political support were weak, there is some evidence in favor of theories focusing on the effects of political socialization and the subconscious, symbolic elements underlying supportive attitudes. Particularly noteworthy are the markedly lower scores accorded the national political community by Quebec Francophones. The relative strength of this relationship is consonant with their historic circumstances as outlined in Chapter 1 – circumstances that have worked to produce long-term group-related differences in support for the Canadian political system.

Government effectiveness

Canadians, like citizens of other contemporary liberal democracies, share a broad consensus concerning the desirability of government intervention in economic and social life (see Chapter 3). Regarding the economy, previous research has demonstrated that political support in part is a product of people's judgments about a government's economic performance.[5] As noted, most of those studies have focused on support for governing parties and their leaders rather than on the national political regime or community. Moreover, most studies also have concentrated on retrospective or contemporaneous evaluations; people have been asked to make judgments about the recent past or the "here and now." Here, we analyze the extent to which not only current and past but also future-oriented evaluations of government's impact on the national economy and one's personal financial condition affect support for the national political community, regime, and authorities.

Regarding judgments about the national economy, even evaluations unmediated by estimates of the quality of the government's stewardship[6] are related to regime and authorities support. These relationships vary in strength, although virtually all of them are statistically significant. For

5 See Chapter 2, note 3.
6 The battery of economic questions and the economic evaluation indices are presented in Chapter 2, note 4.

Table 4.5. *Mean support for national political community, regime and authorities, by national economic evaluations, 1988*

	Community	Government of Canada	Parliament	Civil Service	Judiciary	Party Leaders
Economy over past three or four years						
Better	81	59	55	52	57	50
Same, pro-con	78	50	51	50	55	49
Worse	76	46	46	45	53	47
eta=	.09a	.23a	.17a	.12a	.08a	.09a
N	2152	2136	2021	1774	2065	2177
State of economy now						
Very well	85	61	56	52	59	51
Fairly well, pro-con	79	54	53	51	57	50
Not very well	73	46	46	46	51	46
eta=	.17a	.19a	.16a	.10a	.11a	.11a
N	2161	2145	2029	1780	2072	2127
Economy during the next year or so						
Better	79	60	55	52	58	51
Same, pro-con	79	54	53	51	56	50
Worse	79	44	48	45	49	46
eta=	.01	.23a	.12a	.12a	.12a	.10a
N	1936	1927	1827	1601	1861	1910

Note: a-p ≤ .001

example, in 1988 support for the government of Canada increased by 15 points – from an average of 46 points among those who thought the national economy was not doing very well to 61 among those who believed it was (Table 4.5). In 1983 the comparable increase was even larger, 23 points, from 45 to 68 (data not shown). In contrast, in 1988 support for national civil service increased by only 6 points – from an average of 46 among those stating that the economy was not doing very well to 52 who thought it was doing very well. More generally, in 1983 contemporaneous judgments about the state of the national economy had the strongest effects on regime and authorities support, whereas, in 1988, retrospective, contemporaneous, and prospective judgments tended to have equally strong effects on support at these levels. Community support relationships were less robust, although all but one were statistically significant. In both years contemporaneous judgments about the national economy had the strongest effects. Thus, in 1988 community support increased from an average of 73 points among persons who believed the economy was not performing very well to 85 among those believing it was performing very well (Table 4.5). In 1983, the increase was from 72 to 83 points.

Several of the relationships between judgments about the economy and support increased markedly in strength when we took into account the extent to which government was praised or blamed for its condition. In keeping with previous research, the strongest relationships involved retrospective rather than prospective judgments. By way of illustration, in 1988 there was a 42-point difference in support for the regime (government of Canada) between those who believed that the economy had performed very well over the past four years and that the government had a great deal to do with this, and those who believed the economy had performed poorly and it was the government's fault (Table 4.6). Such judgments also were associated with large differences in support for parliament, the federal civil service, and more modest differences in support for the judiciary. The effect of these retrospective judgments of the national economy on support for party leaders also were substantial. The differences in the strength of the relationships between 1983 and 1988 again reflect the importance of the political context in which economic judgments are made. In the former year unemployment had reached its highest level in over thirty years. In the latter, both joblessness and prices had declined sharply, if unevenly, across much of the country, and public attention had refocused on future uncertainties associated with the proposed U.S.–Canada free-trade agreement.

As was the case for unmediated economic judgments, the weakest correlations involved the national political community. In 1988, community support increased modestly, from an average of 78 points among persons who believed the economy had deteriorated and the government had a great deal of responsibility, to an average of 84 points among those who

Table 4.6. *Mean support by economic performance-impact indices, 1988*

	Canada	Government of Canada	Parliament	Civil Service	Judiciary	Party Leaders
Retrospective-Sociotropic						
Negative -2	78	31	39	41	46	41
-1	78	38	45	45	53	44
0	80	47	51	49	52	49
1	79	58	54	52	57	51
Positive 2	84	73	62	57	60	53
eta=	.07c	.48a	.27a	.21a	.14a	.23a
Prospective-Sociotropic						
Negative -2	79	41	46	45	47	45
-1	78	46	49	44	51	46
0	79	53	52	51	56	50
1	80	60	55	52	61	51
Positive 2	78	63	56	53	56	51
eta=	.03	.24a	.13a	.17a	.14a	.11a
Retrospective-Egocentric						
Negative -2	82	41	44	44	49	44
-1	74	47	48	43	51	46
0	78	53	52	50	56	49
1	83	62	56	52	60	51
Positive 2	81	62	60	59	53	52
eta=	.11a	.22a	.16a	.17a	.11a	.12a
Prospective-Egocentric						
Negative -2	79	41	48	44	50	45
-1	78	46	49	44	54	48
0	79	53	52	50	56	49
1	80	62	56	53	59	52
Positive 2	81	65	59	57	55	52
eta=	.04	.25a	.13a	.16a	.09a	.12a
N (all analyses)	2183	2166	2043	1791	2092	2143

Note: a-p $\leq$.001; c-p $\leq$.05

believed the economy had improved and the government was responsible (Table 4.6). In 1983, this relationship also was weak, and correlations between community support and mediated prospective economic judgments were weaker still.

Relationships involving unmediated evaluations of one's personal economic condition were modest at best. In 1983, the strongest ones were for contemporaneous judgments – how one is doing "now" – with the largest being for community support. The latter increased from an average of 66 among those who were very dissatisfied with their personal economic condition to 80 among those who were very satisfied. Retrospective and future-oriented egocentric evaluations had a negligible impact on support for any object. Similarly, with one exception, all relationships involving retrospective and prospective evaluations were statistically insignificant. In 1988 the picture changes: retrospective and prospective as well as contemporaneous judgements about one's personal financial situation manifested significant, if moderate, associations with support at all three levels, again reflecting the changed context of political debate (Table 4.7).

Table 4.7. *Mean support for national political community, regime and authorities by personal economic evaluations, 1988*

	Community	Government of Canada	Parliament	Civil Service	Judiciary	Party Leaders
Financial condition compared to four years ago						
Better	81	58	55	52	58	50
Same	78	52	51	51	55	50
Worse	78	46	48	46	52	47
eta=	.06a	.18a	.12a	.13a	.09a	.09a
N	2158	2142	2019	1772	2068	2120
Present financial condition						
Very satisfied	82	57	55	53	58	50
Fairly satisfied	79	54	53	50	56	50
Little dissatisfied	76	50	48	49	52	48
Very dissatisfied	72	41	45	40	46	45
eta=	.14a	.14a	.13a	.12a	.12a	.06c
N	2181	2164	2042	1789	2090	2139
Expected financial condition in three or four years						
Better	80	58	54	52	57	50
Same, pro-con	79	53	52	51	56	50
Worse	79	43	49	46	52	46
eta=	.03	.20a	.09a	.11a	.08b	.09a
N	2070	2058	1941	1704	1986	2034

Note: a-p ≤.001; b-p ≤.01; c-p ≤.05

Similar to judgments about national economic conditions, the effects of egocentric evaluations were magnified when attributions of governmental responsibility were taken into account. Canadians who believed their personal financial condition had improved and thought that the federal government was responsible for this were more supportive of the community, regime, and authorities than were those who were very dissatisfied and felt that the government was to blame for their condition (Table 4.6). In both 1983 and 1988 the strongest of these relationships involved support for parliament and authorities, and the weakest were those for the community and the judiciary. Consistent with our hypothesis that the context in which economic judgments are made affects the relative importance of retrospective, contemporaneous and prospective evaluations, we found that the latter have their greatest impact in 1988. Those who believed that their personal financial condition would improve and were willing to credit government for this happy circumstance were more supportive than those who thought their condition would deteriorate and government would be at fault (Table 4.6). Once more, the weakest of these relationships involved support for the community.[7]

Overall, the several analyses revealed that retrospective and contemporaneous economic judgments generally have a greater impact on support than do prospective ones. Additionally, judgments about the national economy and the quality of the government's stewardship thereof have greater effects than do judgments about one's personal financial situation and the extent of government responsibility. In keeping with our hypothesis that context makes a difference, prospective judgments had their greatest impact in 1988, the year in which the issue of free trade raised a host of questions about the country's future. The strongest such effects involved egocentric evaluations and support for the government of Canada, a not unexpected result given that the incumbent Tory Party was the architect and principal proponent of the hotly debated free trade agreement.

People's judgments about the effectiveness of the government's performance in noneconomic policy domains also had considerable influence on support. Relatively strong predictors of regime and authorities support included judgments of how effectively the federal government had safeguarded civil liberties, provided welfare services, protected citizens' lives

---

7 The importance of economic effectiveness evaluations is evident in other analyses as well. In 1983, for example, there was an 18-point average difference in support for the government of Canada between those who thought the government had done very well in keeping inflation under control as compared to those who thought it had not done very well. Differences in support for national political institutions related to judgments about government's handling of inflation were: parliament – 14 points, civil service – 10 points, and the judiciary – 9 points. At the authorities level, the difference was 8 points, and at the community level, 4 points. Relationships of similar orders of magnitude were apparent in analyses involving judgments about government performance regarding unemployment.

and property, and maintained the armed forces.[8] Evaluations of the government's performance in the health, education, and environmental fields did not have as great an impact, and the least powerful predictors were judgments about the effectiveness of government in promoting culture and the arts. As was the case with economic evaluations, judgments about the government's effectiveness in noneconomic areas had less of an impact on support for Canada as a political community than they did on support for the regime and authorities.

The overall impact of these judgments can be better appreciated by employing the summary government effectiveness index[9] introduced in Chapter 3. In both 1983 and 1988 relationships between this index and political support were substantial for the several measures of national regime support. In 1983, for example, as one moves from the most negative to the most positive point on the index, average support for the government of Canada increased by fully 41 points, from 39 to 80 (Figure 4.4). Comparable average increases in support for parliament were from 40 to 75, the civil service, from 42 to 68, and the judiciary, from 37 to 72. The effects on community and authorities support were less powerful, but still substantial. Community support increased from 66 to 87 and authorities support, from 45 to 61. In 1988 all of these patterns again were present, although the strength of the associations involving the three regime institutions and party leaders were slightly weaker.

Equity–fairness

As argued in Chapter 3, democratic theory prescribes that political systems should be judged not only by their effectiveness, but also by the equity and fairness of their procedures, processes and policy outcomes. Empirically, equity–fairness evaluations were related to support in expected ways. The strongest and most consistent predictor was the statement that political parties looked after the best interests of all Canadians and not just those who voted for them.[10] For example, in 1983, agreement–disagreement with this statement was associated with a 4-point average difference in support for Canada, a 12-point difference in support for the government of Canada, an 11-point difference for parliament, a 9-point difference for the civil service, and a 6-point difference in support both for the judiciary and political authorities. More generally, the strongest relationships were those involving statements that referred directly and specifically to the equity–fairness of the way in which a particular political object functioned. Thus, in 1983 the relationship between support for parliament and the statement

---

8 The government effectiveness questions are listed in Chapter 3, note 13.
9 On construction of the summary government effectiveness index see Chapter 3, note 14.
10 The equity–fairness questions are listed in Chapter 3, note 15.

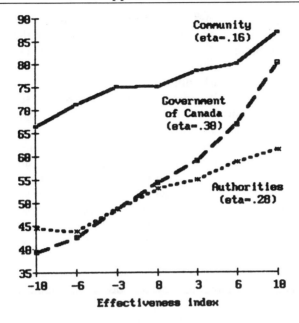

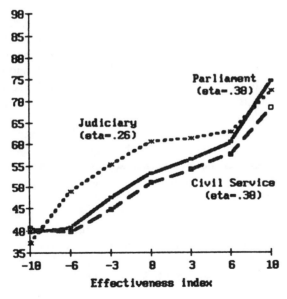

Figure 4.4. *Mean political support by government effectiveness index, 1983*

that parliament doesn't represent everyone fairly was stronger than were the relationships between this statement and support for the civil service and the judiciary. Similarly, the statement that the federal civil service has treated all Canadians equally was more strongly correlated with support for the civil service than with support for other objects.

Like the measures of governmental effectiveness, the summary index of equity–fairness evaluations[11] was associated strongly with support for the national regime and authorities. In 1983, on average, support for the government of Canada increased from 40 to 61 as one moved from the negative to the positive end of the equity–fairness index, and support for parliament, the civil service, the judiciary, and political authorities also increased by substantial amounts (Figure 4.5). The relationship of equity–fairness judgments to community support, in contrast, was very modest, with scores increasing only from 72 to 75. All of these relationships were replicated at the same orders of magnitude in 1988. Not only is community support consistently much higher than support for regime and authorities, but it remains relatively impervious to varying effectiveness and equity–fairness judgments. This finding provides additional evidence for our argument that in liberal democracies people distinguish between the notion of community and those of authorities and regime. The latter two are held accountable for citizens well-being in ways the former is not.

The several analyses confirm that in a democracy such as Canada people make judgments about both the effectiveness and equity–fairness of their political system and society which have strong effects on national regime and authorities support but only very modest ones on community support. However, because these analyses have treated the relationships *seriatim*, they do not inform us whether combinations of effectiveness and equity–fairness evaluations have especially potent effects. One might anticipate that persons who judge that government is both effective and equitable in its operations would be especially strong supporters of the regime and authorities and, perhaps, of the community as well. In contrast, persons who made negative evaluations on both dimensions would manifest particularly low levels of support. The potential importance of such interaction effects at the aggregate level is suggested by the fact that nearly half of those surveyed had average or below average scores on both the effectiveness and the equity–fairness indices, whereas only about one in five had above average scores on both.

We used two-way analyses of variance to test for the presence of effectiveness x equity–fairness interaction effects. Respondents were divided into four groups: those who had above average scores on the two summary indices; those who had average or below scores; and two others who were above average on one measure but below on the other. The 1983 and 1988

---

11 The summary equity–fairness index is discussed in Chapter 3, note 16.

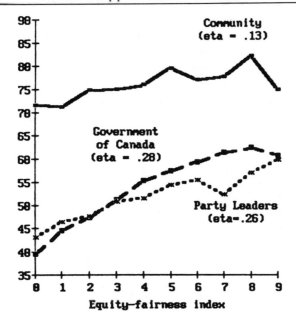

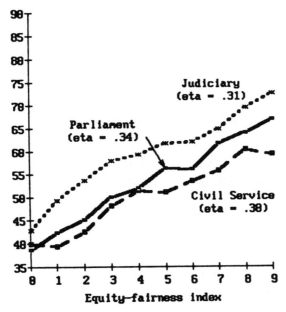

Figure 4.5. *Mean political support by equity–fairness index, 1983*

results replicate those presented above. They indicate that both effectiveness and equity–fairness judgments had strong "main" effects on regime
and authorities support, but much weaker ones for community support.
However, virtually all of the interaction effects were insignificant. The sole
exception concerns support for the civil service in 1983, but even in this
case, the interaction effect was quite modest. Our expectations notwithstanding, effectiveness and equity–fairness judgments constitute basically
"separate streams" of influence on political support.

Support for incumbent political authorities

We have shown that governmental effectiveness and equity–fairness judgments have significant and, in some instances, large relationships with
authorities support as measured by the mean level of affect for the leaders
of Canada's three national political parties. One would expect that in a
parliamentary system these associations will be particularly strong for the
governing party and its leader because, although they are only the
"government-of-the-day," people may have difficulty distinguishing them
from government per se. As argued, this tendency should be especially
pronounced in Canada because the Liberal Party formed the national
government for much of the post-World War II era. Consistent with this
hypothesis, in 1983 the summary effectiveness and equity–fairness indices
were far better predictors of support for the leader of the governing Liberal
Party and Prime Minister Trudeau than they were for Messrs. Clark and
Broadbent, the opposition parties' leaders. This also was true for relationships between the predictors and support for the three parties; the
strongest involved the governing Liberals. Similarly, in 1988, after a Conservative government had been in office for four years, the strongest relationships involved support for that party and its leader.

As was the case with sociotropic economic evaluations more generally,
differences in the magnitude of the correlations between judgments about
economic conditions and support for government and opposition parties
and their leaders increased when they were mediated by beliefs about the
government's role in managing the economy. In 1983 average support for
Prime Minister Trudeau increased by fully 57 points – from 20 among persons who judged that the national economy had performed poorly over the
past few years and that it was the government's fault to 77 among those
who believed the economy had performed well and credited that performance to the government. For the Conservative and New Democratic
leaders, the comparable differences were much smaller, 6 and 10 points,
respectively. The relationships involving mediated contemporaneous and
prospective economic evaluations and support for the governing party and
its leaders were more modest, although still considerably stronger than
those involving opposition parties and their leaders.

Interestingly, government-opposition differences eroded when analyzed in terms of people's judgments about their material condition and the government's responsibility for it. In Chapter 2 we noted the asymmetric character of people's judgments about their personal well-being and the extent to which it was affected by government. Recall that people who felt they were in good shape were not inclined to tip their hats to government, whereas those who were not sanguine about their circumstances were prone to believe that the government did bear some responsibility for their condition. It may be the case that the latter make up a disproportionate number of the Canadians whom we hypothesized would have difficulty distinguishing the government-of-the-day from government per se. An equally plausible alternative, however, is that they were neither more nor less able to make this distinction than more materially favored fellow citizens. It simply may be the case that in a country with a liberal democratic political culture and a market-oriented economy most people take responsibility for their own material condition and government – regardless of whether it is thought of as government qua regime or government qua party in office – is largely irrelevant. In contrast, most people *do* assign responsibility for more global economic conditions to government, and in these areas they *do* make both regime versus government-of-the-day and governing party versus opposition party distinctions.

Various other data are consonant with this interpretation. Regarding governmental effectiveness, for example, in 1983 there was, on average, a 23-point difference (59 versus 36) in support for Mr. Trudeau between people who believed the government was doing very well in controlling inflation and those who judged that the government had failed to check price increases. In contrast, differences in support for opposition party leaders, Clark and Broadbent, were small (3 and 6 points, respectively) and statistically insignificant. Similarly, there was a 16-point difference in support accorded the governing Liberal Party by people who gave the government high as opposed to low marks for handling inflation, but only negligible (two points or less) and statistically insignificant differences in the support ascribed the Conservative and New Democratic parties. Government-opposition differences in support that were associated with judgments about the macroeconomy were not unique, but rather characterized beliefs about governmental performance in noneconomic areas as well.

Relationships between equity–fairness judgments and support for the prime minister and his party also were stronger than those involving the two opposition leaders and their parties. In 1983 the difference in support for the Liberal leader between those who agreed and disagreed with the nine equity–fairness statements averaged 11 points, whereas those for the Conservative and NDP leaders averaged less than 2 points. Moreover, all of the relationships for the Liberal leader were statistically significant, whereas 6 for the Conservative leader and 7 for the NDP leader, were not.

Equity–fairness judgments also were associated with an average difference of 9 points in support for the Liberal Party and less than 4 points for the opposition parties. Finally, effectiveness and equity–fairness judgments did not interact to influence support for governing or opposition parties and their leaders. Tests for interaction effects similar to those performed above were insignificant in all instances and, again, the main effects were much stronger for government than opposition.

To recapitulate, combinations of effectiveness and equity–fairness judgments did not have especially marked consequences for support, even in the case of incumbent parties and their leaders. Although analyses strongly indicate that incumbents, as the government-of-the-day, constitute the primary focal point for public political judgments, the effectiveness and equity–fairness dimensions of such judgments have largely independent effects on political support.

Federalism

Since Quebec's "Quiet Revolution" in the early 1960s disputes concerning the nature of the federal system have been a continuing source of stress on the fabric of the Canadian polity. Much of the conflict concerning federalism has occurred at the elite level and has involved the leaders and principal policy advisors of the federal and provincial governments (Simeon, 1972; Cairns, 1983). As shown in Chapter 3, however, the conflict has resonated among the general public as well, with sizable numbers of Canadians perceiving that the federal system makes their province or region bear unfair costs while bestowing unfair benefits and undue political influence on other provinces and regions. At the height of the debate concerning a constitutional accord in the late 1970s and early 1980s, such perceptions were concentrated in the Western provinces and Ontario. Agreement on a new constitution did not relieve the situation, at least in terms of the breadth of discontent with the federal system. Indeed, in the late 1980s, unhappiness with the costs and benefits of federalism were more widely dispersed across the country than had been the case prior to the implementation of the Canada Act. The new constitution and the presence of a Conservative national government promising cooperation rather than confrontation with the provinces may have reduced the intensity of feelings of discontent, but not their pervasiveness.

This is the case. In 1983, support for the government of Canada, parliament and the federal civil service varied with judgments about how the federal system allocates the costs and benefits of governing Canada, being lower among persons who believed that such inequities existed. For the government of Canada support declined from 55 to 41 points, whereas for parliament and the civil service the decreases were from 52 to 43 and from 50 to 40, respectively. Consonant with arguments that the federal Liberals and their longtime leader, Pierre Trudeau, were seen as the leading proponents of a centralized form of federalism and, more generally, that the distinction between the Liberal Party and the federal government had blurred for many Canadians, support for the Liberals and their leader was strongly associated with judgments about the costs and benefits of federalism. Persons who were unhappy about the operation of the federal system were much less supportive of the prime minister and his party than were those who judged that the system distributed costs and benefits equitably and fairly. For Trudeau the decrease was from 52 to 35 points, whereas for the Liberal Party the decrease was from 51 to 37 points. Again, support for the two opposition parties, the Conservatives and the New Democrats, was much more weakly related to judgments about the federal system. That Conservative support was stronger among those who judged the system harshly likely reflects the fact that by 1983 the party was in power in several provinces which had been deeply involved in the protracted struggle with Ottawa over the contours of a new and more equitable federalism.

The power of perceived inequities in the federal system to influence support for the regime and authorities had dissipated by 1988.[12] Perhaps because memories of the conflicts surrounding the design of a new constitution had faded somewhat or because the Conservatives had enjoyed some measure of success in their efforts to restore harmony between Ottawa and the provinces, relationships between the perceived costs and benefits of federalism and support for the government of Canada, parliament, and the civil service all were considerably weaker in 1988. Relationships between feelings about the federal system and the incumbent political authorities also were weaker than previously.

In 1983 and 1988 support for the national political community and the judicial system were unrelated to beliefs about the costs and benefits of federalism. The latter finding is consistent with the limited role and the generally low profile the judiciary maintained in resolving federal–provincial conflicts in the 1970s and 1980s, whereas the former is suggestive of the general limits of evaluations of the operation of the federal system to affect support for the concept of a continuing political community. However, we will demonstrate in Chapter 5 that such judgments are considerably more important for understanding community support among Québécois.

Unlike cost–benefit evaluations, general orientations toward the federal system influence community support. In 1983 community support averaged 70 points among those who focused their attention on provincial politics as compared to 78 among those who paid more attention to federal politics.[13] The comparable figures for both regime (government of Canada) and au-

---

12 It is possible that the constitutional crisis engendered by the Meech Lake crisis of the spring of 1990 may have reinvigorated the impact of evaluations of the federal system on support.

13 See Chapter 3, note 9.

thorities support were modest, increasing from 49 and 32. Community support scores increased from 68 to 79, depending on whether people regarded the provincial or the federal government as "their" government. The equivalent increases for government of Canada and authorities support were 46 and 53 and 47 and 51, respectively. The cumulative impact of these orientations reflect the same patterns, i.e., stronger effects on community than on regime or authorities support.

We may ask why, unlike the cost–benefit evaluations, the more general orientations toward the federal system affect community support. In our view these latter orientations are proxies for the effects of long-term socialization processes that, as we have noted, are difficult to capture but are nonetheless important. Their effect is to differentially integrate Canadians into their national and their provincial political communities, thus providing a political cultural basis for the ongoing struggles that successive federal and provincial governments have waged for the "hearts and minds" of their citizens.

It is, therefore, tempting to infer that there is an inverse relationship between national and provincial support, i.e., positive feelings toward the provincial regime and community are accompanied by negative feelings toward the national regime and community and vice versa. This image of "divided loyalties" (Black, 1975) between nation and province has strong intuitive appeal. However, it is not supported by the data. In both 1983 and 1988, across the entire country, aggregate- and individual-level differences in support for the national and provincial communities were very small, and analyses by region–ethnicity revealed that only among non-French Quebecers was there a decided national "tilt" (Table 4.8). Similarly, across the country as a whole differences in national and provincial regime support (as measured by feelings about national and provincial governments) were extremely modest. In 1983 these differences were substantial only among non-French Quebecers and Prairie residents, the former being more strongly supportive of the national, and the latter, their provincial government. In 1988 these differences were no longer apparent.

Moreover, there was a positive relationship between national and provincial support. For community support, the strength of the correlation varied with region–ethnicity. However, controls for partisan identifications with governing or opposition parties at the two levels of government had little impact except among Quebec Francophones. The latter finding reflected the strong negative relationship between a Parti Québécois provincial party identification and support for the Canadian political community. This relationship is examined in detail in the next chapter. As for regime support, the relationship without controls for party identification varied markedly by region–ethnicity, but equaled only .06 for the country as a whole. Here, however, controls for federal and provincial party identification were important. For the entire country and among all regional

Table 4.8. *Mean national and provincial community and regime support by region-ethnicity, 1988*

Region-ethnicity	Community Support			Regime Support		
	Canada	Province	Difference*	Canada	Province	Difference*
Atlantic	84	81	3.2	54	60	-6.3
Quebec-French	67	75	-7.4	57	61	-3.3
Quebec-Non-French	86	68	18.6	58	55	2.2
Ontario	83	76	6.8	53	60	-7.4
Prairies	80	76	4.1	52	55	-2.8
British Columbia	82	80	2.4	51	44	6.3
eta=	.34a	.12a	.29a	.11a	.24a	.18a
Canada	79	77	2.4	54	57	-3.7
N	2183	2192	2172	2166	2169	2148

Note: * - mean individual-level difference; a-p ≤.001; b-p ≤.01; c-p ≤.05

ethnic groups the correlations between national and provincial regime support controlling for partisan identifications were positive, although only among Quebec non-French was it stronger than the comparable correlation for national and provincial community support. These positive relationships between national and provincial community and regime support indicate that the existence of a federal form of government has provided important avenues for the mobilization and articulation of ethnolinguistic and regional discontents, and for the ways in which people think about political parties and politics more generally. Overall, however, it has not resulted in sharply divided loyalties. Nor is it the case that Canadians' federal and provincial political worlds are "hermetically sealed" from one another. Rather, political support at the two levels of the system tends to be reinforcing.

DEMOCRATIC CITIZENSHIP AND POLITICAL SUPPORT

Efficacy and trust

Theories of democracy and conventional wisdom alike recognize that democracy is a difficult form of government to operate successfully because it makes strong demands on citizens and political leaders alike. The latter have to make people believe in their ability to lead, to have trust and confidence in them, whereas the former must trust leaders but maintain a measured skepticism about their motives and behavior. Equally important, citizens in a democracy must have confidence in their ability to make their leaders and the system itself change direction when, and if, things are going awry. Absent these attitudes and behavior on the part of leaders and led, the long-term future of a democratic political order is problematic. Therefore, in the context of a democratic political culture, political support should be associated with: (A) the trust citizens have in their leaders; (B) feelings that both the system and its authorities are responsive to citizens' needs and demands (external political efficacy); and (C) the belief that people are capable of making the system and its leaders respond (internal political efficacy).

Empirically, both internal and external political efficacy were positively related to community, regime, and authorities support, although they had a stronger impact on regime and authorities than on community. In every case the effects of externally efficacious feelings were somewhat stronger than the internal variety. Because the two types of efficacy, although conceptually and empirically distinct, are strongly interrelated, we gauged their joint effects on support by constructing a summary efficacy index.[14]

14 The summary efficacy index is the sum of the internal and external efficacy indices described in Chapter 3, note 21.

Table 4.9. *Mean support for national political community, regime and authorities by political efficacy and trust indices, 1988*

	Canada	Government of Canada	Parliament	Civil Service	Judiciary	Party Leaders
Political Efficacy						
Low 0	77	47	47	46	50	47
1	78	50	50	49	54	49
2	80	55	54	52	58	50
3	82	61	58	54	61	52
High 4	84	66	62	56	66	52
eta=	.11a	.29a	.28a	.21a	.24a	.13a
N	2183	2166	2043	1791	2092	2143
Trust in Political Authorities						
Low 0	75	43	43	44	47	43
1	78	48	49	48	53	47
2	80	54	53	50	57	50
3	82	60	58	54	61	52
High 4	79	65	60	58	61	53
eta=	.12a	.32a	.28a	.25a	.24a	.25a
N	2183	2166	2043	1791	2092	2143

Note: a-p ≤.001; b-p ≤.01; c-p ≤.05

The 1988 data indicated that as one moved across the index, average community support scores increased from 77 to 84. Comparable increases for regime support were substantially larger, whereas those for authorities were more modest (Table 4.9). The 1983 results were very similar.

External efficacy involves citizens' perceptions of how responsive the political system is to their attempts to influence it. In both 1983 and 1988 the impact of such perceptions on political support also was manifested in people's responses to a series of questions about the responsiveness of MPs to their views and needs. In 1988, for example, community support increased from 73 to 85 across a summary index measuring perceptions of MPs responsiveness.[15] Support for the government of Canada went from 46 to 61, and support for parliament, the civil service, and the judiciary exhibited similar patterns. Support for authorities rose a more modest but still significant amount, e.g., from 45 to 52 points.

Trust in public officials also was related to differences in support. The weakest relationships were at the community level. In 1988 community scores rose from 75 to 79 in 1988 as trust went from low to high (Table 4.9).[16] For political authorities it increased from 43 to 53. Stronger relationships were found at the regime level, with support for the government of Canada moving from 43 to 65 points, and that for parliament from 43 to 60 points. Support for the civil service and the judiciary were associated with trust in a similar fashion. Although it may be beneficial for the successful functioning of a democracy for citizens to exhibit a measure of skepticism concerning the character and competence of public officials, it is evident that at the individual level support for one such political system is virtually a linear function of levels of trust in such persons.

In democracies governing parties and their leaders are charged with responding to citizen needs and demands and then are judged on that basis. They also are continually subjected to performance evaluations that can have important effects on the public's trust in them. Opposition parties and their leaders, in contrast, typically are able to make untested claims that they will be more responsive to citizen needs and demands, and are worthier of the public's trust than is a current administration. And, fortunately for them, opposition parties generally are not held accountable for the performance of incumbents. Variations in the public's efficacious and trusting feelings thereby should have a more substantial impact on support for an incumbent party and its leader than for opposition parties and their leaders.

The data strongly support these expectations; in 1983, for example, political efficacy was much more strongly related to support for the then prime

15 The measures of perceptions of MPs' responsiveness are presented in Chapter 3, note 19.
16 For the measures of trust in political authorities and the summary trust index see Chapter 3, notes 20 and 21.

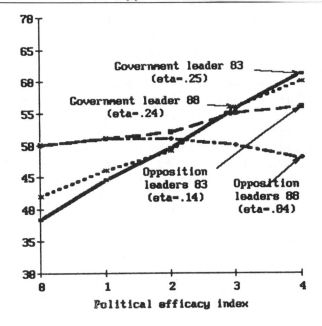

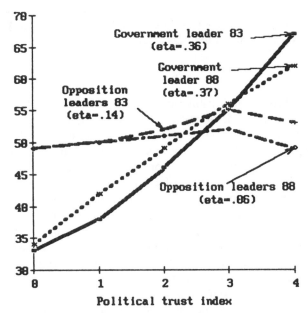

Figure 4.6. *Mean support for government and opposition party leaders by political efficacy and trust in political authorities, 1983, 1988*

minister, Trudeau, than to support for either of the two opposition leaders
(Figure 4.6). The pattern also obtained for trust; movement from the
lowest to the highest position on the trust index was accompanied by a 34
point increase in support for Trudeau, but only 3 and 5 point increases in
support for Mulroney and Broadbent, respectively. Similar government-
opposition differences characterized the relationships between efficacy and
trust and support for the governing Liberal Party, on the one hand, and the
opposition Conservative and New Democratic parties, on the other. The
1988 pattern is identical; as anticipated, the strong relationships involved
the governing party, the Conservatives, and their leader Brian Mulroney.

One would not expect to find that perceptions of MPs responsiveness
sharply differentiate support for the government and opposition parties
and their leaders because MPs are, by definition, local representatives and
the norm of constituency representation is widely shared by MPs of every
party (e.g., Kornberg and Mishler, 1976; Clarke and Price, 1980). Again,
this expectation proved correct. In 1983 relationships between perceptions
of MPs responsiveness and support for the three leaders and their parties
were only slightly stronger in the case of Trudeau and the governing Liberals. In 1988 the strongest relationships obtained for the Conservatives and
Prime Minister Mulroney. However, all of the relationships were rather
weak, a finding consistent with the notion that support for individual MPs
rather than entire parties or party leaders is affected by evaluations of how
responsive MPs are to constituent needs and interests. However, it still is
possible that feelings about MPs indirectly affect support for key objects by
influencing broader-gauged feelings of efficacy and trust.

Interest

We also considered relationships between political interest and support.
From the standpoint of democratic theory, one might anticipate that people who are interested in politics also are more psychologically involved in
the political process and, hence, more supportive of the system. However,
the converse is also plausible: that for at least some less supportive persons, political interest is a product of perceived shortcomings in the system.
To an extent the relationships between interest and support have been
investigated in the previous analyses of the effects of attention to federal
and provincial politics on support. Persons whose primary focus was the
federal political arena were moderately more supportive of the national
political authorities, regime, and community, but a more general measure
of political interest was largely unrelated to support at any level. In 1983
community support was only 3 points higher on average (76 versus 73)
among those who followed politics "very closely" as compared to those
who followed them "not much at all." Support for the government of
Canada actually was higher among the latter group than among the former

(52 versus 49). All of the regime and authorities support political interest correlations were statistically insignificant, as were comparable relationships in 1988. These "null" findings are consistent with the proposition that for some people interest in the political process generates positive support whereas, for others, heightened interest reflects misgivings about politicians and the system more generally. The net result is a canceling effect that is manifested in the very modest and statistically insignificant relationships between interest and support.

SUMMARY

In this chapter we have investigated the incidence, structure and correlates of support for Canada's national political authorities, regime, and community. We found that community support was consistently much higher than that for authorities and the regime, and that the conceptual distinction between support at the three levels corresponded to the way Canadians actually organize their supportive feelings. Moreover, regime support was "not of a piece." Rather, Canadians distinguish support for parliament and the civil service, on the one hand, from that for the judiciary, on the other. This finding is consonant with the historic lack of overt politicization of the latter institution, and it reinforces our conclusion that a multidimensional model of political support is reality-oriented.

Regarding the correlates of support, many of the socioeconomic and demographic characteristics which were intended to proxy Canadians long-term group-related socialization experiences did not have statistically significant effects. Those that did largely involved differences in national community support between Quebec Francophones and other Canadians. Somewhat better predictors of support were other proxies of the socialization process such as people's perceptions of how the media represent the country, the federal government and its politicians, and orientations toward the federal and provincial levels of the political system.

A competing theory of support is that it is largely a product of people's assessments about how effective and equitable government is in its operation. We found that judgments about the government's ability to manage the economy were particularly powerful predictors of support for the incumbent political authorities and the regime. Judgments about governmental effectiveness in noneconomic domains also influenced support. And, with respect to judgments about the equity and fairness of government and the political system more generally, we found that the strongest relationships with support were those that referred directly and specifically to the way in which a particular political institution (e.g., parliament, the judiciary) functions, but that a global index of equity–fairness judgments also had strong relationships with support for authorities and, especially, the regime. Additional analyses reveal that effectiveness and equity–

fairness judgments constitute essentially separate streams of influence on support. We also tested the hypothesis that in a parliamentary system feelings about a governing party and its leader would be more strongly correlated with regime support than would similar feelings about their counterparts in the opposition. This is indeed the case, a point to which we return below.

Federalism is one of the most salient aspects of Canadian government and, as anticipated, regime support was higher among persons who were oriented toward the federal rather than the provincial level of government. Notwithstanding this finding, federalism – and the fact that it has been employed as a vehicle to mobilize and articulate the claims and complaints of various ethnolinguistic and regional groups – has not resulted in dividing the community loyalties of most Canadians. Indeed, for the entire country, aggregate- and individual-level differences in support for the national and provincial political communities were very small. Moreover, other than among Quebec Francophones, the relationship between support for both was positive; strong supporters of their province also tended to be strong supporters of Canada.

Finally, feelings of political efficacy and trust in public officials were associated positively with support for the authorities and the regime and, to a lesser extent, the community. At the authorities level, however, differences in efficacy and trust were much more strongly correlated with support for the prime minister and the governing party than with their opposition counterparts.

Generally, our findings are consonant with the conclusion that support in contemporary representative democracies has a strong *instrumental* component. In such systems, citizens judge the performance of the political system and public officials in light of effectiveness and equity–fairness norms integral to democratic theory. Such judgments have strong effects on support for incumbent political authorities and the regime, and much weaker ones on opposition parties and their leaders, as well as on the political community. The latter finding reflects the ability of citizens in a mature democracy to distinguish the political community, on the one hand, from regime institutions and, especially, authorities, on the other. The fact that relationships between support for authorities and people's judgments about the state of the economy and the government's stewardship thereof are particularly robust can be attributed, in part, to the presence of a Westminster-model parliamentary system. Such a system facilitates the ability of average citizens to hold incumbent authorities accountable for national events and conditions during their tenure in office, and is consonant with the theory of responsible government.

In the Canadian case, the strength of the relationship between economic judgments and authorities support also reflects a condition of one-party dominance; the Liberal Party constituted the incumbent federal government for much of the post-World War II period. Such protracted incumbency by a single party has a negative consequence for the support process in a democracy, however. It encourages citizens to obfuscate the distinction between an incumbent government and the regime. This tendency becomes particularly strong in situations when, as in Canada during the 1970s and early 1980s, a highly visible and articulate head of government becomes the champion of the national regime, which thereby becomes identified in the public mind with the leader and his party.

The relative weakness of most sociodemographic variables in our analyses indicates that they do not have strong direct effects on political support. However, this does not mean that the socialization experiences these variables are intended to proxy are irrelevant to the support process. Rather, we would argue that they operate more subtly and indirectly, by defining a cultural matrix in which support-relevant judgments are made. Recall our findings in Chapters 2 and 3 demonstrating that overwhelming majorities of Canadians believe it is important for government to intervene in most areas of social and economic life, and that many believe that the actions of government will affect the national economy and, to a lesser extent, their own material condition. This argument will guide analyses of support processes and their consequences pursued in subsequent chapters. First, however, we will examine in more detail support and its correlates in the two regions of Canada, Quebec and the West, where public complaints about the political order have been longstanding and, in the former region, threats to its continuing integrity most profound.

5

Regional disaffection: Quebec and the West

We in Quebec think of Canada as a very artificial creation. . . . Confederation was conned upon people who were not consulted. . . . A Canadian is just someone who lives here. That's all.
René Lévesque, *Politics Canada*, 5th ed., p. 191

Western farmers generally see themselves at the mercy of a central government concerned primarily about an industrial and consumer-oriented eastern society.
The Task Force on Canadian Unity: A Time to Speak, p. 216

Deep, reinforcing, and persistent regional cleavages based on ethnolinguistic and economic particularisms have done much to shape the nature of Canadian politics. Preeminent among these societal divisions are those involving Quebec and the Western provinces. Throughout the country's history conflicts engendered by these cleavages frequently have preoccupied politicians and public alike. Both have been concerned that continuing support for the political system was in jeopardy unless suitable accommodations could be reached. In the 1970s and 1980s an interlocking series of "Confederation issues" generated by social, economic, and political developments affecting Quebec, the West, and Canada as a whole posed a genuine threat to national unity. These issues and the protracted and oftentimes acrimonious political struggles they engendered pointedly emphasize the fragility of support for national political authorities, regime, and community in Quebec and, to a lesser extent, the West. Accordingly, in this chapter, we investigate forces that influence political support among residents of these regions.

We will focus much of the discussion on the roles federal and, especially, provincial, political parties have played in the support process. For most of this century the two old-line parties, the Liberals and the Conservatives, have not been able to sustain the loyalty and affection of a majority of Westerners. The rise of the left-of-center CCF–NDP and the right-of-center Social Credit parties in the 1930s and their success in the provincial and federal political arenas reflected deep discontent with the quality of representation provided by the Liberals and Conservatives. The formation of these two protest parties did not alleviate Western grievances, and the region's unhappiness with how its economic interests are represented in national politics continues to strain the fabric of the party system, as witness the emergence of and growing support for yet another such party, Reform, in the late 1980s.

For very different reasons, the national party system failed in Quebec as well. The Union Nationale Party dominated Quebec provincial politics in the 1940s and 1950s and remained a major force until the emergence of the avowedly separatist Parti Québécois in the late 1960s. Unlike their Western counterparts that almost immediately became active in national as well as provincial politics, Quebec protest parties historically have focused their energies almost entirely on provincial politics in Quebec. The Parti Québécois continued this pattern with a vengeance. Indeed, their raison d'être was to separate Quebec politics entirely from those in the rest of Canada. The referendum on sovereignty-association which the Péquistes placed before the Quebec electorate in May 1980 is at once a vivid illustration of their determination to pursue this goal and dramatic testimony of the continuing difficulty of maintaining the integrity of a Canada that includes Quebec. The sovereignty-association referendum was a direct and immediate challenge to that integrity and, without exaggeration, the most important single event in the country's history. Accordingly, in the concluding section of this chapter we focus on this historic event and the manner in which support for the national community affected Quebecers' decision to vote *oui* or *non* for Canada.

Based on the analyses in this chapter we conclude that it may well be beyond the capacity of any party or party system to keep a democracy together without periodic crises of support when a significant proportion of the population concentrated in a particular region have negative feelings about the national political community and support a party that wishes to dissolve that community. In such a circumstance, arguments in favor of the existing political order must be cast entirely in instrumental terms, and instrumental arguments are inevitably open to question as economic conditions change. As the Meech Lake crisis and its aftermath reveal, this has been the case in Canada.

QUEBEC

When the World War II ended in the summer of 1945 Quebec society was largely rural and underdeveloped industrially. Francophone culture of the time was described as insular, withdrawn, conservative, and priest-ridden (Guindon, 1960:533–51). Critics also noted that Francophone Quebec used democratic political institutions such as parliaments and political parties and processes such as elections in defensive and ethnically directed ways – as weapons in the struggle for "survivance."[1]

During the second half of the nineteenth century and the first two decades of the twentieth, traditional French-Canadian nationalism focused on the language and educational rights of French-Canadians living outside of Quebec. As the struggles to establish those rights were lost – in New Brunswick in the 1870s, Manitoba in the 1890s, Alberta in the first decade of this century, and Ontario during World War I – the focus became Quebec itself. The call was for a French nation domiciled in Quebec, Catholic in religion, and agricultural in vocation. "The church, the parish and the family were its essential institutions. The state, the very idea of which implied secularism, played only a marginal role" (Cook, 1985:18).

This traditional nationalism and the definition it gave to French-Canadian society (Christian inspiration and French genius), as well as the Duplessis Union Nationale provincial government that subsequently championed it, were, however, being threatened by the dramatic socioeconomic changes that had begun during World War II. The 1956 Tremblay Royal Commission established by the Duplessis government recognized this, particularly the threat posed by industrialization and urbanization. The commission's Report complained that the culture of industrial capitalism was secular rather than spiritual, scientific and technical rather than humanist, and individualistic rather than communal. The best way to combat these pernicious influences was to insist on Quebec's autonomy because it was a province "pas comme les autres" and to employ the provincial government to safeguard that autonomy. Although critics of traditional nationalism and of its Union Nationale defenders disagreed with this analysis of industrialization and urbanization (arguing instead that these forces should be welcomed), they nonetheless shared the view (indeed emphasized) that there should be an enhanced role for the state.[2] And like their opponents, they also looked to the provincial government – increasingly referred to as L'Etat du Québec – to lead a "Quiet Revolution" to transform the economic and social bases of Quebec society and to rid it of its old religion-centered, rural, and antistatist culture.

1 Perhaps the most trenchant criticism of Francophone attitudes toward democracy and their use (or misuse) of democratic institutions and processes was delivered by Pierre Elliott Trudeau, then a law professor at the University of Montreal. In an article published ten years before he became prime minister he contended that it would "encroach upon eternity" if he were to cite all the evidence in support of his thesis that French Canadians never have understood democracy, or been democrats, and that Anglophone elites have conspired with their Francophone counterparts to keep them that way (Trudeau, 1968:297–314).

2 These included the founders of the magazine *Cité Libre* and the mass circulation newspaper *Le Devoir* after it came under the editorial control of such nationalists as André Laurendeau and Gerard Filion.

Gingras and Nevitte (1983:321) have argued that although the Quiet Revolution was a watershed event ("There is no question that the Quiet Revolution did unleash secular forces in Quebec, enormously significant forces") the changes that occurred were not as complete as many observers have suggested. They contend that "uncritical acceptance of the Quiet Revolution paradigm tends to overdramatize the scope and nature of Quebec sociopolitical change." They maintain that the transformation of Quebec from a traditional religious to a secular society was far from complete because religion was and remains very important, especially among older groups of Québécois.[3] And the more important religion is, the more likely people are to feel that it helps maintain French-Canadian culture. In turn, the more strongly people feel that French-Canadian culture is important, the greater is their opposition to political independence (Gingras and Nevitte, 1983:315, Table 11.5).

The contemporary independence movement in Quebec is usually traced to 1957, with the emergence of an extreme conservative nationalist group, the Alliance Laurentienne. However, the Rassemblement pour l'Indépendance Nationale (RIN), created in 1960, was the first distinct organizational vehicle for the political expression of modern Quebec nationalism. The RIN wanted to promote a nonconfessional social democracy with a mixed economy, where public utility monopolies would be nationalized and worker participation could be encouraged. In 1968 a split in the RIN culminated in a resolution to terminate the party. The demise of the RIN, in turn, facilitated the growth of the newly created Parti Québécois (PQ),

---

3 They acknowledge, however, that "the institutional power of the Church has declined and the once organic relationship between church and state has been ruptured by the introduction of hospital insurance and medicare, the creation of the ministries of Cultural Affairs and of Education, and the establishment of an integrated network of state agencies providing basic as well as specialized health and social services." Other scholars (e.g., Hamelin, 1984) have observed that as early as the 1950s the Church's conservative leaders had recognized their weakened position and have engaged in a strenuous rearguard action over the years to shore it up. However, church attendance has declined, particularly among young people; trade unions have dropped their confessional ties; there has been a sharp drop in the number of recruits to the priesthood, and a significant number of priests have left the church. The unity of those who have remained has been strained by liberation theology on the one hand and a fundamentalism that is personal, devotional, and charismatic on the other. Finally, illustrative of the church's problems regarding its teachings on sexual relations and the family is that Quebec has the lowest birth rate and the highest abortion rate in the country. Evaluating these trends Ramsey Cook (1985:22) noted that "the mighty army of the church, once more numerous in proportion to population than in any country outside of Latin America, has fallen into irreversible decline."

On the role of religion in Canada more generally, Lipset cites a variety of surveys that indicate religion has become more secular and that Catholicism, especially in Quebec, has changed in a number of ways as just noted. In comparison to Americans, Canadians are less religious, moralistic, fundamentalist, puritanical in their attitudes toward sexual behavior and less frequent church attenders. Anglophone Canadians are more like Americans in most regards than are Francophones (Lipset, 1983:125–8). See also Reginald Bibby (1987).

Itself an outgrowth of the Mouvement Souveraineté Association formed in 1967 by René Lévesque, a former cabinet minister in the Liberal provincial government of Jean Lesage. Lévesque, who had been a newspaperman and television personality, had argued, when still a member of the Lesage government, that Quebec needed more economic and political autonomy than the federal system provided. Moreover, French-Canadians had to be recognized as equal partners with English-Canadians in the federation, and if the rest of Canada could not accept genuine binationalism "then we will have to think about separating" (*Le Devoir*, June 3, 1963, p. 9 and November 4, 1963, p. 1).[4] Lévesque viewed the PQ as the political vehicle that would unite all Québécois who believed the time to move toward independence was at hand. In his words, the new party would be "a synthesis of all valid perspectives."

During the first years of its existence the PQ tried to recruit new members, develop a broad program of social welfare measures, and convince the Quebec electorate of the appropriateness of both social democracy and independence (e.g., McRoberts, 1988:ch. 6). In the 1970 provincial election the party won seven seats and 23 percent of the popular vote. Although it captured only six legislative seats in the 1973 provincial election, it increased its share of the vote to 30 percent. In 1976, aided by adverse economic conditions and the scandals, incompetence, and plain bad luck of the Liberal administration of Robert Bourassa, it captured 41 percent of the vote and enough legislative seats to form a majority government.

In this election the PQ was careful to ask the electorate to cast a vote for good government rather than for a mandate to separate. They did, however, promise to hold a referendum on what they termed "sovereignty-association," political independence for Quebec coupled with some form of economic association with the rest of Canada, during their first term in office (Pinard and Hamilton, 1978). After delay and substantial internecine bickering, May 20, 1980 was chosen as the date the public would be asked to give the provincial government a mandate to *negotiate* sovereignty association rather than to simply *assert* Quebec's independence. The wording of the question was carefully chosen to attract maximum public support for the proposition. It represented an effort by the Péquistes "to deflect the discussion away from the theme of basic changes in the Canadian political community and toward the interpretation that what was being proposed

---

4 Throughout the 1960s a variety of protest movements were at work within Quebec. The most notorious was the Front de Libération du Québec (FLQ). The violent activities of the FLQ came to a head in 1970 with the kidnapping and murder of Pierre Laporte, a member of the Quebec Liberal provincial government of the time. The crisis was resolved when Prime Minister Trudeau invoked the draconian War Measures Act, an action widely applauded, even by many Québécois, as "protecting the fundamental unity of French society against the destructive excesses of left-wing intellectuals" (Clift, 1982:95–6).

was a series of changes to the regime" (Pammett et al., 1983:329). If so, they were partially successful. According to Pinard and Hamilton (1980), more than 40 percent of those who voted "yes" in the referendum were voting to start negotiations on a renewed form of federalism rather than sovereignty-association. Irrespective of their underlying motives, Francophone Quebecers divided their votes virtually evenly, whereas Anglophones overwhelmingly voted *non*, thereby decisively rejecting the government's proposal.

Despite this defeat the PQ managed to retain power in the 1981 Quebec provincial election. However, in his anger and disappointment Premier Lévesque refused to make Quebec a party to the 1982 agreement by which the British parliament formally turned over control of Canada's constitution to the Canadian government. Both the PQ's defeat in the subsequent 1985 provincial election and the landslide victory of the Conservative Party in the federal election of the previous year help explain the Meech Lake Accord of April 30, 1987. The failure to ratify it three years later testifies to the continuing problems Canada has faced over the years in becoming a nation as well as a state.

THE WEST

Unlike Alberta and Saskatchewan, which were federal creations carved out of the vast Western territories, British Columbia had to be enticed into Confederation "by the prospect of greater riches than might be had outside of it" (Blake, 1985:7).[5] Included was a promise from the Conservative federal government of the day that by 1885 a transcontinental railroad would be built that would link British Columbia to the rest of Canada. When the Conservatives were defeated in the election of 1874 and the Liberal government delayed completion of the Canadian Pacific Railroad, the British Columbia legislature passed two secession resolutions that were withdrawn only after the Conservative government of John A. Macdonald was returned to power in 1878. Blake (1985:52) contends that nothing has changed much in the past one hundred years; British Columbia still judges federal governments largely by how much they contribute to the economic welfare of the province.

British Columbians share the view of their Prairie neighbors that they are underrepresented in the House of Commons, that their positions on national policy issues do not receive the consideration they deserve and, more generally, that they never have been full and equal partners in Confederation because their interests have been consistently subordinated to those of Ontario and Quebec (Cairns, 1983). In some respects, however,

5 Both Alberta and Saskatchewan formally entered the federal union in 1905. Manitoba and British Columbia had entered in 1870 and 1871, respectively.

the province is different, if not unique. No province, with the possible exception of Quebec, operates two such different party systems at the federal and provincial levels of government. It is the only province in which the two major parties, the Liberal and Conservative, have exercised almost no significant influence in provincial politics since the early 1950s. And, although in some respects, British Columbia politics are the most class-polarized in the country, they do not invariably reflect the province's socioeconomic divisions (Galbraith, 1976). For example, the New Democrats support the entrenchment of property rights in the constitution to allay the concerns of the middle class (Blake, 1985:11). Moreover, some surveys (e.g., Blake, 1985) have indicated that working-class supporters of the NDP, even those whose jobs are dependent on the public sector, are less enthusiastic about an activist state than are members of the middle class. Notwithstanding the fact that the "objective" class basis of party politics periodically is muddied in the political marketplace, the issues of collectivism versus individualism and the appropriate role of the state in society long have been the poles around which party competition in the province has been organized.[6]

The concerns of political leaders during the first thirty years of the province's existence focused largely on "getting the province off the ground." There was overwhelming electoral support for the governing Conservatives because they were viewed as the federal party most committed to fulfilling the terms of union that had been negotiated, terms that were strongly opposed by the opposition Liberals as too generous. The period from 1903 to World War II is regarded as one in which genuine interparty competition developed between Liberals and Conservatives at both levels of the federal system. The parties built organizations that replaced personalistic politics organized around shifting factions within the dominant Conservative Party. According to Robin (1972:28–31), although there was substantial labor militancy during this period, the political left was unable to garner much electoral support. However, an independent British Columbia labor party did emerge during the first years of the Depression which united with other Western labor and socialist parties to form the new CCF (Co-operative Commonwealth Federation) Party. In the 1933 provincial election the CCF obtained major opposition status, a position briefly relinquished in the subsequent election, but thereafter steadfastly maintained until 1972, when it briefly assumed the reins of provincial power in Victoria (Robin, 1972:49).

To keep the CCF from provincial power the Liberals and Conservatives entered into a coalition during World War II. The coalition broke down in

6 According to Galbraith (1976) one set of attitudes emphasizes not only individual achievement but also the desirability of economic growth. The second set focuses on the distribution of wealth and egalitarianism. These conflicting attitudes make the class dimension of British Columbia politics more divisive than in other provinces.

1952 when the right-wing populist Social Credit Party narrowly defeated the CCF and formed a minority government. Social Credit, under the leadership of W. A. C. Bennett, remained in power until 1972 and, according to Blake, represented a triumph of the interior over the metropolitan areas of the province. Bennett defined his platform as free enterprise versus socialism: as a struggle between the left and socialism, on the one hand, and those who supported freedom and free enterprise, on the other (Blake, 1985:24). Bennett's tactics ensured that when Social Credit's defeat came, it would be at the hands of the NDP, the name the CCF had adopted in 1961, when it became the official arm of organized labor in Canada. Social Credit regained provincial power in 1975 and continues to hold it as this is written. Together, Social Credit and the NDP share the votes of an overwhelming majority of the provincial electorate. At the federal level, however, Social Credit is a nonstarter and British Columbians divide their votes among NDP, Conservative, and Liberal candidates for the House of Commons.

Over the years the policies Social Crediters have pursued in British Columbia have aimed largely at diversifying the economy so that it is not excessively reliant on resource extraction. This also has been the case in oil- and gas-rich Alberta. Before oil was discovered in Alberta, there were cattle. Brym (1977, cited in Gibbins, 1980:141–2) has argued that differences in the party systems of Alberta and neighboring Saskatchewan reflected differences in their agricultural economies. Alberta cattle ranchers were more independent and therefore more prone to support a free enterprise system championed by Social Credit, whereas Saskatchewan grain farmers were more dependent upon the government for both the production and marketing of their grain and therefore were more enamored of a collectivist, state oriented party such as the CCF/NDP.

Alberta has been described as having a "quasiparty" system because of long periods of one-partyism in which social and economic conflicts that normally would be mediated between parties in a competitive party system instead were worked out within a single dominant party (Macpherson, 1953). A "quasiparty" system also appears to be both cause and consequence of conflict between levels of government, and some of the antipathy that historically has existed between the Alberta and federal governments has been attributed to the former's peculiar party system. Liberals were in office in Ottawa when Alberta entered the federal union in 1905. That party not only won the first provincial election, it held office until 1917, when sharply declining agricultural prices and increasing support for populist rhetoric led to the formation of the United Farmers of Alberta. The United Farmers won the 1921 provincial election and remained in power until 1935, when they were supplanted by Social Credit.

The latter party and the CCF had their roots in the short-lived Progressive Party and the United Farmers movement, which were responses to the perceived exploitation of the Western provinces by central Canada. One manifestation of the "internal colonialism" to which Westerners felt they were being subjected was that farmers had to sell their principal product, wheat, in world markets, whereas a tariff wall originally erected in the nineteenth century as the centerpiece of the Macdonald Conservatives "National Policy" provided the manufactured products of Ontario and Quebec with a captive domestic market. Gibbins (1980:134) has observed that Saskatchewan Liberals were able to weather the agrarian revolt of the 1920s and early 1930s, but their Alberta counterparts were swept away by it and were never again able to capture power in Edmonton. In fact, since that time no party in Alberta has regained provincial office once having lost it. The Social Credit government, which took office in 1935 under the leadership of William ("Bible Bill") Aberhart, a high school teacher and evangelical minister, remained in power until 1971, when it was supplanted by the currently governing Conservatives. During the 1980s Social Credit virtually disappeared from the provincial political landscape.

When they had held office provincial "Socreds" were in the enviable position of never having to raise taxes because of the enormous oil and gas revenues that began to be generated in the late 1940s. According to Gibbins, these revenues enabled them at one and the same time to preach the virtues of free enterprise, rail against the evils of socialism, and establish a full-blown and lavishly funded welfare state. Ironically, the Socreds success also was responsible for their downfall, in that the province's prosperity encouraged continuous internal migration from less favored parts of Canada. These immigrants had no psychological attachments to Social Credit and they tended to both urbanize and secularize Alberta society. By 1971 the kind of "bible thumping" the Socreds had indulged in earlier was clearly out of fashion, and Peter Lougheed, the leader of a resurgent Conservative Party, was able to represent his fellow Tories as "younger, more technocratically skilled, more urban oriented, and more dynamic Social Crediters" (Gibbins, 1980:138). The Trudeau era in Ottawa largely coincided with Lougheed's leadership and the strongly provincialist focus he gave Alberta politics. Because of the province's wealth and his own popularity Lougheed soon became the principal spokesman of the West's opposition to the centralizing policies of the Liberal administrations of the 1970s and early 1980s. During this period the Alberta premier engaged in continuous and oftentimes bitter disputes with the federal government concerning the appropriate distribution of the riches generated by the sale of oil and other natural resources, the prices of which had escalated dramatically in the wake of the 1973 oil embargo (Richards and Pratt, 1979; Stevenson, 1989).

In Saskatchewan the federal Liberal Party generally, and Mr. Trudeau in particular, were cordially disliked because of their ill-considered and insensitive disparagement of the problems Western farmers faced in selling their wheat in world markets. What made his remarks especially galling was that the Liberals had been able to remain in power in Saskatchewan during the period of agrarian radicalism of the 1920s and 1930s because they then recognized that wheat was the cornerstone of the Saskatchewan economy and that any party wanting to win and hold office needed to protect it. In fact, the ability of both Liberals and Conservatives to monopolize provincial office until 1944 was partially a function of the rhetorical and policy importance they ascribed to agriculture. At that time they were supplanted by the CCF, which governed for the next twenty years. After seven years in the political wilderness the New Democrats were returned to power in 1971 on a platform emphasizing (not surprisingly) the importance of preserving the family farm. Eager (1980:43) has argued that such a platform tells us a lot about Saskatchewan politics: "It shows the contradiction of a conservative electorate which is willing to elect a radical party to office." However, other observers (e.g., Zakuta, 1964; Lipset, 1968) have expressed doubt about the radicalism of both a party that long ago began to soft-pedal its "socialism" and the conservatism of an electorate that over the years has appeared to so enthusiastically embrace a full panoply of welfare state programs.

As was the case in British Columbia, when Manitoba entered Confederation in 1870, and for some years afterward, party politics as such were personalistic, being confined to competition among loosely organized factions. The first real Conservative government was not formed until 1878. Gibbins notes that since that time Manitoba has been the stage upon which major national religious controversies periodically have been played out (Gibbins, 1980:145). He points to the hanging of Louis Riel, who in 1885 led the so-called Northwest Rebellion (an event that today might be labeled a war of national liberation) and to the Manitoba Schools Question, which involved state support for Catholic (and largely Francophone) schools. Ethnicity, then, has been a major source of political cleavage within Manitoba, first pitting Francophones against Anglophones and then those two charter groups against newer arrivals – many of whom migrated from Eastern and Central Europe during the first two decades of the twentieth century. Peterson (1972:78) has contended that following this immigration both Liberals and Conservatives purposely structured party conflict along ethnic rather than class lines, and even the Progressives (and the CCF before it became the NDP) initially targeted their partisan appeals primarily to voters of Anglo-Celtic descent. For example, during one stage of the Winnipeg general strike of 1921 (a class issue if there ever was one, and the single most dramatic event in Canadian labor history to that time) the sainted J. S. Woodsworth, founder of the CCF, assured an audience that "without hesitation, I say, that there was not a single foreigner in a position of leadership" (McNaught, 1959:116).

Many of the foreigners to whom Woodsworth referred settled in the north and center of the capital city of Winnipeg. Their influence in provincial politics and, indeed, the political influence of the entire Winnipeg metropolitan area, which contained the great bulk of the province's population, were severely diluted by the gross overrepresentation of rural areas. This was especially true of representation within the provincial legislature. In fact, a predominately rural-based and rural-oriented Liberal and Progressive coalition, appealing to the electorate of the time on a platform of fiscal conservatism and good government, was able to gain power in the Depression and stay in office for some thirty years. Even after the Conservatives left the coalition in 1950, the remnants, largely Liberals and Progressives, were able to govern the province for another eight years.

It was not until the most grievous of these electoral distortions were ameliorated in the 1960s that the CCF/NDP was able to effectively challenge the then governing Conservatives. The NDP won the provincial election of 1969 and retained power until 1977. Since then these two parties have alternated in office, with the Conservatives winning the two most recent elections and forming governments led by Gary Filmon. Early on he and his government distinguished themselves by their strong opposition to the aforementioned Meech Lake Accord whose principal architect was a fellow Conservative, Prime Minister Brian Mulroney.

Federal politics in the West were transformed in 1957, when one of Mulroney's predecessors, John Diefenbaker – who prior to his selection as national party leader was a small-town lawyer, virtually unknown outside of his native Saskatchewan – led the Conservatives to a close victory and minority government status. In the 1958 electoral campaign the Conservatives under Diefenbaker won what was then the greatest election victory in Canadian history. Diefenbaker's rhetorical style and repeated calls for a developed Canadian Northland in which great new cities would rise and enormous new wealth would be generated fired the imagination of voters during the 1958 election and made him a charismatic figure on the national political stage. Charisma was not enough, however, and he was reduced to heading a minority government after the 1962 election. The next year he was out of office and leader of the opposition. Diefenbaker's sojourn as leader of the Conservatives was associated with some fundamental changes in Canadian electoral politics. His party, which for years had been anathema to Western voters, henceforth made the Prairies its principal bastion. In so doing, it made the Liberals, claim of being the only truly "national" party ring hollow, kept the NDP share of the federal vote relatively constant, and effectively eliminated Social Credit parliamentary representation outside of Quebec. Moreover, as will be shown, the Conservatives eventually were able to make serious inroads into Liberal support in its Quebec heartland.

Importantly, however, these changing patterns of Conservative support did not significantly reduce the disaffection of either Quebec or the West from the central government. Nor were the Liberals able to accomplish this task. David Smith attributes the failure of the two old-line parties to build national regime support in these regions to the policies they pursued since the Diefenbaker era. "The Liberals Pan-Canadian policies were designed to incorporate Quebec, but they estranged the West. The Progressive Conservatives 'One Canada' and their 'community of communities' succeeded in the latter but failed in the former" (Smith, 1985:53). Although these arguments have merit, it is evident that the negative feelings of people in the two regions toward the national regime are grounded in historic and structural factors that antedate events of the past quarter century.

As argued in Chapter 1, in Quebec's case disaffection is rooted in the conditions that have made it a kind of "nation within a state." The failure to ratify the Meech Lake Accord in June 1990 and Quebec's reaction to the intense and bitter disputes occasioned by the Accord make it unlikely that these conditions will change in the foreseeable future. In contrast, problems of support in the West are grounded in longstanding perceptions that the region was exploited in the best colonial fashion for most of the first century of the country's existence, and because of demographic and political-structural factors (i.e., a Westminster-model parliamentary system and the failure of the Senate to represent regional interests effectively), it continues to be sacrificed or, at best, unfailingly short-changed. The historic tendency of Westerners to vent their grievances by forming "third parties" continues. The most recent such effort has involved the rapidly growing Reform Party, which, as of May 1990, had the support of as much as one-third of the electorate in the three Prairie provinces. That this party was able to generate this much support after only a few years of existence lends force to Andrew Malcolm's contention that Western discontent, although less visible than that associated with the ethnolinguistic grievances of Québécois, threatens "to jeopardize the future of the country at least as much as its more publicized language division" (Malcolm, 1985:71).

Recognition that powerful centrifugal forces long have been at work in the West as well as Quebec prompts us to analyze the correlates of political support among inhabitants of these two regions. After doing so, we conclude the chapter by investigating voting behavior in the Parti Québécois 1980 sovereignty-association referendum that was the centerpiece of the party's strategy to achieve an independent Quebec. By so doing, we may better comprehend how the country was able to survive what, thus far, has been its most serious challenge, and why it periodically teeters on the brink of falling apart. First, however, we will discuss how disaffection in Quebec and the West has been reflected in the ebb and flow of support for national political authorities by examining trends in the partisan identifications of the electorates of the two regions.

PARTY SUPPORT IN QUEBEC AND THE WEST

The preceding overview of the historical development of the party systems of Quebec, the Prairies and British Columbia has emphasized the evolution of differing patterns of public support for federal and provincial parties. Our national survey data enable us to document these regional differences and to examine trends within them over the past two decades. We first will map the direction and cross-level consistency of federal and provincial party identifications, and then consider their strength and stability.

Direction

Until very recently the Liberal Party has been the dominant force in federal politics in Quebec and substantial majorities of Quebecers (60 percent across the 1965–80 national surveys) identified themselves as federal Liberals. During the 1980s, however, the percentage of Liberal identifiers declined substantially, falling to 42 percent in 1984 and to only 28 percent immediately after the 1988 federal election. One-party dominance also has characterized the Prairies, but here the Progressive Conservatives have had the upper hand. Between 1965 and 1988 federal PC identifications in the Prairies averaged 45 percent, and since 1974 no other party has had the support of more than 28 percent of the electorate. The British Columbia pattern is different; on average, identification with the three national parties has been much more equally distributed than in Quebec or the Prairies. Between 1965 and 1988 the Liberals and the PCs both averaged 29 percent, and the NDP, 28 percent. However, these overall figures mask a sharp decrease in Liberal support and an accompanying increase in PC identification in the 1970s, as well as a decline and subsequent rebound in federal PC strength between 1985 and 1988.

Even larger differences in party identification are apparent at the provincial level in the three regions. As noted, since the late 1960s provincial party competition in Quebec has revolved around the struggle over the province's constitutional status and the possibility that Quebecers might sever their ties with Canada. The Parti Québécois has been the vehicle of the "indépendantistes," whereas the provincial Liberals have championed the cause of a renewed Canadian federal union. A reflection of the centrality of this conflict is the overwhelming numbers of Quebecers who have identified with one of these two parties. Between 1974 and 1988, the Liberals enjoyed a decided advantage in provincial party identifiers, averaging 51 percent to the PQ's 30 percent, but this largely has been a function of Liberal strength among non-Francophones. Age differences also have been very significant. After its formation in 1968 the Parti Québécois quickly attracted the enthusiastic support of many younger Francophones and, although the nexus between age and party identification has moderated somewhat since then, it remains readily apparent. As will be discussed below, the strength of the PQ appeal for younger Quebecers reflects their relatively low levels of national regime and community support and the resulting attractiveness of the Péquistes project for an independent Quebec.

Provincial party identification in the Prairies resembles its federal counterpart. In five surveys conducted between 1974 and 1988, Tory identification averaged 53 percent, whereas the Liberals and NDP each averaged approximately 18 percent. The extent of PC strength in the region as a whole in great part reflects the massive support enjoyed by the party in Alberta. No party has a comparable level of support in the other two Prairie provinces (Manitoba and Saskatchewan), although the Conservatives have large numbers of identifiers in these provinces as well.

In British Columbia, the distribution of provincial party identifications is very different than anywhere else in Canada. The duopolistic competition between the Socreds and New Democrats is reflected in a distribution of provincial party identifications in which a very large majority of the BC electorate regularly has identified with these parties. This pattern has been very stable since the late 1970s. However, despite the Socreds repeated electoral victories, the balance of Social Credit and NDP partisans has remained almost even over this period, the average percentages of their identifiers being 36 percent and 37 percent, respectively. These data on the direction of federal and provincial party identifications in Quebec and the four Western provinces are one illustration of the complexity of the Canadian party system. Even within regions characterized by relative economic and geographic homogeneity there are marked differences in patterns of partisanship.

Inconsistency

The inconsistency of party identifications at the national and subnational levels of government is another striking feature of party support. The pronounced differences in the strength of various parties in federal and provincial politics in Quebec and British Columbia suggest that large numbers of persons in those two provinces do not identify with the same party at both levels of government. This is, in fact, the case. In 1983, for example, 32 percent of Quebecers and 48 percent of British Columbians identified with different federal and provincial parties. Five years later, the percentage of "split" identifiers in Quebec climbed to 49 percent. Partisan inconsistency in Quebec and BC has been much greater than in the Prairies, where 79 percent of the respondents in our 1983 survey had the same federal and provincial party identifications and only 11 percent had split identifications. In 1988 these figures were substantially unchanged. These patterns of federal and provincial party identifications are not unique to the 1980s.

Rather, partisan inconsistency is a longstanding feature of political attitudes in Canada (Figure 3.3), and there are good reasons to believe that striking differences in federal and provincial party identification have obtained in British Columbia since at least the early 1950s and, in Quebec, since at least the 1930s. The Prairies again are a contrasting case in that the rapid demise of Social Credit in Alberta in the early 1970s and the growth of support for the PCs at that time was accompanied by a decrease in partisan inconsistency in that province. Because countervailing trends did not occur in Manitoba or Saskatchewan, the change in Alberta lowered levels of inconsistent partisanship in the region as a whole.

Patterns of federal and provincial party identification in Quebec and the West have been quite fluid in recent years. During the 1970s and early 1980s, despite the sharp disagreements between the federal Liberals and the Péquistes concerning Quebec independence, large minorities (35 to 40 percent) of Péquistes remained federal Liberals and only about 10 percent were Conservatives. However, the PQ–Liberal nexus eroded in the 1980s as Péquiste identifiers began moving strongly to the federal Tories. By 1988 over half (51 percent) of the Péquistes were PCs and only 9 percent were Liberals. The latter party's loss of support in Quebec is critical for understanding Conservative successes in that province in the 1984 and 1988 federal elections.

In the Prairies and British Columbia patterns of inconsistent federal and provincial party identifications also have involved Liberal identifiers. In 1988, for example, 22 percent of British Columbia federal Liberals identified with the provincial NDP, and twice as many identified with Social Credit. In the Prairies, 9 percent of federal Liberals were provincial New Democrats and nearly three times as many were provincial PCs. The Prairies and British Columbia differ, however, in the provincial distributions of federal Conservative support. In British Columbia a large majority of federal Tories are provincial Socreds. In the Prairies, in contrast, virtually all of them also identify with the PCs provincially. Given the size of the cohort of federal PCs in the Prairies, this latter pattern does much to explain the relatively high level of partisan consistency. Party loyalty among Prairie New Democrats also is relevant, however; an overwhelming percentage of NDPers maintain the same party ties in national and provincial politics. British Columbia New Democrats also exhibit strong cross-level partisan consistency, thereby indicating that the high level of split party identification in this province is due largely to the prevalence of Social Credit provincial identifications among federal Liberals and PCs.

Recall that in the nineteenth century the Liberals were able to build strong party support at the provincial level and to utilize this as a springboard for success in national politics in the twentieth century. Over the past half century, however, the party's strength has eroded throughout the West, and this has negatively affected their ability to marshal support in federal elections as well as provincial ones. In contrast, although during the same period many Quebecers identified first with the Union Nationale and more recently with the Parti Québécois provincially, they continued to identify with and to vote for the federal Liberals. In the 1980s, however, identification with and electoral support for the federal Liberals declined, and Quebec, like the West, returned Conservative MPs to the House of Commons.

Strength

In comparison to a country such as the United States, Canada's federal system is highly decentralized. The importance of the provinces is widely recognized by political elites and the general public alike. Provincial party attachments are as strong and as influential as their national counterparts. In fact, provincial party identifications actually are stronger than federal ones in every region except Ontario. The relative strength of provincial partisanship is especially evident in Quebec and British Columbia. In 1983, for example, 30 percent of Quebecers held "very strong" provincial party identifications but only 19 percent were "very strong" federal party identifiers. In BC the comparable percentages were 32 percent and 22 percent, respectively. The provincial "edge" in partisan strength also exists in the Prairies, although the difference is less pronounced. An overall "strength of party identification index"[7] tells the same story. Provincial party identification is consistently stronger than its federal counterpart in every region but Ontario, with the biggest differences being in British Columbia and Quebec. That many Canadians in the West and Quebec identify more strongly with provincial parties than with their federal counterparts is yet another illustration of the difficulties the latter have experienced in generating the public support needed to transcend longstanding regional particularisms.

Stability

A principal reason that party identification held "pride of place" in early studies of support for political authorities was its presumed stability. As such, it was a long-term element in the "funnel of causality" that affected support both directly and indirectly (Campbell et al., 1960, 1966). In the past two decades this assumption has been challenged in research conducted in the United States and elsewhere (e.g., Budge, Crewe, and Farlie, 1976; Fiorina, 1981) and, as shown in Chapter 3, it certainly lacks validity in Canada. Analyses of five panel surveys conducted between 1974 and

---

7 The index is created by scoring "very strong" identifiers + 3; "fairly strong" identifiers + 2; "not very strong" or 'leaning" identifiers + 1; and nonidentifiers 0.

1988[8] reveal high levels of partisan instability in all regions over even relatively brief time intervals. Between 1983 and 1984, for example, the percentages of unstable federal party identifiers were 20 percent in the Prairies
and 38 percent in both Quebec and British Columbia. Provincially, the
percentages were 17 percent in the Prairies, 27 percent in Quebec, and 32
percent in British Columbia. Party identifications in Quebec and the West
clearly are not "unmoved movers" in the skein of causal forces influencing
political support at either level of the federal system.

The most recent illustration of the mutability of partisan attachments is
the rise of the Reform movement and its subsequent institutionalization as
the Reform Party. The party was only established in 1987 with its base
in Calgary, Alberta. Like its predecessors of the 1930s, CCF and Social
Credit, Reform entered almost immediately into national politics. Led by
Preston Manning, the son of a longtime Alberta Social Credit provincial
premier, the party advocates a conservative social and economic agenda,
together with such traditional Western political causes as Senate reform. In
1989 it had gained a foothold in both the Senate and the House of Commons (one member in each). More important, in a December 1990 survey
it claimed the allegiance of nearly 4 percent of the Canadian electorate.
Not surprisingly, its newfound partisans were concentrated almost entirely
in the West. In the three Prairie provinces as a whole 16 percent were
Reform identifiers in national politics, and in energy-rich Alberta, where
discontent with national political arrangements has been most intense during the past twenty years, fully one voter in five identified with the party.
More detailed analyses indicate that many Reform partisans formerly identified with the Conservative Party in both national and provincial politics.

In summary, the characteristics of party support in Quebec and the West
make clear that Canadian parties have difficulty in performing some of the
functions democratic theorists ascribe to them. More specifically, although
they periodically attract the attention and loyalties of significant proportions of the public, they have not been able to sustain these loyalties over
time. Nor have they been able to generate issue agendas or, when in office,
implement public policies that transcend purely regional interests, whether
cultural or economic. Their failure in these regards helps explain why
seemingly trivial as well as consequential political and economic events
periodically have served to catalyze regional disaffection and generate
crises of support in the national political system.

THE BASES OF POLITICAL SUPPORT IN QUEBEC AND THE WEST

The analyses in Chapter 4 revealed that evaluative variables are important
predictors of political support. What is true nationally is also true regional-

8 The panels are: 1974–79, 1979–80, 1980–83, 1983–84, and 1984–88.

ly. In both Quebec and the West people's judgments about the economy's good health and the government's ability to manage it successfully were significant predictors of support for Canada as a political community, the government of Canada, and political authorities. Although aggregate support for the national political community is significantly lower in Quebec than in the West, the effects of economic judgments on variations in support for Canada were stronger for Quebec residents (Figure 5.1). This finding is consistent with the belief expressed by political and media pundits at the time of the 1980 sovereignty-association referendum that in the privacy of the voting booth fears about the economic future may have helped make thousands of Quebecers into *"non"* voters. Additional evidence in support of this supposition is that the correlation (eta) between community support and one's own material condition was twice as great for Quebecers as for Westerners (Figure 5.2). Further, people's judgments about the national economy and their own financial circumstances had strong effects on support for both parliament and the federal bureaucracy and a more modest, but still significant, impact on support for the judiciary in both Quebec and the West (data not shown). All of the relationships between judgments about the equity–fairness of the political system and federal government effectiveness, on the one hand, and support for the political community, the government of Canada, regime institutions, and the authorities, on the other, also were statistically significant in both regions (Figures 5.3 and 5.4).

The evaluative variables, together with sociodemographic and attitudinal factors, were entered in a series of regression analyses to predict support for the national political community, regime, and authorities. These analyses indicate that with regard to the attribution of support, there is really not one Quebec but two: Francophones and identifiers with the Parti Québécois constitute one group, and non-French and Liberal Party identifiers the other. Partisanship also is important in the West; an identification with the national Liberal Party is a kind of anchor of support for Ottawa, i.e., for both the government of Canada and the national political authorities – as one might anticipate in a region that has been governed provincially for significant periods of time over the past half century by parties, the CCF–NDP and Social Credit, that have their historic roots in Western discontent. Equally important were: (A) economic judgments about the current and future conditions of the economy and the federal government's ability to manage it successfully; and (B) the fairness and effectiveness of the federal government. Economic judgments also significantly affected support in Quebec as did trust in political authorities and orientations to the federal as opposed to provincial governments. Lastly, although on average we are able to predict approximately 25 percent of the variance in our support measures, this was not the case for the analysis of support for Canada among Westerners. This is because there is no analogue in the

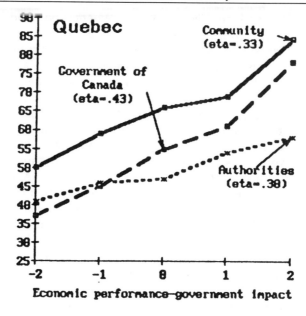

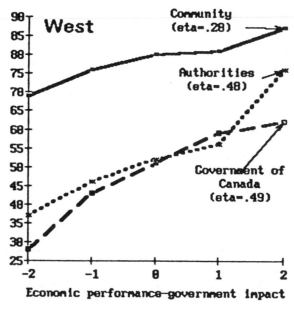

Figure 5.1. *Mean support for national political community, government of Canada, and national political authorities by national economic performance–government impact, Quebec and the West, 1983*

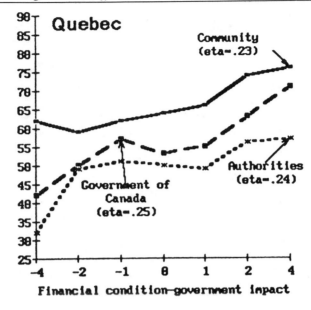

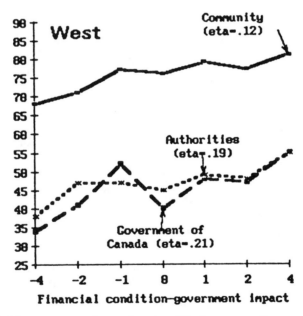

Figure 5.2. *Mean support for national political community, government of Canada and national political authorities by personal financial condition– government impact, Quebec and the West, 1983*

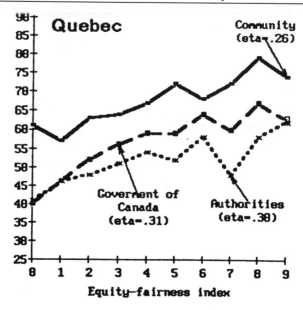

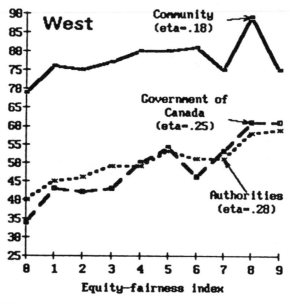

Figure 5.3. *Mean support for national political community, government of Canada and national political authorities by equity–fairness index, Quebec and the West, 1983*

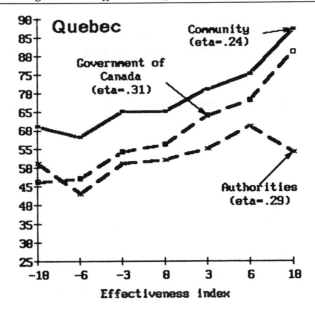

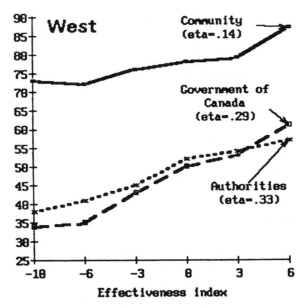

Figure 5.4. *Mean support for national political community, government of Canada, and national political authorities by government effectiveness index, Quebec and the West, 1983*

West for the explanatory power of long-term socialization effects proxied by French ethnicity in Quebec and, relatedly, because support of the Canadian political community is stronger and less variable in the former region than in the latter.

COMMUNITY SUPPORT AND COMMUNITY CHOICE

Quebec or Canada?

We observed at the beginning of this book that the May 1980 sovereignty-association referendum constituted a profound test of Quebecers support for Canada and its political system because never before in the country's history had continuation in its current form been put to the test of a public vote. The Parti Québécois had come to power in November 1976 promising to hold a referendum on the province's future relationship with Canada. At that time PQ leaders understood that only a minority of Quebecers favored either sovereignty-association or outright independence. Consequently, the idea of a deferred referendum was an important element in the PQ's *étapiste* (step-by-step) strategy, a means of uncoupling a vote for the party in the 1976 provincial election from the larger issue of the desirability of a sovereign Quebec. Péquiste strategists assumed that over time support for their project would grow; that their party could use the instruments and resources of the provincial government to facilitate its growth; and that the magnitude of the shift in public opinion would be sufficient for a referendum proposal to pass before the party's five-year term of office expired. These assumptions were problematic because, despite the party's efforts to deflect attention from it, the PQ's electoral victory was viewed in both Quebec and in the rest of Canada as a "clear and present danger" to the future of the country. Federalist forces quickly mobilized and various plans for limited change or "renewed federalism" were presented to attract the growing number of Quebecers who might not be ready for either independence or sovereignty-association, but who nonetheless were dissatisfied with the constitutional status quo. Consequently, the PQ quickly found itself embroiled in a bitter struggle for the "hearts and minds" of the Quebec electorate.

The battle proved difficult. Contrary to their initial expectations, PQ strategists found that almost three years after coming to power, public support for independence remained weak. Our May 1979 survey data show, for example, that only 16 percent favored it and fully 75 percent were opposed (Table 5.1).[9] Prospects for sovereignty-association looked better;

---

9 The question sequence on constitutional options was prefaced by the following statement: "I am going to mention several constitutional options for Quebec. As I read *each* over, please tell me if you are very favorable toward it, somewhat favorable, somewhat un-

Table 5.1. *Quebecers' attitudes toward constitutional options, 1979, 1980 (in percent)*

	Constitutional Options								
	No Change		Renewed Federalism		Special Status		Sovereignty Association		Independence	
	79	80	79	80	79	80	79	80	79	80
Favorable	32	28	38	62	35	41	27	45	16	25
Unfavorable	59	68	25	31	32	38	43	51	75	72
No opinion, don't know	8	5	37	7	34	21	30	4	9	3

Note: 1979 national election survey, N = 752(question asked in Quebec only); 1980 Quebec sovereignty-association referendum, N = 325.

although only 27 percent favored it, nearly a third (30 percent) were un-decided. Similarly, when asked how they would vote in a hypothetical sovereignty-association referendum, although only 28 percent said they would vote *oui*, just as many were unsure. However, a large majority continued to oppose the status quo, and nearly two-fifths favored some sort of renewed federalism.

In the following year the struggle between the PQ and its federal-ist adversaries intensified as both sides presented detailed briefs on the projected economic, political and social consequences of sovereignty-association. The number of Quebecers undecided about this and other con-stitutional options decreased. However, 1979–80 panel data indicated that those who had been undecided in 1979 split almost evenly – 11 percent moved to approval, whereas 10 percent moved to disapproval. About twice as many of those switching their opinions on sovereignty-association in this period moved to a favorable position (9 percent versus 4 percent), but these numbers were relatively small. Although the proposal gained popu-larity in the run-up to the referendum, it still lacked majority approval, and when the vote actually was held in May 1980, only 45 percent said that they favored it (Table 5.1).

Faced with discouraging news from public opinion polls and the impend-ing expiration of their term in office, PQ leaders decided to soften the wording of the question to be posed in the referendum. Voters would be called on only to grant the government authority to open negotiations with their federal counterparts. By putting the question this way, the Péquistes

---

favorable, or very unfavorable." The options were: (a) no change, (b) renewed federal-ism, (c) special status for Quebec in Confederation, (d) sovereignty-association, (e) in-dependence. In our analyses the "very" and "somewhat" favorable responses have been collapsed as have the "very" and "somewhat" unfavorable ones.

hoped to obfuscate the issue enough to muster the additional votes required to win and to claim they had received a mandate to open discussions with Ottawa. If the federal government refused to negotiate, other courses of action might be entertained – even a unilateral declaration of independence was considered within the realm of possibility by some observers.

The party's decision to hold a referendum may have been a logical extension of its hitherto successful *étapiste* strategy, but its ability to win with even a softened question wording was doubtful because the percentage of voters favoring some form of renewed federalism had increased substantially since 1979. At the time of the referendum 62 percent favored this option. Much of the support for renewed federalism came from persons who had been undecided in 1979, but some of it came from people who had changed their minds. Between May 1979 and May 1980, almost twice as many Quebecers (12 percent) came to favor renewed federalism as those who decided that they were opposed to it (7 percent). Clearly, if the PQ was to obtain its mandate, it had to shift the public's attention away from sovereignty-association and focus it instead on the popularity of the party and its charismatic leader, René Lévesque. Not only was it unable to do so, but perhaps the bitterest pill to swallow was that the referendum question was approved by only a tiny majority of Francophone voters.

Political support and competing constitutional options. Long before the referendum balloting, and despite the PQ's strenuous attempts to blur the issue, sovereignty-association was widely seen as a grave threat to the continued existence of Canada. Attitudes toward sovereignty-association and the principal competing constitutional option, renewed federalism, were closely associated in the public mind with regime and community as well as authorities sentiments. On the eve of the referendum, support for the governing Parti Québécois decreased from 80 points among those strongly favoring sovereignty-association to only 32 points among those strongly opposing it. Support for the provincial Liberals, in contrast, increased from 30 to 74 points as attitudes toward sovereignty-association moved from strongly positive to strongly negative. The correlations between party support and attitudes toward renewed federalism were equally strong, and were mirror images of those for sovereignty-association.

Impressive relationships also characterized attitudes toward competing constitutional options and feelings for Canada and the national political system. Average support for Canada increased from 53 among those strongly favoring sovereignty-association to 85 among those opposing it, and support for the Canadian government and parliament increased from 43 to 75 and from 50 to 65, respectively, among these groups (Figure 5.5). Relationships involving renewed federalism were precisely the opposite – support for Canada, the Canadian government and parliament all decreased sharply as feelings about renewed federalism moved from positive to negative.

These striking patterns demonstrate that Quebecers understood that the sovereignty-association referendum was much more than a conventional authorities-level battle between an incumbent provincial government, on the one hand, and its Liberal opposition in Quebec City and its counterpart in Ottawa, on the other. As Pammett et al. (1983:330) note: "[o]ne major factor enhancing the importance of community-level voting in the referendum was the conviction of a large part of the Quebec population that the real goal of the PQ was not sovereignty-association but independence." Relationships between our support measures and attitudes toward independence underscore the point. Correlations between regime and community support, on the one hand, and independence, on the other, were very strong, and closely paralleled those for sovereignty-association. Persons favoring independence had much lower support scores than did those who opposed it (Figure 5.5). These correlations were important because, as noted, many voters believed that sovereignty-association was independence "in disguise." A year before the referendum 40 percent of the public defined sovereignty-association as involving either "independence" or "separation" for Quebec, and at the time of balloting attitudes toward the two options were tightly linked ($\varphi = 53$); 24 percent favored both sovereignty-association and independence and 51 percent opposed both options. Virtually all of the remainder (23 percent) favored sovereignty-association but opposed independence. To have any hope of winning the PQ needed to secure the votes of all of the latter group because they were the ones who could distinguish between the two concepts.

Oui or Non?   During the decade preceding the referendum, opinion surveys had shown that support for sovereignty-association and independence was largely confined to younger Québécois (e.g., Pinard and Hamilton, 1977; 1978). This strong relationship persisted in the referendum itself. The percentage voting "oui" declined monotonically from 83 percent among those aged 18–25 to only 26 percent among those over 65. Persons with higher levels of formal education, those with higher incomes and professional occupations and men also were more likely to cast a *oui* ballot, but these correlations were quite modest. A probit analysis of referendum voting[10] using these sociodemographic variables as predictors accounted for 33 percent of the variance, with age, language and gender, but not education, income, or (professional) occupation, exerting significant effects (Table 5.2, Model A). The several sociodemographic predictors were able to classify 68 percent of the referendum voters correctly.[11]

As observed above, feelings about the Canada and its political regime are related to several attitudinal and evaluative variables. Although mea-

10 In these analyses the dependent variable, referendum voting, is scored *oui* = 1, *non* = 0.
11 The proportion of cases correctly classified is inevitably high when the dependent variables is highly skewed (Aldrich and Nelson 1984:56–7). This is not a problem here: the sample vote shares are 47 percent *oui* and 53 percent *non*.

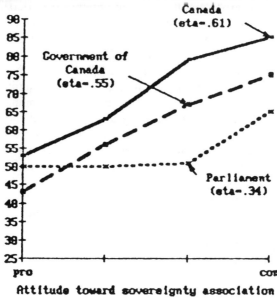

Attitude toward sovereignty association

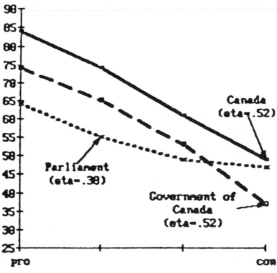

Attitude toward renewed federalism

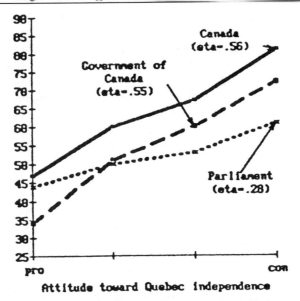

Figure 5.5. *Mean support for Canada, the government of Canada, and parliament among Quebecers by attitudes toward constitutional options, May 1980*

Table 5.2. *Probit analyses of voting in sovereignty-association referendum*

	Model				
Predictor Variables	<u>A</u>	<u>B</u>	<u>C</u>	<u>D</u>	<u>E</u>
Age cohort	-.30a	-.16c	-.14c	-.15c	-.00
Education	.01	.00	.00	-.00	-.00
Gender	-.31c	-.26d	-.13	-.01	-.38d
Income	.01	.12	.12	.14	.15
Language	1.01a	.96b	.59d	1.05a	.35
Professional occupation	.00	-.01	-.35	-.19	-.32
Federal government effectiveness	t	-.11c	-.01	-.01d	-.00
Political system equity-fairness	t	-.01b	-.01c	-.01d	-.01c
Federal v. provincial orientation	t	-.38a	-.26c	-.30b	-.29b
Economic evaluations: egocentric	t	-.01	-.00	.00	.01
future	t	.00	.01	.01	.33d
MP responsiveness	t	-.01d	-.03	-.00	-.01c
Costs-benefits of federal system	t	.23b	.13	.13	.24c
Support: federal government	t	t	t	-.003a	t
national community	t	t	-.01a	t	t
Parti Quebecois	t	t	t	t	.01a
Constant	.00	-.44	3.04a	1.20d	-3.57a
Estimated R² =	.33	.60	.88	.89	.90
% correctly classified=	68	82	85	82	89

Note: t - variable not included in model; a-p ≤.001; b-p ≤.01; c-p ≤.05; d-p ≤.10; one-tailed test

sures of efficacy, trust and sociotropic economic evaluations were unavailable in the referendum survey, we did have versions of the others and, thus, we can assess how they affected referendum voting. Employing them in a probit analysis revealed that several behaved as expected (Table 5.2, Model B). Positive evaluations of governmental effectiveness, equity-fairness, and MPs responsiveness all reduced the probability of a *oui* vote. Those whose orientations toward the federal system were national rather than provincial were less likely to vote *oui* and those who believed that the costs and benefits of the federal system were unfairly distributed had a higher probability of doing so. Collectively, these variables increased the variance explained to 60 percent – nearly double that for the analysis in which only the sociodemographic characteristics were employed. Similarly, the percentage correctly classified climbed to nearly 82 percent.

We next considered the impact of supportive feelings about authorities, regime and community. The latter two types of support were highly inter-correlated, making it difficult to disentangle their individual effects on referendum voting. Accordingly, we entered support for Canada and the government of Canada in separate analyses. When community support was entered the variance explained increased to 88 percent, and when regime support was entered it increased to 89 percent. In these two analyses, the percentages of voters correctly classified were 85 percent and 82 percent, respectively (Table 5.2, Models C and D). Provincial authorities support (support for the Parti Québécois) also had strong (negative) relationships with community and regime support. Substituting PQ support for the measures of regime and community support revealed that the former had a very impressive impact on referendum voting – it boosted the explained variance to fully 90 percent, with 89 percent of the voters being correctly classified (Table 5.2, Model E).

In interpreting these findings, it is important to remember that negative feelings about the national government and Canada among Quebecers motivated the formation of the Parti Québécois. Those feelings continued to be an important – perhaps the most important – source of the party's appeal in the period before the referendum. Thus, the total effects of national regime and community support on behavior in the referendum were partially mediated by feelings about the PQ and thus were even greater than those indicated by our probit analyses which capture direct effects only. Similarly, analyses discussed earlier in this chapter have shown that several attitudinal and evaluative variables in our referendum voting models had significant effects on Quebecers feelings about the national regime and community. Such attitudes and evaluations thereby affected referendum voting indirectly by influencing support at the regime or community levels, which, in turn, affected feelings about the political authorities.

Non and Oui. When the referendum votes were tallied, nearly three Quebecers in five (59 percent) rejected the Parti Québécois request for a mandate to negotiate sovereignty-association with Ottawa. Although the emotionally charged atmosphere surrounding the event created great anxiety, in retrospect, the outcome was not surprising because the PQ clearly faced an uphill struggle in their battle to rally a *oui* majority. Attitudes toward sovereignty-association and the major competing constitution option, renewed federalism, were closely associated not only with support for the PQ, but also with feelings about Canada and its political system. However, although a near majority of Quebecers (49 percent) felt positively about the PQ, many more (64 percent) were positively disposed toward the government of Canada, and fully 75 percent felt this way about Canada. The PQ had waged its successful 1976 campaign by carefully focusing public attention on the failures of the then incumbent provincial Liberals rather than on sovereignty-association or independence. By so doing, it successfully decoupled voting choice from questions of support for the Canadian polity. But despite the Péquistes best efforts, such a separation was impossible in the referendum campaign. The PQ had important strategic advantages grounded in its status as the governing party in Quebec City, but profederalist forces worked mightily to ensure that voters understood that a sovereignty-association proposal, however worded, challenged the continued viability of the national regime and Canada itself. Because they did – and because a majority of Quebecers continued to support both – the referendum failed.

SUMMARY

We began this chapter by observing that Quebec has changed dramatically since the end of World War II. It has become urbanized, industrialized, and increasingly secular, although perhaps not quite as secular as often has been assumed. The Quiet Revolution of the 1960s accelerated the transformation of its economic and social bases, the erosion of a religious-centered, rural and antistatist culture, and laid the groundwork for the coming to power of the Parti Québécois, whose raison d'être was the establishment of an independent Quebec.

The PQ did its best to obfuscate the issue of independence in its 1980 referendum by employing a soft question and by arguing that a *oui* vote would lead to an unlocking ("déblocage") of the province's gridlocked relations with the federal government. However, a great majority of Quebecers understood that sovereignty-association was a euphemism for a process that eventually would culminate in a Canada *sans* Quebec. The sovereignty-association referendum failed for a number of reasons. Political support in Quebec is a function of ethnicity, language, economic evaluations, partisanship, and considerations of the relative effectiveness and fairness of the federal government. Importantly, however, although many Quebecers rejected the constitutional status quo, at the time the referendum was held a majority remained sufficiently positively disposed toward

Canada, its government, and national political leaders to reject the
Péquiste option of a politically sovereign Quebec.

In Western Canada language and ethnicity are not significant correlates
of support, but economic evaluations and judgments about the effective
and equitable operation of the federal government are. The West, like
Quebec, has changed since World War II, in the sense that the region has
become more urbanized, developed a broader economic base, and most
important, the two most westerly provinces have become economic
"haves" rather than "have nots" within the federal system. However, these
favorable economic developments have not overcome the long-held Western belief that the federal playing field is tilted against them. Indeed, the
new prosperity may well have had the opposite effect. Federal-provincial
conflicts in the 1970s and early 1980s over the distribution of wealth generated by the West's oil and other natural resources seemed to provide Westerners with proof positive that their disadvantaged position in the Canadian federation remained unchanged. Consistent with this interpretation,
our surveys conducted in the 1970s and 1980s show that many Westerners
expressed misgivings about the quality of representation provided by the
existing parliamentary system and negatively assessed the effectiveness and
equity–fairness of the operation of the national government and existing
federal arrangements. These negative judgments diminished support for
the national authorities, regime, and community.

A number of times we have noted that Canada continues to experience
national integration problems that other mature democracies put behind
them long ago. Analyses indicating how important people's perceptions of
fair and equitable treatment by the federal government are in explaining
support can be interpreted as reflecting the bases of Quebec's and the
West's disaffection. However, their histories indicate that their respective
interpretations of what constitutes fair and equitable treatment are different. For Quebecers it has meant recognition by the rest of Canada that
Quebec, at the very least, is an equal partner in the national enterprise
called Canada. But it is a partner that generally has wanted to be left to
develop in its own way – to be *maître chez nous*. In contrast, for the West
fair and equitable treatment has meant being regarded as a major player on
a "level" national political playing field. Like the Rodney Dangerfield
character, the West long has wanted "respect" from central Canada and
the "feds." The defeat of the sovereignty-association referendum, the 1984
election of a national Conservative government, that government's
attempt via the Meech Lake Accord to recognize Quebec's "special status"
while making it a "full partner" in Confederation, and the 1988 reelection
of the Conservatives – a party whose electoral stronghold remains the West
but which now enjoys substantial support in Quebec – suggest that residents of both regions now may believe that they are getting somewhat
more of the fair and equitable treatment they so long have desired. At the

same time, the rise of the Reform Party and the concomitant weakening of Conservative strength in the West since 1988 suggest that Westerners are hardly satisfied with the actions of the Tory government in Ottawa. Also, that government's inability to obtain the requisite consent of all ten provinces to the Meech Lake Accord indicates that consensus on vital constitutional issues has not been achieved. The frequently strident and even apocalyptic rhetoric of the debate surrounding the failure to ratify the Accord and the accompanying reinvigoration of separatist sentiment in Quebec emphasize that deep and longstanding disagreements about the nature of the Canadian federation remain unresolved. Emotionally charged regional and ethnolinguistic cleavages persist, and they render political support in Canada highly problematic in the 1990s.

6

Elections and political support

Elections are basic means by which the people of a democracy bend government to their wishes. In both their symbolism and their reality free elections
distinguish democratic regimes.

V. O. Key, Jr., *Public Opinion and American Democracy*, p. 458

In a definition that has become famous, Joseph Schumpeter (1942:269)
contended that elections are what democracy is all about. A democracy is
an "institutionalized arrangement for arriving at political decisions in
which individuals acquire the power to decide by means of a competitive
struggle for the people's vote."[1] At their most fundamental level elections
can be thought of as institutionalized alternatives to revolution. It is argued
that when elections are genuinely free and competitive they help safeguard
freedom; make possible peaceful transitions of political power; promote
political stability by providing ordinary citizens with their principal vehicle
of participation in political life; encourage them to engage in other forms
of conventional political behavior; and provide them with a crash course
on major problems confronting their country. In addition, elections are
credited with helping democracies to achieve, or come close to achieving,
formal political equality through the mechanism of one person, one vote.
Perhaps most important from the perspective of democratic theory, elections are designated as the principal institutional mechanisms for providing
ordinary citizens with regular opportunities to influence the policies of persons whom they select to lead them, and some scholars have contended
that in periodic "critical elections" changes in the content and direction of
those policies can be profound indeed (e.g., Key, 1955:3–18; Campbell, et
al., 1960:531–8; Burnham, 1970).

Even those who contend that for a variety of reasons elections really do
not give people either genuine choices among alternative policy options, or

---

1 Anthony Downs's (1957) and Robert Dahl's (1971) works are probably the two best-known
attempts by theorists to set out the conditions that make elections so fundamental to democracy. See also Mayo (1960); Lipset (1963); Bachrach (1967); Pateman (1970); Macpherson
(1977); Pennock (1979); Powell (1982); and Sartori (1987).

the ability to influence what those options are, acknowledge that elections provide opportunities to choose between competing candidates and, relatedly, to reward or punish incumbent elected officials for their behavior in office.[2] They thereby enhance the accountability of political authorities to constituents they represent. At a minimum, even when elections do not adequately fulfill conditions set forth by democratic theorists (e.g., Dahl, 1971), they help legitimate the actions of political leaders and provide a measure of symbolic reassurance to the general public.

Because they seemingly perform both instrumental and expressive functions (e.g., Ginsberg, 1982), there has been a great deal of research on why people do and do not vote in elections.[3] Among the explanations given for voting are: citizens identify psychologically with political parties and candidates; the costs of voting are negligible; in close elections the votes of individuals can be of pivotal importance; even if they are not pivotal, people derive sociopsychological benefits from voting such as a sense of gratification from fulfilling their citizen duties and avoiding the social stigma associated with nonvoting. Explanations for failing to vote include a variety of psychological, cultural and structural factors such as: the lack of interest on the part of ordinary citizens; the high costs of acquiring and processing political information; the irrationality of bothering to go to the polls when the probability of casting a decisive ballot is infinitesimally small; the lack of politically efficacious and trusting feelings; disaffection with or outright alienation from the political system; and voter registration procedures that involve citizen rather than state initiatives.

However, other than a concern with the way in which elections can help drain political tensions within an electorate (Burnham, 1970), Dennis's (1970) study of public support for the institution of elections, and Ginsberg's (1982) claim that even when elections do not operate in accordance with the canons of democratic theory they still generate popular support for both political authorities and the regime itself, there has been surprisingly little consideration and virtually no empirical analyses of the role elections play in the support process, broadly conceived. Because we view

2 Ginsberg has summarized the arguments of scholars who assert that elections have limited consequences in democracies such as the United States under four categories: (1) in a modern democratic state most of the important day-to-day policy decisions are made by appointed administrators rather than by elected officials; (2) candidates for elected public office are primarily responsible to powerful elite groups rather than to the geographic constituencies they represent because the former provide them with a substantial proportion of the funds that enable them to conduct campaigns; (3) elected public officials are more concerned with organized interest groups than with the mass public they represent because the former rather than the latter influence major policy decisions (a variation of the elite argument); (4) vital decisions are made on a day-by-day basis by experts with specialized knowledge and not by politicians (Ginsberg and Stone, 1986:8)

3 See, for example, Milbrath and Goel (1977); Reiter (1979); Wolfinger and Rosenstone (1980); Seligman (1982); Bennett and Bennett (1986); and Miller (1986:1–36).

elections as regular, constitutionally sanctioned opportunities that – net of
any other functions they may perform – can help sustain democratic political systems, in this chapter we will focus on the ways in which national
elections affect political support in Canada. We begin with a delineation of
Canadians' evaluations of national elections in their country. We then determine whether there are dimensions underlying their evaluations that
give them a kind of unity and coherence that would merit them being
labeled an "ideology" of elections. Next we focus on whether their views
about elections are systematically related to support for national political
authorities and the political regime. In addressing this latter topic, we will
analyze the two most recent national elections: the 1984 contest which
ended a long period of Liberal Party hegemony, and the 1988 one that
maintained an incumbent Conservative administration in office.

THE ROLE OF ELECTIONS

Respondents in the preelection wave of our 1988 national study were presented with nine "agree–disagree" statements about federal elections in
Canada. These were:

(A) Elections help to keep politicians honest.
(B) There is often a big difference between what a party says it will do and what it
actually does if it wins an election.
(C) In election campaigns people don't learn about the *really* important problems
facing the country.
(D) Elections are unfair because the party with the most money usually wins.
(E) In elections the political parties give people *real* choices.
(F) Rewarding or punishing the governing party is what elections are really all
about.
(G) Parties that win elections usually know exactly what the people want them to
do.
(H) Elections do more to divide the country than to bring it together.
(I) The benefits of elections far outweigh the costs.

Items (A) and (F) were intended to determine whether Canadians view
elections as instruments of accountability. Items (B), (E), and (G) were
intended to assess their views about the policy mandate function of elections. Item (C) is oriented to the educative function elections supposedly
perform and items (D), (H), and (I) focus on the quality of the electoral
process and its consequences for democracy.

Regarding item "(F)", elections as devices for rewarding or punishing
the governing party, we found that nearly 60 percent do not believe that
this is "what elections are really all about" (Table 6.1). Although the popularity of "Keysian" (Key, 1966) retrospective voting models (e.g., Fiorina,
1981) might tempt one to interpret these responses as a negative commentary on the quality of Canadian democracy, in thinking further about their
responses we were uncertain whether some of those who disagreed with

Table 6.1. *Evaluations of federal elections, 1988 (in percent)*

	Agree	Disagree	Don't know
A. Elections help to keep politicians honest	55a	41	4
B. There is often a big difference between what a party says it will do and what it actually does if it wins an election	90	8	2
C. In election campaigns people don't learn about the really important problems facing the country	65	32	2
D. Elections are unfair because the party with the most money usually wins	27	67	6
E. In elections the political parties give people real choices	48	47	5
F. Rewarding or punishing the governing party is what elections are really all about	36	58	6
G. Parties that win elections usually know exactly what the people want them to do	36	60	4
H. Elections do more to divide the country than to bring it together	30	63	7
I. The benefits of elections far outweigh the costs	57	35	8

Note: a - horizontal percentages; N = 2215 for all items

the proposition did so because they believed that a principal function of elections is to provide prospectively oriented choices between alternative parties and policies, or whether they agreed with the statement, but felt elections also serve other functions. Given the ambiguity of responses to this item we decided not to employ it in subsequent analyses. We used factor analyses to assess the dimensionality of the evaluations of elections measured by the remaining eight items. Before proceeding with these analyses we will present the distribution of responses to the election evaluation items, report on variations in them across important sociodemographic groups and determine whether positive views about elections increase or decrease as the day of decision approaches.

Election evaluations

Responses to the nine statements (Table 6.1) reveal that with the exception of the item concerning the proclivity of winning parties to renege on their campaign promises, Canadians are divided in their evaluations of the role elections play in their political system. On the one hand, many believe that elections facilitate the accountability process, give them genuine choices among competing policy alternatives, and are not simply ritualistic occasions that may make them feel good but leave real power in the hands of economic elites and the politicians who represent their interests. Pluralities or majorities also believe that elections help to keep politicians honest and their benefits greatly outweigh their costs. Further, they disagree with the propositions that elections are unfair because the party with the most money usually wins, and that elections do more to divide than to unify the country. On the other hand, many question the effectiveness of elections as educative mechanisms – two-thirds doubt that elections enable people to learn about the important problems facing the country. They also take with a grain of salt the claim invariably made by winning parties and their leaders that the electorate has given them a "mandate" – some three-fifths doubt that elections provide winning parties with information about what the people want them to do. Canadians "mixed reviews" of elections are further reflected in a summary index we constructed based on their "positive" responses to the eight items.[4] The mean score of this index is 3.9; the median and mode are both 4.0.

Given the protracted and oftentimes heated disputes concerning the inadequacy of regional and ethnic/linguistic representation at the national level of Canada's political system, we anticipated that evaluations of elections would be most negative in Quebec and the West, areas where complaints about representation have been loudest. A regional analysis of the eight election items suggests that such tendencies are discernable, particularly among Quebecers, but they are quite weak. Additional evidence is provided by an analysis in which the elections evaluation index was regressed on our standard sociodemographic variables. As anticipated, residents of Quebec and the four Western provinces had less positive views about them than did residents of the country's heartland, Ontario. However, only the Francophone Quebec variable attained statistical significance. Canadians election evaluations were largely independent of regional/ linguistic and other sociodemographic cleavages.

We next considered whether views regarding elections change as an election approaches. One might expect views to become more positive, because elections provide the great majority of citizens with the opportunity to feel they are a part of and contributing to a major event in the life of a democracy. They might become less positive, however, because of disapproval of negative campaigning, disappointment with the performance of their party's candidates and leaders, or with the prospect that their favorite party or candidate appeared to be losing ground. For this purpose we generated a mean election evaluation index score for groups of respondents interviewed in each of the six weeks before the 1988 election. Although the views of those in the "end of campaign" group were more

4 For items (A), (E), (G), and (I) "agree" responses are coded 1, and "disagree" responses 0; for items (B), (C), (D), and (H) "disagree" responses are coded 1, and "agree" responses 0.

positive than those in the "early campaign" group, the increase was both slight and unsystematic.

Structure. Our next concern was how Canadians organized their views about the electoral process. One might anticipate, for example, that a person who agreed with item "A," that elections help keep politicians honest, might also agree with item "I," that the benefits of elections far outweigh the costs. One might also assume that those who feel that election campaigns do not provide voters with an opportunity to learn about important problems facing the country (item "C") might also feel that the political parties do not give people real choices (item "E") and, moreover, that there is a disjunction between what parties promise to do during election campaigns and what they actually do afterward (item "B"). However, they might believe the latter and still believe that political parties give voters choices during elections and usually know what they want them to do if they win. One need not be a cynic about the role that parties – especially governing parties – play in the political process to accept the fact that conditions might arise that would make it difficult, if not impossible, for even the best-intentioned leaders of a governing party to fulfill their campaign promises. Such a possibility suggested the need to proceed empirically to determine if the public's election evaluations were structured in terms of one or more underlying dimensions.

There also was a theoretical reason to hypothesize that more than one dimension might underlie the judgments Canadians make about elections. A quarter century ago, in his landmark article on the belief systems of mass publics, Philip Converse (1964:211) argued that the ability to think in ideological terms is "an act of creative synthesis characteristic of only a minuscule proportion of any population." This was because an ideology or a "belief system" (as he labeled it) is characterized by constraint or functional interdependence among its ideational elements and by a relatively wide range of objects that are referents for the ideas and attitudes in the system. To the extent elements of ideologies become socially diffused, they typically reach mass publics in the form of small "packages" that are substantially unconstrained by more general principles or propositions constituting core elements of an ideology. Converse demonstrated his argument empirically by showing that relationships (as measured by interitem correlations) among the ideational elements of the American public's beliefs within the domestic and foreign policy domains were weak and that relationships between elements in the two domains were weaker still.

Our data tend to support Converse's findings. The correlations among people's judgments of elections are quite modest – not entirely unexpected, because we purposely structured statements that would delineate their views across a range of functions ascribed to elections by both their celebrants and critics. Nevertheless, an exploratory factor analysis of a random half sample of the data indicated that their evaluations are structured in terms of three underlying factors, and the pattern of item loadings suggests that the factors can be interpreted in a fashion consistent with both common sense and democratic theory. The first factor reveals the presence of a "process" dimension. It is dominated by the "elections unfair," "elections divide the country," and "elections help educate" items. Items related to the choices elections provide, the information they convey to winning parties, and the behavior of parties in office vis-à-vis their campaign promises load on a second factor. This factor is clearly related to the notion of elections providing winning parties with popular mandates. Only two items – "elections keep politicians honest" and "the benefits of elections outweigh costs" – load heavily on a third factor, suggesting that people see elections as vehicles that contribute positively to democracy by facilitating the accountability of elected officials to the public through the implied sanction of removal from office. We labeled the first factor "process," the second "mandate," and the third "accountability."

We used confirmatory factor analysis to test this three-factor model. All items loading at .40 or greater in the exploratory analysis were hypothesized to load on that factor. The model fit the random half-sample fairly well, but clearly there was room for improvement ($\chi^2_{16} = 43.40$, p < .001). Inspection of LISREL diagnostic statistics indicated the fit would improve if selected error terms were correlated and if item "E" ("elections give real choices") were permitted to load on the "process" factor. The resulting modified model fit the half-sample data very well ($\chi^2_{12} = 19.91$, p = .069). All parameter estimates were statistically significant and various diagnostic statistics had acceptable values. The case for this model was strengthened by testing it using a second random half-sample. The fit was again excellent. We therefore accepted the modified three-factor election evaluation model and obtained parameter estimates for the entire sample. The pattern and strength of factor loadings for this model (Table 6.2) were similar to those in the exploratory analysis and, so we retained the labels "process," "mandate," and "accountability," respectively, for each of the three factors.[5] Factors two and three were strongly correlated ($\varphi = .73$). The first factor, in contrast, had much weaker correlations with the second and third (i.e., φ's = .19 and .25, respectively). Thus, there are significant relationships among Canadians beliefs about elections but the overall degree of constraint is relatively modest.

5 For purposes of construct validation we investigated relationships between the election evaluation factors and political efficacy. Democratic theory suggests that these relationships should be positive. Empirically, all six ϕ correlations between the three election factors and the two efficacy factors were positive; five were statistically significant; and four were moderately strong (range .51–.53). The weakest correlations involved the "accountability" factor – the ϕ's between this factor and the external and internal efficacy factors were .21 and .04, respectively.

Table 6.2. *Confirmatory factor analysis of evaluations of federal elections, 1988*

	Factor Matrix (λ)		
Election evaluations	Factor 1	Factor 2	Factor 3
Elections keep politicians honest	.00	.00	.51c
Parties don't do what they say	.00	.58c	.00
Don't learn important problems	.41c	.33	.00
Elections unfair	.79c	.00	.00
Elections give real choices	.26c	.62c	.00
Winning parties know what people want	.00	.42c	.00
Elections divide country	.48c	.00	.00
Benefits of elections outweigh costs	.00	.00	.36c

$$\chi^2_{13} = 23.31, \ p = .038, \ AGFI = .992$$

Inter-factor correlations (ϕ)

	F1	F2	F3
F1	1.00		
F2	.19c	1.00	
F3	.25c	.73c	1.00

Note: c–p $\leq$.05; N = 1716, listwise deletion of missing data; WLS estimates

Election evaluations and regime support

Our next task was to determine whether judgments about elections were systematically associated with support for the national political regime. We assumed that the most straightforward such relationship would obtain between Canadians views about elections and support for parliament, the linchpin of government in a representative democracy. Figure 6.1 reveals this is, in fact, the case. It also indicates that election evaluations have a slightly stronger relationship with judicial than with civil service support. One might have thought otherwise: that the judiciary would be regarded as the less manifestly "political" institution and thus less tightly tied to views about elections.[6]

6 This is because the organizational, procedural, and support systems of the judiciary are the responsibility of ministers of the Crown – the federal justice minister and the provincial attorneys general. The assumption is that it enables judges to perform their adjudicative function without fear or favor. They are relieved of administrative chores and hence freed of the possibility of making decisions that might be based on administrative feasibility. Judicial scholar Carl Baar (1977:242–74) has contended that as a consequence Canadian judges, unlike their American counterparts, have not tried to enhance their status by increasing the size of their judicial bureaucracies. Instead, they have emphasized the distinctive characteristics of judges, courts, and the judicial process. By focusing attention on their own importance and by arguing that they need to be insulated from nonjudicial tasks, judges have been able to simultaneously enhance their own status and avoid being stigmatized as "politicians" or "bureaucrats."

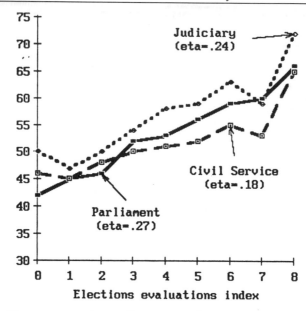

Figure 6.1. *Mean support for parliament, civil service, and judiciary by evaluations of federal elections, 1988*

A number of times we have observed that in Canada average citizens would have difficulty distinguishing between government-as-regime and government-as-the-party-in-power. Canada is a country in which a key symbol of the regime, the governor general, opens every session of parliament with a Throne Speech in which he or she routinely describes the policy proposals of an incumbent prime minister and the Cabinet as those of "the" or "my" government. Given the association of "government" per se with a current administration, it can be assumed that in this instance support for parliament, the bureaucracy and judiciary will be influenced by people's support for the governing Conservative Party and its most conspicuous symbol, the prime minister. Figure 6.2 indicates that support for the Conservatives did vary significantly and positively with evaluations of elections – increasing from 38 to 75 across the elections index – whereas the relationships for the opposition Liberal and New Democratic parties were negligible. These findings led us to control for feelings about the Conservative government-of-the-day in a covariance structure analysis performed to determine the effects of the three election evaluation factors on parliamentary, bureaucratic, and judicial support. And, because the mandate and accountability factors were highly intercorrelated, to avoid any multicollinearity problems, we performed the analysis twice, eliminating each of them in turn.

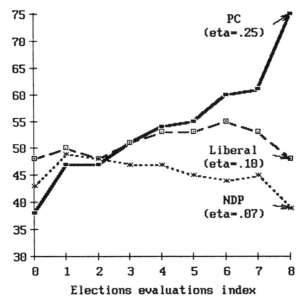

Figure 6.2. *Mean support for federal political parties by evaluations of federal elections, 1988*

The results reveal election evaluations *do* influence support, even when feelings about the incumbent government are controlled. For example, when the accountability factor was omitted (Model I), both the mandate and process factors had statistically significant and positive effects on support for parliament (Table 6.3). The same was true of the process and accountability factors when the mandate factor was eliminated (Model II). It also is evident from an inspection of the standardized β's that both the mandate and accountability factors had stronger effects on parliamentary support than did the process factor. Additionally, and consistent with our more general argument about the flow of support in a Westminster-model parliamentary democracy, orientations toward the incumbent government had a positive impact on feelings about parliament net of controls for the election evaluation factors.

The civil service and judicial support analyses were somewhat different. In the civil service analysis, the mandate and the accountability factors were significant but the process factor was not, whereas, in the judiciary analysis, all three election evaluation factors were significant. The proportions of explained variance in support for the three regime components declined monotonically, being highest for parliament, the most manifestly political institution, lower for the bureaucracy, and lower still for the politi-

Table 6.3. *Covariance structure analyses of support for parliament, civil service, and judiciary by evaluations of federal elections and orientations toward incumbent government, 1988*

Predictors	Model I		Model II	
	β	Std. β	β	Std. β
Parliament				
Election evaluation factors				
Process	.11c	.08	.12c	.10
Mandate	.41c	.21	t	t
Accountability	t	t	.45c	.26
Orientations toward incumbent government	.34c	.31	.33c	.30
R^2 =	.22		.24	
χ^2_{27} =	39.88, p = .05		34.86, p = .14	
AGFI =	.994		.995	
Civil Service				
Election evaluation factors				
Process	-.01	-.01	.04	.01
Mandate	.29c	.17	t	t
Accountability	t	t	.20c	.20
Orientations toward incumbent government	.32c	.29	.30c	.29
R^2 =	.14		.15	
χ^2_{27} =	31.86, p = .24		28.22, p = .40	
AGFI =	.995		.995	
Judiciary				
Election evaluation factors				
Proccess	.18c	.15	.17c	.14
Mandate	.28c	.16	t	t
Accountability	t	t	.36c	.23
Orientations toward incumbent government	.11c	.10	.10c	.09
R^2 =	.09		.11	
χ^2_{27} =	47.13, p = .01		34.56, p = .15	
AGFI =	.993		.995	

Note: c–p $\leq$.05, t – not included in model; WLS estimates

cally "neutral" judiciary – a pattern that is both plausible and theoretically compelling.

Table 6.4 presents the results of a summary covariance analysis in which we simultaneously assessed the effects of the three election factors on support for parliament, bureaucracy, and the judiciary. Here, we modeled the mandate and accountability factors as indicators of a second-order factor labeled "popular control." Also, in keeping with results presented in Chapter 4 (Table 4.2), we modeled two regime factors, one for parliament and the civil service, and one for the judiciary. The covariance analysis reveals that the popular control and process factors had positive and statistically significant effects on both the parliament/civil service and the judiciary

Table 6.4. *Summary covariance structure analysis of national regime support by election evaluation factors and orientations toward incumbent government, 1988*

	Regime Support Factors					
Predictors	Parliament-Civil Service			Judiciary		
	γ	β	s^+	γ	β	s^+
Election evaluation factors						
Process		.15c	.14		.22c	.20
Popular control: mandate	.21c		.25	.19c		.21
accountability						
Incumbent government orientations		.38c	.40		.13c	.13
	R^2 = .28			R^2 = .12		
			χ^2_{27} = 50.27, p = .21			
			AGFI = .994			

Note: c – p $\leq$.05; + – standardized coefficients; WLS estimates

support factors. The popular control factor had a stronger effect on parliamentary/civil service support than did the process factor (.25 and .14, respectively). In contrast, the popular control and process factors had equally strong effects on judicial support (.21 and .20, respectively), whereas feelings about the incumbent Conservative government had a greater impact on support for parliament and the civil service than on the judiciary.

ELECTIONS AND THE MOBILIZATION OF SUPPORT

In Chapter 4 it was noted that support for the political community and regime declined in 1983 from what it had been when measured in 1980 and rose again after the 1984 national election campaign. This pattern implied that elections help mobilize support for key political objects and that during the interim between elections support declines. However, our previous analysis of changes in people's judgments of elections over the six-week period preceding the 1988 election revealed that neither their positions on the elections evaluations index nor their judgments about each of the eight items making up the index underwent any systematic or statistically significant changes during the course of the actual campaign. This was also the case with respect to support for key political objects and feelings of political efficacy, interest and trust, all of which did not increase or decrease in any patterned way during the campaign. Notwithstanding the absence of evidence of any systematic changes in support and related attitudes in the campaign period, when we measured average support for Canada, the gov-

Table 6.5. *Paired t-tests: support for national political community and regime, 1980–83, 1983–84 and 1988 national panels*

		Panel				
		1980-83		1983-84		1988 pre-post
		80	83	83	84	pre	post
Canada	$\overline{X}$ =	84	76	75	82	79	84
	t =		11.83a		-14.00a		-9.94a
Government of Canda	$\overline{X}$ =	61	51	50	65	54	61
	t =		12.92a		-19.30a		-14.64a
Parliament*	$\overline{X}$ =	59	50	50	57	53	59
	t =		10.59a		-14.64a		-10.75a
Civil Service	$\overline{X}$ =		t	47	52	51	55
	t =				-8.17a		-6.53a
Judiciary	$\overline{X}$ =		t	56	57	57	59
	t =				-0.69		-6.23a

Note: a-p $\leq$.001; one-tailed test; * - 1979-83 comparison; t - variable not available

ernment of Canada, parliament, the civil service and judiciary *after* the 1988 election, we found that in every instance support had risen. Average scores on indices of political efficacy, trust, interest, and MPs responsiveness also increased.

These were aggregate changes. Our panel data enable us to also measure individual-level changes and provide additional and more compelling evidence that elections do indeed mobilize support for key political objects and stimulate increases in the kind of attitudes which, in theory, characterize a democratic citizenry. For example, the analyses displayed in Table 6.5 reveal that each of three paired comparisons in the first panel (1980–83), and the five comparisons in the second panel (1983–84), differed significantly, as did the five pre- and post-1988 election comparisons. As might be anticipated from analyses presented in Chapter 4, the sharpest differences were in the support levels of Conservative identifiers, whose party came to power in the mid-1980s after spending all but nine months of the preceding two decades in the political wilderness (data not shown). Their support for the government of Canada declined by 13 points when they were in opposition (1980–83), increased by 14 points after the 1984 election in which their party won a smashing victory, and increased by 7 points after the 1988 election, when they again were victorious. Overall, all but 6 of 39 paired comparisons in levels of political support attained statistical significance.

Elections also influence individual-level changes in attitudes such as polit-

Table 6.6. *Paired t-tests: political attitudes, 1980–83, 1983–84 and 1988 national panels*

			Panel		
		1980–83	1983–84	1988 pre–post	
		80 83	83 84	pre post	
Internal political efficacy	X̄ =	.86 .65	.72 .83	.83 .85	
	t =	4.78a	−5.10a	−1.04	
External political efficacy	X̄ =	.83 .67	.67 .76	.71 .75	
	t =	4.02a	−3.74a	−1.88c	
Overall political efficacy	X̄ =	1.69 1.32	1.39 1.59	1.53 1.59	
	t =	5.65a	−5.66a	−1.95c	
MP responsiveness	X̄ =	t	t	7.49 7.69	
	t =			−4.00	
Political authorities trust*	X̄ =	2.05 1.99	1.91 2.01	1.96 2.13	
	t =	1.01	−3.07a	−6.28a	
Political interest	X̄ =	1.98 1.81	1.79 1.87	1.87 1.92	
	t =	5.41a	−4.30a	−3.93a	

Note: a–p ≤.001; b–p ≤.01; c–p ≤.05; one-tailed test; * – 1979–83 comparison; t – variable not available

ical efficacy, perceptions of MPs' responsiveness, trust in political authorities, and interest in politics more generally. Paired comparisons employing the panel data reveal that 13 of 16 comparisons were statistically significant and all 16 pairs of changes were in the right direction. That is, they declined during the 1980–83 period and increased in both 1983–84 and between the preelection and postelection waves of the 1988 panel (Table 6.6). Similar analyses were conducted for each group of party identifiers, and again, the most dramatic changes occurred among Conservative partisans (data not shown). Levels of efficacy, trust and interest declined between 1980 and 1983, and increased between 1983 and 1984, and after the 1988 election.

To recapitulate, Canadian views about elections are somewhat constrained, but not enough to merit being labeled an "ideology" of elections. Briefly, three factors underlie their views, which we labeled "process," "mandate," and "accountability" because these seem to us to be the ways in which people think about the role elections play in the political process. A second issue we addressed was whether views about elections become more positive during an election campaign. We found no support for this hypothesis. However, support for the national political community and regime institutions fell during the interim between elections and increased afterward. Moreover, political interest, trust, efficacy, and perceptions of the responsiveness of MPs also rose and fell in a similar fashion. The patterns were sharpest for identifiers with the Conservative Party, winners in the last two national elections. Whether it is an election campaign, the expressive and instrumental functions of an election itself, its outcome, or some combination of all these that provide the catalyst, elections in Canada do seem to mobilize public support, at least temporarily, for key political objects and stimulate attitudes vital to the healthy functioning of a democratic polity.

That the pattern of increased support after the 1984 and 1988 national elections should have been greatest for Conservative partisans is not surprising given the party's success after a long period in opposition. The party system both reflects and contributes to support processes for a variety of reasons, three of which are especially notable. First, the system is so complex that one could reasonably argue that the country has not one but several party systems. For example, as noted in Chapters 3 and 5, both the identities of the contesting parties and the pattern of interparty competition between and among them can vary sharply from province to province. And, within individual provinces, party competition at one level of government often seems to be unrelated to competition at the other. Second, although there are nominally several national parties, virtually from the beginning of the country's history there has been a tendency toward one-party domination. It bears repeating that at the federal level the Liberal Party governed for 33 of the 39 years between the end of World War II and 1984. Its hegemony rested in large part on continuing success in Quebec; the party received fully 54 percent of that province's vote in thirteen elections between 1945 and 1980 (Feigert, 1989:163–203). The distortion produced by the first-past-the-post electoral system also contributed. In ten of the thirteen elections the Liberal share of parliamentary seats exceeded its share of votes and on five occasions a minority of votes produced a majority of parliamentary seats. The tendency toward one-partyism also has been operative at the provincial level; the success of the New Democrats in Saskatchewan, Social Credit in Alberta and British Columbia, the Conservatives in Ontario, and Liberals in Newfoundland come quickly to mind. Third, tendencies toward one-partyism notwithstanding, there is a curious periodicity to the fortunes of Canada's political parties. After years of electoral success they fall from grace, and when they do, their demise is often rapid and precipitous. Examples include the demise of the provincial Social Credit party in Alberta in the early 1970s, the provincial Progressive Conservatives in Ontario in the 1980s, and the federal Liberals in the Prairies in the late 1950s (Feigert, 1989, passim).

This periodicity reflects the weakness and continuing instability of partisan identifications discussed previously. When coupled with an appropriate mix of short-term issue and leadership forces, the result can appear to be what V. O. Key (1955) termed a "critical election" in which there is a basic and enduring redistribution of partisan support. In such a circumstance, a long-governing party is driven from office to be replaced by an opposition party which then enjoys a new era of one-party dominance. In 1984 it initially seemed that the perennially governing Liberals had fallen victim to such an election, and that the Conservatives were the beneficiaries of their demise. Little more than a year later, however, the longstanding pattern of volatility in party support had begun to reassert itself. Indeed, by 1987, the Tory tide that had swept the Liberals out of office three years earlier had become a trickle. Indicative of this volatility is that at times during this period the New Democrats, always a minor party on the national political stage, seemed to be on the verge of coming to power. At other times, it seemed that in the next election the Liberals might regain enough support to return to office. In Chapter 1 we hypothesized that political support in Canada flows upward – from authorities, to regime, to community. Thus, analyses of factors influencing support for the incumbent Conservatives and the other national political parties in the 1984 and 1988 elections are important for illuminating the matrix of forces affecting public support for the national political regime and community.

NATIONAL ELECTIONS AND PARTY SUPPORT

1984: The Tory tide

The evening of September 4, 1984, was not a pleasant one for John Turner, erstwhile crown prince of the Liberal Party and Canada's recently appointed prime minister. It grew worse as the electoral returns from Quebec confirmed that the Liberals might be in for a defeat as great as the one they suffered in 1958 when their party won only 34 percent of the popular vote and 18 percent of the then 265 parliamentary seats. Most of the initial explanations for the Liberals dramatic loss of support offered by political cognoscenti centered on several egregious errors committed by Mr. Turner on the campaign trail.[7] These included his agreement to and subsequent defense of a number of high-level patronage appointments foisted on him by his predecessor, long-time Prime Minister Pierre Trudeau; his midcampaign dismissal of top operatives and their replacement by some of the old guard associated with Trudeau; his agreement to a nationally televised debate in French with the fluently bilingual Mulroney; and his gaffes in publicly patting the derrieres of two prominent female members of his party (one of whom returned the favor).

   In fact, neither the magnitude of the Liberal defeat nor the Conservative victory could be fully explained by tactical errors Turner and his advisors committed. For one thing, only in Quebec was his party more highly regarded by the electorate than he was. For another, for the first time in history the Conservatives won the largest share of the popular vote in every

7 See Frizzell and Westell (1985) and Penniman (1988).

province from Newfoundland to British Columbia. Indeed, so great was their margin of victory among every major group in the country that it appeared that the 1984 election was "critical" in the sense of signaling a basic redistribution of partisan support in Canada. However, we shall demonstrate that the outcome of the contest was not a product of partisan realignment. Rather, similar to other Canadian federal elections held in the past two decades, the 1984 result was strongly influenced by short-term forces associated with party leader images and orientations toward salient issues.

Leaders and issues – the Conservative advantage.   Our 1984 survey data reveal that in the struggle for the hearts and minds of the Canadian public, Mr. Mulroney and the Conservatives won in a walk. Feeling thermometer scores revealed that the average Canadian accorded much greater support to Brian Mulroney and his party than to the Liberal and New Democratic parties and their respective leaders, John Turner and Ed Broadbent (Table 6.7). As noted, only in Quebec did Mr. Turner run behind his party. However, he did not run far enough ahead in other areas to justify the hopes invested in him by the hundreds of Liberal insiders who for years had treated him as a kind of "emperor in exile" and who had pleaded with him to enter the leadership fight when Trudeau announced his intention to return to private life. Those Liberal insiders and their counterparts in the Conservative Party seemed convinced that the public was so disaffected from both Pierre Trudeau and Conservative leader Joe Clark that neither party might win an election if they remained at the helm. Although it was not immediately apparent, the Conservatives gained far more from their change of leaders than did the Liberals. At the time of the 1984 election, support for Mr. Mulroney was fully 13 points greater (61 versus 48) than that for his predecessor, Clark. In sharp contrast, Turner's support actually was slightly lower than former Prime Minister Trudeau's (47 versus 49), even though the latter was then at the nadir of his popularity after some fifteen years as head of government.

Issues, particularly economic ones, were very important in 1984. As shown in Chapter 2, economic issues long have been matters of great concern and throughout most of the 1970s various combinations of the "twin evils" of inflation and unemployment bedeviled the country's stagflated economy. After the Trudeau-led Liberals returned to office in 1980 the misery continued – a severe recession in 1982 sharply reduced the rate of inflation, but at the cost of large increases in joblessness. Data presented in Chapter 2 (Table 2.1) demonstrated that in the autumn of 1983 a majority of the electorate felt the condition of the economy left much to be desired, and that future prospects were dim. Moreover, fully half of the voters believed that the government had done a poor job in managing the economy and only 3 percent felt it had done a very good job.

Table 6.7. *Party leader images, 1984–88*

*Leader and Party Thermometer Scores**

Leader and Party	1984	N	1987	N	1988 Pre	N	1988 Post	N
Turner	47	1857	44	1710	46	2165	44	1985
Liberal party	45	1860	51	1710	51	2147	51	1972
Mulroney	61	1866	41	1756	48	2176	50	1989
PC party	60	1840	44	1740	53	2159	54	1988
Broadbent	56	1851	53	1695	54	2157	54	1977
NDP	46	1802	47	1688	46	2134	46	1966

*Leader Character and Competence Ratings***

		1987	N	1988 Post	N
Turner:	character	t		5.3	1909
	competence	t		4.8	1963
Mulroney:	character	4.9	1709	5.5	1951
	competence	4.7	1779	5.7	1985
Broadbent:	character	t		6.4	1928
	competence	t		5.8	1950

Note: * - mean scores on 100-point scale; ** - mean scores on 10-point scale; t - question not asked in 1987 survey

As we have argued throughout this study, long periods of Liberal government since World War II, structural factors such as cohesive parliamentary parties, and a tradition of single-party rather than coalition government made it a virtual certainty in 1984 that large numbers of voters would associate the federal government with the Liberal Party. As a consequence, not only did a majority feel the "economy" was the most important issue[8] and that the Conservatives were closest to them on that issue (Table 6.8), most of them also blamed the Liberal Party qua government for the economy's impoverished state, and for a variety of noneconomic problems as well. In fact, except for "social" and "human rights" matters, majorities stated the Conservatives were closest to them on virtually all such issues. As we shall see, overwhelming public support for the Tories in 1984 owed much to short-term factors related to people's pro-Conservative issue orientations.

Partisan volatility and political support.   Prior to 1988, three successive federal elections produced a turnover of government; a 1979 minority Conservative government gave way the following year to a majority Liberal administration, which was turned out four years later when voters elected 75 percent of the Conservative candidates offered them. These simple facts alone argue that a model of Canadian voting behavior should give pride of place to short-term forces. Research conducted over the past decade indicates that both electoral choices and more general orientations toward political parties are subject to considerable individual-level instability produced by changing support for party leaders and public judgments about party performance on salient issues (e.g., Clarke et al., 1984; Archer, 1987).

Panel data show that many voters had unstable federal party identifications in the 1980–84 period. But, data from the 1970s presented in Chapter 3 (Table 3.4) show that rates of partisan instability in fact were no greater in the early 1980s than previously. What *was* different was the *direction* of partisan movement: In the 1970s exchanges of identifiers among the parties were relatively balanced and, hence, the parties' aggregate levels of support were largely undisturbed. In the early 1980s, especially between 1980 and 1983, however, those switching their support moved heavily towards the Conservatives. As a result, between 1980 and 1984 the percentage of federal PC identifiers increased from 28 to 40, whereas the percentage of Liberal identifiers dropped from 45 to 32 (the NDP share was 15 percent in both

---

8 Respondents were asked: "In your opinion, what was the *most* important issue in the election?" Those providing an answer were asked: "Which party is closest to *you* on this issue?" and "How important was that issue to you in deciding how to vote in the election – very important, fairly important, or not very important?"

Table 6.8. *Party closest on most important issue, 1984 federal election (in percent)*

Issue category	Most Important issue**	Party Closest				
		Liberal	Conservative	NDP	Other	None/Don't Know
Economic+	60	14a	53	21	X	12
Confederation: New Constitution/National Unity	2	9	53	3	18	16
Resource	1	11	70	9	5	6
Social	2	30	39	15	0	16
Other						
Leaders, leadership	3	17	58	11	0	14
Parties, electoral change	10	4	77	10	0	9
Human rights, women's rights	3	14	44	31	0	12
Honesty in government	1	10	61	16	5	8
Miscellaneous	3	*	*	*	*	*
None, don't know	3	-	-	-	-	-
All issues	22	13	55	18	1	12

Note: ** – multiple response, N = 1928, vertical percentages; X – less than 0.5 percent; * – varies by specific issue; + – includes unemployment = 31%, state of the economy = 22%, deficits and currency = 5%, inflation = 1%, taxes = 1%; a – horizontal percentages

years).[9] If the 1984 distribution of partisan support had been maintained after the election, the case for party realignment would be much stronger. However, the post-1984 period was one in which partisan instability continued apace.

Our contention that party identifications in Canada reflect short-term forces does not mean they are simply expressions of current vote intentions. Political socialization studies (e.g., Kornberg, Smith and Clarke, 1979:ch. 2) indicate that many Canadians first form party attachments during childhood or adolescence, and although a substantial proportion report one or more changes in party identification, others state that they always have identified with the same party. Recall data cannot accurately gauge levels of partisan stability over the life cycle (Gutek, 1978; Niemi, Katz, and Newman, 1980) but, even allowing for substantial measurement error, the percentages of "recalled stable identifiers" in Canadian election studies also suggest that a sizable number of voters always have identified with the same party. Relatedly, although our panel studies cover only a segment of the life cycle, they too reveal that a majority of the electorate have stable party identifications over several years. At any time, then, public support for Canadian parties reflects a mixture of long- and short-term forces.

In addition, as shown in Chapters 3 and 5, large numbers of voters fail to identify with the same party in federal and provincial politics. Also, recall that such partisan inconsistency influences the stability of party identification and electoral choice at both levels of the federal system. Because it does, a model of federal voting behavior should include measures of federal and provincial party identifications as well as variables capturing short-term forces, i.e., orientations toward important issues and support for party leaders. The likelihood that identifications both influence and are influenced by issue and leader effects complicates the construction of such a model. One approach is to specify a nonrecursive model with reciprocal causal linkages between party identification, on the one hand, and issue and leader variables, on the other (e.g., Archer, 1987). However, the estimation of coefficients in such a model is problematic because it may be difficult to specify theoretically meaningful and statistically powerful exogenous variables (Fiorina, 1981:188; Beck, 1986:261).

A convenient alternative is to employ our panel data and hypothesize that the 1984 vote is a function of prior federal and provincial party iden-

---

9 Individual-level "*conversion*" is not the only source of aggregate change in the distribution of party identification. The other is *replacement*, i.e., the exit of older persons from the electorate and their replacement by new voters. Replacement effects contributed to the growth of Conservative partisanship in the electorate between 1980 and 1984 – newly eligible voters (persons aged 18 to 21) were more likely than older persons to be Tories (45 percent versus 39 percent) and slightly less likely to be Liberals (28 percent versus 33 percent).

tifications (i.e., those in 1983), as well as issue and leader orientations measured in 1984. In such a model the two identification variables serve as summary measures of party support that are a product of long- and short-term forces operating at earlier points in time.[10] This use of the party identification measures is consistent with our argument that partisanship in Canada has both long- and short-term components and is analogous to the conceptualization of party identification proposed by Fiorina in his influential "retrospective voting" theory of electoral choice (1981:90). Here, we will treat retrospective evaluations of governmental performance as one component of a larger set of forces influencing current party identification and the vote itself.

Our model of the vote, then, may be stated as:

$$V_t = a + b_1 FPID_{t-1} + b_2 PPID_{t-1} + \Sigma b_i IS_t + \Sigma b_j LE_t + e_t$$

where:

V_t = vote for Liberals, PCs or NDP at time t

a = constant

$FPID_{t-1}$ = federal party identification at time $t - 1$

$PPID_{t-1}$ = provincial party identification at time $t - 1$

IS_t = issue orientations at time t

LE_t = leader orientations at time t

e_t = error term

We measured support for party leaders with 100-point feeling thermometers. In addition to using such variables for Mulroney, Turner, and Broadbent in each of the analyses, in one instance we also included a measure of support for former Liberal leader, Pierre Trudeau. We did so because feelings about him were so varied and intense, and his departure from political life so recent, it was reasonable to hypothesize that they continued to influence party support. Issue orientations were measured in two ways. The first was whether a respondent stated unemployment or another economic issue was "most important." The second was a measure of perceptions of which party, if any, was "closest" on the issue judged most important, with the measure weighted for the issue's reported importance in the vote decision.[11] The use of the first "unmediated" economic

10 The federal and provincial party identification variables used in the model depend on which party's vote is being analyzed. For example, in the Conservative vote analysis, federal and provincial party identifications are scored: "very strong" Conservative = + 3, "fairly strong" Conservative = + 2, "not very strong" or "leaning" Conservative = + 1, nonidentifier = 0, "not very strong" or "leaning" other party identifier = − 1, "fairly strong" other party identifier = − 2, "very strong" other party identifier = − 3.

11 The construction of this variable varies depending on whether Liberal, Conservative, or NDP voting is being analyzed. In the case of Conservative voting, for example, persons selecting the Conservatives as closest on their "most important issue" are scored + 1; those selecting another party, − 1; and those not selecting a party or not designating an

variable is consonant with the "reward-punishment" hypothesis (Key, 1966) that in times of economic adversity economic issues work *against* governing and *for* opposition parties. The use of the second is prompted by previous analyses of the conditions under which issue voting occurs: namely, that even salient issues must be linked in voters' minds with a particular political party (Butler and Stokes, 1976:ch. 14). Such linkages are not automatic, but rather are contingent upon the nature and outcome of political debate in particular campaign contexts.

Probit analyses[12] indicate that a majority of the predictor variables perform as hypothesized. In all nine cases federal party identification exerted significant effects and, in all but three (Conservative voting), provincial party identifications did so as well (Table 6.9). Leader effects on party support also were abundantly evident and consistent with expectations. Thus, for Liberal voting, support for the current Liberal leader was positively associated with the likelihood of a Liberal vote, whereas support for the Conservative and NDP leaders had negative effects. Support for former Liberal leader, Pierre Trudeau, had a significant positive impact on Liberal voting and a negative impact on Conservative voting, but no effect on NDP voting. The model's strong explanatory power is suggested by R^2 statistics which range from .63 to .78.

As in previous voting studies (e.g., Clarke and Stewart, 1985) unmediated economic variables did not have significant effects, a result that might seem paradoxical given the importance assigned to them in 1984. However, this result can be explained if one recalls that large numbers of voters favored the Conservatives on all issues, and not merely economic ones. When issues were linked to parties, the anticipated strong effects on party support appeared. In every case, voters who preferred a particular party on an issue they regarded as "most important" were more likely to vote for that party regardless of all other considerations. Their commanding lead on all issues enabled the PCs to translate these individual-level issue effects on electoral choice into handsome aggregate vote totals that strongly influenced the election outcome.

The magnitude of these issue effects on party support are not immediately apparent because probit coefficients do not have straightforward interpretations analogous to those for ordinary least squares regression coefficients. The impact of issues can be appreciated by constructing a scenario in which we assign plausible values to other predictor variables and then

---

issue, 0. These scores are weighted by multiplying them by the perceived importance of the issue to the vote decision. The latter variable is scored: "very important" = + 3, "fairly important" = + 2, "not very important" or "no important issue" = + 1.

12 In the Conservative vote analysis, Conservative voters are scored + 1, other voters, 0; in the Liberal vote analysis, Liberal voters are scored + 1, other voters, 0; and in the NDP vote analysis, NDP voters are scored + 1, other voters, 0.

Table 6.9. *Probit analyses of voting in 1984 federal election*

Predictor variables	1984 Vote		
	Liberal b	PC b	NDP b
Including economic issues			
Federal party identification, 1983	.32a	.31a	.31a
Provincial party identification, 1983	.14a	-.00	.13a
Party leader affect: Turner	.03a	-.02a	-.01c
Mulroney	-.02a	.05a	-.03a
Broadbent	-.01a	-.02a	.04a
Economic issues mentioned: unemployment	-.03	-.02	.09
other	.05	-.14	.12
Constant	-.96a	-.72a	-.67
Estimated R²	.65	.69	.63
% correctly predicted	86	82	88
Including party closest on most important issue			
Federal party identification, 1983	.27a	.24a	.25a
Provincial party identification, 1983	.13a	-.00	.11c
Party leader affect: Turner	.03a	-.02a	-.00
Mulroney	-.01a	.04a	-.02a
Broadbent	-.01b	-.02a	.03a
Party closest on most important issue	.37a	.35a	.33a
Constant	-.79a	-.58a	-.78a
Estimated R²	.71	.76	.68
% correctly predicted	88	86	91
Including party closest on most important issue and Trudeau affect			
Federal party identification, 1983	.18a	.18a	.25a
Provincial party identification, 1983	.10a	-.00	.11c
Party leader affect: Turner	.03a	-.02a	-.00
Mulroney	-.01a	.04a	-.02a
Broadbent	-.01b	-.02a	.03a
Trudeau	.02b	-.01c	.00
Party closest on most important issue	.36a	.35a	.33a
Constant	-1.48a	-.27	-.81a
Estimated R²	.74	.78	.68
% correctly predicted	90	87	91

Note: a—p ≤.001; b—p ≤.01; c—p ≤.05; one-tailed test

manipulate the values of the issue variable (Aldrich and Nelson, 1984:41–4). In our scenario we assume that a voter identifies "fairly strongly" at both levels of government (in 1983) with the party whose vote is being analyzed. Substantively, this amounts to assuming that prior (long- and short-term) forces predispose a person to vote for that party. We also assume that a voter's support for the three party leaders and the former Liberal leader is "typical" of the electorate as a whole (i.e., the leader variables are set equal to their means). Given these assumptions, we determined how the probabilities of voting for the three parties were influenced by changes in party-issue linkages and variations in the perceived importance of issues in the voting decision.

The likelihood of voting for a party increased markedly as the value of the issue variable changed. The Conservative case is illustrative. The probability of casting a PC ballot was slightly less than .5 if a voter either was unable to select a party closest on a most important issue or failed to designate such an issue. However, if the voter selected the Conservatives and believed the issue was very important in deciding how to vote, the probability of PC voting increased markedly, to .84. In contrast, for voters selecting *another* party on the most important issue, the probability of a Tory vote was well under .5 and fell to only .14 if the issue was judged "very important" in the voting decision. The patterns of Liberal and NDP vote probabilities were similar.

A similar scenario can be used to assess the effects of support for leaders. Consider one in which a voter identifies with the Liberal Party "fairly strongly" at both levels of government, favors the Conservatives on the most important election issue, but does not think the issue is particularly important in deciding how to vote, and ascribes average levels of support to Mulroney and Turner. Under those conditions, the probability of a Liberal vote was .48. If, however, levels of support for Mulroney and Turner were reversed, the probability of voting Liberal increased to .70 and the probability of voting Tory dropped from .61 to .28.

These changes in vote probabilities under varying assumptions about party leader support illustrate the strong influence of leader effects in Canadian federal elections. They tempt one to conclude that if *only* the voters had been able to support Turner more strongly, the outcome of the 1984 election might have been different. Undoubtedly, a stronger showing by their new leader would have helped the Liberal cause. One must remember, however, that our scenario assumes a voter was a "fairly strong" Liberal identifier both federally and provincially. At the time Turner became Liberal leader in the spring of 1984 the number of such persons was much smaller than it had been four years earlier. To stem the 1984 Tory tide a more highly regarded John Turner would have had to bring large numbers of party identifiers back into the Liberal fold in the run-up to the election. Although the sensitivity of party identification to feelings about party leaders might have made this possible, in fact it did not happen. Turner was very unpopular and his party suffered a crushing defeat. Four years later, although the mix of short-term forces had changed significantly, strongly negative "Turner effects" were still at work.

1988: The "risky business" of free trade

Soon after taking office in 1984 the Conservatives began a precipitous slide in the polls such that in early 1987 they trailed both the Liberals and the New Democrats and had lost the support of nearly 40 percent of the entire electorate.[13] Paralleling this slide the group of Conservative identifiers fell to 30 percent by the autumn of 1985, and to 24 percent in 1987 (Figure 3.4). Fortunately for the Tories, the post-1984 erosion in their partisan base was accompanied by an incomplete revival of Liberal identifications, and by very modest increments in the NDP's. Still, the latter party, the perennial "plus" in Canada's "two party plus" national party system (Epstein, 1964), profited handsomely in the short-term from the Tories loss of support. By 1987 the New Democrats led the field with what for them was an unprecedented 37 percent vote intention rating. But their hopes for a major breakthrough were soon dashed. In the spring of 1988 they had fallen to third place in the polls, and our October–November 1988 preelection survey revealed only 16 percent were NDP identifiers.

Individual-level partisan instability also continued after 1984. However, unlike the early 1980s when the Liberals suffered very large losses, each of the three parties lost approximately 25 percent of their identifiers between 1984 and 1988. These data and the additional fact that increasing numbers of Canadians did not identify with any federal party in the first three years of the new Conservative government indicate that the 1984–88 period was one of growing partisan *dealignment* in an electorate long distinguished by the presence of many voters with weak party ties. The weakness and volatility of support for the national parties meant that the 1988 election outcome would be determined by short-term forces generated by party leader images and salient issues.

Free trade: "Let the people decide." The year 1988 will be remembered as the free trade election.[14] As noted in Chapter 1, relations with the United States always have had a major influence on Canadian politics, society and economy. Thus, Prime Minister Mulroney's decision to enter into a free trade agreement with the United States virtually guaranteed that the pact would be an issue in a forthcoming election. The Liberals decision to oppose the pact, to use their majority in the Senate to thwart its passage through Parliament, and the prime minister's decision to use the action as a pretext for calling an election meant that it would be a salient one. However, when the election writs were issued it was not apparent that free trade would totally dominate the issue agenda. At the time, Tory strategy was to soft-pedal free trade, while focusing public attention on and claiming credit for the reinvigoration of the economy that had occurred after their party had taken the reins of power.

13 Although the Canadian economy improved after 1984, favorable economic trends did not offset the effects of a continuing series of scandals, each of which eroded Tory support. See Chapter 3, note 5.
14 See Frizell, Pammett, and Westell (1989) and Leduc (1989).

The dynamics of the campaign quickly overturned this strategy. Liberal leader John Turner was under heavy fire within his own party for its lackluster showing in the early polls, and there were rumors that he might even be deposed. Because removing a leader during an actual campaign is a recipe for disaster, vigorous opposition to free trade became the obvious, perhaps the only, option for the Liberals.[15] Besides its uncertain economic effects, free trade might be represented to the public as a policy that could have a multiplicity of negative *noneconomic* consequences – namely, that it would open Canadian borders to American cultural and political domination. By casting the free trade issue in this way the Liberals could appear as the champions of national independence struggling to save the country from both the Conservatives and the rapacious Americans. Free trade held another important advantage for the Liberals. As the leaders of the anti-free trade forces they could effectively marginalize the NDP, which, as we have noted, had threatened to displace them as the principal opposition party. The Liberals chance to exploit the issue in this way was enhanced by the New Democrats less than vigorous campaign and their indecision as to how much emphasis to place on free trade as compared to other issues.

To reap these benefits the Liberals needed an opportunity to dramatize their opposition to the agreement. The nationally televised debates between the party leaders provided it, and Turner rose to the occasion. In the immediate aftermath of the debates, polls showed that many voters believed that the Liberal leader had outshone his rivals. More importantly, they revealed a dramatic shift in party support in the Liberals favor, and some polls even showed them surging ahead of the Conservatives.[16] As a consequence, the remainder of the campaign was dominated by a heated debate between the two parties concerning free trade and Canada's future.

The extent to which the debate over the issue helped capture public attention is shown in their responses to the "most important election issue" question in our 1988 postelection survey. Fully 89 percent cited free trade, with no other issue being mentioned by as many as 2 percent (Table 6.10). Such dominance of the issue agenda is unprecedented for elections for which national survey data are available. Although free trade was *the* issue, its status as a *position* issue meant that its impact on party support de-

---

15 As a *position* issue free trade was quite different from most other economic issues such as inflation and unemployment that have played prominent roles in previous Canadian elections. Although it is not logically necessary (see Alt, 1979: ch. 1), the latter have been *valence* issues in the Canadian context, and political debate has focused on which party is best able to deal with problems such as price increases and joblessness. See Clarke et al. (1984: ch. 4).

16 In our postelection survey 50 percent stated that Turner had impressed them "most favorably" in the leader debates. Mulroney and Broadbent favorably impressed 23 percent and 12 percent, respectively. Poll data on trends in party support in the campaign are reported in Frizzell, Pammett, and Westell (1989:95).

Table 6.10. *Party closest on most important issue, 1988 federal election (in percent)*

Most important election issue	Most important issue*	Party Closest Liberal	Conservative	NDP	Other	None/Don't Know
Free trade	89.4	26a	47	15	1	12
Other economic: deficit	1.4					
taxes	.2					
unemployment	.2					
Other: abortion	.8	12	28	18	10	31
daycare	.1					
environment	.7					
Meech Lake	.9					
Miscellaneous	2.8					
None, don't know	3.6					
All issues		24	44	15	2	16

Note: * - single response, N = 2010, vertical percentages; a - horizontal percentages

pended heavily on the distribution of public opinion and the dynamics
thereof. Also, because free trade was a *prospectively* oriented issue, its
long-term effects on the country's economy, society and polity were uncertain and, hence, open to debate.

With the sole exception of a strong consensus that the pact would hurt
some sectors of the economy, public opinion on its economic consequences
was deeply divided. Before the election 31 percent believed that free trade
would benefit all regions and 36 percent thought it would ensure the country's future prosperity (Figure 6.3).[17] These opinions did not change much
after the election and many voters continued to harbor reservations about
the pact's economic impact. Opinion regarding noneconomic effects also
was divided, but favored the pro-free trade forces. Before the election, for
example, only 37 percent believed free trade would threaten Canadian culture and the arts and 44 percent worried about a possible threat to the
country's political sovereignty. Similarly, the pact's opponents failed to
convince a majority that it endangered highly popular social programs.

Over the course of the campaign opinion on free trade moved in the
government's direction. In the preelection survey 39 percent favored free
trade, 45 percent were opposed and 16 percent were undecided; immediately after the election, 50 percent favored it, 40 percent were opposed
and 10 percent remained uncertain. This is not to say that the movement
of opinion was linear; the electorate's reaction to the party leaders heated
discussion of the issue in the television debates strongly suggests otherwise.
Analyzing our preelection survey responses by date of interview reveals
that opinion regarding the pact was almost evenly divided at 41 percent
before the debates, that opposition increased to 50 percent immediately
afterward, with support for the pact declining to 35 percent. Although
the balance of opinion fluctuated thereafter, a movement toward free trade
was evident among those interviewed in the closing week of the campaign.

To determine the sociodemographic and political characteristics of those
in favor of or opposing free trade we employed an additive index[18] of the

17 The following "agree–disagree" statements were used: (A) "The free-trade agreement
ensures Canada's future prosperity"; (B) "The free trade agreement threatens Canada's
political independence"; (C) "Economically the free trade agreement helps some *indus-
tries* but it hurts others"; (D) "The free-trade agreement threatens Canadian culture and
the arts"; (E) "The free-trade agreement economically benefits *all* of Canada, not just
certain regions or provinces"; (F) "The free-trade agreement could threaten important
programs such as unemployment insurance and medical care." Items (A) through (E) were
asked in both waves of interviewing; item (F) was asked in the postelection wave only.
18 For the free-trade items (see note 17 above), (A) and (E) "disagree" responses are scored
1; "agree" responses, 0. For items (B), (C), (D), and (F), "agree" responses are scored 1;
"disagree" responses, 0. Confirmatory factor analyses of these items using LISREL 7
weighted least squares procedures (Joreskog and Sorbom, 1988) indicate that Canadian
thinking about free trade was structured in terms of two *highly* correlated ($\phi = .75$) factors
($\chi^2_7 = 5.81$, p = .562). The general prosperity, political sovereignty, culture and the arts,

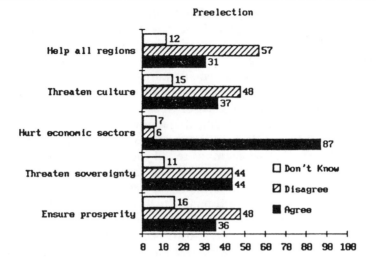

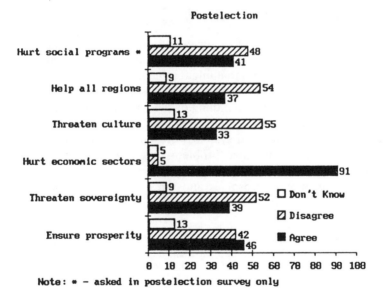

Note: * - asked in postelection survey only

Figure 6.3. *Opinions on the consequences of free trade, 1988 preelection and postelection surveys (in percent)*

number of problems people perceived with free trade as the dependent variable in a regression analysis of our 1984–88 panel data. Predictor variables included the measures of voters sociotropic, egocentric, and future-oriented economic judgments, as well as their more general evaluations of governmental effectiveness and equity–fairness introduced in Chapters 2 and 3.[19] The rationale for including these evaluative measures is that arguments concerning the benefits of free trade were articulated by the *governing* party and those arguments required voters to make complex prospective assessments. It seemed reasonable to expect that an important basis for making such assessments were judgments about the government's performance. Voters who believed that the government was effective and equitable and fair in its operations and expected more of the same in the future should have been more receptive to Tory arguments that free trade held more payoffs than problems, and that the government could implement the agreement successfully. Also, because of the close association between support for the Conservatives and pro-free trade sentiment, we included measures of *1984* federal and provincial party identifications. Their use enabled us to determine the extent to which opinions on free trade were products of previously established partisan sentiments. Finally, we included our standard set of sociodemographic variables (age, annual family income, gender, level of formal education, region–ethnicity) to provide controls for other forces that might influence feelings about free trade.

Regression analyses demonstrated that persons who had favorable evaluations of the government's handling of the national economy and its performance in several policy domains, and those who believed the government and the larger political system were operating equitably and fairly were more likely to minimize problems associated with the free trade agreement. So too were persons who were sanguine about their own and the country's economic prospects and the government's ability to affect

---

and social programs items loaded on factor one, and the sectoral and regional economic items on factor two. Although an alternative single-factor model does not perform as well ($\chi^2_9 = 35.52$, p = .001), the latter's fit is not bad considering the sample size (N = 2.010) (Carmines 1986:40–1), and all items except (C) (which has little variance) have impressive loadings (range = .75–.90). These results, and the desire to avoid multicollinearity problems occasioned by using strongly correlated variables in subsequent multivariate analyses, prompted us to adopt a single-factor measurement model of perceived problems with free trade. For ease of interpretation of the probit analyses below, the recoded free-trade variables are summed to produce a "free-trade problems" index ranging from 0 (no problems) to 6 (six problems).

19 The sociotropic, egocentric, and future-oriented economic evaluation measures are factor-scores based on a principal components analysis (varimax rotation) of six variables tapping retrospective, contemporaneous, and future-oriented judgments about national and personal economic conditions. See Chapter 2. The governmental effectiveness and equity–fairness indices are described in Chapter 3, notes 13 and 14, and 15 and 16, respectively.

them. Federal and provincial PC identifiers also were less likely to find problems with the pact. Finally, opinion divided along region–ethnicity and income lines; Francophone Quebecers and residents of the Prairies and British Columbia were less likely than Ontarians (the reference category) to see anything wrong, as were persons with higher incomes. These relationships reflect both historic region–ethnicity discontents with the Canadian political economy documented in Chapter 5, and the likelihood that free trade would hold different risks for different occupational groups, being greatest for blue collar (lower income) workers.

Leaders – Questions of character and competence. The "brokerage" electioneering strategies of Canadian parties (e.g., Schwartz, 1967; Clarke et al., 1984; Brodie and Jenson, 1990) help ensure that party leader support will have significant effects on voting behavior. Throughout much of the Trudeau era (1968–84) these strategies had worked strongly to the Liberals advantage because their leader was more favorably regarded by the public than were his NDP and, especially, his Tory rivals. When John Turner became Liberal leader this changed. As noted, after the Liberals 1984 debacle, support for him declined so sharply that efforts were made to oust him. He survived these efforts as well as a caucus revolt in the autumn of 1987, but there still was open discussion of replacing him when the 1988 campaign began. Even his unexpectedly strong debate performance had little lasting impact on his public support, which averaged only 46 and 44 points, respectively, in our preelection and postelection surveys (Table 6.7).

Public support for Conservative and NDP leaders followed different courses. In 1984 Mulroney's support score was 61, the third highest recorded for any party leader in the several national surveys. Public affection for the new prime minister soon declined as the aforementioned scandals began to take their toll. By 1987 his support stood at a dismal 41 points. However, as his party's fortunes improved in the polls, he made a modest comeback as well, so that in our 1988 preelection and postelection surveys his support scores stood at 48 and 50, respectively. Public feeling about Ed Broadbent, the NDP chieftain, also remained steady over the course of the campaign, his preelection and postelection ratings being 54 in both instances. This represented only a very slight decline from the 56 mark he had received in 1984. Broadbent differed from Turner and Mulroney, however, in that he received more support than his party in every section of the country. This "he's OK but what about his party?" pattern was one that also had characterized NDP leaders in earlier elections.

Although none of the party leaders enjoyed great support in 1988, most voters did distinguish among them. In relative terms, 37 percent gave their highest score to Mulroney, 35 percent favored Broadbent, and Turner trailed badly with only 16 percent. Even more indicative of the extent of

Turner's unpopularity, only 40 percent of his own party's identifiers ranked him ahead of his rivals. In sharp contrast, 70 percent and 87 percent of the Conservative and NDP identifiers, respectively, preferred their own party's leader.

Two crucial dimensions of party leader images are "character" and "competence" (Kinder and Abelson, 1981; Kinder, 1983). In 1988, all three leaders received mediocre rankings (means of 4.8 to 6.4) on 10-point "performance" and "honesty and ethics" scales (Table 6.7), with Broadbent's scores being the highest and Turner's the lowest.[20] Similar scores and patterns obtained among most regional/ethnic categories. Only among Francophone Quebecers did Mulroney have higher performance and honesty/ethics ratings than Broadbent. Turner consistently ranked last in performance but received marginally higher honesty/ethics scores than Mulroney in Ontario, British Columbia and among non-Francophone Quebecers. Comparisons with 1987 data show that the Conservative leader's performance and honesty/ethics ratings improved in the year preceding the election. The improvement was not dramatic, but it was enough to move him ahead of his Liberal rival on both dimensions in the run-up to the 1988 contest.

Risky business – the 1988 vote. Our model of the 1988 vote is one in which federal and provincial party identifications are measured in 1984 and feelings about leaders and issues in 1988. As in the 1984 analyses, we used probit for estimation purposes. Feelings about party leaders again were measured with the 100-point thermometer scales, and two issue variables were used – a "party closest on the most important issue" modified by evaluations of the importance of that issue in the voting decision, and an index of the number of perceived problems with the free trade agreement. The probit results indicated that the party closest on the most important issue had significant, positive effects on Liberal, Conservative, and NDP voting (Table 6.11). Predictable party leader effects also were evident. In the Liberal case feelings about Turner had positive effects, whereas feelings about Mulroney and Broadbent had negative ones. In the PC and NDP analyses comparable effects could be detected, although feelings about Turner were not a significant predictor of NDP voting. Also, as anticipated, federal party identification had significant positive effects, and in the Liberal case, provincial party identification was significant as well. The model's explanatory power was impressive with estimated R^2s varying from .77 to .81. Substituting the free trade problems index for the party

---

20 Respondents were asked: "Using a scale from 1 to 10, with 1 being *very bad* and 10 being *very good*, how would you rate Mr. Mulroney's *overall performance* as prime minister?" "And how would you rate Mr. Mulroney's *honesty* and *ethics*?" Comparable questions were asked about Messrs. Turner and Broadbent in 1988.

Table 6.11. *Probit analyses of voting in 1988 federal election*

Predictor variables	Liberal b	Conservative b	NDP b
Including party closest on most important issue			
Federal party identification, 1984	.18a	.17a	.20a
Provincial party identification, 1984	.10c	.01	.08
Party leader affect			
Turner	.02a	-.01b	-.00
Mulroney	-.02a	.02a	-.01c
Broadbent	-.01c	-.01c	.02a
Party closest on most important issue	.42a	.51a	.34a
Constant	-.22	-.34	-1.41a
Estimated R²	.81	.77	.80
% correctly predicted	88	86	91
Including free trade problems index			
Federal party identification, 1984	.20a	.12b	.26a
Provincial party identification, 1984	.12b	.04	.10c
Party leader affect			
Turner	.03a	-.02a	-.01c
Mulroney	-.02a	.03a	-.01c
Broadbent	-.02a	-.01	.03a
Free trade problems index	.24a	-.32a	.18a
Constant	-.94a	.32	-2.22a
Estimated R²	.76	.72	.62
% correctly predicted	84	86	88

Note: all variables except federal and provincial party identification
are from the 1988 post-election survey; a-p $\leq$.001; b-p $\leq$.01; c-p $\leq$.05;
one-tailed test

closest on the most important issues variable yielded similar results and, as
expected, the index had positive effects for the Liberals and NDP and a
negative one for the Conservatives (Table 6.11).

Overall, the vote models revealed that both orientations toward free
trade and party leaders had significant influences net of previously established partisan attachments. To determine the magnitude of these effects
we calculated the probabilities that voters would cast a Conservative,
Liberal or NDP ballot as their perceptions of free trade and feelings about
party leaders changed. We first computed these probabilities for persons
perceiving varying numbers of problems with free trade. We assumed that
a voter identified with the party in question at both the federal and provincial levels in 1984 and also assumed that the voters had average party leader affect scores. The results indicated that Tory identifiers with average
feelings about the leaders had a .86 probability of casting a Conservative
ballot if they failed to see problems with free trade. This declined to .55 if
they felt the agreement had the average number of problems and to only
.20 if they viewed it as having the maximum possible number of problems,

i.e., six. Liberal and NDP vote probabilities were mirror images, increasing rapidly as the number of problems cited increased. Clearly, the extent to which free trade was seen as risky business did much to determine electoral choice in 1988.

We focused on John Turner in analyzing the impact of leadership on voting choice. To determine Liberal voting probabilities if Turner had been held in higher esteem, we considered a scenario in which a voter perceived an average number of problems with free trade and had average feelings for rival leaders. Turner's popularity was successively set to his 1984 thermometer score as well as those for his predecessor, Pierre Trudeau, in the 1968–80 election surveys. We considered these changes for seven sets of federal and provincial party identifiers, ranging from those with very strong federal and provincial Liberal identifications to those with very strong identifications with another party. A more popular John Turner would have influenced Liberal vote probabilities most strongly (by .21 to .23) among his own party's identifiers, and equally large "Turner effects" were discernible among nonidentifiers. However, even if he had been as popular as his predecessor was twenty years earlier the Liberal vote probability still would have remained below .50 for those without a party identification. The consequences of more positive feelings about the Liberal leader among identifiers with *other* parties were considerably smaller, and even "Turnermania" would have left the probability of a Liberal vote among such persons well below .5.

Parties, issues, and the volatility of political support

We would argue that in a very real sense the 1988 election was a reprise of the 1980 sovereignty-association referendum analyzed in Chapter 5. In both cases the Liberal Party represented the debate as one involving a fundamental question of national community support. In the referendum campaign the Liberals argued vigorously that sovereignty-association required Quebec voters to choose between a Canadian political community that either did or did not include Quebec. Similarly, in the 1988 election, they again contended the vote involved the future of Canada, only this time the choice was one for all Canadians. This was a vote for an independent Canada, on the one hand, or the country's subordination – perhaps even its eventual absorption – by its powerful neighbor, on the other. In contrast, in 1980 the Parti Québécois argued that sovereignty-association was a regime- and authorities-level issue; Quebec voters were being asked merely to demonstrate their support for the PQ government and its plans to reorder unsatisfactory federal arrangements. In 1988 the Conservatives did not invest free trade with even regime-level significance. Rather, they portrayed it as a typical election issue involving a choice between the economic policy proposals offered by competing parties. Their proposal promised continued and even greater economic prosperity through increased access to the important markets of their neighbor to the south; the opposition's promised economic stagnation. Messrs. Turner and Mulroney's increasingly bitter charges and counter charges on the issue climaxed in the second of their nationally televised debates in which Mr. Turner accused the prime minister of selling out the country for the proverbial mess of pottage.

In both 1980 and 1988, then, the contesting parties tried to invest the voting decision with dramatically different meanings. In the first instance, the Péquistes failed in their attempt to minimize the significance of the decision for support for the national community; in the second, the Conservatives were successful. That they employed such a strategy is hardly surprising. Nor, given the volatility of the Canadian electorate, is it surprising that the outcomes of the contests were in doubt until the ballots were actually counted. As we have demonstrated, the volatility of support for Canada's political parties and their leaders is a longstanding phenomenon, one which is intimately related to the continuing instability of party and class identifications among voters and their frequent inability to apply ideological labels either to themselves or to the parties that compete for their favor. These conditions are both cause and consequence of the parties' brokerage electoral strategies, whereby they generally eschew comprehensive and clearly articulated packages of policy proposals in favor of a politics of leader images and short-term "fixes" for salient economic and social problems. Although it can be argued that such strategies are rational from the perspective of vote-maximizing parties, they effectively obfuscate much of the political choice that elections in democracies are supposed to provide. Such obfuscation, in turn, effectively decouples society and polity and serves to stimulate and reinforce the low levels of political efficacy and authorities trust shown in Chapter 3. Moreover, because support for political authorities has significant effects on the regime (a topic to which we return in the next chapter), the highly variable and frequently negative cast of Canadians feelings about political authorities has important consequences for support throughout the system.

SUMMARY

Elections perform a variety of instrumental and expressive functions that facilitate the maintenance of a democratic political order. Their position of centrality notwithstanding, there has been little consideration and no empirical investigation in a non-American setting of the role elections play in the overall support process. That has been the subject of this chapter. We began by delineating how respondents in our 1988 survey evaluated national elections. We found that Canadians gave them mixed reviews. Many believed that elections facilitate the accountability process and give people genuine choices among competing policy alternatives, but they also questioned the effectiveness of elections as educative mechanisms, and the claim almost invariably made by winning parties that they have been given a mandate by the electorate. Moreover, although evaluations of elections were largely independent of regional/linguistic and other salient sociodemographic cleavages, they were structured in terms of three underlying dimensions which we labeled "process," "mandate," and "accountability."

Our next task was to determine whether judgments about elections were systematically related to people's regime support. We found that election evaluations do influence regime support, even when people's attitudes toward the incumbent government are controlled. Moreover, notwithstanding the absence of any substantial or patterned change in people's judgments about elections during the course of a campaign, we found that when we measured average support for Canada, the government of Canada, parliament, the civil service, and judiciary before and after the 1988 national election, in every instance support had risen, as had people's feelings of political efficacy, trust, interest, and their perceptions of the responsiveness of MPs. These were aggregate changes but they also were reflected at the individual level, especially among identifiers with the Conservative Party, the party that was victorious in both the 1984 and 1988 national elections.

We then analyzed the forces associated with those victories, and found that in both cases short-term factors – notably issues and feelings about the three national parties and their leaders – in great part determined why the Conservatives won. Despite a massive triumph in 1984, the erosion of Tory support that began almost immediately afterward indicated that a second victory in the 1988 election was extremely problematic. In preparation for the 1988 election the prime minister undoubtedly was aware that his search for renewed support might be most successful in the province that not only is his home but which, together with Ontario, has decided the outcome of virtually every election since Confederation. As we showed in Chapter 5, during the 1980s federal party identification in Quebec was highly unstable, and at the time of the 1988 election there were fewer federal Liberal and more Conservative identifiers in the province than at any time since 1965. To woo Quebec voters Mulroney made excellent use of the patronage at his disposal and, although the subsequent failure of the Meech Lake Accord may have disastrous consequences for the Conservatives and, indeed, for the entire country, in 1988 it was popular among ordinary Quebecers and was strongly endorsed by Premier Robert Bourassa and his governing provincial Liberals.[21] Also, support for free trade, *the* issue in 1988, was widespread in the province.

---

21 In the 1988 preelection survey 66 percent said they had heard of the Meech Lake Accord. Among this group, 62 percent of Quebecers and 37 percent of non-Quebecers favored it, and 21 percent and 44 percent, respectively, opposed it. The rest were uncertain

Tory strength in Quebec in both the 1984 and 1988 elections, however, did not signal the onset of an era of Conservative hegemony in national politics such as the Liberals enjoyed during the past half century. There are three reasons why this is the case. One is that there has not been a genuine partisan *realignment* in Quebec. Although the Conservatives gained identifiers in the run-up to the 1988 election the overall impression conveyed by the 1980s survey data is one of extreme volatility in party support. All parties, not just the Conservatives, have significant opportunities, but no guarantees in the province, particularly in the wake of the Meech Lake Accord. A second is that in the crucial province of Ontario the Liberals have not as yet experienced a decline of federal party identifiers comparable to that in Quebec. Ontario remains very much an electoral battleground where no party occupies the high ground. Third, the impression of continuing volatility in party support is very much reinforced by recent trends in public opinion in which rapid and massive Conservative losses have been coupled with large Liberal and NDP gains. Propelled by the resignation of the unpopular Liberal leader, John Turner, and the massively negative public reaction to a government proposal to institute a general goods and services tax (the GST), Conservative popularity slipped from 49 percent immediately after the 1988 elections to 26 percent a year later, when the party fell to third place behind the Liberals and the NDP. PC strength continued to deteriorate in reaction to mounting economic difficulties, the implementation of the GST, and the continuing constitutional crisis created by the impasse over the Meech Lake Accord.

Despite the impoverished state of Conservative support, the changeable nature of the Canadian electorate means that the Tories will have significant opportunities to practice the arts of brokerage politics before another federal election is held. The brokerage strategies traditionally employed in Canadian elections are both cause and consequence of the volatility of support for political authorities that we have demonstrated in this and earlier chapters. The consequences of this volatility extend well beyond the electoral arena and affect the support process at the regime and community levels. In Chapter 7 we explore that process and its consequences in greater detail.

7

Causes and consequences of political support

It is better to coerce fewer people than more, to get voluntary observance rather than coerced obedience.
           Henry Mayo, *An Introduction to Democratic Theory*, p. 224

The notion of political participation is at the center of the concept of the democratic state.
           Samuel Barnes and Max Kaase, *Political Action*, p. 28

The skein of political life in democracies is complex and tightly woven. In this chapter we attempt to unravel several of its most important strands. We begin by developing and testing a multivariate model of the support process in which the dependent variables are the authorities, regime and community support factors identified in Chapter 4. The significance of economic and more general government effectiveness evaluations in the support model prompts us to assess their generality by investigating the impact of economic and other variables on support for democratic regimes in a broader comparative context. One of the problems that has bedeviled previous studies of political support is a failure to demonstrate that it has consequences for important political attitudes and behavior in a democracy. Because one of the proudest claims of democracies is that they are governments of "laws not of men," we next consider how people's willingness to voluntarily comply with authoritative edicts of government are affected by differences in support for the political authorities, regime, and community, as well as by other factors relevant to the support process. Finally, because citizen involvement is a sine qua non of democratic politics, we examine participation in conventional electorally oriented activities as well as more unconventional ones such as sit-ins and potentially violent protests, and determine the extent to which these are affected by variations in political support and related factors. These analyses demonstrate that support does indeed have significant consequences for two of the most important aspects of political life of a democracy.

THE FOUNDATIONS OF POLITICAL SUPPORT:
A MULTIVARIATE ANALYSIS

Analyses in presented Chapter 4 reveal that Canadians distinguish between support for the national political community and regime and support for incumbent authorities. Moreover, at the regime level, they distinguish support for parliament and the civil service, on the one hand, and support for the judiciary, on the other. We employed several predictor variables in our multivariate model of these four support factors. One of the predictors was federal party identification. Because party identification may affect and be affected by other predictor variables in the model and because we wished to capture the long-term effects of partisan attachments, we used the 1980–83 and 1984–88 panel data and measured party identification in the first wave of each panel.[1] We also included measures of people's evaluations of government effectiveness and the equity–fairness of the political system. Regarding the former, we employed both the general effectiveness index as well as our three measures of people's perceptions of general and personal economic conditions and government's impact thereon – what we termed sociotropic, egocentric, and future-oriented economic evaluations in Chapter 2.[2] Since judgments about the national economy are one component of people's evaluations of government effectiveness captured in our general index, we performed the analyses twice, once using the general index, and once using the sociotropic economic variable. In Chapters 1, 4, and 6 we argued that in the context of a democratic political culture, evaluations of the electoral process, feelings of political efficacy, and trust in public officials should influence support at various levels of the political system. In addition, the salience of federalism in Canadian politics suggests that support for national authorities, regime, and community should be influenced by the extent to which individuals are oriented toward national as opposed to provincial politics. Accordingly, measures of election evaluations,[3] political efficacy, authorities trust, and federal-provincial orientations[4] all were included in the model.

1 The party identification variable is described in Chapter 3, note 4.
2 For the government effectiveness and equity–fairness indices see Chapter 3, notes 13–16. The sociotropic, egocentric, and future-oriented economic judgment indices are factor scores based on an exploratory factor analysis of the variables described in Chapter 2, note 4.
3 The election evaluations index is available only in 1988. The measure is described in Chapter 6, note 4.
4 See Chapter 3, notes 18, 20, and 21 re: the construction of the efficacy and trust indices. For reasons of data availability the federal–provincial orientation measure used here is obtained by subtracting a respondent's province thermometer score from that for Canada. Those with positive scores on the resulting variable are considered to be federally oriented; those with negative scores, provincially oriented; and those with scores of 0, equally oriented to both levels of the political system. In both the 1980–83 and 1988 analyses federal-provincial orientations are measured using data from the first wave of the panel.

The model also incorporated our standard sociodemographic variables. Québécois and Westerners are the two groups which historically have manifested the greatest discontent with the Canadian political system, and so we focused on the impact of being a Francophone Quebecer or a resident of one of the four Western provinces.[5] These measures and the other sociodemographic characteristics should help to detect long-term, group-related socialization experiences that might affect support over and above more proximate attitudinal and evaluative influences. Finally, because we hypothesized that political support in Canada flows upward, from authorities to regime to community, we expected that support for regime institutions (parliament, civil service, judiciary) would be influenced by support for incumbent authorities. Support for the national community, in turn, would be affected by feelings about regime institutions and authorities. However, since support also might flow downward, from community to regime and authorities, and from regime to authorities, we investigated the possibility of these causal linkages as well.

Covariance structure analysis enables us to analyze the determinants of authorities, parliament/civil service, judiciary, and community support simultaneously, and diagnostics facilitate the detection of reciprocal causal linkages among the support factors.[6] The analyses proceeded in three steps. First, we permitted each independent variable to affect each dependent variable (support factor). Second, we reestimated the model using significant predictors only. Third, we examined diagnostic information and tested for the presence of nonrecursive linkages. Generally, the model performed well – for the 1980–83 panel the variance explained in incumbent authorities, parliament and civil service, and national community support ranged from .41 to .50 (Figure 7.1). Support for the judiciary was less well explained, although the R^2 (.25) was quite respectable. Examining the results in detail revealed that authorities support was influenced by prior (1980) party identification and trust in public officials. Also important were general government effectiveness evaluations. When we replicated the analysis substituting sociotropic economic judgments for the general effectiveness measure, we found that sociotropic judgments had a very strong

5 French-Quebecers are scored 1, and other respondents, 0. Similarly, the West variable is scored 1 for residents of Manitoba, Saskatchewan, Alberta, and British Columbia, and 0 for other respondents.

6 Since it may be assumed that the independent variables in the model are not error-free, CSA permits us to derive estimates of their effects net of measurement error. However, because a CSA that attempted to estimate error terms for the many indicators of the several predictor variables in the structural portion of our model would be extraordinarily complex, we adopted an alternative strategy of assuming plausible values for the error variance in these variables (Hayduk, 1987:119–22). Specifically, 10 percent of the variance in the attitudinal and evaluative variables was assumed to be error variance. This assumption was also made for income, and the other sociodemographic variables were assumed to be measured without error.

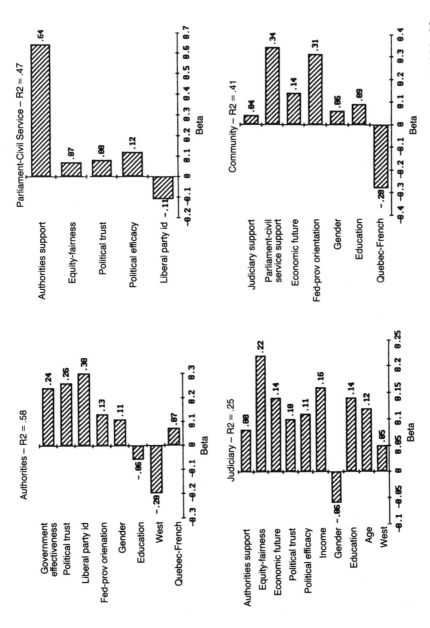

Figure 7.1. *Covariance structure analysis of national authorities, regime and community support, 1980–83 national panel, significant predictors only*

effect on support for political authorities ($\beta - .40$, data not shown). Federal-provincial orientations and region/ethnicity were influential at the authorities level as well. In addition, (and also as anticipated) given the presence of a Liberal government in Ottawa in 1983, federally oriented persons and Quebec-French were more supportive, and Westerners less supportive, of the incumbent authorities.

The determinants of regime support differed for parliament–civil service as opposed to the judiciary. As expected, feelings about the incumbent authorities had a very strong influence on support for the former ($\beta = .64$), whereas the impact on the latter was much less pronounced ($\beta = .08$). Additionally, although general government effectiveness judgments did not influence support for either regime factor, when we substituted socio-tropic economic judgments in the model, we found they that they had significant effects on support for parliament and the civil service. In contrast, future-oriented economic judgments and, especially, equity–fairness evaluations influenced judicial support. The effects of the sociodemographic variables on the two regime support factors also differed, none of them affected the parliament–civil service factor, whereas several had a significant influence on support for the judiciary.

As we had hypothesized, community sentiments were strongly affected by federal-provincial orientations and parliament–civil service support, with federally oriented people and those with positive feelings about the regime being the strongest community supporters. Additionally, with the sole exception of future-oriented economic judgments (those making positive judgments about the country's and their own economic future were more positively disposed), none of the evaluation variables had significant effects on community support. Again, as expected, being a Quebec-Francophone had large negative effects on national community support ($\beta = -.28$). Finally, the diagnostics provided by the covariance structure analyses revealed no evidence that support flows downward as well as upward. Analyses of the 1988 data revealed that the model again was able to account for sizable percentages of variance in authorities, parliament–civil service and community support (R^2s ranging from .30 to .47) and, once more, judiciary support was less well explained ($R^2 = .21$) (Figure 7.2). At the authorities level, prior (1984) party identification had the greatest impact ($\beta = .41$). Trust in authorities was influential, as were equity–fairness, general government effectiveness and egocentric and future-oriented economic judgments. Regarding the effects of region–ethnicity, the coefficient for Quebec Francophones was significant and positive – a result that is consistent with the strong support they gave the incumbent Progressive Conservative government in the 1988 federal election. In contrast to the 1980–83 results, the coefficient for Western residence was positive in 1988. This finding, in our view, reflects the presence of a Conservative govern-

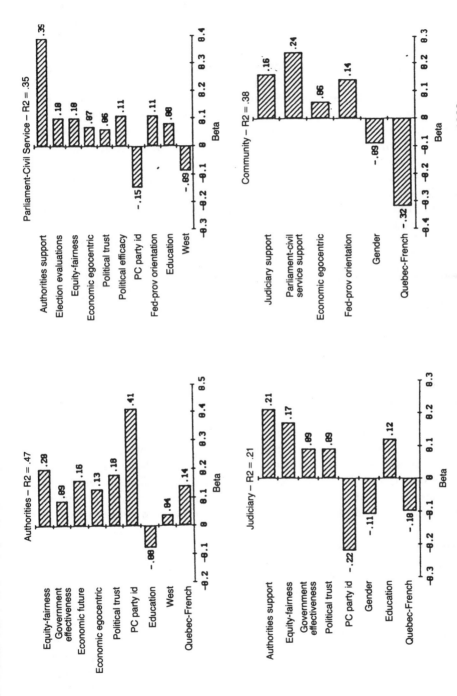

Figure 7.2. *Covariance structure analysis of national authorities, regime and community support, 1988 national panel, significant predictors only*

ment in Ottawa in 1988 coupled with the strong support Westerners have accorded the Conservative Party since the late 1950s (see Chapter 5).

As was the case in our 1980–83 analyses, parliament–civil service support in 1988 was strongly and positively associated with feelings about incumbent authorities ($\beta = .39$). More generally, the set of significant predictors was somewhat larger in 1988 than in 1980–83. Among the evaluative measures, favorable judgments about the equity–fairness of the political system and one's personal financial condition, and positive feelings about the electoral process enhanced parliament–civil service support. Political efficacy and authorities trust did so as well, and federally oriented persons again were more supportive. The effects of the sociodemographic characteristics on this type of regime support again were weak. Several variables also affected judiciary support, the most notable being the positive associations for authorities support, governmental effectiveness and fairness, and the negative one for Quebec Francophones.

One other finding in the 1988 regime support analyses merits comment. Unlike the strong positive association between Conservative Party identification and authorities support, PC partisanship is negatively related to parliament–civil service and judiciary support. We interpret this pattern as reflecting the historic tendency of Progressive Conservatives to regard "Ottawa" as a foreign country, indeed, a kind of "alien entity." Nor is this surprising given Liberal Party control of the national government for most of the last half century. Relatedly, recall our discussion in Chapter 5 about longstanding Western complaints about the quality of representation provided their interests by Ottawa, as well as the overwhelming shift in partisan support by Westerners to the federal Conservatives during the Diefenbaker era.

As in 1980–83, national community support was positively influenced by parliament–civil service and judiciary support. Again, there was a strong negative relationship between being a Quebec Francophone and community support ($\beta = -.32$). The effects of the federal-provincial orientations also were similar to those for the earlier period and, once more, model diagnostics had failed to indicate that support flows downward as well as upward.

Viewed more generally, it is evident that sociodemographic characteristics and political attitudes and economic and other evaluations have a variety of effects on support for the Canadian political system. However, their strength varies markedly across the authorities, regime and community levels. Sociodemographic variables consistently have their strongest effects on community and their weakest ones on parliament–civil service support. In 1980–83, for example, they accounted for 36 percent of the explained variance in community support, but only 10 percent of that for parliament and the civil service. The 1988 figures were 41 percent and 11 percent, respectively (data not shown). Sociodemographic effects also varied over time; they accounted for 34 percent of the variance in feelings about incumbent authorities in 1983, but for only 11 percent in 1988. This was also true of economic evaluations. Egocentric judgments had positive effects on several support objects in 1988, but not in 1980–83. Future-oriented judgments operated in both analyses, whereas judgments about the national economy and government's stewardship of it had a powerful impact on authorities support in 1980–83, and a more modest but still strong one in 1988.

These findings support our general hypothesis that neither political support nor its determinants are "of a piece." Predictably, long-term forces associated with membership in the Québécois ethnolinguistic community have their strongest impact on feelings about Canada as a political community. Even here, however, differences between Québécois and other Canadians do not explain everything. Throughout the 1980s support for the regime (parliament–civil service) had a strong influence on community support. At the regime level, parliament–civil service support was not greatly affected by sociodemographic characteristics, but support for the incumbent authorities, evaluative orientations and partisan attachments had major effects. Partisan identifications also strongly affected feelings about incumbent authorities. Again, as we argued in Chapter 1, national community support is partially the product of the *indirect* effects of people's judgments about governmental performance and the equity–fairness of the political system, as well as their support for political parties and their leaders.

As for the determinants of regime support, the impact of support for authorities on parliament–civil service support is impressive, especially in circumstances of one-party dominance, such as prevailed circa the early 1980s. Authorities and regime support are not synonymous, however, and the impact of the former is considerably weaker on the judiciary than on parliament–civil service. Also, although evaluations of government performance and sociodemographic characteristics influence both types of regime support either directly or indirectly, the size of these effects varies. The pattern is replicated for authorities support, in that it is affected by long-term partisan attachments and enduring group memberships, but short-term reactions to government performance in economic and other policy fields are influential as well. Trust in public officials also is important. As discussed in Chapter 6, public perceptions of incumbent authorities can change rapidly as citizens react to the actions of a government-of-the-day and its leaders. In the Canadian case, however, these perceptions are superimposed on a more general and persistent mistrust of both federal and provincial authorities (Chapter 3). We have argued that this latter condition is in part at least a product of electoral strategies pursued by vote-maximizing politicians operating in a particular sociopolitical context. The implication of these findings is that authorities support, like that for the regime and community, is a complex product of long- and short-term forces at play in the Canadian political system.

Economic performance and regime support in comparative perspective

This study has been concerned with delineating the support process in representative democracies through an intensive and systematic investigation of its sources, distribution and consequences for key political objects in one such democracy, Canada. One of our principal findings has been that political support in Canada is strongly influenced by citizen evaluations of the performance of the economy. These findings accord well with arguments that stress the importance of public reactions to changing economic conditions for explaining political support in contemporary Western democracies. Although a great deal of research has been done on this topic, the vast bulk of it has been confined to how economic trends affect support for governing parties and their leaders. The question of whether public reactions to economic conditions also influence support for democratic *regimes* remains unanswered, as does the effects of elections and other kinds of political interventions on feelings about such regimes. Our analyses in Chapter 6 indicate that in Canada elections are events that have a positive effect on regime and community support. One of the purposes of the present chapter is to determine whether such effects operate in other democracies as well. Answering these questions will help us to assess the level of generality of our Canadian findings.

As in Chapter 3, we employed the Euro-Barometer data on citizens' feelings of satisfaction with democracy in various Western European countries to address these questions. They enable us to determine the extent to which feelings about democratic regimes respond to changing economic conditions and various political events. We consider satisfaction with democracy in eight countries (Belgium, Denmark, France, Great Britain, Ireland, Italy, the Netherlands, and West Germany) over the 1976–86 period. These countries vary in theoretically interesting ways such as the length of their experience as democracies, the continuity of their regimes and, relatedly, the presence or absence of fascist dictatorships in the 1930s and 1940s, the nature of their party systems, the mix of politically relevant social and economic cleavages, and levels of and trends in their economic development.

Recall that levels of satisfaction with democracy varied across those eight countries as well as within them over time (see Chapter 3). Also, in some cases, such as France and Great Britain, marked changes in satisfaction occurred over brief time periods, and coincided with important domestic and international events such as an election outcome or success in an international conflict. Such country differences and short-term dynamics suggest that satisfaction with a democratic regime is related to longstanding political cultural and structural factors as well as to trends in economic well-being and transitory political events and conditions.

These data are suggestive, but formal time series analyses are needed to test hypotheses about the effects of economic conditions and political interventions on satisfaction with democratic regimes. Our analysis of the impact of economic conditions focuses on inflation and unemployment rates, typically matters of great public concern. Information on them is readily available via the mass media, the market place, and various channels of interpersonal communication. The 1976–86 period was one of economic hardship in many Western countries as first inflation and subsequently unemployment increased greatly. The public reacted by moving prices and then jobs to the top of the issue agenda and, in several cases, by withdrawing support for incumbent governments and removing them from office. Regarding the impact of elections and other political interventions, attention is restricted here to two especially salient ones, the 1981 French presidential election and British involvement in the Falklands War.

The GLS–ARMA variant of pooled cross-sectional time series analysis[7] was utilized to determine if inflation and unemployment and the two political interventions affected levels of satisfaction with democratic regimes.[8] The estimates[9] revealed that all of the predictor variables behaved as expected. Both inflation and unemployment had significant negative effects on satisfaction with democracy; as inflation or unemployment rose, satisfaction decreased (Table 7.1). The impact of unemployment was somewhat

7 Depending upon the nature of the pooled data set and the purposes of one's analyses, there are several possible approaches to estimation. Stimson (1985:927) notes: "GLS–ARMA becomes relatively desirable when design is time dominant and when explanatory variables are dynamic. . . . [W]here there are significant between-unit effects, error will be nonstationary and GLS–ARMA is inappropriate unless modified by the addition of dummy variables." The present data clearly have a strong time component (eleven time points for each of eight countries), and GLS–ARMA procedures enable us to control for time series dependencies that otherwise would bedevil attempts to assess the influence of macroeconomic conditions.

8 The dependent variable is the percentage in each country in each year who are very or fairly satisfied with the operation of democracy. Inflation and unemployment series are from OECD (1988:39, 83). The 1981 French election is scored 1 for France in 1981 and 0 for all other countries and years. The Falklands war is scored 1 for Great Britain in 1982 and 1983, and 0 for all other countries and years. Evidence supporting the assumption that the effect of the war on public opinion persisted into 1983 at the authorities level is presented in Norpoth (1987). Note also that part of the 1983 effect may reflect the general election held that year.

9 A preliminary analysis using inflation, unemployment, and the two political interventions as predictors indicated the presence of heteroscedasticity in the residuals that was controlled by incorporating dummy variables for six of the units (countries). Autoregressive and moving average parameters were specified on a country-by-country basis using diagnostics provided by an OLS regression that included country dummies. An alternative model using a pooled estimate of first-order autoregressive effects provided very similar results to those reported here.

Table 7.1. Pooled cross-sectional time series analysis of the impact of inflation and unemployment on democracy satisfaction in eight Western European countries, 1976–86

Predictor variables	b	t
Consumer price index*	-0.89	-5.71a
Unemployment rate**	-1.17	-4.88a
Country		
Belgium	-5.84	-2.03c
Denmark	10.61	4.55a
France	-12.41	-6.39a
Ireland	6.66	2.35c
Italy	-31.41	-16.83a
West Germany	11.37	6.98a
Interventions		
France 1981	18.57	5.51a
Britain 1982-83	9.42	2.49b
Constant	75.10	27.87a

$$\bar{R}^2 = .89$$

Note: * - year to year percentage change; ** - percentage change of total labor force; a-p $\leq$.001; b-p $\leq$.01; c-p $\leq$.05; one-tailed test for consumer prices, unemployment and interventions, two-tailed test for country dummy variables

greater than that of inflation; a 1 percent increase in joblessness lowered satisfaction with democracy by slightly over 1 percent, whereas a similar increase in inflation had an effect of slightly less than 1 percent. Because both types of economic adversity grew markedly in most of the eight countries between the mid-1970s and mid-1980s, these estimates indicate that the impact of rising prices and joblessness on lowering satisfaction with democracy was substantial in this period.[10]

However, the economy was not the whole story. Both political interven-

10 Considering all eight countries, unemployment ranged from 3.3 percent (West Germany, 1979 and 1980) to 17.4 percent (Ireland, 1985 and 1986). Inflation ranged from 0.2 percent (the Netherlands, 1986, and West Germany, 1986) to 21.2 percent (Italy, 1980). It is also noteworthy that the impact of economic evaluations on satisfaction with democracy operates at the individual level as well. The October 1983 Euro-Barometers for France, Great Britain, Italy, and West Germany included questions measuring judgments about national and personal economic conditions over the past year. The questions were: "How do you think the general economic situation in this country has changed over the past 12 months?" and "How does the financial condition of your household now compare with what it was 12 months ago?" The response categories were "a lot better," "a little better," "stayed the same," "a little worse," "a lot worse." Regression analyses revealed that in every country but Britain both types of evaluations influenced satisfaction with democracy net of feelings about incumbent governments (as measured by vote intention "if a general election were held tomorrow"). In the British case, national economic evaluations were significant, and personal ones just failed to be so (t = 1.59).

tions were highly significant; the 1981 presidential election in France produced a temporary increase of nearly 19 points in satisfaction with democracy in that country, whereas the Falklands war had a positive impact of over nine points in Britain. The "country effects" are noteworthy as well. Consistent with the national differences in average levels of satisfaction with democracy observed in Chapter 3, the coefficients for the country variables were large and statistically significant. For example, controlling for other factors, feelings about democracy were fully 31 points lower among Italians, and nearly 11 points higher among Danes. Although unpacking the meaning of these country effects is beyond the scope of the present inquiry, they strongly suggest that support for democratic regimes is a product of enduring political cultural and structural differences as well as more dynamic forces associated with economic trends and transient political events and conditions.

These findings accord well with the results of our Canadian analyses. Recall, for example, that either inflation, unemployment, or both, were almost continuously on the minds of many Canadians throughout the 1970s and early 1980s. People's perceptions of the state of the economy and their judgments about the government's ability to manage it were significant predictors of support for authorities and regime institutions. Moreover, our analysis of voting behavior in the 1984 election revealed that Canadians reacted to rising unemployment by moving joblessness to the top of the issue agenda. Their belief that the then opposition Conservative Party could handle the unemployment problem better than the incumbent Liberals was one of the principal causes of the latter's defeat after many years in power. Recall also that analyses of the Canadian panel data (Tables 6.5 and 6.6) revealed that the mere occurrence of an election stimulated a significant, albeit temporary, increase in support for key political objects, as well as increases in related attitudes such as political efficacy and trust. In sum, our European analyses increase our confidence that the results of our Canadian study are not idiosyncratic products of analyzing a country where support for the political system is especially problematic.

THE CONSEQUENCES OF POLITICAL SUPPORT

Compliance

Although democratic theory emphasizes that political systems and their leaders should respond to citizen needs and demands, the converse is also true. Democracies, like other forms of government, make demands on their citizens. Some of them – requests for the provision of tax monies and the human resources needed to counter external and internal threats to national and personal security – are not peculiar to democracies, but rather are common to all political systems. However, democratic norms and

Table 7.2. *Percentages agreeing with political compliance statements,*
1983, 1984, 1988

Compliance Statement	1983	1984	1988
People should pay their federal taxes even if they are used to support programs they don't like	76	77	75
The laws of Parliament should be obeyed as long as they don't violate people's basic rights	94	95	95
People should be willing to serve in the armed forces if the government asks them, even if they don't want to	49	48	42
If a policeman orders you to do something, you should do it even if you disagree	53	60	48
Canadians should be willing to go along with what the federal govenment decides even if they do not personally support the political party in power	57	62	53
N	2117	1928	2215

values shape and constrain what can be required of the public, and pre-
scribe the manner in which they may be formulated and expressed. Nevertheless, democracies resemble other systems in that widespread, although
not necessarily universal, public compliance with the demands of authorities is a prerequisite for effective governmental performance and system
stability.

To measure compliance orientations the 1983, 1984, and 1988 surveys
included five "agree–disagree" statements concerning adherence to the
laws of parliament and the decisions of the federal government, obedience
to orders from the police, and willingness to pay taxes and serve in the
armed forces. In all three surveys overwhelming majorities (averaging 95
percent) believed that the laws of parliament should be obeyed as long as
they do not violate basic rights (Table 7.2). Somewhat smaller, but still
large, majorities (averaging 76 percent) felt that federal taxes should be
paid, even if the monies are used to fund programs they do not personally
favor. However, there was much less agreement about the necessity of
adhering to the decisions of the federal government if a person does not
support the party in power, to serve in the armed forces, or to unques-
tioningly obey orders from the police. From one-half to three-fifths of the
public agreed with the first two of these propositions, but only two-fifths to
one-half with the third.

Compliance attitudes varied among different groups in the population.
With the exception of willingness to obey the laws of parliament, younger
persons consistently expressed less willingness to comply than did older

ones. Perhaps not surprisingly, since young people are most frequently called on for this purpose, the strongest difference involved service in the armed forces; in 1988 only 30 percent of those twenty-five years old or younger were willing to do so as compared to 61 percent of those over 65, a number of whom undoubtedly had served during World War II. Also, perhaps because they generally have less to risk materially and have fewer familial responsibilities, younger people also were much less likely to agree that the orders of the police should be obeyed without question; nor did they as often believe that one always should go along with what the federal government decides. Region–ethnicity differences were apparent as well, the most salient being that Francophone Quebecers declared themselves less willing to serve in the armed forces, obey orders from the police, or agree that federal taxes should be paid. Educational level and gender also correlated with compliance, with better educated individuals being more likely to agree that taxes should be paid, but less likely to agree that one should serve in the armed forces, obey the police, or adhere to the decisions of the federal government. Women generally were somewhat less compliant than men.

Confirmatory factor analysis enabled us to ascertain whether there was an underlying structure to these compliance orientations.[11] A one-factor model applied to the 1983 data was problematic ($\chi^2_5 = 33.40$, p = .00). LISREL diagnostics suggested that a two-factor alternative with the "pay federal taxes," "obey laws of parliament," and "adhere to federal government decisions" items loading on the first factor and the "serve in armed forces" and "obey police" items loading on the second was preferable. This model fit the 1983 data extremely well and, accordingly, it was retested using the 1984 and 1988 data. The fit was acceptable in these cases as well (Table 7.3). Moreover, although the two factors were strongly correlated in all three years (ϕ's ranging from .62 to .77), they clearly were not coterminous. Based on the item loadings we labeled the two factors "federal laws and regulations" and "service and obedience," respectively.

How stable are compliance orientations? One possibility is that a person's willingness to adhere to the demands of government may be mutable, changing as evaluations of system performance and feelings about political authorities, regime and community change. Another is that compliance attitudes are deeply rooted products of early-life socialization processes and, as such, highly resistant to the changing mix of political events and

11 In these analyses respondents indicating the presence of a compliance orientation by "agreeing" with a compliance statement are scored 1; "disagree" responses are scored 0. On the assumption that some respondents might be unwilling to indicate openly their unwillingness to comply, "don't know" responses also are scored 0. The percentage of such responses ranges from 2.5 percent to 7.8 percent in 1983, from 2.3 percent to 8.2 percent in 1984, and from 1.5 percent to 8.0 percent in 1988. Rerunning the analyses omitting these respondents (listwise deletion) leaves the results essentially unchanged.

Table 7.3. Confirmatory factor analyses of compliance orientations, 1983, 1984, and 1988 national surveys

Compliance statement	1983		1984		1988	
	Laws	Service	Laws	Service	Laws	Service
Should pay taxes	.61a	.00	.62a	.00	.52a	.00
Should obey laws of parliament	.50a	.00	.47a	.00	.56a	.00
Should serve in armed forces	.00	.53a	.00	.56a	.00	.57a
Should obey police	.00	.70a	.00	.64a	.00	.63a
Should go along with federal government	.68a	.00	.68a	.00	.58a	.00
ϕ	.62a		.77a		.65a	
	$\chi^2_4 = 2.43$, p = .66		$\chi^2_4 = 13.88$, p = .01		$\chi^2_4 = 10.91$, p = .03	
	AGFI = .998		AGFI = .990		AGFI = .998	
	N = 2117		N = 1928		N = 2215	

Note: a-p ≤.001; WLS estimates

conditions and the reactions they engender. Analyses of our panel data indicate that, in fact, compliance orientations do vary over time. This was especially true of the federal laws and regulations factor; the correlations (ϕ) for the 1983–4 and 1984–8 panels were .62 and .48, respectively. Service and obedience attitudes were somewhat more stable, but they were subject to change as well, the ϕ's for the two panels being .71 and .76. Feelings of compliance, then, can "wax and wane" over even relatively brief time intervals.

Covariance structure analyses of the 1983 and 1988 survey data were employed to ascertain the determinants of compliance. Predictor variables included support for incumbent authorities, parliament–civil service, the judiciary, and the national community. Also included were evaluations of the economic and more general performance of government, the perceived equity–fairness of the political system, and evaluations of the electoral process. In the context of a democratic political culture such as Canada's these evaluations should have important effects on citizens willingness to comply with the demands of political authorities. Feelings of political efficacy and trust in these authorities also should be influential and therefore were included, as were the sociodemographic characteristics used to proxy the impact of long-term socialization processes.

The predictors accounted for sizable amounts of the variance in laws and service compliance (R^2's ranging from .42 to .47) (e.g., Table 7.4). In both 1983 (data not shown) and 1988 national community support had positive effects on compliance with federal laws and regulations, and in one of the 1988 analyses, it had a positive impact on service–obedience compliance as well. At the regime level, support for the judiciary had a positive influence in 1983, whereas parliament–civil service support had significant negative effects on both types of compliance in 1988. The latter finding suggests that the parliament–civil service factor may tap feelings about the values and procedures that undergird a democratic regime, as well as attitudes toward specific regime institutions. As anticipated, support for incumbent authorities also had positive effects on laws compliance (in 1983), and trust in authorities had positive effects on this type of compliance in both years. Indeed, authorities trust had the greatest impact on laws compliance, and it positively affected service compliance in 1983.

Citizens evaluations of system performance also played important roles in the compliance models. Equity–fairness judgments were the most consistent; favorable judgments were associated with increased laws and service compliance. General governmental effectiveness evaluations had a positive impact on laws compliance in both years, and on service compliance in the latter year. Judgments concerning one's personal financial circumstances and government's impact thereon were significant in both 1983 and 1988. They were positively associated with laws compliance and,

Table 7.4. *Covariance structure analysis of political compliance factors, 1988*

Predictor variables	1988	
	Laws	Services
	γ	γ
Region-ethnicity		
Atlantic	.01	-.02
Quebec-French	.10c	-.19a
Quebec-Non-French	-.04	-.00
Prairies	.02	.11a
British Columbia	.02	.02
Age	.26a	.40a
Education	.12b	-.02
Gender	-.06	-.18a
Income	.06c	.04
Political efficacy	.02	-.06
Political trust	.29a	.01
Economic evaluations		
Egocentric	.04c	.02
Sociotropic	t	t
Future	-.01	.00
Federal government effectiveness	.14a	.20a
Political system equity-fairness	.14a	.15a
Evaluations of federal elections	.09b	.03
Authorities support +	.13a	.05
Parliament-civil service support	-.09b	-.10b
Judiciary support	.03	-.01
National community support	.13a	.05
R^2 =	.47	.42

Note: entries are standardized Gamma coefficients; t - variable not included in analysis; + - mean incumbent government party and party leader thermometer scores; a-p ≤.001; b-p ≤.01; c-p ≤.05; one-tailed test.

in the former year, with service compliance as well. Also, net of all other considerations, favorable evaluations of the national electoral process had a positive impact on laws compliance in 1988 (the only survey for which the elections measure is available).

Compliance attitudes also were associated with several sociodemographic characteristics (Table 7.4). Older Canadians were more likely to be high on both types of compliance. Quebec Francophones tended to have much lower scores than Ontarians (the reference category) on the service factor, whereas Prairie residents had lower scores in 1983, but higher ones in 1988. This reversal suggests the importance of feelings about incumbent authorities for understanding compliance. In 1983 the Trudeau-led Liberals were on the government benches and, as noted in Chapter 5, many Prairie residents had strongly negative feelings about the prime minister and his party. Five years later, the Mulroney-led Conservatives were in office and, although Westerners were less than enthralled with some of the decisions made by the new prime minister and his colleagues,[12] relatively speaking, the region remained a bastion of Conservative strength.

In summary, sociodemographic, attitudinal and evaluative variables all have important influences on compliance. Although long-term socialization processes are only imperfectly captured by sociodemographic charac-teristics, the significance of variables such as age and region–ethnicity in the multivariate analyses that control for attitudinal and evaluative factors suggests that socialization effects are indeed at work. However, long-term forces are not the whole story. Compliance feelings are mutable, reacting to a complex mixture of attitudes and evaluations, at least some of which can change rapidly. Trust in authorities, support for them and the national political community, judgments regarding governmental performance and equity–fairness, and evaluations of national elections are relevant as well. We conclude that compliance in a democracy such as Canada cannot be taken for granted, but rather must be continually regenerated by the ongoing political process.

Participation

Democratic politics is about citizen participation, and representative democracies provide numerous "pathways to politics." Many of these routes lead to and through the electoral arena. Voting is, of course, the most basic form of electoral participation, but people also can try to con-vince others how to vote, campaign on behalf of candidates or parties, donate money to these individuals and organizations, or stand for elective office themselves. In the interim between elections they may continue to do party work, discuss politics with friends, family, and co-workers and, either alone or collectively, contact public officials to press their concerns. All of these activities long have been accorded legitimacy by prevailing cultural norms, but there are other participation pathways as well and, in contem-porary democracies some of these trails are well-traveled, while others re-main off the beaten track. Among the former are activities such as organiz-ing or simply signing petitions, engaging in marches and rallies, boycotting goods and services, while the latter include participating in wildcat strikes, sit-ins, and other types of demonstrations. Many of these activities are peaceful and lawful and they are considered appropriate and effective by large percentages of the publics of Western countries (Barnes, Kaase et al., 1979; Jennings, Van Deth et al., 1989). Some, however, have the potential

---

12 For example, in the autumn of 1986 the Conservative government decided to award the Air Canada CF–18 maintenance contract to Canadair in Montreal and not to Bristol Aerospace in Winnipeg. The decision was widely interpreted in the West as a blatant display of favoritism to Quebec.

to become violent and are of questionable legality. Nonetheless, the incidence of and legitimacy ascribed to several of these "unconventional" activities have increased over the past three decades, thereby expanding what Barnes, Kaase et al. (1979) have felicitously termed the "repertoire" of citizen political action.

Activity levels. On average 75 percent of the Canadian electorate have cast ballots in the eight federal elections held since 1965 (Feigert, 1989) and, although turnout varied somewhat over this period, the pattern is one of fluctuation rather than a systematic trend. Voting in Canadian federal elections, although high in comparison with some countries such as the United States, is lower than that in many others. Circa the early 1980s, Canada ranked in the bottom quarter of democratic countries in turnout (Crewe, 1981:234–7). Nor does turnout in provincial elections change the picture. In some provinces voting in provincial elections tends to be greater than in federal contests, whereas in others, the opposite is the case.

Regarding other activities, data from national surveys conducted since 1965 tell a consistent story – the Canadian political arena is the preserve of "active minorities." In the 1988 preelection survey, for example, although 70 percent reported that they discuss politics at least "sometimes," only 18 percent tried to convince friends how to vote, 14 percent attended a political meeting, and 25 percent contacted public officials (Figure 7.3). Working for political parties or candidates was even more exotic; over 90 percent of those in the 1988 postelection survey never had done so and only 3 percent did so often. Again, Canadians do not eschew the national arena in favor of provincial and local alternatives. Rather, rates of public involvement are very similar at all levels of the political system (Mishler, 1979; Uhlaner, 1982).

As with voting turnout, there is no evidence that involvement in these various conventional and mainly electorally related activities is systematically increasing or decreasing over time. More specifically, the 1974–88 data reveal that participation fluctuates within a narrow range. The sole exception is discussing politics, which increased dramatically between the 1988 preelection and postelection surveys. In the former 29 percent said they discussed politics often, whereas in the latter 45 percent did so. The preelection figure resembles those for earlier surveys, and we attribute the postelection increase to the 1988 campaign, which sharply focused public attention, if only temporarily, on the highly salient free trade issue and its potential impact on the country's future (see Chapter 6). Although other forms of participation did not increase across the preelection and postelection waves of interviewing, the sharp rise in public discussion during the 1988 campaign indicates that elections can foster citizen involvement. That it occurs only rarely reflects the ideologically muted, "problem-" and leader-oriented electioneering strategies favored by Canada's major polit-

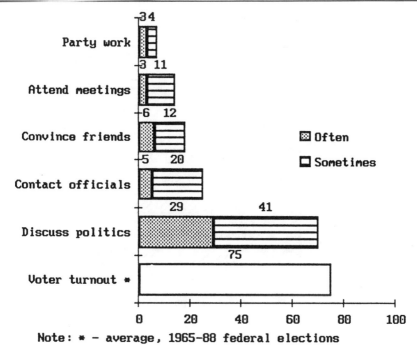

Figure 7.3. *Participation in conventional political activities, 1988 (in percent)*

ical parties, a theme we stressed in Chapter 6, and one to which we return in our concluding chapter.

The 1983 and 1988 surveys also included questions about several other activities. Large majorities (68 percent) stated that they had signed a petition at some point in their lives, nearly two-fifths said that they had engaged in boycotts (38 percent in both surveys), and about one-fifth to one-quarter (20 percent in 1983, 24 percent in 1988) reported that they had participated in a march or rally (Figure 7.4). Other activities were clearly the preserves of very small minorities; in 1983 only 5 percent said they had ever taken part in a "sit-in" and 4 percent had engaged in a protest "where there was a chance of violence." The comparable 1988 figures were somewhat larger – 8 percent in both cases.

Approval, effectiveness.   Judgments about which activities were considered legitimate and effective varied markedly. Nearly nine of ten people interviewed in 1983 approved of petitions, and more than seven in ten believed they could be effective (Figure 7.4). About half recognized the legitimacy and effectiveness of marches and rallies. Sit-ins and potentially

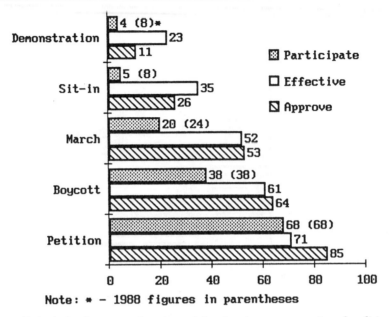

Figure 7.4. *Attitudes toward and participation in unconventional political activities, 1983, 1988 (in percent)*

violent protests, in sharp contrast, were regarded as effective by only one-quarter to slightly over one-third of the public. Further, although one person in four believed sit-ins were legitimate, only one in ten approved of demonstrations that might turn violent.

These figures resemble those from the 1981 Social Change Survey, which asked whether several activities, including boycotts, marches, rallies, sit-ins, and violent protests could be justified. Although only small minorities (no more than 20 percent) said that any of them could be justified "often," large majorities thought that boycotts, marches, and rallies were legitimate "sometimes," and about one-half felt this way about sit-ins. Violent protests, again in contrast, met with massive disapproval; over 90 percent stated that they were "never" justified. Thus, although their political action repertoire extends well beyond election-related activities, an overwhelming majority of Canadians draw the line when it comes to disruptive and potentially violent behavior. These remain beyond the pale for all but very small groups.

Who? Voluminous research has indicated that electoral participation is related to socioeconomic status, age, and gender (e.g., Verba and Nie,

1972; Milbrath and Goel, 1977). Persons with higher income and education and those with middle class or upper middle class occupations are more likely to be active, as are men and middle-aged rather than older or younger persons. Participation in unconventional activities is different; although situational considerations are important,[13] young, well-educated men tend to be the most active (e.g., Barnes, Kaase et al., 1979; Muller, 1979; Jennings, Van Deth et al., 1989). The Canadian data are generally consistent with these patterns. In 1988, for example, better educated persons were more likely to have participated in all of the unconventional activities and, in some cases (boycotts, petitions, marches), the relationships were fairly strong. Also, women were somewhat less likely than men to have participated in conventional activities, and less likely to have engaged in certain unconventional ones (sit-ins or possibly violent demonstrations) as well. Younger persons were more likely to have performed these latter acts, with the sharpest distinction being between those who reached the age of majority in the late 1960s or later and those who did so earlier. Participation in most conventional activities and in boycotts and petitions, in contrast, was greatest among the middle-aged and it declined among both younger and older persons. Also, as anticipated, those with higher incomes generally were more active. Regarding region–ethnicity, Québécois were noticeably more likely than others to have been involved in sit-ins or potentially violent demonstrations, and least likely to have talked about politics, tried to convince others how to vote, or to have attended meetings or rallies. However, most of the region–ethnicity relationships were quite weak, suggesting that outside of Quebec the incidence of citizen participation is basically the same across the country.

Structure.   Early studies argued, or simply assumed, that participation formed a unidimensional hierarchy (e.g., Milbrath, 1965:16). People who engaged in more demanding activities such as working for political parties or standing for public office also performed less demanding ones such as going to the polls, discussing politics, or trying to convince others how to vote as well. In the past two decades this unidimensional model has been challenged on conceptual and empirical grounds. Research on conventional types of participation, especially that by Verba and Nie (1972), as well as studies concerned with a broader range of activities (Barnes, Kaase et al., 1979; Jennings, Van Deth et al., 1989) have demonstrated or strongly suggested the existence of "multimodal" models of citizen action in which various forms of participation other than voting are the preserves of different, but possibly overlapping groups.

Confirmatory factor analysis enabled us to evaluate the appropriateness

13 On the importance of the context of participation see Kaase (1989:50–7).

of these alternative unidimensional and multidimensional models.[14] We began by analyzing a random half-sample of our 1983 data to test a simple single-factor model of nine conventional and unconventional activities (discuss politics, convince friends how to vote, attend meetings, work for party or candidate, sign petition, march or demonstrate, boycott, engage in sit-ins, or join possibly violent protests). The model's fit was very unsatisfactory ($\chi^2_{27} = 314.22$, p = .00). Better, but still unacceptable, was a two-factor model that distinguished between conventional, largely electorally oriented, activities and others. Clearly, a more elaborate multidimensional model was needed. To develop such a model we made three distinctions. The first was between conventional, electorally oriented activities and unconventional ones. The second was between "words" and "deeds," i.e., between verbal and other forms of behavior. The third was between nonconfrontational and confrontational protests. The former included signing a petition and joining a boycott, whereas the latter involved marches and other demonstrations, sit-ins, and potentially violent protests. Based on these three distinctions we hypothesized that four factors – verbal persuasion, campaign activity, nonconfrontational protest, and confrontational protest – characterize citizen political activity in Canada. The four-factor model performed markedly better than the one- and two-factor alternatives ($\chi^2_{21} = 25.49$, p = .23).

We next replicated the analysis using the second 1983 half sample and the full 1988 sample, and in both instances the fit again was excellent (Table 7.5). All factor loadings were large and statistically significant and diagnostic statistics were acceptable. These findings strongly argue in favor of a multimodal participation model. Although the number of factors in such a model might increase if additional activities were considered (e.g., contacting public officials, local community action), the items included in the four-factor model enable us to analyze forces affecting both electorally related activities that traditionally have played crucial roles in the support process, as well as various protest activities that have become increasingly important in these Western countries since the mid-1960s.

Before proceeding, it is noteworthy that all of the interfactor correlations for the four-factor model were positive, suggesting that people who engage in one type of activity tend to participate in others. However, the correlations varied substantially, being strongest for verbal persuasion and campaign activity ($\phi = .72$ in 1988) and confrontational and nonconfronta-

---

14 In these analyses persons responding that they "often" or "sometimes" engage in a particular political activity are scored 1; "seldom" and "never" responses are scored 0. On the assumption that some respondents might be unwilling to indicate that they are not active participants in the political process, "don't know" responses (which, depending on the item, constitute from .1 percent to 5 percent of the responses) also are scored 0. Rerunning the analyses eliminating these respondents (listwise deletion) does not change the results.

Table 7.5. *Confirmatory factor analysis of political participation, 1988 panel*

	Political Participation Factor			
Political Activity	Verbal Persuasion	Campaign Activity	Nonconfrontational Protest	Confrontational Protest
Discuss politics	.67a	.00	.00	.00
Convince friends how to vote	.72a	.00	.00	.00
Attend meeting or rally	.00	.89a	.00	.00
Work for party or candidate	.00	.85a	.00	.00
Sign petition	.00	.00	.67a	.00
March or demonstrate	.00	.00	.00	.97a
Boycott	.00	.00	.78a	.00
Sit-in	.00	.00	.00	.61a
Possibly violent protest	.00	.00	.00	.81a

$$\chi^2_{21} = 22.71, \ p = .359, \ \text{AGFI} = .995$$

Inter-factor correlations (ϕ)

	Verbal Persuasion	Campaign Activity	Nonconfrontational Protest	Confrontational Protest
Verbal persuasion	1.00			
Campaign activity	.72a	1.00		
Nonconfrontational protest	.44a	.25a	1.00	
Confrontational protest	.32a	.31a	.62a	1.00

Note: N = 1516, a-p $\leq$.001; WLS estimates

tional protest ($\phi = .62$ in 1988) (Table 7.5). The relative strength of these correlations confirms the validity of the basic distinction between conventional and unconventional activities, and the good fit of the four-factor model in comparison with the simpler two-factor (conventional versus unconventional activity) alternative indicates that distinctions within these categories also are appropriate. More generally, none of the interfactor correlations approached 1.0 and several were quite modest, thus suggesting "participation specialization" among imperfectly overlapping groups of active minorities.

Causes. Although studies of forces affecting political participation are legion, much remains to be learned. Particularly intriguing is the impact of authorities, regime, and community support, and the effects of compliance attitudes, judgments about government effectiveness and equity–fairness, and the quality of the electoral process. Do these orientations influence the propensity to engage in different forms of political activity and, if so, how? Regarding the second question, there would seem to be a fundamental difference between conventional activities, on the one hand, and confrontational protest activities, on the other. One would anticipate that regime and community support, and compliance attitudes would have positive relationships with the former, and negative ones with the latter. Expectations about nonconfrontational activities such as boycotts and petitions are more difficult to formulate. Although these activities do not involve elections or party organizational work, as we have seen, they meet with widespread approval, and seemingly are regarded as options in the accepted repertoire of political action. If so, we might anticipate that engaging in them would be positively related to regime and community support and compliance orientations.

Another important distinction concerns positive versus negative motivations for involvement. Do people become active because they are satisfied with government performance or because they are dissatisfied? Presumably, protest activities are products of dissatisfaction, but the situation regarding conventional activities such as discussing politics or working for a party or candidate is less clear. People might do these things because they are satisfied with the performance of the incumbent authorities or the political system more generally or, alternatively, they might do them because they are discontented and want to "throw the rascals out."

Covariance structure analysis was used to answer these questions. The independent variables included authorities, regime and community support, compliance and governmental performance evaluations, as well as several variables identified in previous research as having significant effects on various forms of political participation (Milbrath and Goel, 1977; Verba and Nie, 1972; Barnes, Kaase et al., 1979). The latter included political interest and efficacy, strength of party identification, trust in political authorities and sociodemographic characteristics (age,[15] education, gender, income, region–ethnicity). Two measures of socialization experiences that might dispose people to become active also were included. The first was involvement in decision-making in the family, school, and workplace, and the expression of opinions in such settings. Participatory democratic theorists (e.g., Pateman, 1970; Macpherson, 1977) have claimed that such involvement fosters attitudes that encourage political activity, and some researchers have reported findings consistent with their arguments (e.g., Almond and Verba, 1963; Greenberg, 1981). Such effects might be substantial in the Canadian case. In our 1984 survey 22 percent stated that they had "a great deal" to say about family decisions that affected them and another 39 percent said they had some say. Similarly, nearly one-third recalled expressing their opinions "often" in school and another third did so "sometimes." At least some involvement in decision-making in the workplace also was fairly common; nearly two-fifths reported that they did so "often" and another one-third, "sometimes." It also has been hypothesized that early life socialization experiences in families in which parents were

15 Age is treated as a series of dummies to capture possible curvilinearities or cohort effects. Cutting points are established to delineate groups entering the electorate in the mid-1970s, the mid-1960s, and the post-World War II era. Persons entering before World War II are the reference group.

Table 7.6. *Covariance structure analysis of political participation factors, 1983–84 panel*

| | Political Participation Factors | | | |
Predictor variables	Verbal Persuasion	Campaign Activity	Nonconfrontational Protest	Confrontational Protest
Region-ethnicity				
Atlantic	-.07c*	.10a	-.12b	-.02
Quebec-French	.18a	.07c	.12b	.27a
Quebec-Non-French	.09b	.00	.03	.09b
Prairies	.03	.06c	-.02	-.05
British Columbia	.06c	.05	.03	.06c
Age cohorts				
18-26	.01	-.03	.02	.19a
27-41	-.01	.02	.30a	.20a
42-65	-.01	.05	.25a	.03
Education	.03	.02	.37a	.17a
Gender	-.07c	.04	.01	-.13c
Income	.05	-.02	.01	.00
Political efficacy	.13a	.09b	.09c	.03
Political trust	-.06	-.01	-.03	-.01
Federal government effectiveness	-.08b	-.02	-.14b	-.02
Political system equity-fairness	-.02	.01	-.19a	-.13a
Parental political involvement	.11a	.09a	.08c	.05
Involvement non-political decisions	.15a	.17a	.08c	.04
Strength of federal party identification	.21a	.17a	.03	-.01
Political interest	.53a	.28a	.09c	.12a
Authorities support+	-.05	-.05	-.09c	-.04
Parliament-civil service support	-.02	.04	.02	.04
Judiciary support	.07c	.04	.02	.08c
National community support	-.05	-.04	.02	-.08c
Compliance				
Laws	-.04	.02	.08c	-.07c
Service	.02	.00	-.06	-.11b
$R^2 =$	.56	.24	.46	.31

Note: * entries are standardized Gamma coefficients; + mean incumbent government party and party leader thermometer scores; a-p $\leq$.001; b-p $\leq$.01; c-p $\leq$.05; one-tailed test

politically interested and active encourage later life political involvement, and evidence from studies comparing party activists and nonactivists offers empirical support (Kornberg, Smith, and Clarke, 1979:ch. 2). The 1983 survey reveals that about one-quarter of the interviewees recalled that their parents were "very interested" in politics and over half had parents who were "somewhat interested." Slightly less than one in five reported that one or both parents at some point in their lives had done something on behalf of a party or candidate.

We employed our 1983–84 and 1988 panel data to investigate the impact of the several variables discussed above. In both cases, their collective explanatory power was substantial, being greatest for verbal persuasion, somewhat less for nonconfrontational and confrontational protest, and smallest for campaign activity (e.g., Table 7.6). Regarding confrontational protests, many of the predictors behaved as anticipated. In 1983–84, engaging in protests such as sit-ins and potentially violent demonstrations was negatively associated with community support and both types of compliance orientations (laws and regulations, service and obedience) (Table 7.6). Also, as anticipated, persons making negative judgments about the equitable and fair operation of the political system and those who were more interested in politics were more likely to protest. Several of the sociodemographics were influential as well; confrontational protesters tended to be Québécois, well-educated, men, and those who entered the electorate during or after the mid-1960s.

Nonconfrontational protest was negatively related to support for incumbent political authorities. Relationships with equity–fairness and government effectiveness judgments were negative as well. Both of the political socialization variables – parental political involvement and participation in decision-making in nonpolitical milieux – were associated with enhanced participation. Also, Québécois, the well-educated and those in the two intermediate age cohorts (27–41, 42–65) were more active than other persons. Finally, although neither regime nor community support was significant, laws compliance was, but the effect was positive. This finding is consistent with the previous observation that Canadians view petitioning and boycotting very differently from confrontational protests. Because they do, it may be that those with positive orientations toward compliance with federal laws and regulations choose nonconfrontational rather than confrontational means to press their grievances. Verbal persuasion and campaign activity had the expected positive relationships with variables such as political interest, efficacy, and strength of party identification. Also consistent with previous research, both of these participation factors were positively associated with socialization experiences involving politically active parents and decision-making in nonpolitical settings. To learn about the effects of economic evaluations per se, we substituted the three economic evaluation factors for the general effectiveness measure. Overall, the results were largely unchanged. Persons who made unfavorable evaluations about their own economic condition or that of the country as a whole and attributed responsibility to government for these circumstances were more apt than others to engage in conventional and unconventional forms of political action.

In 1988, support for the national political community, support for the judiciary and the service-obedience compliance factor all were negatively associated with confrontational protest (data not shown). Additionally, persons who made unfavorable effectiveness and equity–fairness judgments were more likely to protest, as were those with high levels of political efficacy and interest. As in 1983–84, Quebec-French, the well-educated, men, and younger persons also were more likely than others to protest. Several of these predictors had significant effects on nonconfrontational protest as well. Particularly noteworthy were the negative effects of governmental performance and equity–fairness evaluations and authorities support. As in 1983–84, laws compliance was also positively related to non-confrontational protest, as were several of the sociodemographics. Like confrontational protest, nonconfrontational protest was positively associated with heightened interest and efficacy, and the determinants of conventional participation in 1988 also resembled those operative in 1983–84. Once again, future-oriented economic judgments did not influence any type of political activity in 1988. Egocentric and sociotropic ones, in contrast, were influential; people making unfavorable judgments participated more frequently. Unfavorable egocentric judgments also were associated with heightened campaign activity, and unfavorable sociotropic ones with attempts at verbal persuasion.

Confrontational protest in Quebec.   The salience and significance of confrontational protests in Quebec since the mid-1960s suggest the utility of examining the determinants of these activities in greater detail. We did so by replicating our participation analyses for Quebec residents only.[16] The predictor variables in the Quebec models explained substantial amounts of variance in confrontational protest in the province (in 1983–84 $R^2 = .48$, and in 1988, .34), and several variables that were significant predictors for the country as a whole were significant in Quebec as well (data not shown). As expected, low levels of support for the national political community were associated with increased protest, and in 1983–84, low levels of support for the judiciary worked this way too. Negative evaluations of the equity–fairness of the political system also were related to increased protest in 1983–84, and in 1988, negative government effectiveness evaluations and negative service/obedience compliance orientations did so. As expected, well-educated, male Quebecers were the most prone to protest, and in 1983–84 persons in the two youngest age groups (those 41 or younger) were the most active. The age relationships were different in 1988, with the very youngest group (those 30 or younger) being the least likely to be active. This may reflect the entry of a 1980s "postsovereignty-association" cohort into the electorate. In the wake of the defeat of the sovereignty-association referendum in 1980, public interest in and discussion of Quebec's future ebbed dramatically. Although the abortive Meech Lake constitutional accord and disputes concerning the language legislation reinvigorated proseparatist sentiments as the 1990s began, Québécois who had come of age in the immediate postreferendum period may have undergone different socialization experiences from those who reached maturity in the turbulent, emotionally charged 1960s and 1970s.

16 Confirmatory factor analyses demonstrated that the four-factor participation model fit the Quebec subsample extremely well, i.e., 1983–4, $\chi^2_{21} = 20.30$, p = .50; 1988, $\chi^2_{21} = 26.03$, p = .21.

SUMMARY

This chapter has focused on the causes and consequences of political support. In earlier chapters we hypothesized that support has two sources: political socialization experiences and evaluations of the effectiveness and equity–fairness of government and the larger political system. We also argued that because political parties play vital roles in linking citizens to a democratic political order, attitudes toward parties are important in support processes. As anticipated, partisan attachments affect support primarily at the authorities level, but because feelings about incumbent authorities "spill over" to influence regime support, feelings about parties reverberate throughout the support process more generally. These effects are sizable because of Canada's Westminster-model parliamentary system and protracted periods of one-party dominance.

We again proxied the empirically elusive effects of socialization experiences with several sociodemographic variables. These affect authorities, regime and community support and, as expected, the strongest impact occurs at the community level; controlling for all other factors Quebec Francophones have significantly lower levels of support for the Canadian political community. Also indicative of the importance of socialization experiences, orientations toward the federal as opposed to the provincial level of the political system are associated with enhanced community support.

Effectiveness and equity–fairness evaluations have significant effects on support as well. Performance evaluations influencing support involve reactions to an incumbent government's management of the economy and its activity in several other policy areas. Important too are equity–fairness judgments; in a representative democracy such as Canada, citizen attitudes toward the political system are governed by evaluations of whether it is operating according to democratic norms. Although we have distinguished analytically between the effects of evaluations and political socialization experiences, it is important to recognize that the former are grounded in the latter. Standards of government effectiveness and equity–fairness are not generated *ab nihilo*, but rather are products of socialization experiences within a particular cultural context. In Canada, that context is one in which democratic norms and values are the rule. Relatedly, and consistent with this argument, evaluations of one of the most important aspects of democratic government, the electoral process, influence regime support, controlling for all other considerations.

The Canadian analyses are consistent with the oft-advanced proposition that political support reflects public reactions to changing economic conditions. We assessed the generality of our Canadian findings in a broader comparative context by analyzing public satisfaction with the operation of democracy in eight European nations. Two of the features of the economy, inflation and unemployment rates, negatively affected people's satisfaction with how democracy worked in their countries. As in Canada, the occurrence of elections also had significant, albeit transient, effects on the dynamics of support for democracy in the eight nations. However, large "country effects" were evident as well, suggesting the importance of long-term cultural and structural forces.

We also have analyzed the *consequences* as well as the *causes* of political support. Democratic theory holds that the successful functioning of a democratic system of governance is predicated on citizen compliance with the edicts of duly constituted authorities and extensive participation in the political process. Despite the theoretical importance of this proposition, the effects of variations in political support on people's compliance with government's edicts and their participation in the system have been neglected in previous research. We found that in Canada compliance attitudes have a bi-dimensional structure and, although Canadians generally are quite willing to observe the laws and regulations promulgated by government, they are much less willing to offer unquestioning service and obedience to it. Whereas noncompliant attitudes were especially prevalent among younger persons and Quebecers, they were not confined to these groups. Compliance orientations are not fixed in stone, but instead vary over time in response to other political attitudes. Trust in political authorities, positive evaluations of the government's effectiveness and equity–fairness and favorable assessments of the electoral process all enhance compliance. Support is relevant as well; positive feelings about the national political community are associated with a heightened willingness to adhere to the federal government's laws, regulations, and requests for service and obedience.

Citizen participation is the "red thread" in the tapestry of democracy. Like other contemporary representative democracies, the political action repertoire in Canada is diverse and multidimensional. Quebecers are more likely than other Canadians to engage in confrontational protests. Although they have not been the only ones to march, sit-in, or take part in violent protests, since the mid-1960s these activities have been a highly salient, if episodic, feature of the province's political life. Many of these protests have involved those wanting to sever Quebec's ties with the rest of Canada. Beginning with the bombing of mailboxes to symbolically protest the federal government's presence in the province, political violence in Quebec escalated as the 1960s progressed. It culminated in the 1970 "October crisis" when British trade official James Cross and former provincial Liberal cabinet minister Pierre Laporte were kidnapped and the latter murdered by members of the radical FLN (Front de libération du Québec). Their acts of terrorism caused a sensation in Canada's "peaceable kingdom," and prompted Prime Minister Trudeau to invoke the emergency War Measures Act, to bring out troops and tanks, and to suspend the right of habeas corpus.

After the crisis passed, terrorism subsided, but marches and demonstrations continued, as proponents of Quebec sovereignty periodically "took to the streets" to dramatize their cause. When the Parti Québécois came to power in 1976, its legislation to protect and advance the status of French language and culture became a new focal point for protests. In recent years, the passions of both proseparatists and antiseparatist groups again have been inflamed as by similar measures undertaken by the Liberal provincial government of Robert Bourassa. In 1988 the Bourassa government invoked the "notwithstanding" clause (Section 33) in the new constitution to ensure that their language law (Bill 178) forbidding non-French signs was not overturned in the courts by groups claiming protection under the constitution's Charter of Rights and Freedoms. This markedly heightened tensions between Francophones and non-Francophones, and prompted protests within and outside of the province.

As for other Canadians, after voting in periodic elections, most abandon the political arena to overlapping groups of active minorities. Nevertheless, large numbers are not "voters only" in that they at least occasionally discuss politics with friends and family, sign petitions, or boycott various goods and services. Vast majorities, however, avoid confrontational protests such as sit-ins and potentially violent demonstrations because they believe such activities are illegitimate. The determinants of participation vary according to the type of activity. Negative motives frequently prompt involvement, and unfavorable reactions to political authorities are associated with a propensity to engage in nonconfrontational protests such as petitions and boycotts. Similarly, negative evaluations of government effectiveness and equity–fairness stimulate protest activities, and low levels of regime (judiciary) and community support and service-obedience compliance increase the likelihood of confrontational activities.

Political support thus has a variety of important consequences. By documenting them, the analyses presented in this chapter have laid the groundwork for a more general assessment of the present status of and future prospects for political support in Canada and other contemporary representative democracies.

8

Political support in representative democracies

Canada is whole again. Quebec has joined the Canadian family.
> Prime Minister Brian Mulroney, Meech Lake, April 1987

Well if that's what you think, f—you!
F—you too!
> Exchange of views between Quebec Premier Robert Bourassa and Newfoundland Premier Clyde Wells over the Meech Lake Accord, Ottawa, June 1990

Democracies have few political heroes. Even the popularity of such redoubtable wartime giants as Winston Churchill and Charles de Gaulle proved to be ephemeral, whereas the periods in which merely mortal political leaders have strutted and fretted their hours on the political stage to the applause of citizen audiences generally have been brief indeed. That they have both makes the task of maintaining public support for democracies difficult and is a source of their greatest strength. We began this study by arguing that citizen support for a political regime and its leaders, and for the community of which they are a part, flows from both political socialization experiences and evaluative judgments regarding the performance of political objects generally and the extent to which they provide for one's personal well-being and that of cherished others. In turn, each of these twin pillars of support has two parts: effectiveness and equity–fairness assessments, in the case of political objects and processes, and group identities and democratic norms, in the case of political socialization. We noted that political socialization is one component of a more general process through which people become social beings. As a consequence there are times in the life of a democracy when the support accorded certain social objects and processes will be higher than that accorded manifestly political ones.[1]

One reason is the sporadic and haphazard character of political socializa-

---

1 For example, data presented in Chapter 3 that show social and political trust and competence are significantly related but not coterminous.

tion In democracies, a condition that also makes it extremely difficult to delineate the impact of socialization effects on political support. A second, related, reason is the content of what is being transmitted through the socialization process; the information that socializing agents provide about the political system and its leaders is not always positive or flattering to them. Still another reason is the distinction between what is public and what is private. In representative democracies, including Canada, socialization experiences work to define separate and well-demarcated public and private spheres. That defined as private includes a large and diverse array of activities taking place in hometowns, neighborhoods, workplaces, and myriad other formal and informal social groups. They do much to structure the content of people's daily lives but often are not seen as being connected to what government does. Nonetheless, in the past half century, the public sphere has been greatly expanded. In addition to traditional functions such as protecting people's lives and property and maintaining national security, governments are accorded major responsibility for the state of the economy and for a broad range of social programs including health care, education, family allowances, job training, old age pensions, and unemployment insurance. Recently, governments have been charged with implementing programs designed to protect and restore the environment, redress regional and other group-related economic inequalities, foster culture and the arts, and secure the rights and improve the status of historically disadvantaged groups such as women, the handicapped, and visible minorities.

Although in part a response to the hazards of life in modern industrialized societies, the expansion of the scope of governmental activity is also a product of the willingness of political leaders of all ideological hues not only to assume responsibility for current programs but, under conditions of intense interparty competition, to promise and then to generate new ones. Until the 1970s the unstated assumption was that an ever-expanding economy would ensure that such programs would not unduly strain the public purse. The stagflation that plagued many Western economies during the 1970s and early 1980s rendered these assumptions problematic but, importantly, it did not transform public thinking about the desirability of such programs.

Citizens of all democratic societies expect their government to maintain an economic climate in which the weather is always sunny, but in some of them – certainly in Canada – judgments about the government's economic performance tend to be asymmetric. People are less willing to praise government when things are going well than they are to blame it when they are going poorly. This asymmetry, we believe, reflects a complex mix of cultural assumptions and values concerning a capitalist economy's ability to generate personal and national prosperity, the managerial competence and fairness of public authorities, and the efficacy of individual effort. To attribute responsibility to government for unhappy circumstances seems reasonable, for example, given the oft-articulated claims of democratic political leaders pursuing electoral office that they can manage a nation's economy successfully and their perceived inability to live up to their claims. Another incentive is the psychological need to avoid blaming one-self for one's condition. In some countries, such as the United States and, to a lesser extent, Canada, classic liberal shibboleths concerning equality of opportunity and individual responsibility continue to have resonance, and to be invoked periodically by societal leaders and ordinary citizens alike. Even in these countries, however, the ability of such ideas to circumscribe political demand is limited by the presence of a substantial interventionist element in the political culture.

There also is evidence of another kind of asymmetry. Irrespective of whether people judge that economic conditions are good or bad nationally, they tend to believe that they and their local communities are in at least reasonably good shape. The ability to distinguish between one's own finan-cial and more general well-being and that of others extends to judgments about a variety of noneconomic matters as well. *Pace* relative deprivation theory, in democracies such as Canada, most people feel *relatively advan-taged* rather than deprived, a feeling that can and does help sustain a polit-ical system during periods of social, economic, and political travail. We have argued that a factor contributing to the disjunction between people's perceptions of national social and economic conditions, on the one hand, and their own, on the other, is that global attitudes and judgments tend to be based on information acquired from the mass media. In a democracy the media report fully and continuously on a variety of social pathologies as well as on national economic conditions – about which "nits can be picked" even in the best of times. In contrast to relying on the media for informa-tion about the country, people rely more heavily on personal experiences in forming opinions about their own condition, and those of family, friends, neighbors, and the community in which they live.

An additional explanatory factor concerns the salience of social class and its impact on public attitudes and behavior. In Canada about half of the public ordinarily do not think of themselves as members of a social class and, of those who do, their self-perceptions are very unstable. Further-more, at any point in time a large majority of those with class self-images see themselves as part of an amorphous "middle class." Such mutable and poorly defined self-perceptions inhibit the ability of voters to link their objective social and economic circumstances with what is or is not happen-ing in the political arena. The weakness of class cleavages in Canadian politics is reinforced by the brokerage strategies of the two major national parties, the Liberals and the Conservatives, both of which consistently cast their electoral appeals in nonclass terms.

In all democracies psychological attachments to political parties and pat-terms of party support are part and parcel of the political process. In Canada feelings about parties are important but their effects are limited by the weakness and instability of partisan ties. Substantial partisan dealignment in Canada is longstanding, and in the past two decades party allegiances have weakened in several other Western democracies as well.[2] For perhaps as much as one half of the Canadian electorate, party identification seems little more than a convenient score card for recording issue concerns and party leader evaluations that may change over relatively brief periods of time. The implication for the support process is that party identification is both a cause and consequence of other political attitudes, beliefs and opinions. One of these surely is judgments about the state of the economy and the quality of its management by government. If the asymmetric character of Canadians' judgments about government's responsibility for the economy noted above reflects a common pattern of thinking among citizens of other democracies, it seems clear that regime support is more easily eroded than enhanced by the actions governments take or fail to take to ensure national prosperity.

We would argue that generally the strength of the linkage between economic judgments and regime (and ultimately community) support should be influenced by several factors, including the structure of government, patterns and intensity of interparty competition, party issue priorities and ideological positions, as well as the intensity and durability of people's partisan attachments. Regarding structural factors, the impact of economic evaluations on political support should be stronger in parliamentary/unitary than in presidential-congressional/federal systems. The decoupling of executive and legislative functions of government and the division of responsibilities between national and subnational units in a system such as the United States should diminish the strength of the relationship between public judgments about the economy and support for an incumbent administration, on the one hand, and, at least in theory, between administration and regime support, on the other. The relationship should be most robust in a parliamentary/unitary system such as Great Britain, where executive and legislative powers are fused in a single body, and it should be of intermediate strength in countries such as Canada and Australia, which combine Westminster-model parliamentary systems with federalism. In the Canadian case, however, we find, despite a highly decentralized form of federalism, that regime and authorities support is compressed and strongly correlated. We have argued that this condition is largely a product of protracted periods of one-party dominance in national and provincial politics.

2 See, *inter alia*, Budge, Crewe, and Farlie (1976); Sarvik and Crewe (1983: ch. 12); Clarke and Stewart (1984); Dalton, Flanagan, and Beck (1984); Le Duc et al. (1984); Dalton (1988: ch. 9).

The condition is exacerbated by the self-serving practices of provincial and federal officials who, irrespective of the party labels they bear, represent themselves as sole spokespersons of *their* regimes and even *their* communities.

The varying strength of the relationship between authorities and regime support evident in our 1980–83 and 1988 Canadian analyses illustrates how interparty competition can affect the political economy of support for both an incumbent government and a democratic regime. The federal Liberals controlled the national government for approximately forty-two of forty-nine years between 1935 and 1984, and in the struggle for constitutional change in the 1970s and early 1980s the Liberals and their longtime leader, Pierre Trudeau, were the principal exponents of a "renewed federalism" with strong central government powers. As a consequence, in 1983 the Liberal Party and the national regime had become virtually synonymous for many people, and this is reflected in the strong linkages between authorities and parliament–civil service support in our 1980–83 analyses. In contrast, these correlations are weaker in our 1988 analysis because the Conservatives had been in office for only four years.

The extent to which political parties have distinctive issue priorities and ideological positions should influence the strength of the effects of different kinds of government effectiveness judgments on political support. Narrow issue and ideological distances between parties make it likely that retrospective judgments about the economy and an incumbent government's ability to manage it will dominate the support process. In contrast, prospective economic judgments – indeed, prospective judgments more generally – should have stronger effects on support in situations in which parties have relatively distinct issue priorities and ideological positions because such differences raise the possibility of major policy departures should a change of government occur.

In Canada there is little ideological differentiation between the two major national parties. During election campaigns the Liberals and the Conservatives typically represent themselves as problem solvers, claiming that they are best suited to deal with pressing issues such as inflation, unemployment, or national unity, while downplaying or eschewing specific policy proposals designed to handle such problems. As a result, many voters believe that a change of government will not produce major policy innovations and, consequently, retrospective judgments about government performance dominate prospective ones in our model of authorities support. Analyses of our 1980–83 data gathered at a time when unemployment (a quintessential problem issue) was the preeminent concern illustrate this pattern. In atypical situations when the parties *do* divide over a highly salient issue, prospective judgments become more important. This pattern is illustrated by analyses of our 1988 data gathered during a

heated interparty debate over the economic, social and political consequences of a free trade agreement with the United States for the future of
the Canadian political community.

The *strength* of partisanship also is important. Party ties have eroded in a
number of Western democracies since 1970, resulting in partial dealign-
ments similar to that which long has characterized Canada. We hypothesize that the stronger and more durable party attachments are, the less
important economic judgments (of whatever kind) will be in the support
process. In Canada economic evaluations presently have strong effects on
support and, if partisanship should weaken further, these effects should be
magnified. Because economic judgments influence political support in
other Western democracies as well, if dealignment continues in those countries, such judgments should become even more influential in the 1990s.
This is important because the political economy of support always entails
an element of risk for incumbent governments and democratic regimes.
Political leaders – however wise their policies and impressive their managerial skills – cannot guarantee prosperity, and thus economically based support must always be problematic in a democracy.

Less problematic for support may be people's perceptions of democracy
and elections. If the Canadian case is typical, the great majority of citizens
in Western countries believe that their countries are democracies, but they
vary in their views about what democracy does and should entail. Average
citizens, then, as well as political philosophers, differ in their conceptions
of democracy. Our analyses indicate that there are essentially two streams
of thought – "expansive" and "restrictive." Those having an expansive conception emphasize, for example, that free speech should be extended even
to people who would like to destroy democracy, and that democracy as a
political process should entail more than just voting in elections. Those
with a restrictive view believe that democracies should provide for equality
of opportunity but not of outcome, that a democracy has a right to protect
itself from internal subversion, and that it can limit individual and group
rights for the benefit of the entire community.

National elections are integral to democratic theory and practice. If the
views of Canadians can be generalized, in democracies citizens also are
divided in their evaluations of the roles elections play. Some believe that
elections facilitate the accountability process, provide real choices among
policy alternatives, and are not simply ritualistic occasions that do little
more than make them feel good. However, others question the effectiveness of elections as educative mechanisms, doubting that such contests enable them to learn much about important problems facing the country.
They also express skepticism about the perpetual claims of winning parties
that they have received a mandate from the people, and an overwhelming
majority believe that once in office, parties renege on their campaign
promises. In Canada evaluations of the national electoral process are not

idiosyncratic, but rather are structured in terms of readily recognizable accountability, mandate and process factors, the first two of which are subsumed by a more general popular control factor. Evaluations of the electoral process matter – they influence regime support controlling for all other variables in our support models.

Elections are important in other ways as well. Although they have attracted a great deal of scholarly attention, existing research has focused heavily on explaining individual voting behavior or the outcome of specific elections. However, elections also may be viewed as recurring interventions that periodically affect important political attitudes and behavior – they are events that bolster, even if only temporarily, support for and satisfaction with democracy. Our Canadian and Western European analyses support this proposition. The Canadian data also reveal that elections have positive effects on feelings of external political efficacy and trust in political authorities. They increase immediately after elections, decline in the interim between them, and then rise again when another election is in the offing.

This study has focused on public attitudes and behavior. Obviously, however, what happens at the level of the citizen is influenced by political elites. For example, the mixed reviews average Canadians give national elections likely reflect the tendency of party leaders to emphasize the three "Cs" during an election campaign – charisma, character, and competence – which, of course, they claim to possess in abundance in contrast to their opponents, who are said to be remarkably deficient in all three. Also relevant is the aforementioned tendency of Canadian party leaders to downplay discussions of specific policy alternatives and to emphasize valence rather than positional issues. Encouraged by the media, especially television, party leaders thus help trivialize elections by representing them to the public as personality and quasiathletic contests. In Canada, typically, it is only after an election that major economic policy initiatives such as a comprehensive energy program (the National Energy Programme) or a national sales tax (the Goods and Services Tax) materialize. Even such basic matters as constitutional reform (e.g., the Meech Lake Accord) seldom find their way onto the issue agenda during an actual campaign. The fevered debate between Prime Minister Mulroney and Liberal leader John Turner over the government's proposed free trade agreement that dominated the 1988 campaign was an anomalous result of the dynamics of a particular campaign context. It occurred not because the parties had changed their minds about the efficacy of brokerage electioneering strategies, but rather because the Liberals, fearful of losing a second consecutive election and possibly even being displaced as the official opposition by the New Democrats, seized on the issue out of desperation. Indeed, by attempting to portray the free trade agreement as a challenge to the continued integrity and independence of the Canadian political community rather than as a disagreement over the economic consequences of a government policy initiative, the Liberals hoped to convert the proposal into the kind of valence issue that is a major component of such strategies.

Party scholar John Meisel (e.g., 1975:217–52; 1979:119–35) contends that during the post-World War II era much of the blame for these obfuscatory brokerage strategies could be laid at the doorstep of the long-dominant Liberals. However, the Liberals were hardly unique in their approach to electioneering; the strategies they and the other parties pursue are both a cause and consequence of the sociopolitical milieu in which they operate. Rather than being a kind of elite conspiracy against hapless voters, brokerage strategies represent a rational response by politicians attempting to maximize their vote shares under a condition in which deep, reinforcing ethnolinguistic cleavages, weak social class identities, and unstable partisan attachments define the context of electoral competition. But the process is circular; the practice of brokerage politics reinforces the conditions that give rise to it.

Some would argue that deficiencies in the electoral process produced by brokerage electioneering strategies are part and parcel of a more general and pervasive elitism in Canadian society – an elitism that historically has had profoundly deleterious effects on the development of a democratic political culture and an integrated nation–state (e.g., Lipset, 1990; Stevenson, 1979, 1989). One of the leading exponents of this type of argument, sociologist John Porter, claimed that over the years Canadian political leaders have combined pious exhortations to unite with themes and practices that divide. "The major themes in Canadian political thought emphasize those characteristics, mainly regional and provincial loyalties, which *divide* the Canadian populations. Consequently integration and national unity must be constantly reiterated to counter such divisive sentiments" (Porter, 1965:368).

Although Porter's classic study was published a quarter of a century ago, the elitist strand in Canadian political culture remains a sturdy and enduring one. An excellent example is the protracted process of constitutional renewal that took place in the 1970s and early 1980s, a process in which the leading actors were the eleven governments of the federal system, each of which sought "not some abstract goal of legitimacy for the system as a whole, but a version of legitimacy designed to serve *its* present and future interests" (Cairns, 1983:380). A more recent example is the ill-fated Meech Lake Accord. Like the constitutional agreement, the 1987 Accord was a product of negotiations among federal and provincial first ministers which were devoid of any significant public involvement. The Accord would have been a "done deal" if all of the provincial governments had accepted it. Meech Lake was a nonissue in the 1988 federal election, and only became one at the eleventh hour, in the spring of 1990, when it was apparent that unanimous provincial consent might not be forthcoming before the June 23 deadline for ratification. As a consequence, the realization that their country was in the throes of yet another constitutional crisis caught many average Canadians by surprise.

Meech Lake and the crisis of national community support it precipitated are eloquent testimony to the continuing strength of the elitist thrust in Canadian politics. That said, it also is the case that democracies such as Canada are dynamic entities in which the content of political culture and associated patterns of behavior change over time. Thus, for example, in the 1960s and 1970s Canada often was described as a nation of passive spectators rather than participants in the game of politics (e.g., Van Loon, 1970; Presthus, 1973). In the 1980s, however, we found that the Canadian electorate consisted of overlapping groups of active minorities whose repertoire ranged from attempts at verbal persuasion and involvement in conventional, electorally related activities to protests of various kinds. Another illustration of this dynamism is the difference we found in levels of unconventional participation in 1983 and 1988. Over a brief five-year period the frequency of protest demonstrations increased substantially. Moreover, Canadians are not as deferential toward authority as they were said to have been in the 1950s and 1960s, and which Lipset (1990) contends they still are today. And, like political participation, Canadians' willingness to comply with the authoritative edicts of government can change quickly. In sum, if our Canadian findings can be generalized to other democracies, the context within which a public's attitudes and values develop and are expressed in a democracy matters, and people's willingness to comply with what a government is asking of them cannot simply be taken for granted by political authorities, or assumed by political theorists.

In the Canadian case, for example, support at the authorities and regime levels is quite mutable, and at any point in time large numbers of people are less than enthusiastic about their political leaders and major institutions of the federal government such as parliament, the civil service, and judiciary. What makes this finding especially important is that in Canada, support flows upward, with feelings about the incumbent authorities and regime influencing those about the national political community. Because some of these feelings, particularly those about authorities, are driven by highly changeable effectiveness and equity–fairness judgments, and authorities support, in turn, influences – either directly or indirectly – regime and community support, Rogowski (1974) is correct in arguing that support at all levels has a contingent rather than a "once and for all" quality.

To illustrate this point, we have developed a six-fold classification of support types defined as follows:

1. *Supporters* These are people with community support scores of 75 or more, regime scores of 51 or more, and global authority support scores of 50 or more.[3]
   They are, in brief, persons who are very supportive of the national community,

---

3 To maintain sample integrity, missing values for the community, regime, and authorities support variables are reassigned randomly across the 1–100 range.

at least positively disposed toward the regime, and at least neutral, on balance, in their overall attitudes towards the incumbent government and its opposition counterparts.

2. *Oppositionists* These are people with highly positive (75 or more) community scores, positive (51 or more) regime scores, but with negative (49 or less) authority scores.
3. *Discontented* This type comprises people with community support scores of 75 or more, regime scores that are negative (49 or less), and authorities scores that can be either positive or negative.
4. *Instrumentalists* These individuals have modestly positive or negative community feelings (scores less than 75), positive regime scores (of 51 or more), and authority scores that can be either positive, neutral, or negative.
5. *Partially alienated* Similar to the instrumentalists, they have moderately positive or negative community scores (less than 75). Their authority scores are either positive, neutral, or negative, and their regime scores are neutral or negative.
6. *Totally alienated* This type consists of individuals with negative feelings about the political authorities, regime, and community.

These are not stringent criteria, and they do not require Canadians to be overwhelmingly enthusiastic about the national community, regime, and authorities to be considered "supporters" of the political system. Notwithstanding the ease with which the label can be acquired, in 1983 only one in five qualified, and in 1988 only one in four did so (Figure 8.1). Moreover, in both years supporters were minorities in *every* region of the country; in 1983 they ranged from a low of 14 percent among Quebec-French to a high of 35 percent among Quebec non-French, and in 1988, from 15 percent among the former to 33 percent among residents of the Atlantic provinces.

It requires a lower level of authorities support to qualify as an "oppositionist," and one would anticipate that this group might be the modal type in democracies where interparty conflict is intense and party identifications are strong. Oppositionists show strong affection for the national community, they feel positively about the regime, but have marked reservations about at least some parties and party leaders other than their own. However, consistent with the weakness and instability of partisanship in Canada, they constituted only 11 percent of the public in 1983 and 14 percent in 1988.

The "discontented" were a much larger group in both years. In 1983 there were twice as many discontented as there were oppositionists, and in 1988 they outnumbered the oppositionists by a margin of three to two. What distinguishes the discontented, of course, is that they have negative support for the principal institutions of the regime. We have argued that in part this is because Canada has a Westminster-model parliamentary system, a situation that lends itself to blurring the distinction between the government-of-the-day and regime. As we also have argued, this tendency is reinforced by long periods of one-party dominance at both the national and provincial levels of government.

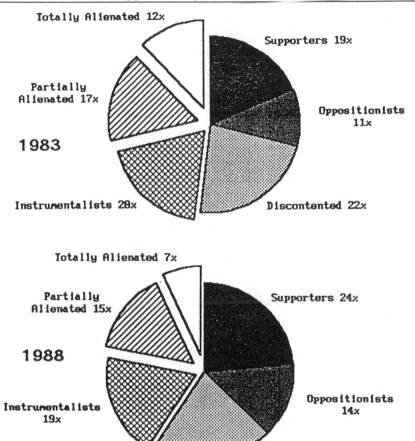

Figure 8.1. *Political support typology, 1983, 1988 (in percent)*

The proportion of the public whom we have labeled "instrumentalists" also was substantial, constituting one-fifth of the 1983 and 1988 samples. They do not especially like the political community, but they remain basically positive about the regime, perhaps in many cases because it appears to have utilitarian value. They are concentrated in Quebec, where, over the past two decades, the term "profitable federalism" has been a staple element in the arguments of Liberal Party elites in Ottawa and Quebec City about why the province should remain part of Canada. More generally, the instrumentalists may be common in democracies troubled by regional cleavages based upon cultural and economic particularisms of various kinds.

The two alienated groups are sizable. The largest, the partially alienated, have only lukewarm regard for the community and feel either neutral
or negative toward the regime. In contrast, the totally alienated are just
that – they are negatively disposed toward the country's political authorities, regime and community. In 1983 nearly three of ten Canadians were in
one of these two categories, and collectively they outnumbered supporters
by a ratio of three to two. Illustrative of the mutability of support, in 1988
the combined percentage of partially and totally alienated declined to 22
percent but, importantly, the two groups together remained almost as large
as the supporter category (24 percent).

As anticipated by our earlier analyses, the alienated were concentrated
in regions marked either by economic disadvantage (the West and the
Atlantic provinces) or cultural disaffection (Quebec). In 1983, fully 42 percent of Quebec Francophones were in one of the alienated groups, and 31
percent and 29 percent of Prairie and Atlantic residents, respectively, were
as well. Five years later the percentage of alienated had declined almost by
half in the Atlantic provinces, but by much smaller margins in the other
regions (Table 8.1). Although the trend affected Québécois as well, nonetheless, over one-third of them were in one of the alienated categories in
1988, and collectively the alienated and the instrumentalists comprised
over two-thirds of the Quebec electorate.

Comparisons of the extent to which the supporters and totally alienated
engaged in confrontational and nonconfrontational protests and expressed
strongly positive compliance attitudes indicate the importance of the patterns of political support delineated by our typology. The 1983 data are
illustrative. Supporters and alienated were about equally likely to have
strong "service" compliance orientations, but twice as many supporters (61
percent versus 32 percent) expressed a strong willingness to adhere to
federal laws and regulations (Figure 8.2).[4] Similarly, the two groups differed only marginally in their level of participation in nonconfrontational
protests such as boycotts and petitions, but the alienated were twice as
likely to have engaged in confrontational activities such as marches, sit-ins,
and, possibly, violent demonstrations.

Viewed more generally, the distribution of the several types of supporters points to the fact that the concentration of alienated citizens in one
region of the country is what makes the continued viability of the Canadian
political community problematic. Our comparative analyses suggest that
all democracies have a cohort of dissatisfied citizens and, undoubtedly,
a smaller cohort of alienated ones. Although the latter group may not be

---

4 The compliance and participation measures are described in Chapter 7. For purposes of the
  present analysis, persons with strong "laws and regulations" compliance attitudes are those
  who provide positive answers to the three items loading on this compliance factor. Similarly, those with strong "service" attitudes provide positive answers to the two items loading
  on this factor.

Table 8.1. *Political support typology by region-ethnicity, 1983, 1988 (in percent)*

Political support types	Region-ethnicity					
	Atlantic	Quebec-French	Quebec-Non-French	Ontario	Prairies	British Columbia
1983						
Supporters	23	14	35	22	15	19
Oppositionists	12	7	9	14	13	10
Discontented	20	5	17	30	28	27
Instrumentalists	19	32	25	15	13	19
Alienated: partial	19	22	15	12	19	13
total	10	20	0	7	12	12

V = .16, p ≤ .001; N = 2117

Political support types	Atlantic	Quebec-French	Quebec-Non-French	Ontario	Prairies	British Columbia
1988						
Supporters	33	15	30	28	22	24
Oppositionists	15	7	24	17	14	15
Discontented	24	8	22	27	26	26
Instrumentalists	13	35	14	13	15	14
Alienated: partial	11	23	7	11	17	15
total	5	12	2	4	7	6

V = .16, p ≤ .001; N = 2215 (pre-election survey)

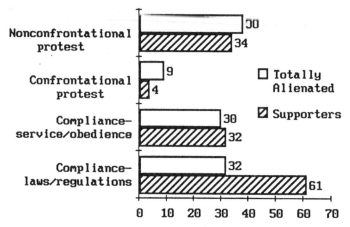

Figure 8.2. *Compliance and protest, extreme political support types, 1983 (in percent)*

as large as it is in Canada, generally its size may not be as important for the maintenance of a political system as its concentration, coupled with the availability of a structure such as a subnational unit of government that can be employed to threaten the integrity of the national system. Ironically, then, federalism, a system of government designed to accommodate ethnolinguistic and other types of cultural particularisms within a democratic society, under certain conditions, can become an instrument of political disintegration. Many would argue that this now is the case in Canada, and that the country is in the midst of a genuine and serious crisis of political support.

One might dispute this conclusion by arguing that the 1983 data, showing more people were alienated from the political system than supported it, were atypical – a reflection of especially sour, but transitory, public attitudes engendered by a protracted period of economic distress and constitutional wrangling presided over by a Trudeau-led Liberal government, which had become decidedly unpopular among large segments of the population. However, when the proportion of alienated remains almost as large as the proportion of supporters (as was the case in 1988), even after a change in the national government, the implementation of a new constitution, and several years of increasing economic prosperity, there is definitely a problem. Moreover, if the country continues to be one of the freest and most affluent in the world (as was the case in June 1990) but three-fifths of those in one region of the country (Quebec) state to public opinion pollsters that they favor some form of political independence,[5] and pictures

5 The data were gathered in a national CIPO (Gallup) poll conducted in early May 1990. See *Maclean's*, June 4, 1990, p. 28.

of young Québécois trampling on the flag appear on national television while their counterparts in English Canada are simultaneously burning the Quebec provincial flag, the problem is critical. And, when provincial premiers castigate each other with obscenities and the prime minister reacts to the failure of Meech Lake by warning his fellow citizens that they cannot take the continued existence of the country for granted, the problem has reached crisis proportions.

The crisis is widely acknowledged, but reactions to it have varied substantially. Many non-Canadians simply express incomprehension. Stephen Lewis, former leader of the Ontario New Democratic Party and Canada's chief delegate to the United Nations until 1988, captured their puzzlement succinctly when he stated "It's simply beyond their [non-Canadians] imagination that a country like Canada with so much that other countries can envy could engage in this orgy of self-immolation" (*New York Times*, June 28, 1990). For their part, many Canadians were either resentful or outraged. Distinguished novelist Margaret Atwood, for example, suggested that much of the fault lay with Quebec, where historic resentment outweighs efforts in recent decades to satisfy Quebecers cultural and linguistic demands: "I understand the historical background, the desire to protect an identity, but I don't feel I am stepping on anyone's neck." Another noted author, Mordecai Richler, portrayed the problem as a "childish tribal squabble" generated by the Quebec provincial government's imposition of illiberal French-only language laws (*New York Times*, June 28, 1990).

More ominously, some Canadians, many of whom live in the West, now appear not only to be resigned to the breakup of the country, they look forward to it. As University of Calgary political scientist Barry Cooper wrote: "moralizing appeals for 'national unity' . . . simply meant the continued rule by Ontario and Quebec in the interests of Ontario and Quebec, nothing more. . . . No wonder increasing numbers of Westerners are . . . starting to contemplate the departure of Quebec with equanimity. Some, indeed, would prefer to see Quebec expelled from the country. Their only concern is over the terms of separation" (*Globe & Mail*, May 20, 1990, pp. 22–8).[6]

In our view, the problem of political support in Canada goes far beyond the impasse over Meech Lake and the disputes it has engendered. The problem is grounded in a variety of longstanding economic and political as well as cultural and sociological factors that we have delineated in this study. Meech Lake is only the most recent manifestation of support difficulties facing the Canadian political community that have been evident from the very inception of the country in 1867. These difficulties and the

6 See also the special report in *Maclean's*, March 20, 1990. Particularly noteworthy are the articles by Lisa Van Dusen, "An Insecure Identity: Quebecers Fear of Assimilation," pp. 22–3; and John Howse, "A Quiet Fury in the West: Where are Anglophone Rights?", pp. 26–7.

periodic crises they have produced have repeatedly frustrated Canadians and many now are angry, confused, and worried about the future. As the above quotations illustrate, these feelings are not confined to the general public, but also typify important segments of elite opinion as well.

The present situation notwithstanding, some would argue that there are good reasons why Canada's prospects are not as bleak as some pessimistic observers have concluded. A principal strength of Canada and other contemporary democracies that enables them to survive is that they *are* democracies. As such they are systems in which public needs and demands are widely recognized as having paramount importance. This is not to say that there is not a gap between what people expect of a democratic system and their perceptions of the effectiveness and fairness of what is delivered. This disjunction and the attendant lack of political trust, interest, and efficacy associated with it and with variations in support are abundantly evident in Canada, but, as shown in Chapters 3 and 7 a similar syndrome characterizes the publics of other democracies as well.

The fact that a disequilibrium between demand and supply of goods and services may be real, and perhaps even sizable at any particular time in the life of a democracy, does not mean that its citizens are ready to overthrow it. The promise of democratic government is that such disequilibria are dynamic and short-lived. A genius of existing democracies that has enabled them to be sustained over time is that they do deliver *enough* of the goods for a satisfying life for *enough* of their citizens to enable their leaders to govern political communities which in part, or even in whole, can be profoundly sullen at times, but rarely mutinous. On the one hand, their sullenness may be an inevitable consequence of living in political communities in which the *idea* of progress (e.g., Nisbet, 1980) is a major component of the liberal element of a democratic political culture, but where, to many people, regression and progress seem to alternate as the order of the day. On the other hand, the disjunction between the idea of progress and its realization may contribute to the tendency of citizens in democracies to feel advantaged rather than disadvantaged relative to their fellow citizens. Even if they believe that societal conditions generally and economic conditions in particular are in decline, they, their family, and community are in good shape and likely to remain so.[7]

A second genius of democracies is public involvement and an attendant dynamism of support for political authorities. Most notably, elections in democratic systems offer citizens regular, constitutionally sanctioned opportunities to replace an incumbent government with another and, with varying frequency, this is exactly what they do. Democratic elections may lack the drama of revolutionary change, but they also lack the violence and

---

7 The finding that differences in life satisfaction are not correlated strongly with sociodemographic factors in Canada and a number of other Western democracies illustrates the power of cultural norms such as the idea of progress to transcend societal cleavages.

destruction that almost invariably characterize revolutions, and this is one of their great virtues. "Throwing the rascals out" by peaceful means is no small achievement, and it does much to make the distinction between authorities and regime a reality in democracies. Also, elections, however important, do not exhaust the potential for citizen participation; in the past two decades Western democracies have witnessed a progressive expansion and legitimation of the range of public political action.

Both "outcome" and "process" arguments are basic elements in justifications of democratic government. As recent events in Eastern Europe remind us, these arguments have enormous persuasive power among those to whom democracy has been denied. The problem for those for whom democracy long has been a reality, however, is that its benefits are so familiar to them, there is a danger they will be taken for granted. Moreover, in most democracies, the power of the *idea* of democracy for maintaining the integrity of the national political system may be weakened by the fact that the range of realistic options to the status quo is restricted to alternative democratic arrangements. In Canada, for example, except for a handful of extremists, over the past twenty years proponents of a sovereign Quebec have not argued against Western-style democracy; on the contrary, they have maintained that an independent Quebec will actually enhance democracy for Québécois. Similarly, Westerners arguing for reform of the Senate and other institutions of the central government have made their case in terms of providing more democratic (elected, effective, and equal) representation of Western interests in Ottawa. This, it is claimed, will enable the West to secure its proper and historically denied share of the benefits of being part of the Canadian federation.

A related difficulty concerns assumptions about community. In the Canadian case, all parties to the debate over the country's future assume that regional and ethnolinguistic groups constitute communities that deserve not only recognition and acceptance by all others of their social reality, but also recognition, acceptance, and fulfillment of their political needs and demands. But this assumption is not always made about Canada and Canadians as an integrated nation–state. There is a strong temptation instead to view Canada as merely "a community of communities," as former Conservative Prime Minister Joe Clark put it. The "community of communities" formulation lends itself neatly to the prevailing elitist style of Canadian politics, and more specifically to the practices of "executive federalism" and "federal–provincial diplomacy" discussed at various points in this volume. For more than a generation the prime minister and the ten provincial premiers have bargained behind closed doors in repeated efforts to resolve both the major policy issues that (however knotty) regularly beset all democracies and the constitutional issues that so often have affected Canada.

Executive federalism and the elitist preferences that flow from it deny the reality of a democratic Canadian political community and, in so doing, weaken it. Justifications of the politics of elite accommodation that have been made in Canada and other democracies accept the weakness of the national political community and the strength of subnational communities, but argue that societal conflict will be minimized and political stability maximized if intergroup contact is restricted to interactions among elites. "Consociational democracy" arguments of this kind are seriously flawed because they rest on the assumption that elites always will share an overriding goal, that of maintaining the integrity of the political system and the community of which it is a part. In Canada this assumption has been demonstrably invalid at least since the Parti Québécois came to power in the 1976 Quebec provincial election. Equally important, the case for elite accommodation implies a very restrictive "outcome-oriented" conception of democracy. Such a conception fails to recognize the potential of the democratic process for building political community.

A democratic political community is a "community of citizens," the interests of which transcend those associated with narrower communities based on regional, ethnolinguistic, or other sociocultural divisions in a population. Such a community is unlikely to arise, indeed, perhaps *cannot arise*, in a country characterized by deep societal cleavages unless there is appropriate public involvement in vital political decisions. Canadians have at least as many opportunities to participate in politics as do the people of other democracies. What they have lacked from the very beginning of their history has been the opportunity to have a genuine "say" in the most basic aspects of what they are about as a nation and as a political system. As noted in Chapter 1, it often has been remarked that some of the problems of political support in Canada stem from the lack of a revolutionary experience that fused an emerging sense of nationhood with a commitment to a set of political principles and their institutional expression. Greater public involvement in the ongoing process of constitutional renewal may serve as an effective surrogate – generating the kinds of overarching community sentiments that can overcome the persistent centrifugal forces generated by subnational allegiances of various kinds.

To recapitulate, "delivering the goods" is an acknowledged genius of democracy. The instrumental basis of political support is real and important, and arguments about the "profitability" of existing political arrangements do have resonance. Nevertheless, when the choice is not between an authoritarian regime and a democracy but between two democratic ones, arguments about the instrumental value of the status quo lose prima facie validity. In such a situation a victory in a "battle of the balance sheets" may not be enough to maintain support for a democratic political system unless it can be convincingly demonstrated that the utilitarian value of current arrangements far outweigh those of alternatives. Moreover, as events and conditions of the past two decades throughout the West have demonstrated, continuously expanding economic prosperity cannot be assumed. For these reasons, support for existing democracies is imperfectly grounded, *if economics is all.*

Adding the warmth of community to the coldness of the marketplace is a solution rooted in democratic theory. As the Canadian experience abundantly indicates, building a community of citizens cannot be accomplished by political elites acting alone. However, another genius of democratic politics, citizen involvement, may succeed where elites have failed. We say "may" in the Canadian case because the hour is late and the opportunity for effective nation-building may have passed. Yet, we strongly suspect that many Canadians remain anxious to respond to the famous rhetorical question of "Who will speak for Canada?" posed by former Prime Minister Trudeau a decade ago by answering "We do!" Democratic theory and historical experience argue that they should be given their chance.

Appendix: Data sources

Our principal sources of Canadian data are national cross-sectional and panel surveys conducted in 1983, 1984, and immediately before and after the 1988 federal election. The 1983 survey also contains a panel component composed of persons interviewed in the 1979 and 1980 national election surveys. The 1983, 1984, and 1988 surveys are the centerpieces of two research projects: "Sources, Distribution and Consequences of Political Support in Canada" and "Support for Democratic Polities: The Case of Canada" (co-principal investigators Harold D. Clarke and Allan Kornberg). The studies were funded by the National Science Foundation (grants SES 831–1077 and SES 882–1628). Fieldwork for the surveys was conducted by Canadian Facts Ltd., Toronto, Ontario under the supervision of Canadian Facts' Senior Project Director, Mary Auvinen. Additional Canadian data were gathered in national cross-sectional surveys conducted in 1985, 1986, 1987, and 1989, with the fieldwork for these studies being conducted by Canadian Facts Ltd. as part of their monthly "Monitor" survey. Funding for these latter studies was provided by research grants from the Canadian Embassy, Washington, D. C., the Canadian Studies Center, Duke University, the International Political Economy Program, Duke University, and the Duke University Research Council and Provosts' Funds. All of these survey data and related technical information are available from the authors upon request.

We also employed Canadian data gathered in the 1974, 1979, and 1980 national election and panel surveys and two surveys carried out at the time of the Quebec sovereignty-association referendum. The principal investigators for the election studies were Harold D. Clarke, Jane Jenson, Lawrence LeDuc, and Jon Pammett, using research funds provided by the Canada Council and the Social Sciences and Humanities Research Council of Canada. One of the referendum surveys was conducted as part of a project "The Quebec Referendum, the Media, and the Maintenance of the National Integrity of Canada" (principal investigators: Allan Kornberg and Joel Smith) funded by the National Science Foundation (grants SOC–7915420). A second was the "Quebec Referendum Study" carried out by Clarke, Jenson, Leduc, and Pammett in conjunction with their 1974–80 national election surveys. The latter research was supported by the Social Sciences and Humanities Research Council of Canada. The 1974 election study is described in Clarke et al. (1979:397–400), and information regarding the other surveys can be obtained from the principal investigators.

Other data sources included the 1965, 1968, and 1984 Canadian national election surveys, the 1977, 1979, and 1981 "Quality of Life: Social Change in Canada" surveys, Canadian Institute of Public Opinion (CIPO) polls, 1976–86 Euro-barometer surveys for Belgium, Denmark, France, Great Britain, Ireland, Italy, the Netherlands, and West Germany, and the Eight Nations Study data gathered in the mid-1970s. The 1965 election study was conducted by Philip Converse, John Meisel, Maurice Pinard, Peter Regenstreif, and Mildred Schwartz; the 1968 study was carried out by John Meisel. Ronald Lambert, Steven Brown, James Curtis, Barry Kay, and John Wilson were principal investigators in 1984. The Quality of Life project was carried out by Tom Atkinson et al. Jacques-Rene Rabier, Ronald Inglehart and associates conducted the Euro-Barometer surveys, and Samuel Barnes, Max Kaase et al., the Eight Nations surveys. The 1974, 1979, 1980 and 1984 Canadian election survey data and those for the Euro-Barometer and Eight Nations projects are available from the Interuniversity Consortium for Political and Social Research, University of Michigan. The three Quality of Life surveys are archived at the Institute for Behavioural Research, York University, and the CIPO polls, at Carleton University, Ottawa.

Sample sizes

The sampling design employed in the Political Support surveys, as well as those used in the National Election and Quality of Life surveys, ensure the presence of several hundred cases in each region of Canada by oversampling in smaller provinces. Weights are then employed to yield correct regional proportions for representative national samples. See Clarke et al. (1979:397–400). The weighted sample sizes for the several Canadian studies are as follows:

Political Support Surveys: national cross-sections – 1983 = 2117, 1984 = 1928, 1985 = 1853, 1986 = 2000, 1987 = 1877, 1988 pre-election = 2215, 1988 post-election = 2010, 1989 = 1845; adjacent national panels – 1980–83 = 834, 1983–84 = 1294, 1984–88 (pre-election) = 868, 1988 pre-post election = 1516.

National Election Surveys: national cross-sections – 1965 = 2729, 1968 = 2767, 1974 = 2445, 1979 = 2670, 1980 = 1786, 1984 = 3380; adjacent national panels – 1974–79 = 1353, 1979–80 = 1786.

Quality of Life: Social Change in Canada Surveys: national cross-sections – 1977 = 3290, 1979 = 2982, 1981 = 2948.

Quebec Referendum Surveys: provincial survey = 325; Three-Cities pro-

Table A.1. *Weighted sample sizes: Region-ethnicity*

Region-ethnicity	1974	1979	1980	1983	1984	1988I	1988II
Atlantic	220	252	168	193	169	200	183
Quebec-French	608	680	463	525	457	531	470
Quebec-Non-French	94	72	46	47	60	46	56
Ontario	878	938	622	743	692	808	730
Prairies	393	447	299	365	329	372	338
British Columbia	252	280	188	245	223	259	232
Total*	2445	2670	1786	2117	1928	2215	2010

Note: * - some totals differ from summed column totals by one case because of rounding; 1988I - 1988 preelection survey; 1988II - 1988 postelection survey

ject surveys – Trois Rivieres = 350, Peterborough = 308, Lethbridge = 303.

Regional Samples: Two variables frequently employed in the analyses are region (Atlantic, Quebec, Ontario, Prairies, British Columbia) and region/ethnicity (Atlantic, Quebec-French, Quebec-Non-French, Ontario, Prairies, British Columbia). The sample sizes for these variables are shown in Table A.1.

References

Aldrich, John H., and Forrest D. Nelson. 1984. *Linear Probability, Logit, and Probit Models*. Beverly Hills, Calif.: Sage.

Alford, Robert R. 1963. *Party and Society: The Anglo-American Democracies*. Chicago: Rand McNally.

Allardt, Erik. 1978. "Objective and Subjective Social Indicators of Well-Being." *Comparative Studies in Sociology* 1:142–73.

Almond, Gabriel, and Sidney Verba. 1963. *The Civic Culture*. Princeton, N.J.: Princeton University Press.

(eds.) 1980. *The Civic Culture Revisited*. Boston: Little, Brown.

Alt, James. 1979. *The Politics of Economic Decline*. Cambridge: Cambridge University Press.

Arblaster, Anthony. 1984. *The Rise and Decline of Western Liberalism*. New York: Basil Blackwell.

Archer, Keith. 1987. "A Simultaneous Equation Model of Canadian Voting Behaviour." *Canadian Journal of Political Science* 20:553–72.

Asher, Herbert. 1983. "Voting Behavior Research in the 1980s: An Examination of Some Old and New Problem Areas." In Ada W. Finifter, ed. *Political Science: The State of the Discipline*. Washington, D.C.: American Political Science Association.

Baar, Carl. 1977. "Patterns and Strategies of Court Administration in Canada and the U.S." *Canadian Public Administration* 20:242–72.

Bachrach, Peter. 1967. *The Theory of Democratic Elitism*. Boston: Little, Brown.

Banting, Keith, and Richard Simeon. 1983. *And No One Cheered: Federalism, Democracy and the Constitution Act*. Toronto: Methuen.

Barber, Benjamin R. 1984. *Strong Democracy: Participatory Politics for a New Age*. Berkeley and Los Angeles: University of California Press.

Barnard, F. M. 1965. *Herder's Social and Political Thought*. Oxford: Oxford University Press (Clarendon Press).

Barnes, Samuel H. 1986. "Politics and Culture." Unpublished manuscript. Ann Arbor, University of Michigan.

Barnes, Samuel H., and Max Kaase, et al. 1979. *Political Action*. Beverly Hills, Calif.: Sage.

Beck, Paul Allen. 1986. "Choice, Context, and Consequence: Beaten and Unbeaten Paths toward a Science of Electoral Behavior." In Herbert F. Weisberg, ed. *Political Science: The Science of Politics*. New York: Agathon Press.

Behiels, Michael D. 1989. *Prelude to Quebec's Quiet Revolution: Liberalism Versus Neo-Nationalism, 1945–1960*. Montreal: McGill-Queen's University Press.

Belknap, George, and Angus Campbell. 1952. "Political Party Identification and Attitudes Toward Foreign Policy." *Public Opinion Quarterly* 15:601–23.

Bell, David, and Lorne Tepperman. 1979. *The Roots of Disunity: A Look at Canadian Political Culture.* Toronto: McClelland & Stewart.

Bennett, Lance W. 1988. *News: The Politics of Illusion.* New York: Longman.

Bennett, Stephen E., and Linda M. Bennett. 1986. "Political Participation." In Samuel Long, ed. *Annual Review of Political Science.* Vol. 1. Norwood: Ablex Publishing Corporation.

Bernard, A. 1978. *What Does Quebec Want?* Toronto: Lorimer.

Bibby, Reginald. 1987. *Fragmented Gods: The Poverty and Potential of Religion in Canada.* Toronto: Irvine.

Black, Edwin R. 1975. *Divided Loyalties: Canadian Concepts of Federalism.* Montreal: McGill-Queen's University Press.

Black, Edwin. R., and A. C. Cairns. 1966. "A Different Perspective on Canadian Federalism." *Canadian Public Administration* 9:27–44.

Blake, Donald E. 1982. "The Consistency of Inconsistency: Party Identification in Federal and Provincial Politics." *Canadian Journal of Political Science* 15:691–710.

    1985. *Two Political Worlds: Parties and Voting in British Columbia.* Vancouver: University of British Columbia Press.

Bollen, Kenneth A. 1989. *Structural Equations with Latent Variables.* New York: Wiley Interscience.

Boynton, G. Robert, and Gerhard Loewenberg. 1973. "The Development of Public Support for Parliament in Germany, 1951–59." *British Journal of Political Science* 3:169–89.

Braestrup, P. 1978. *Big Story.* New Haven, Conn.: Yale University Press.

Breton, Raymond, Jeffery G. Reitz, and Victor Valentine. 1980. *Cultural Boundaries and the Cohesion of Canada.* Montreal: Institute for Research on Public Policy.

Brittan, Samuel. 1978. "Inflation and Democracy." In Frederick Hirsch and John H. Goldthorpe, eds. *The Political Economy of Inflation.* Cambridge: Harvard University Press.

    1983. *The Role and Limits of Government: Essays in Political Economy.* Minneapolis: University of Minnesota Press.

Brodie, Janine, and Jane Jenson. 1990. "The Party System." In Michael Whittington and Glenn Williams, eds. *Canadian Politics in the 1990s.* 3rd ed. Toronto: Nelson.

Brody, Richard A., and Paul M. Sniderman. 1977. "From Life Space to Polling Place: The Relevance of Personal Concerns for Voting Behavior." *British Journal of Political Science* 7:337–60.

Brym, Robert J. 1977. "Explaining Regional Variations in Canadian Populist Movements." Paper presented at the 1977 Annual Meeting of the Canadian Sociology and Anthropology Association, Fredericton, New Brunswick.

Buchanan, James M., and Gordon Tullock. 1962. *Calculus of Consent: Logical Foundations of Constitutional Democracy.* Ann Arbor: University of Michigan Press.

Buchanan, James M., and R. E. Wagner. 1977. *Democracy in Deficit: The Political Legacy of Lord Keynes.* New York: Academic Press.

Budge, Ian, Ivor Crewe, and Dennis Farlie, eds. 1976. *Party Identification and Beyond.* New York: Wiley.

Budge, Ian, and Dennis Farlie. 1983. *Explaining and Predicting Elections.* London: Allen & Unwin.

Burnham, Walter Dean. 1970. *Critical Elections and the Mainsprings of American Politics*. New York: Norton.

Cairns, Alan C. 1971. "The Judicial Committee and Its Critics." *Canadian Journal of Political Science* 4:301–45.

1977. "The Governments and Societies of Canadian Federalism." *Canadian Journal of Political Science* 10:695–726.

1983. "Constitution-Making, Government Self-Interest, and the Problem of Legitimacy." In Allan Kornberg and Harold D. Clarke, eds. *Political Support in Canada: The Crisis Years*. Durham, N.C.: Duke University Press.

Campbell, Angus, Philip E. Converse, Warren E. Miller, and Donald E. Stokes. 1960. *The American Voter*. New York: Wiley.

1966. *Elections and the Political Order*. New York: Wiley.

Campbell, Angus, Philip E. Converse, and W. L. Rodgers. 1976. *The Quality of Life*. New York: Russell Sage.

Campbell, Angus, Gerald Gurin, and Warren E. Miller. 1954. *The Voter Decides*. Evanston, Ill.: Row, Peterson.

Campbell, Colin. 1978. *The Canadian Senate: A Lobby from Within*. Toronto: Macmillan.

Campbell, Colin, and George J. Szablowski. 1979. *The Superbureaucrats: Structure and Behaviour in Central Agencies*. Toronto: Macmillan.

Carmines, Edward. 1986. "The Analysis of Covariance Structure Models." In William D. Berry and Michael S. Lewis-Beck, eds. *New Tools For Social Scientists*. Beverly Hills, Calif.: Sage.

Chappell, H. W., and W. R. Keech. 1985. "A New View of Political Accountability for Economic Performance." *American Political Science Review* 79:10–27.

Citrin, Jack. 1974. "Comment: The Political Relevance of Trust in Government." *American Political Science Review* 68:973–88.

Citrin, Jack, Herbert McClosky, Merrill Shanks, and Paul Sniderman. 1975. "Personal and Political Sources of Political Alienation." *British Journal of Political Science* 5:1–31.

Clark, S. D. 1968. *The Developing Canadian Community*. 2nd ed. Toronto: University of Toronto Press.

Clarke, Harold D., Jane Jenson, Lawrence LeDuc, and Jon Pammett. 1979. *Political Choice in Canada*. Toronto: McGraw-Hill Ryerson.

1984. *Absent Mandate: The Politics of Discontent in Canada*. Agincourt: Gage Publishing Ltd.

Clarke, Harold D., and Allan Kornberg. 1989. "Public Reactions to Economic Performance and Political Support in Contemporary Liberal Democracies: The Case of Canada." In Harold D. Clarke, Marianne C. Stewart, and Gary Zuk, eds. *Economic Decline and Political Change*. Pittsburgh: University of Pittsburgh Press.

Clarke, Harold D., Allan Kornberg, and Marianne C. Stewart. 1984. "Parliament and Political Support in Canada." *American Political Science Review* 78:452–69.

Clarke, Harold D., and Richard G. Price. 1980. "Freshman MPs' Job Images: the Effects of Incumbency, Ambition, and Position." *Canadian Journal of Political Science* 13:583–606.

Clarke, Harold D., and Marianne C. Stewart. 1985. "Short-Term Forces and Partisan Change in Canada: 1974–80." *Electoral Studies* 3:15–36.

1987. "Partisan Inconsistency and Partisan Change in Federal States: The Case of Canada." *American Journal of Political Science* 31:383–407.

Clarke, Harold D., Marianne C. Stewart, and Gary Zuk. 1986. "The Political Econonly of Party Support in Canada: 1980–84." *European Journal of Political Economy* 2:25–45.

1988. "Not For Turning?: Beliefs About the Role of Government in Contemporary Britain." *Governance* 1:271–87.

Clarke, Harold D., and Gary Zuk. 1987. "Economics, Politics and Party Support in Canada 1974–79." *Comparative Politics* 20:299–316.

Clement, Wallace. 1975. *The Canadian Corporate Elite: An Analysis of Economic Power*. Toronto: McClelland & Stewart.

Clift, Dominque. 1982. *Quebec Nationalism in Crisis*. Montreal: McGill-Queen's University Press.

Converse, Philip E. 1964. "The Nature of Belief Systems in Mass Publics." In David E. Apter, ed. *Ideology and Discontent*. New York: Free Press.

1972. "Changes in the American Electorate." In Angus Campbell and Philip E. Converse, eds. *The Human Meaning of Social Change*. New York: Russell Sage.

Cook, Ramsay. 1969. "Provincial Autonomy, Minority Rights and the Theory of Confederation, 1867–1921." Study no. 4 of the *Royal Commission on Bilingualism and Biculturalism*. Ottawa: Queen's Printer.

1985. "The Quiet Revolution and the New Nationalism." *Zeitschrift der Gesellschaft fur Kanada Studies* 5:15–30.

Cooper, Barry, Allan Kornberg, and William Mishler. 1988. "The Resurgence of Conservatism in Britain, Canada, and the United States: An Overview." In Barry Cooper, Allan Kornberg, and William Mishler, eds. *The Resurgence of Conservatism in Anglo-American Democracies*. Durham, N.C.: Duke University Press.

Crewe, Ivor. 1981. "Electoral Participation." In David Butler, Howard R. Penniman, and Austin Ranney, eds. *Democracy at the Polls: A Comparative Study of Competitive National Elections*. Washington, D.C.: American Enterprise Institute for Public Policy Research.

Crewe, Ivor, and Donald D. Searing. 1988. "Ideological Change in the British Conservative Party." *American Political Science Review* 82:361–84.

Crozier, Michel, Samuel P. Huntington, and Joji Watanuki. 1975. *The Crisis of Democracy*. New York: New York University Press.

Dahl, Robert A. 1971. *Polyarchy: Participation and Opposition*. New Haven, Conn.: Yale University Press.

1982. *Dilemmas of Pluralist Democracy: Autonomy vs. Control*. New Haven, Conn.: Yale University Press.

Dalton, Russell J. 1988. *Citizen Politics in Western Democracies*. Chatham: Chatham House Publishers.

Dalton, Russell J., Scott Flanagan, and Paul Allen Beck, eds. 1984. *Electoral Change in Advanced Industrial Societies*. Princeton, N.J.: Princeton University Press.

Dennis, Jack. 1970. "Support for the Institution of Elections by the Mass Public." *American Political Science Review* 64:819–35.

Dogan, Mattei, and Dominique Pelassy. 1984. *How To Compare Nations: Strategies in Comparative Politics*. Chatham: Chatham House Publishers.

Dogan, Mattei (ed.). 1988. *Comparing Pluralist Democracies: Strains on Legitimacy*. Boulder, Colo.: Westview Press.

Downs, Anthony. 1957. *An Economic Theory of Democracy*. New York: Harper & Row.

Dryzek, John, and Robert E. Goodin. 1986. "Risk-sharing and Social Justice: The Motivational Foundations of the Post-War Welfare State." *British Journal of Political Science* 16:1–34.

Durocher, R. 1978. "The Evolution of Canadian Federalism, 1867–1976." In *The Political Economy of Confederation*. Kingston: The Institute of Intergovernmental Relations, Queen's University.

Easton, David. 1965. *A Systems Analysis of Political Life*. New York: Wiley.

——— 1975. "A Re-Assessment of the Concept of Political Support." *British Journal of Political Science* 5:435–48.

——— 1976. "Theoretical Approaches to Political Support." *Canadian Journal of Political Science* 9:431–48.

Eckstein, Harry. 1966. *Division and Cohesion in Democracy: A Study of Norway*. Princeton, N.J.: Princeton University Press.

Elkins, David J., and Richard Simeon. 1980. *Small Worlds: Provinces and Parties in Canadian Political Life*. Toronto: Methuen.

Englemann, Frederick C., and M. A. Schwartz. 1975. *Political Parties and the Canadian Social Structure*. 2nd ed. Scarborough, Ont.: Prentice-Hall.

Epstein, Leon D. 1964. "A Comparative Study of Canadian Parties." *American Political Science Review* 58:46–60.

Falcone, David, and Richard J. Van Loon. 1983. "Public Attitudes and Intergovernmental Shifts in Responsibility for Health Programs: Paying the Piper Without Calling the Tune." In Allan Kornberg and Harold D. Clarke, eds. *Political Support in Canada: The Crisis Years*. Durham, N.C.: Duke University Press.

Feigert, Frank. 1989. *Canada Votes: 1935–1988*. Durham, N.C.: Duke University Press.

Finifter, Ada W. 1970. "Dimensions of Political Alienation." *American Political Science Review* 64:389–410.

Fiorina, Morris. 1981. *Retrospective Voting in American National Elections*. New Haven, Conn.: Yale University Press.

Flathman, Richard E. 1980. *The Practice of Political Authority: Authority and the Authoritative*. Chicago: University of Chicago Press.

Flora, Peter, and Arnold J. Heidenheimer. 1981. *The Development of the Welfare State in Europe and America*. New Brunswick: Transaction Books.

Friedman, Daniel A. 1977. "Political Socialization and Models of Moral Development." In Stanley Allen Renshon, ed. *Handbook of Political Socialization*. New York: Free Press.

Frizzell, Alan, Jon H. Pammett, and Anthony Westell. 1989. *The Canadian General Election of 1988*. Ottawa: Carelton University Press.

Frizzell, Alan, and Anthony Westell. 1985. *The Canadian General Election of 1984: Politicians, Parties, Press and Polls*. Ottawa: Carelton University Press.

Galbraith, Gordon S. 1976. "British Columbia." In David J. Bellamy, Jon H. Pammett and Donald C. Rowat, eds. *The Provincial Political Systems*. Toronto: Methuen.

Gamson, William A. 1968. *Power and Discontent*. Homewood, Ill.: Dorsey Press.

Gibbins, Roger. 1980. *Prairie Politics and Society*. Scarborough, Ont.: Butterworth & Company.

Gingras, Francois-Pierre, and Neil Nevitte. 1983. "Nationalism in Quebec: The Transition of Ideology and Political Support." In Allan Kornberg and Harold D. Clarke, eds. *Political Support in Canada: The Crisis Years*. Durham, N.C.: Duke University Press.

Ginsberg, Benjamin. 1982. *The Consequences of Consent: Elections, Citizen Control and Popular Acquiescence*. Reading, Mass.: Addison-Wesley.

Ginsberg, Benjamin, and Alan Stone, eds. 1986. *Do Elections Matter?* Armonk, N.Y.: M. E. Sharpe.

Globe and Mail. 20 May 1990, pp. 22–8.

Grant, George. 1970. *Lament For a Nation*. Toronto: McClelland & Stewart.

Gratton, Michael. 1988. *So, What Are the Boys Saying?: An Inside Look at Brian Mulroney in Power*. Toronto: Paperjacks.

Greenberg, Edward S. 1981. "Industrial Democracy and the Democratic Citizen." *The Journal of Politics* 43:964–81.

Greenstein, Fred I. 1965. *Children and Politics*. New Haven, Conn.: Yale University Press.

Guindon, Hubert. 1960. "The Social Evolution of Quebec Reconsidered." *Canadian Journal of Economics and Political Science* 26:533–51.

Gutek, B. 1978. "On the Accuracy of Retrospective Attitudinal Data." *Public Opinion Quarterly* 42:390–401.

Habermas, Jurgen. 1973. *Legitimation Crisis*. Boston: Beacon.

Hall, Peter, ed. 1989. *The Political Power of Economic Ideas: Keynesianism Across Nations*. Princeton, N.J.: Princeton University Press.

Hayduk, Leslie. 1987. *Structural Equation Modeling with LISREL*. Baltimore: Johns Hopkins University Press.

Hiller, Harry H. 1986. *Canadian Society: A Macro Analysis*. Scarborough, Ont.: Prentice-Hall.

Hochschild, Jennifer L. 1981. *What's Fair? American Beliefs about Distributive Justice*. Cambridge: Harvard University Press.

Horowitz, Gad. 1966. "Conservatism, Liberalism and Socialism in Canada: An Interpretation." *Canadian Journal of Economics and Political Science* 32: 144–71.

Hougham, George, M. 1972. "The Background and Development of National Parties." In Hugh G. Thorburn, ed. *Party Politics in Canada*. 3rd ed. Scarborough, Ont.: Prentice-Hall.

Inglehart, Ronald. 1977. *The Silent Revolution: Changing Values and Political Styles Among Western Publics*. Princeton, N.J.: Princeton University Press.
    1990. *Culture Shift in Advanced Industrial Society*. Princeton, N.J.: Princeton University Press.

Inkeles, Alex. 1950. *Public Opinion in Soviet Russia: A Study in Mass Persuasion*. Cambridge: Harvard University Press.

Irving, John A. 1959. *The Social Credit Movement in Alberta*. Toronto: University of Toronto Press.

Jennings, M. Kent, and Jan Van Deth, eds. 1989. *Continuities in Political Action*. New York: Walter de Gruyter.

Jewell, Malcolm E., and Chong Lim Kim. 1976. "Sources of Support for the Legislature in a Developing Nation: The Case of Korea." *Comparative Political Studies* 8:461–89.

Johnston, Richard. 1986. *Public Opinion and Public Policy in Canada*. Toronto: University of Toronto Press.

Joreskog, Karl G., and Dag Sorbom. 1988. *LISREL 7: A Guide to the Program and Applications*. Chicago: SPSS Inc.

Kaase, Max. 1988. "Political Alienation and Protest." In Mattei Dogan, ed. *Comparing Pluralist Democracies: Strains on Legitimacy*. Boulder, Colo.: Westview Press.
    1989. "Mass Participation." In Jan W. van Deth and M. Kent Jennings, et al., eds. *Continuities in Political Action*. New York: Walter de Gruyter.

Keech, William R., Robert H. Bates, and Peter Lange. 1989. "Political Economy Within Nations." Durham, N.C.: Duke University Program in Political Economy, Papers in International Political Economy: Working Paper Number 83.

Key, V. O. 1955. "A Theory of Critical Elections." *Journal of Politics* 17:3–18.

1966. *The Responsible Electorate*. New York: Random House (Vintage Books).

1967. *Public Opinion and American Democracy*. New York: Knopf.

Keynes, John Maynard. 1936. *The General Theory of Employment, Interest and Money*. London: Macmillan.

Kiewiet, D. Roderick. 1983. *Macroeconomics and Micropolitics: The Electoral Effects of Economic Issues*. Chicago: University of Chicago Press.

Kim, Chong Lim, Joel D. Barkan, Illya Turan, and Malcolm E. Jewell. 1984. *The Legislative Connection: The Politics of Representation in Kenya, Korea and Turkey*. Durham, N.C.: Duke University Press.

Kinder, Donald R. 1983. "Diversity and Complexity in American Public Opinion." In A. W. Finifter, ed. *Political Science: The State of the Discipline*. Washington, D.C.: American Political Science Association.

Kinder, Donald R., and R. Paul Abelson. 1981. "Appraising Presidential Candidates: Personality and Affect in the 1980 Campaign." Paper prepared for the 1981 annual meeting of the American Political Science Association, New York, September 3–6, 1981.

Kinder, Donald R., and D. Roderick Kiewiet. 1979. "Economic Discontent and Political Behavior: the Role of Personel Grievances and Collective Economic Judgments in Congressional Voting." *American Journal of Political Science* 23:495–527.

1981. "Sociotropic Politics: The American Case." *British Journal of Political Science* 11:129–61.

Kohn, Hans. 1961. *The Idea of Nationalism*. New York: Macmillan.

Kornberg, Allan. 1970. "Parliament in Canadian Society." In Allan Kornberg and L. D. Musolf, eds. *Legislatures in Developmental Perspective*. Durham, N.C.: Duke University Press.

Kornberg, Allan, Harold D. Clarke, and Lawrence LeDuc. 1978. "Some Correlates of Regime Support in Canada." *British Journal of Political Science* 11:129–61.

1980. "Regime Support in Canada: A Rejoinder." *British Journal of Political Science* 10:410–16.

Kornberg, Allan, Harold D. Clarke, and Marianne C. Stewart. 1979. "Federalism and Fragmentation: Political Support in Canada." *Journal of Politics* 41:889–906.

1980. "Public Support for Community and Regime in the Regions of Contemporary Canada." *American Review of Canadian Studies* 10:75–93.

Kornberg, Allan, and Samuel J. Hines. 1977. "Parliament's Role in the Integration-Modernization of Canadian Society, 1865–1876." In Albert Eldridge, ed. *Legislatures in Plural Societies*. Durham, N.C.: Duke University Press.

Kornberg, Allan, and William Mishler. 1976. *Influence in Parliament: Canada*. Durham, N.C.: Duke University Press.

Kornberg, Allan, William Mishler, and Harold D. Clarke. 1982. *Representative Democracy in the Canadian Provinces*. Scarborough, Ont.: Prentice-Hall.

Kornberg, Allan, William Mishler, and Joel Smith. 1975. "Political Elite and Mass Perceptions of Party Locations in Issue Space: Some Tests of Two Positions." *British Journal of Political Science* 5:161–85.

Kornberg, Allan, Joel Smith, and Harold D. Clarke. 1979. *Citizen Politicians Canada*. Scarborough, Ont.: Prentice-Hall.

Kornberg, Allan, and Harold D. Clarke (eds.). 1983. *Political Support in Canada: The Crisis Years*. Durham, N.C.: Duke University Press.

Kramer, Gerald H. 1983. "The Ecological Fallacy Revisited: Aggregate Versus

Individual-Level Findings on Economics and Elections and Sociotropic Voting." *American Political Science Review* 77:92–111.

Krieger, Leonard, 1977. *Leopold Ranke: The Meaning of History*. Chicago: University of Chicago Press.

Kuklinski, John H., and Darrell M. West. 1981. "Economic Expectations and Voting Behavior in United States House and Senate Elections." *American Political Science Review* 75:436–47.

Kwavnick, David, ed. 1973. *The Tremblay Report: Report of the Royal Commission of Inquiry on Constitutional Problems*. Toronto: University of Toronto Press.

Lane, Robert E. 1959. *Political Life: How and Why People Get Involved in Politics*. New York: Free Press.

Laxer, R., ed. 1973. *(Canada) Ltd.: The Political Economy of Dependency*. Toronto: McClelland & Stewart.

LeDuc, Lawrence. 1989. "The Canadian Federal Election of 1988." *Electoral Studies* 8:163–7.

Le Devoir. 3 June 1963; 4 November 1963.

Lefever, Ernest W. 1974. *TV and National Defense: An Analysis of CBS News, 1972–1973*. Boston, VA: Institute for American Strategy Press.

Lemieux, Vincent. 1972. "Heaven Is Blue and Hell Is Red." In Martin Robin, ed. *Canadian Provincial Politics: The Party Systems of the Ten Provinces*. Scarborough, Ont.: Prentice-Hall.

Lévesque, René. 1982. "French Canada." In Paul W. Fox, ed. *Politics: Canada*. 5th ed. Toronto: McGraw-Hill Ryerson Ltd.

Levitt, Kari 1970. *Silent Surrender: The Multinational Corporation in Canada*. Toronto: Macmillan.

Lewis-Beck, Michael S. 1986. "Comparative Economic Voting: Britain, France, Germany, Italy." *American Journal of Political Science* 30:315–46.

1988. *Economics and Elections: The Major Western Democracies*. Ann Arbor: The University of Michigan Press.

Lipset, Seymour Martin. 1968. "Social Structure and Political Activity." In B. Blishen, et al., eds. *Canadian Society: Sociological Perspectives*. Toronto: Macmillan.

1983. "Canada and the United States: The Cultural Dimension." In Charles F. Doran and John H. Sigler, eds. *Canada and the United States: Enduring Friendship, Persistent Stress*. Englewood Cliffs, N.J.: Prentice-Hall.

1990. *The Continental Divide: The Values and Institutions of the United States and Canada*. New York: Routledge.

Loewenberg, Gerhard. 1971. "The Influence of Parliamentary Behavior on Regime Stability: Some Conceptual Clarifications." *Comparative Politics* 3:177–200.

Long, J. Scott. 1983. *Confirmatory Factor Analysis: A Preface to Lisrel*. Beverly Hills, Calif.: Sage.

Lower, Arthur R. M. 1958. "Theories of Canadian Federalism – Yesterday and Today." In Arthur R. M. Lower, Frank R. Scott, John A. Corry, F. H. Soward, and Alexander Brady, eds. *Evolving Canadian Federalism*. Durham, N.C.: Duke University Press.

Lumsden, Ian. 1970. *Close the 49th Parallel etc.: The Americanization of Canada*. Toronto: University of Toronto Press.

Macpherson, C. B. 1953. *Democracy in Alberta: The Theory and Practice of a Quasi-Party System*. Toronto: University of Toronto Press.

1962. *The Political Theory of Possessive Individualism: Hobbes to Locke*. Oxford: Oxford University Press (Clarendon Press).

1977. *The Life and Times of Liberal Democracy*. Oxford: Oxford University Press.

Malcolm, Andrew H. 1985. *The Canadians*. New York: Times Books.

Mallory, J. R. 1965. "The Five Faces of Federalism." In P. A. Crepeau and C. B. Macpherson, eds. *The Future of Canadian Federalism*. Toronto: University of Toronto Press.

Marshall, T. H. 1965. *Class, Citizenship and Social Development*. New York: Doubleday.

Martinez, Michael D. 1989. "Partisan Reinforcement in Context and Cognition: Canadian Federal Partisanships, 1974–1979." Paper presented at the Annual Meeting of the Midwest Political Science Association, Chicago, Ill.

Mayo, Henry. 1960. *An Introduction to Democratic Theory*. New York: Oxford University Press.

McClosky, Herbert. 1964. "Consensus and Ideology in American Politics." *American Political Science Review* 58:361–82.

McKelvey, Richard D., and William Zavoina. 1975. "A Statistical Model for the Analysis of Ordinal Level Dependent Variables." *Journal of Mathematical Sociology* 4:103–20.

McNaught, Kenneth. 1959. *A Prophet in Politics: A Biography of J. S. Woodsworth*. Toronto: University of Toronto Press.

McRoberts, Kenneth. 1988. *Quebec: Social Change and Political Crisis*. 3rd ed. Toronto: McClelland & Stewart.

Meisel, John. 1975. "Howe, Hubris and '72: An Essay On Political Elitism." In *Working Papers on Canadian Politics*. 2nd ed. Montreal: McGill-Queen's University Press.

——— 1979. "The Decline of Party in Canada." In Hugh Thorburn, ed. *Party Politics in Canada*. 4th ed. Scarborough, Ont.: Prentice-Hall.

Milbrath, Lester. 1965. *Political Participation*. Chicago: Rand McNally.

Milbrath, Lester, and M. L. Goel. 1977. *Political Participation*. 2nd ed. Chicago: Rand McNally.

Miller, A. H. 1974a. "Political Issues and Trust in Government 1964–1970." *American Political Science Review* 68:951–72.

——— 1974b. "Rejoinder to 'comment' by Jack Citrin: Political Discontent or Ritualism?" *American Political Science Review* 68:989–1,001.

Miller, Nicholas R. 1986. "Public Choice and the Theory of Voting: A Survey." In Samuel Long, ed. *Annual Review of Political Science*. Vol. 1. Norwood: Ablex Publishing Corp.

Miller, William L. 1989. "Studying How the Economy Affects Public Attitudes and Behavior: Problems and Prospects." In Harold D. Clarke, Marianne C. Stewart, and Gary Zuk, eds. *Economic Decline and Political Change: Canada, Great Britain, the United States*. Pittsburgh: University of Pittsburgh Press.

Milne, David. 1986. *Tug of War: Ottawa and the Provinces under Trudeau and Mulroney*. Toronto: Lorimer.

Mishler, William. 1979. *Political Participation in Canada*. Toronto: Macmillan of Canada.

Monroe, Kristen Renwick. 1984. *Presidential Popularity and the Economy*. New York: Praeger.

Morton, William. 1950. *The Progressive Party in Canada*. Toronto: University of Toronto Press.

Muller, Edward N. 1970. "The Representation of Citizens by Political Authorities: Consequences for Regime Support." *American Political Science Review* 64:1,149–66.

——— 1979. *Aggressive Political Participation*. Princeton, N.J.: Princeton University Press.

Muller, Edward N., and Thomas O. Jukam. 1977. "On the Meaning of Political

Support." *American Political Science Review* 71:1,561–95.

Muller, Edward N., Thomas O. Jukam, and Mitchell A. Seligson. 1982. "Diffuse Political Support and Antisystem Political Behavior: A Comparative Analysis." *American Journal of Political Science* 26:240–64.

Muller, Edward N., and C. J. Williams. 1980. "Dynamics of Political Support-Alienation." *Comparative Political Studies* 13:33–59.

New York Times. 28 June 1990.

Newman, Peter. 1977. *The Canadian Establishment*. Vol. 1. Toronto: McClelland & Stewart.

　1979. *The Canadian Establishment*. Vol. 2. Toronto: McClelland & Stewart.

　1982. *The Establishment Man: A Portrait of Power*. Toronto: McClelland & Stewart.

Niemi, Richard, Richard Katz, and David Newman. 1980. "Reconstructing Past Partisanship: The Failure of the Party Identification Recall Questions." *American Journal of Political Science* 24:633–51.

Nimmo, Dan, and James E. Combs. 1983. *Mediated Political Realities*. New York: Longman.

Nisbet, Robert. 1980. *History of the Idea of Progress*. New York: Basic.

Niskanen, W. A., Jr. 1971. *Bureaucracy and Representative Government*. New York: Aldine-Atherton.

Norpoth, Helmut. 1987. "Guns and Butter and Government Popularity in Britain." *American Political Science Review* 81:949–59.

Nozick, Robert, 1974. *Anarchy, State and Utopia*. New York: Basic.

O'Connor, James. 1973. *The Fiscal Crisis of the State*. New York: St. Martin's.

　1986. *Accumulation Crisis*. Oxford: Basil Blackwell.

OECD. *See* Organization of Economic Cooperation and Development.

Offe, Claus. 1972. *Struckturprobleme des Kapitalistischen*. Frankfurt am Main: Sukrkamp.

　1984. *Contradictions of the Welare State*. London: Hutchinson.

Organization for Economic Cooperation and Development. 1988. *Historical Statistics 1960–1986*. Paris: OECD.

Pammett, Jon H. 1987. "Class Voting and Class Consciousness in Canada." *Canadian Review of Sociology and Anthropology* 24:269–89.

Pammett, Jon H., Harold D. Clarke, Jane Jenson, and Lawrence LeDuc. 1983. "Political Support and Voting Behavior in the Quebec Referendum." In Allan Kornberg and Harold D. Clarke, eds. *Political Support in Canada: The Crisis Years*. Durham, N.C.: Duke University Press.

Parenti, Michael. 1986. *Inventing Reality: The Politics of the Mass Media*. New York: St. Martin's.

Pateman, Carole. 1970. *Participation and Democratic Theory*. Cambridge University Press.

　1979. *The Problem of Political Obligation: A Cultural Analysis of Liberal Theory*. New York: Wiley.

Patterson, Samuel C., Ronald D. Hedlund, and G. Robert Boynton. 1975. *Representatives and Represented: Bases of Public Support for the American Legislatures*. New York: Wiley.

Patterson, Samuel C., John Wahlke, and G. Robert Boynton. 1973. "Dimensions of Support in Legislative Systems." In Allan Kornberg, ed. *Legislatures in Comparative Perspective*. New York: David McKay.

Penniman, Howard. 1988. *Canada at the Polls, 1984: A Study of the Federal General Elections*. Durham, N.C.: Duke University Press.

Pennock, J. Roland. 1979. *Democratic Political Theory*. Princeton, N.J.: Princeton University Press.

Peterson, T. 1972. "Ethnic and Class Politics in Manitoba." In Martin Robin, ed. *Canadian Provincial Politics: The Party Systems of the Ten Provincesf1. Scarborough, Ont.: Prentice-Hall.*

Phillips, A. W. 1958. "The Relationship Between Unemployment and the Rate of Change of Money Wage Rates in the UK 1861–1957." *Economica* 25:283–99.

Pinard, Maurice, and Richard Hamilton. 1977. "The Independence Issue and the Polarization of the Electorate: The 1973 Election." *Canadian Journal of Political Science* 10:215–60.

_____ 1978. "The Parti Québécois Comes to Power: An Analysis of the 1976 Quebec Election." *Canadian Journal of Political Science* 11:739–76.

_____ 1980. "Les Québécois votent NON: Le sens du vote." Montreal: Université McGill, unpublished paper.

Pitkin, Hanna. 1967. *The Concept of Representation.* Berkeley and Los Angeles: University of California Press.

Porter, John. 1965. *The Vertical Mosaic: An Analysis of Social Class and Power in Canada.* Toronto: University of Toronto Press.

Powell, G. Bingham. 1982. *Contemporary Democracies: Participation, Stability, and Violence.* Cambridge: Harvard University Press.

Presthus, Robert. 1973. *Elite Accommodation in Canadian Politics.* Toronto: Macmillan.

_____ 1974. *Elites and the Policy Process.* Toronto: Macmillan.

Preston, Richard 1972. *The Influence of the United States on Canadian Development.* Durham, D.C.: Duke University Press.

Prothro, James W., and Charles M. Grigg. 1960. "Fundamental Principles of Democracy: Bases of Agreement and Disagreement." *Journal of Politics* 22:276–94.

Quinn, Herbert F. 1963. *The Union Nationale: A Study in Quebec Nationalism.* Toronto: University of Toronto Press.

Rawls, John. 1971. *A Theory of Justice.* Cambridge: Harvard University Press.

_____ 1980. "Kantian Constructivism in Moral Theory: The Dewey Lectures 1980." *The Journal of Philosophy*, vol. 77, no. 9.

Reid, Escott M. 1972. "The Rise of National Parties in Canada." In Hugh G. Thorburn, ed. *Party Politics in Canada.* 3rd ed. Scarborough, Ont.: Prentice-Hall.

Reiter, H. L. 1979. "Why Is Turnout Down." *Public Opinion Quarterly* 43:297–311.

Revel, Jean-François. 1984. *How Democracies Perish.* New York: Doubleday.

Richards, John, and Larry Pratt. 1979. *Prairie Capitalism: Power and Influence in the New West.* Toronto: McClelland & Stewart Ltd.

Robin, Martin, ed. 1972. *Canadian Provincial Politics: The Party Systems of the Ten Provinces.* Scarborough, Ont.: Prentice-Hall.

Robinson, Michael J. 1977. "Television and American Politics." *The Public Interest* 48:3–39.

Rogowski, Ronald. 1974. *Rational Legitimacy: A Theory of Political Support.* Princeton, N.J.: Princeton University Press.

_____ 1983. "Political Support for Regimes: A Theoretical Inventory and Critique." In Allan Kornberg and Harold D. Clarke, eds. *Political Support in Canada: The Crisis Years.* Durham, N.C.: Duke University Press.

Romanow, Roy, John Whyte, and Howard Leeson. 1984. *Canada . . . Notwithstanding: The Making of the Constitution 1976–1982.* Toronto: Carswell/Methuen.

Rose, Richard, and Guy Peters. 1978. *Can Government Go Bankrupt?* New York: Basic.

Rothman, Stanley. 1979. "The Mass Media in Post-Industrial America." In Seymour Martin Lipset, ed. *The Third Century: America as a Post-Industrial Society*. Stanford, CA: Hoover Institute Press.

Sartori, Giovanni. 1987. *Theory of Democracy Revisited*. Vol. 1. Chatham: Chatham House Publishers.

Schlozman, Kay L., and Sidney Verba. 1979. *Injury to Insult: Unemployment, Class and Political Response*. Cambridge: Harvard University Press.

Schmitter, P. C. 1981. "Interest Intermediation and Regime Governability in Contemporary Western Europe and North America." In Suzanne Berger, ed. *Organizing Interests in Western Europe*. Cambridge University Press.

Schumpeter, Joseph A. 1942. *Capitalism, Socialism, and Democracy*. New York: Harper & Row.

Schwartz, Mildred A. 1967. *Public Opinion and Canadian Identity*. Berkeley and Los Angeles: University of California Press.

1974. *Politics and Territory: The Sociology of Regional Persistence in Canada*. Montreal: McGill-Queen's University Press.

Seigel, Arthur. 1983. *Politics and the Media in Canada*. Toronto: McGraw-Hill.

Shanks, Merrill, and Jack Citrin. 1975. "The Measurement of Political Alienation: Strategic and Methodological Issues." Paper delivered at the Conference on Political Alienation, Iowa City, Iowa.

Sigelman, Lee. 1982. "The Nonvoting Voter in Voting Research." *American Journal of Political Science* 26:47–56.

Simeon, Richard. 1972. *Federal-Provincial Diplomacy: The Making of Public Policy in Canada*. Toronto: University of Toronto Press.

1977. *Must Canada Fail?* Montreal: McGill-Queen's University Press.

Smiley, Donald V. 1980. *Canada in Question: Federalism in the Eighties*. 3rd ed. Toronto: McGraw-Hill Ryerson.

Smith, David E. 1985. "Party Government, Representation and National Integration in Canada." In Peter Aucoin, ed. *Party Government and Regional Representation in Canada*. Toronto: University of Toronto Press.

Smith, Joel, and Allan Kornberg. 1983. "The Quebec Referendum: National or Provincial Event?" In Allan Kornberg and Harold D. Clarke, eds. *Political Support in Canada: The Crisis Years*. Durham, N.C.: Duke University Press.

Smith, Joel, Allan Kornberg, and Neil Nevitte. 1988. "Structural Factors in the Conservative Resurgence." In Barry Cooper, Allan Kornberg, and William Mishler, eds. *The Resurgence of Conservatism in Anglo-American Democracies*. Durham, N.C.: Duke University Press.

Smith, Peter J. 1987. "The Ideological Origins of Canadian Confederation." *Canadian Journal of Political Science* 20:3–29.

Sniderman, P. M. 1981. *A Question of Loyalty*. Berkeley and Los Angeles: University of California Press.

Sniderman, P. M., and R. A. Brody. 1977. "Coping: the Ethic of Self-Reliance." *American Journal of Political Science* 21:501–21.

Soderlund, Walter C., Walter I. Romanow, E. Donald Briggs, and Ronald H. Wagenberg. 1984. *Media and Elections in Canada*. Toronto: Holt, Rinehart & Winston.

Spragens, Thomas A., Jr. 1981. *The Irony of Liberal Reason*. Chicago: University of Chicago Press.

Stark, Andy. 1990. "Tongue Tied." *The New Republic* (April 23):17–19.

Stein, Herbert. 1988. *Presidential Economics: The Making of Economic Policy From Roosevelt to Reagan and Beyond*. 2nd. ed. Washington, D.C.: American Enterprise Institute for Public Policy Research.

Stevenson, Garth. 1979. *Unfulfilled Union: Canadian Federalism and National Unity*. 1st ed. Toronto: Macmillan of Canada.
1989. *Unfulfilled Union: Canadian Federalism and National Unity*. 3rd ed. Agincourt, Ont.: Gage.
Stewart, Marianne C. 1986. "A State of Heart, a State of Mind: Political Support in Canada." Ph.D. dissertation. Durham, N.C.: Duke University.
Stewart, Michael. 1986. *Keynes and After*. 3rd. ed. Harmondsworth, Middlesex: Penguin Books.
Stimson, James A. 1985. "Regression in Time and Space: A Statistical Essay." *American Journal of Political Science* 29:914–47.
Sundquist, James L. 1983. *Dynamics of the Party System*. Washington, D.C.: Brookings Institution.
The Task Force on Canadian Unity. 1979. *A Time to Speak: The Views of the Public*. Ottawa: Ministry of Supply and Services Canada.
Thomas, Norman C. 1989. "Adapting Policy-Making Machinery to Fiscal Stress: Canada, Great Britain, and the United States." In Harold D. Clarke, Marianne C. Stewart, and Gary Zuk, eds. *Economic Decline and Political Change: Canada, Great Britain, the United States*. Pittsburgh: University of Pittsburgh Press.
Thompson, D. 1970. *The Democratic Citizen*. Cambridge University Press.
Trudeau, Pierre, Elliott. 1968. *Federalism and the French Canadians*. Toronto: Macmillan of Canada.
Uhlaner, Carole Jean. 1982. "The Consistency of Individual Political Participation Across Governmental Levels in Canada." *American Journal of Political Science* 26:298–311.
Urban, George, ed. 1972. *The Miracles of Chairman Mao*. London: Nash.
Van Loon, Richard J. 1970. "Political Participation in Canada: The 1965 Election." *Canadian Journal of Political Science* 3:376–99.
Van Loon, Richard J., and Michael S. Whittington. 1981. *The Canadian Political System: Environment, Structure, and Process*. 3rd ed. Toronto: McGraw-Hill Ryerson.
Verba, Sidney, and Norman H. Nie. 1972. *Participation in America*. New York: Harper & Row.
Verney, Douglas. 1986. *Three Civilizations, Two Cultures, One State: Canada's Political Traditions*. Durham, N.C.: Duke University Press.
Wahlke, John 1971. "Policy Demands and System Support: The Role of the Represented." *British Journal of Political Science* 1:271–90.
Wattenberg, Ben J. 1985. *The Good News Is the Bad News Is Wrong*. New York: Simon & Schuster.
Wolfinger, Raymond D., and Steven J. Rosenstone. 1980. *Who Votes?* New Haven, Conn.: Yale University Press.
Wright, J. D. 1976. *Dissent of the Governed: Alienation and Democracy in America*. New York: Academic Press.
Wylie, Margaret. 1962. *Children of China*. Hong Kong: Dragonfly Books.
Young, Walter D. 1969. *The Anatomy of a Party: The National CCF 1932–1961*. Toronto: University of Toronto Press.
Zakuta, Leo. 1964. *A Protest Movement Becalmed*. Toronto: University of Toronto Press.
Zimmermann, E. 1979. "Crises and Crises Outcomes: Towards a New Synthetic Approach." *European Journal of Political Research* 7:67–115.

Index

Aberhart, William, 152
age: and compliance, 226–7, 230–1; and
  political participation, 234–5, 238; and
  political support, 22, 35, 55, 90, 104, 116,
  118, 169
Alberta, 50, 51, 80, 82, 146, 149, 151, 152,
  157, 158, 160, 190, 216
Alliance Laurentienne, 147
amending formula procedure, 1
Atwood, Margaret, 259
Authorities, political support for, 9, 19–33,
  104, 105, 106–4, 125, 126–9, 130–2, 141–
  3, 161, 177, 178, 191, 211, 214, 253, 254

Bennett, W. A. C., 151
Bourassa, Robert, 2, 148, 212, 244, 245
British Columbia, 70, 80, 149, 150, 151, 156,
  157, 158, 159, 190, 192, 207, 208, 216;
  social class cleavage in, 150
British North America (BNA) Act, 1–2, 14
Broadbent, Ed, 108, 111, 130, 131, 140, 192,
  194, 197–8, 207–9

Canada Act (1982 constitution), 2, 132
Charter of Rights and Freedoms, 1–2, 244
Churchill, Winston, 245
Cité Libre, 146
community, political support for, 9, 62, 105–
  6, 107–11, 122–3, 133–6, 141–3, 166–73,
  191
compliance: in democracies, 29, 225–6, 243;
  effects of political support on, 30, 33,
  225–31, 237–41; effects of sociodemographic variables on, 229, 230–1; laws and
  regulations, 29, 226–31, 241, 256; service
  and obedience, 29–30, 243, 256; stability
  and change, 227–9
Confederation, 11, 12, 13–14, 15, 18, 144,
  174, 212; fathers of, 11–3; theories of, 14
conservatism: as a political ideology, 17;
  revitalization in 1970s, 8, 84
Conservative Party (PC): effects of scandals
  on after 1984, 201, 207; support after

1984 election, 73–4, 95, 200, 200–1, 213;
  support after 1988 election, 109, 189;
  support in Quebec, 154, 156–60, 213;
  support in West, 145, 154–5, 156–60, 190
Consociational democracy, 262
constitution: Canada Act, 2, 103; Canada,
  and British North America Act, 1, 14;
  Canada, and Meech Lake Accord, 2–3,
  4, 213, 251
Cooperative Commonwealth Federation
  (CCF), *see* New Democratic Party (NDP)

de Gaulle, Charles, 245
democracy: Canada as, 3, 4, 5, 61, 66, 68, 69,
  70, 102, 231, 261; conceptions of, 65, 69–
  70, 102, 250; crisis of, 3–4, 58, 103, 168;
  effects of political events on satisfaction
  with, 56, 68; functions of elections in, 9,
  63, 104, 108, 176–8, 211, 250, 260–1;
  norms and values, 29, 34–5, 56, 59, 90–1,
  225–6, 242; public beliefs about, 61, 65–
  6, 67, 68, 70, 102, 103, 120; satisfaction
  with and economic conditions, 59, 69–70;
  satisfaction with in Western Europe, 67–
  8, 70, 222–5, 242–3; Soviet Union as, 4,
  31, 66, 70, 102; United States as, 66, 70,
  102
Diefenbaker, John, 154–5
Duplessis, Maurice, 146

Eastern Europe, revolutions in, 4
economic theory: Keynesian, 83–4;
  monetarism, 84; supply-side, 84
economic evaluations: and government
  responsibility attributions, 30, 36–7,
  39–41, 48–9, 88, 117, 125, 131, 141,
  192; asymmetric, 35, 41, 59, 60, 246;
  dimensions of, 42–4, 182, 186; dynamism
  of, 188–9; egocentric, 42, 43, 44, 125–6,
  206, 215, 221, 241; national, 30, 35, 43,
  117; personal, 27-8, 35, 41, 50, 69, 122–6,
  131, 189; prospective, 28, 42, 118, 120–6,
  130, 206, 215, 218, 221, 241; retrospec-